Storable Votes

Storable Votes

Protecting the Minority Voice

ALESSANDRA CASELLA

OXFORD
UNIVERSITY PRESS

OXFORD
UNIVERSITY PRESS

Oxford University Press, Inc., publishes works that further
Oxford University's objective of excellence
in research, scholarship, and education.

Oxford New York
Auckland Cape Town Dar es Salaam Hong Kong Karachi
Kuala Lumpur Madrid Melbourne Mexico City Nairobi
New Delhi Shanghai Taipei Toronto

With offices in
Argentina Austria Brazil Chile Czech Republic France Greece
Guatemala Hungary Italy Japan Poland Portugal Singapore
South Korea Switzerland Thailand Turkey Ukraine Vietnam

Published by Oxford University Press, Inc.
198 Madison Avenue, New York, New York 10016
www.oup.com

Casella, Alessandra.
Storable votes : protecting the minority voice / Alessandra Casella.
p. cm.
Includes bibliographical references and index.
ISBN 978-0-19-530909-6 (cloth : alk. paper) – ISBN 978-0-19-530908-9
(pbk. : alk. paper) 1. Voting–Mathematical models. 2. Elections–Mathematical
models. 3. Decision making. 4. Decision making–Mathematical models. I. Title.
JF1001.C24 2011
324.6'501519–dc22

2010049340

ISBN-13: 978-0-195-30909-6 (cloth)

1 3 5 7 9 8 6 4 2

Printed in the United States of America
on acid-free paper

Per Lex e Camilla

Contents

Preface

Imagine a committee responsible for deciding whether to approve each of a number of proposals. The committee may be small – a corporate board, a parents' association in a school, a tenants' group in a condominium, a city council, a faculty committee – or it may be large – a shareholders' meeting, a legislature, a population asked to vote on a series of referendums. The decisions are taken by vote, and in each case the side with the higher number of votes wins. We have all been in a situation of this type. Typically, most of the proposals leave us quite indifferent, but there are a few about which we feel strongly. What we wish we could do is abstain from voting proposals that do not concern us and store all our votes for the ones that really matter. This is the idea discussed in this book.

I am an economist and it is natural for me to think in terms of prices. Operating together with a budget constraint, the price system induces consumers to express demands that reflect their priorities: given the income at their disposal, consumers choose their consumption bundles by comparing the relative prices of different goods to their own individual needs and preferences. In the case of votes, however, even suspending ethical considerations, a market would not work well. An individual selling or buying votes affects all other voters, and the market has no built-in system inducing traders to take these effects into account. If, in addition, individual budgets differ, and they do, not only are fundamental principles of democratic equality violated, but votes will be bought and sold for reasons that are unrelated to the strength of individuals' preferences.

This book does not talk about a market for votes, where the right to vote is sold and bought across individuals. It proposes instead to apply the intuitions derived from the price system to a scheme in which the *same* individual can exchange the right to cast one vote on each issue for the right to abstain on some of them and cast more votes on the remainder. The individual pays for his added influence on some decisions by trading in his influence on some others. By choosing how many votes to store and how to allocate them, the voter develops something similar to a system of individualized prices: given the total number of votes at his disposal – his budget constraint – the relative numbers of votes cast on different decisions reflect his relative willingness to spend (vote) on these decisions, mirroring the relative importance he assigns to them.

Because the mechanism relies on voters' ability to store votes for the decisions they choose, I have called it *storable votes*. It has close relatives in the theory and practice of voting rules, but no twin. Voting schemes are typically designed for choosing among several alternatives in a single election. This book studies instead multiple elections, each of which concerns a simple yes/no decision. The traditional focus is closer to the institutions of indirect democracy and to the choice of a winning candidate among many. Storable votes are an instrument of direct democracy, where a group must decide whether to implement a number of decisions.

Intuitive enough to be described in few words, storable votes have a number of desirable properties: they encourage voters to reveal their intensity of preferences truthfully; they treat every voter identically and yet make it possible for a minority to win at times; they result in minority victories only when the minority cares intensely about the outcome of a decision while the majority does not, and thus when the cost of the defeat for the majority is small; and they are close enough to existing systems of voting to be easily implementable. The different chapters of this book analyze these features one by one, studying in detail scenarios that are modified only incrementally, just enough to capture the emphasis on different aspects of the voting rule as the book proceeds.

Storable votes' theoretical properties rely on voters being able to see through not-so-simple strategic questions. Presumably, with enough experience, the difficulties would be solved; however, if they are not, could voters mishandle the mechanism enough to make its flexibility counterproductive? In the first four chapters of the book, the question is addressed by complementing the theoretical analysis with laboratory experiments in which students interacting via computer terminals make voting choices over a set of abstract elections. The chapters discuss decision-making in small committees, and the theoretical results lend themselves easily to testing in a laboratory. The last two chapters of the book study instead large elections, and here testing took place through a survey matched with field data during actual student elections at Columbia University.

The most difficult decision the book required was its style. The intuition behind storable votes is so immediate that I see no reason to address the book only to political economists, and only to those comfortable with mathematical models. However, avoiding all mathematical tools would inevitably reduce the rigor of the analysis. The book can thus be read on three levels. The text itself is discursive and nonmathematical, presenting the theoretical discussion through the simple logic that drives it. For readers who find a more formal approach clearer, each chapter has one or two boxes that summarize, in mathematical notation, the assumptions and precise results described more loosely in the text. I hope the boxes will be useful, but they can be ignored by any reader who does not feel the need for them. Finally, for anyone who would like to work on storable votes, the formal proofs of the results and the derivations of the figures are presented in detail in the second half of the book, together with the instructions for one experimental session for each experiment. All experimental data are available for download at http://www.oup.com/us/StorableVotes. Again, the second part of the book can be overlooked by readers not interested in proofs or in replicating the experiments.

The text has no mathematical notation, but inevitably its root in formal modeling remains. For better or for worse, it shows the careful, slow development of logical thought in formal models. From one section to the other, from one chapter to the other, additional results are obtained slowly and in small increments – and yet I believe they build our understanding of the voting rule, bringing us much beyond what can be seen through less disciplined thought. Thus, one possible reading of the book is methodological. Stripped of all mathematical derivations, and thus addressed to all, the book still offers an example of the use of formal mathematical modeling in social sciences. At the same time, the discursive tone allows more discussion of the limits of the analysis, and of the possible interpretation of the narrow theoretical results in practical applications. The laboratory experiments provide the first bridge from the abstract nature of the theoretical analysis to the observation of actual voting behavior, including the strategic mistakes observed in the laboratory and the crucial question of the possible effects of such mistakes.

The style of this book differs from the style of academic articles, but the work it discusses builds on several of them. Storable votes were first discussed in Casella (2005), but the specific model studied in that paper is not presented here. Other articles are more closely related to the analysis in the book. Chapter 1 and the first part of Chapter 4 build on Casella (2011); Chapter 2 is based on Casella, Gelman, and Palfrey (2006); Chapter 3 is based on Casella, Palfrey, and Riezman (2008); Chapter 5 is based on Casella and Gelman (2008); and Chapter 6 is based on Casella, Ehrenberg, Gelman, and Shen (2010). The model and the experiment in the second part of Chapter 4 were previously unpublished. In all cases, I have altered the presentation substantially from the original papers to match the different tone of this book and to highlight the results I consider most relevant. I have also deviated from academic norms by limiting footnotes and references to a bare minimum to maintain the intuitive flow that the book is striving to achieve.

This book would not exist without the collaboration of friends and students. Among them, Andrew Gelman and Tom Palfrey have been a constant presence: four of the six chapters of this book draw on joint work with one or both of them. Without their clear thinking, their generosity, and their sense of humor I doubt that *Storable Votes* would have proceeded beyond the initial article. Tom introduced me to experimental methods, and I am happy to hold him responsible for the experimental tilt that the book has acquired. Ray Riezman, Shuky Ehrenberg, and Jie Shen have also coauthored some of the material discussed in the book, and I am very grateful for their contributions. Shuky, at the time still finishing his undergraduate work, designed and implemented the test described in Chapter 6, cheerfully overcoming the university's bureaucratic hurdles. Bogachen Celen participated in the design of the experiments in Chapters 1 and 4. A special thanks goes to Sébastien Turban, who over a long summer reviewed all mathematical proofs, identifying imprecise statements, opaque logical steps, and just plain mistakes. You may not read the second part of this book, but if you do, you too have reasons to be grateful to Sébastien. Several other students have worked on the material discussed in these chapters: Raj Advani, who did the programming for all experiments, and Adam Sacarny for the work described in Chapter 6; Uliana Popova and Geoff McCarney helped to run the experiments; Nobuyuki Hanaki, Brian Rogers, and Kyle Gerry analyzed some the experimental data; Solomon Hsiang helped develop some of the theory discussed in Chapter 4; and Brandon Storm read in detail and offered comments on all chapters.

Many other people played important roles in the project by discussing its findings and offering feedback. In addition to the participants in many seminars and conferences, and to the students in many classrooms, I am in particular debt to Avinash Dixit, John Ferejohn, Matt Jackson, and Eric Maskin, whose steady confidence in the ideas discussed in this book made it possible to overcome the inevitable rough patches. Anna Schwartz's company, her belief in my work, and her extraordinary example have been an exceptional source of energy and inspiration. Terry Vaughn, Catherine Rae, and Lora Friedenthal at Oxford University Press have seen the manuscript to completion, calmly and competently. Finally, I am deeply grateful to the institutions that made this book possible. The experimental laboratories at Caltech (SSEL), UCLA (CASSEL), Princeton (PLESS), and NYU (CESS) generously hosted me; during the splendid year I spent there as Member, the Institute for Advanced Study in Princeton inspired the ambition to collect scattered results into a unified treatment; the National Science Foundation and the Guggenheim Foundation funded much of the work and the essential academic leave that saw the birth of this book; Columbia University made it possible for me to accept the opportunities I was offered; the New York office of the National Bureau of Economic Research was, and is, my home away from home; and for many years, the Ecole des Hautes Etudes en Sciences Sociales and Groupement de Recherche en Economie Quantitative d'Aix Marseille made the splendors of La Vieille Charité in Marseilles my home still further away from home.

Introduction

In November 2009, voters in Maine were asked to vote on seven propositions. The topics varied from school districts' consolidation (confirmed) to tax relief for new or clean energy cars (rejected) to state dispensaries for marijuana devoted to medical use (approved). Two propositions attracted intense campaigning: Question 1 on the ballot concerned the repeal of a 2009 state law allowing same-sex marriage (repealed), and Question 4 proposed submitting increases in state taxes to popular referendum (rejected). Many voters may have felt that these last two issues indeed dominated the ballot, but it seems likely that not everybody did – chemotherapy patients and their families, groups opposed to car excise taxes who had spent their resources to put the initiative to a vote, and families in isolated communities without schools in close proximity. Even among voters focused on Questions 1 and 4, priorities probably differed: Question 1 concerned social rules, Question 4 economics, and many may have considered one much more important to them than the other. Now, suppose that in addition to a regular vote on each question, each voter had at his disposal a number of "bonus votes," that is, extra votes that could be cast on any proposition as the voter saw fit. The decision would then be taken according to the majority of all votes cast, including the bonus votes. A voter who felt that the school district question was central to his family's well-being could cast all bonus votes on that question; anti-tax voters would presumably reserve most of their bonus votes for Question 4, possibly casting a few toward reducing the excise tax on cars; and voters who came to the poll mostly in reaction to the same-sex marriage question could concentrate all their bonus votes on that. Would such a scheme be a good idea? Before dismissing it out of hand, read this book.

The logic behind the idea is easy to see. Everybody is given the same number of bonus votes, and thus everybody is treated identically.

Still, the minority can prevail on an issue if it casts more bonus votes than the majority does, but *only* if it casts more bonus votes than the majority, and thus only if voters on the minority side care more about the issue than voters on the majority side. This is exactly the case of "intense minority" and "apathetic majority" that in political theory casts doubts on the desirability, if not on the legitimacy, of majority rule. Note that the larger the difference in size between the two groups, the larger the discrepancy in the use of bonus votes must be for the minority to prevail. A large enough majority cannot be beaten, unless it chooses not to go to the polls, an outcome that can in itself be interpreted as evidence of weak preferences, but that seems less likely to occur when the majority feels less secure, as it would in the presence of bonus votes.

Could matters go wrong? Voters will not want to spend bonus votes on proposals they are sure to win or to lose anyway; thus, they will need to forecast others' voting behavior and condition their own votes on what they expect others to do, with the result that strategic considerations may interfere with casting the bonus votes according to one's priorities. The added complexity of the decision may confuse the electorate, or at least a part of the electorate, presumably the weaker part, which we particularly want to protect. In addition, the budget of bonus votes creates a link among the different proposals – what is spent on one cannot be spent on another – and may increase the importance of controlling the agenda. Proposals could be put on the agenda with the sole purpose of draining bonus votes from specific groups of voters. If the bonus-votes decision depends on forecasts of others' voting, manipulating and distorting the forecasts could be advantageous. Finally, the effect of the bonus votes is to make minority victories possible. However, the possibility of minority victories must be considered with great caution: every time the majority loses, the greater part of the voters will have to live with decisions they oppose.

I hope it is becoming clear why a whole book was necessary to begin analyzing these questions.

Storable votes and majority rule

I call the voting rule I just sketched *storable votes* because the central idea is the possibility of shifting one's own votes from one contest to another, of *storing* votes not spent on decisions that are low priorities for use on decisions that matter more. The details can vary: the electorate may be large, as in the case of a popular vote, or small, as in the case of specialized committees; the different proposals may be presented simultaneously, as in the example of multiple propositions submitted to referendum, or be voted upon over time, as in the case of a committee that meets at regular dates – for example, the board of a central bank convening monthly to decide interest-rate policy. The agenda may be known, as in the case of multiple referendums or of the bank board, or unknown, if the committee's role is sufficiently wide that new questions can arise. However, two conditions are required. First, each decision has only two alternatives. There are of course cases in which voters are asked to choose between two candidates only, but in the choice of representatives a field limited to two candidates is not the norm. Storable votes are more naturally suited to committee decision-making and to direct democracy, where each proposal either passes or fails. Second, the group faces several decisions, and these decisions are separable – each can be judged on its own merits and pass or fail independently of how other decisions are resolved. The two conditions limit the applicability of the voting scheme but, as the example of the Maine propositions shows, can still be satisfied in realistic, and in fact important, scenarios. For example, looking more widely at the November 2009 election, a total of 26 propositions were on state ballots; one of them was presented alone to New Jersey voters; all others were in bundles of several propositions (seven in Maine, eleven in Texas, three in Ohio, two in New York, and two in Washington State), and in all cases the propositions on the same ballot were unrelated. If we take the agenda as given, an important point to which I will return below, the two conditions are routinely satisfied by committees of very different types, from corporate boards to school boards, from professional associations to faculty committees in universities. Indeed, if we take the agenda as given, the group of voters could be a city council, a government committee, or a legislature.

Majority rule – defined here as enacting the alternative preferred by the larger number of voters – is a particularly desirable rule when a group needs to make a single decision, choosing between two alternatives only. It guarantees that individuals have no incentive to misrepresent their preferences, regardless of how others are voting. It treats the two alternatives identically (as opposed, for example, to supermajority requirements to overcome the status quo). More important, it treats every voter identically and responds nonpathologically to shifts in voters' preferences: an increase in the number of voters favoring one alternative can only increase the likelihood that the alternative wins. Not only does majority rule have these properties, but it is the *only* voting rule that does.[1] In fact, there is only one obvious difficulty that in the case of two alternatives majority rule cannot solve – what democratic theory has called the *problem of intensity*: "What if a minority prefers an alternative much more passionately than the majority prefers a contrary alternative? Does the majority principle still make sense?" (Dahl, 1956, p. 90)

It is a single difficulty, but an important one. On ethical grounds, if majority rule runs counter to our intuitive moral sense in some circumstances, its entire foundation seems fragile. On pragmatic grounds, the one failing is at the origin of much that is decried about committee decision-making: the private deals, the horse trading, the back rooms that are at least metaphorically smoky. What is more dangerous, if the composition of the passionate, losing minority remains constant over many decisions, the minority is effectively disenfranchised, and the stability of the political system threatened.

A large body of literature has debated whether the very concept of intensity is logically rigorous. When applied to a single individual, intensity relies on a cardinal measure of preferences that acquires meaning from the comparison to some unspecified unit of value – a *numeraire*. For example, I can say that I prefer alternative A to alternative B four times more intensely than to alternative C if I am willing to devote four times more of my time to defeat alternative B than to defeat alternative C. When applied to the legitimacy of the majority's choice, however, the question becomes one of interpersonal comparisons. We can say that Camilla prefers B to A three times more intensely than to C, but we have learned nothing about the relative intensity of preferences between Camilla and me in the choice of A versus B. If intensity cannot be measured across individuals, the goal to protect "intense" minorities cannot be defined, let alone achieved. In these terms, the objection has

---

1. The observation that misrepresenting one's preferences can never be advantageous is straightforward; the other properties are known as May's theorem (May (1972)).

no good answer. A more modest and more pragmatic approach in my opinion is more productive. In Dahl's words, "We shall continue to believe not only that we can guess intelligently but that we must guess intelligently about such things" (1956, p. 100).[2] Storable votes are an attempt to attack the problem of intensity by minimizing the amount of guesswork involved. They are not a fundamental answer to the difficulties of social choice but a practical suggestion for group decision-making in specific circumstances.

Objectives

Storable votes work by linking multiple binary decisions through a single budget constraint, the limited number of votes that individuals can shift across the different decisions. Because casting more votes translates, on average, into exercising more influence, individuals choose the use of the votes at their disposal according to the relative strength of their preferences, and the number of votes cast becomes the observable measure of intensity. There are complications, but notice first what storable votes attempt to do.

First, by allowing each individual to cast more votes on decisions that matter to him more, storable votes also allow him to increase the probability of winning decisions he considers important, at the cost of a lower probability of winning where it matters to him less. Thus, in a body of voters homogeneous enough that all expect to be in the minority with similar frequency, an individual will expect to fare better, on average, than he would under majority rule, even though he also expects to be on the losing side more often than he would with majority voting. He will be on the losing side when it matters less.

Second, the possibility of minority victories arises even though each single decision is taken according to the majority of votes cast, and, what is most important, every individual is treated identically: over the full set of decisions, every voter has the same total number of votes, and every vote has the same weight, regardless of the identity of the voter. Over any one decision, different voters may well choose to cast a different number of votes; indeed, if they do not, the voting rule reverts to majority rule,

2. See also the more extensive discussion in Dahl (1989).

but this is a choice that any of them makes freely. In a market, two consumers will choose to buy different quantities of a given good, but if their resources are equal and they face the same price, the different purchases are not evidence of unequal treatment.

Finally, storable votes are a plausible tool for addressing the problem posed by systematic minorities, groups of voters who consistently find themselves on the minority side of most decisions. With majority rule, such groups are effectively disenfranchised. Social choice theorists have suggested reverting in these cases to rules of *fair division*, rules that rather than granting all decision-making power to the majority recast it as proportional to the relative size of the two groups – for example, establishing turns in dictating the outcome, with frequency proportional to size; or assigning the power to control the outcome with probabilities again proportional to size.[3] The rules are clever and please our intuitive sense of justice, but they remain a theoretical suggestion. Unless they are adopted always, routinely allowing for minority rule, they demand the judgment that an exceptional situation has been reached requiring a deviation from the standard voting system. But who makes the judgment? And why should the majority agree?

Storable votes, on the other hand, do not require a different voting rule to respond to minority and majority interests. Even a systematic minority can prevail occasionally, if it cumulates its bonus votes on a few decisions only, and if the majority has different priorities. The voting rule that works well when individuals find themselves changing roles – sometime on the minority's side, more often on the majority's – works well when the roles are much more rigid. Storable votes cannot protect minority interests when the electorate is not only consistently divided but also highly polarized: the same minority always disagrees with preferences that the majority holds strongly. In this case, however, rules of fair division are also unlikely to be applied. The union of the group seems deeply fragile and possibly unwise.

---

3. The canonical reference is Brams and Taylor (1996); see also Brams (2005). Gerken (2005)'s concept of *second order diversity* – diversity across representative bodies, as opposed to within bodies – and its identification in existing U.S. institutions can be read as suggesting an empirical counterpart to theories of fair division. The focus on legal thought and jurisprudence is neatly complementary to the abstract arguments of social choice scholars and philosophers.

Assumptions

The theory of storable votes relies on methodological assumptions that need to be discussed up front. First of all, and expanding on a point raised earlier, because storable vote addresses the problem of intensity, the theory has no choice but to view voters' preferences as cardinal: voters are faced with multiple decisions, and their preferences specify the precise relative importance that each of them assigns to the different decisions. It is not enough to say that I care about proposal A more than about proposal B, and more about B than about C – an ordinal ranking; cardinality requires that I be able to say that I care three times more about A than about B and two times more about B than about C – a cardinal ranking. Note that the absolute measure of intensity is irrelevant and, indeed, undefined; it is the *relative* intensity that matters. An intuitive, if a bit loose, interpretation is to suppose that voters divide the different proposals into classes of importance. For example, voters may think in terms of four classes – *very important, important, somewhat important, not important* – and assign a minimal weight of 1 to proposals in the lowest category, increasing the weight by 1 with each jump of category. The weight, or the importance assigned to each proposal, represents the *intensity* of a voter's preferences. Of course, nothing prevents a finer classification.

Cardinal intensity becomes problematic in interpersonal comparisons, but the focus on multiple decisions helps. With multiple decisions, it becomes natural to concentrate not on the intensity with which any one decision is felt but on the *range* of intensities that a voter experiences over the whole set of proposals. If the analysis is to apply beyond the specificity of a given set of proposals, the essential ingredient becomes the *distribution* of intensities – the range and the relative probabilities – over the full set of potential decisions, the universe of decisions that fall under the competence of the committee. It is this measure of intensities that allows the voter, and us, to form expectations about the functioning of the voting rule and its properties independently, better, *before* the exact realization of the proposals being debated at any precise meeting. Interpersonal comparisons of intensities then take the form of assumptions about the distributions of intensities associated with different individuals. Faced with the impossibility of taking a reasoned stance on individual differences, we can restrict all distributions to be identical without in any way imposing identical realizations of intensities over any specific set of proposals. The assumption instead amounts to requiring that all voters evaluate the importance of different decisions using the same scale. For example, returning to the four-category classification described earlier, all voters might classify 5 percent of all possible decisions as "very important," 20 percent as "important," 25 percent as "somewhat important" and 50 percent as "nonimportant."[4] *Which* decisions belong to which class is free to vary across individuals, and any realization of a specific set of proposals need neither cover the full set of categories for any individual nor be ranked similarly across individuals in any systematic fashion. Only over a large number of realizations are the frequencies expected to be realized. Restricting all distributions to be identical remains an arbitrary assumption; it rules out the possibility that committee members have different views about the overall importance of the issues under the committee's jurisdiction, relative to other aspects of their lives, or the possibility that differences in personality be reflected in objectively different intensities of feelings. It need not be the correct assumption but seems a safer choice than any other obvious alternative.

One benefit is that it allows us to evaluate the performance of the voting rule through its effect on a utilitarian welfare criterion, giving each individual the same weight. I will not argue here in general defense of a utilitarian criterion; it is the meter that fits most naturally the methodological approach of this book, and it matches the book's emphasis on equal treatment for each voter. Utilitarian welfare functions depend on interpersonal comparisons of intensities, however, and would be more difficult to accept without the assumption of identical distributions of intensities. The *intensity* of a voter's preferences is understood to represent the increase in utility that a voter associates with the choice of his preferred option, relative to the alternative. A measure

4. Distributions of intensities differ from distributions of preferences, because the latter include not only the intensity but also the preferred direction of a vote (whether the individual prefers the proposal to pass or to fail). In the case of systematic minorities, for example, once individuals are identified as majority or minority members, their distributions of preferences differ, because members of the minority always, or at least more frequently, agree among themselves and disagree with the majority. The distributions of intensities, however, may well remain identical. (See Chapter 3).

of how well a voter expects to fare with a specific decision-making rule should depend not on whether the rule allows him to prevail in any one concrete instance but on whether the rule allows his to fare well on average. Better yet, on whether the rule allows an average individual to fare well on average. *Ex ante utility* is utility evaluated "under the veil of ignorance," before specific proposals are brought to the table and specific preferences realized. It is a voter's estimate of his probability to prevail over different decisions and of the utility he derives if he does, together with the probability that the different decisions will be called for a vote. "Under the veil of ignorance," the probability of siding with the majority or the minority is equal across all members, and if the voting rule treats them all equally and the distributions of intensities are identical, then all face identical prospects, and ex ante utility is identical for all voters. It thus becomes the natural welfare criterion for the group as a whole. To see what the problem could be, suppose that distributions of intensities were allowed to differ across individuals. To take an extreme example: imagine that Camilla, a jaded teenager, considers all decisions "not important" and assigns to them an intensity of 1, while Lex, a more enthusiastic personality, considers them all "very important" and assigns to all an intensity of 4. A utilitarian criterion that was to sum ex ante individual expected utilities would be identical to a criterion that assigned the same intensity to both Camilla and Lex but weighted Lex's utility four times as much as Camilla's. The distinction between individual weights in the utilitarian welfare function and individual distributions of intensities cannot be made. Again, assigning equal distributions and equal weights need not be the correct assumption, but outside of specific examples it seems the least problematic.

Finally, even within the restricted methodological approach of this book, storable votes are too simple to have ambitions of optimality. Other decision-making rules exist that on average a voter would prefer, but whether these rules can be implemented through a voting scheme is a different matter. From the theory of mechanism design we know that, under some conditions, an appropriate system of taxes and transfers can lead individuals to reveal their preferences and can select the policy alternative that maximizes utilitarian welfare. However, the correct transfers are complex, their design requires knowledge of the voters' distributions of preferences, and, if the budget is to be balanced, individuals may need to be forced to participate in the system.[5] Mechanisms without transfers would be preferable: procedures that ask individuals to send messages and select the winning alternative on the basis of those messages alone – in other words, voting rules. If we focus on voting rules, even when the choice is between two alternatives only, optimality results have been obtained so far only in limited cases, when either the number of decisions or the number of voters becomes arbitrarily large. Even in these cases, the design of the correct rule requires detailed knowledge of the circumstances in which the voting takes place – in particular, knowledge of the distribution of preferences of the voters. And even if such knowledge were available, the voting rule would need to change when circumstances change, making its political acceptance extremely unlikely.[6]

Storable votes have a more modest but more practical purpose: they are a simple, intuitive rule that can be implemented in practice. The immediate question, then, is not whether storable votes are the best possible rule, but whether they are preferable to existing alternatives.

---

5. The mechanisms rely on Clarke-Groves-Vickrey taxes – finely engineered conditional side-payments that induce individuals to report their preferences sincerely (Clarke (1971), Groves (1973), Vickrey (1961), d'Aspremont and Gérard-Varet (1979)). Their limitations are discussed in Green and Laffont (1979), Laffont and Maskin (1983), Mailath and Postlewaite (1990), and Crémer, d'Aspremont and Gérard-Varet (1990), among others.

6. An exception is the *Alternating Selection Mechanism* proposed by McAfee (1992), in which two individuals dissolve a partnership by taking turns choosing one of many objects. The mechanism behaves well if there are only two individuals, the number of objects is very large, the distributions of preferences are identical, and the individuals' preferences are independent over different objects. The other details of the environment – in particular the specific distribution of preferences – need not be known. The text refers to two specific contributions in the literature. Jackson and Sonnenschein (2007) study an environment with multiple binary decisions, as in this book, and suggest asking each individual not only his preferred alternative, but also the importance assigned to each decision, restricting the reports to mimic the known distribution of intensities. For example, returning to the four-category classification described earlier, if it is known that the probability of a decision with intensity 4, a "very important" decision, is only 5 percent, a voter is not allowed to report an intensity of 4 for more than 5 percent of the decisions he faces. As the number of decisions becomes very large, individual reports mimic, more and more closely, the actual distribution of preferences and the outcome approaches the utilitarian optimum. When a single binary decision is at stake, Ledyard and Palfrey (2002) show how a simple yes/no referendum approaches the utilitarian optimum as the number of voters becomes very large, if the threshold for acceptance is chosen correctly, reflecting the electorate's distribution of intensities.

With binary decisions, the concrete relevant alternative is simple majority voting, and it is to majority voting that storable votes are compared throughout this book. The final conclusion, built over different models and different possible applications, is that storable votes are not *always* superior, but they are superior with sufficient frequency and in a sufficiently systematic manner to justify, in my opinion, both the attention this book devotes to them and further study, with an eye to actual implementation.

Storable votes versus other voting rules

Comparison to majority voting is required because majority voting is the existing default rule in binary choices. However, how do storable votes fare relative to other possible voting systems? If we suspend for a moment ethical considerations, the immediate comparison is to vote trading. Suppose first that voters all had the same budget and were allowed to buy or sell votes, either for money or in exchange for votes over future decisions. As in the case of storable votes, the system leads voters to express the intensity of their preferences by varying the number of votes that an individual casts on different decisions, and it is on this basis that it has at times been deemed desirable.[7] Is it then equivalent to storable votes? The short answer is *no*: storable votes allow individuals to shift their own votes across decisions, as opposed to trading with others. The difference has a number of important implications.

First, contrary to storable votes, it is remarkably difficult to predict how vote trading would function, even in simple cases. In decentralized exchanges, in which a pair of voters enters a private agreement, the outcome depends on the details of the bargaining game. The problem

7. In the 1960s and 1970s especially, the debate between proponents and skeptics was lively. Buchanan and Tullock (1962), Coleman (1966), Haefele (1971), and Mueller (1973), all stressed the potentially beneficial aspects of markets for votes. Others, in particular Brams and Riker (1973), pointed out the externalities that bilateral vote trading imposes on third parties and, thus, the possibility of inferior outcomes. The exchange was cooled substantially by Ferejohn (1974), who summarized the state of the literature by stating that outside of some examples "... we really know very little about vote trading. [We don't know] when it will occur, or how often, or what sort of bargains will be made. We don't know if it has any desirable normative properties ..." (p. 25). More recent, noticeable contributions are Philipson and Snyder (1996) and Piketty (1994).

is that if we try to build intuition by reverting to general principles of market exchange, we cannot find a price, either in terms of money or of future votes, at which supply and demand of votes are equal. Consider, for example, a group of three voters who disagree over whether to approve a specific proposal, and suppose that the decision is taken by majority but voters are allowed to buy or sell votes for money. If the minority voter succeeds in buying one vote – and there is no reason to buy more than one – the remaining vote on the majority side has zero value, and at any positive price its owner then prefers to sell it, too. Thus, if any trade takes place, at any positive price the market has excess supply. If, on the other hand, the price is zero, and majority voters thus have no interest in selling, the minority voter is certainly interested in buying and raising the price: the market has excess demand. The example considers trading votes for money, but the difficulty remains if votes are exchanged for votes.

In practice, this means that any market would result in rationing: there would be voters interested in engaging in trade at the current terms but shut out of all transactions. Who these voters are depends on the specific rules through which traders are chosen. Thus – and this is the second observation – as with decentralized exchange, auxiliary procedural rules assume a crucial role in determining the properties of the exchange. Unless these rules are ideally designed, the outcome is unlikely to be desirable. By shifting the balance of votes, any exchange affects everybody's welfare, but the two parties involved in a trade will not take these effects into consideration. Only if the right to trade is allocated in such a manner as to force them to internalize the consequences on others will the trade be beneficial in terms of overall welfare. For example, if the voters actually trading are selected randomly among those interested in doing so, a market in which votes are exchanged for money will generate outcomes that are typically inferior to simple majority, in terms of expected utilitarian welfare.[8] Finally, if we consider how a market for votes is likely to function in practice, two additional considerations deserve a remark. First, the rationing rules add a further layer of possible manipulations: the instinctive reluctance to accept vote markets as legitimate institutions mirrors in part unease with the

8. This is the conclusion of Casella, Llorente-Saguer, and Palfrey (2010).

lack of transparency and oversight through which deals are concluded. Second, whether trade occurs through money or through future votes, differences among individuals in terms of monetary or political power will introduce constraints in trading that are unrelated to strength of preferences. Not only do these constraints appear unethical, but they will also interfere with the welfare performance of the market.

An interesting but different question is whether introducing storable votes would de facto encourage vote trading. The answer is likely to be negative: if votes are storable, and thus can be saved for the future, their value is higher than it is under simple majority rule. A vote on a decision of little importance can always be shifted to a different decision, as opposed to being offered for trade, and one's own future votes are more reliable exchanges than others' promises.

A voting system does exist that storable votes resemble closely, and it is to be found among semi-proportional systems used for candidates' elections in multi-member districts. When several representatives are to be elected, *cumulative voting* grants each voter a specified number of votes and lets him cumulate as many as he sees fit on any individual candidate. Suppose, for example, that five seats are to be filled from a field of twelve candidates. Voters are endowed with multiple votes – commonly five, if there are five seats – and allowed to cast them as they wish, concentrating the votes on as few candidates as a single one, or spreading them over five, or choosing any intermediate option. Cumulative voting is designed to protect minority interests: if voters were limited to a single vote per candidate, a party representing more than 50 percent of the voters and fielding five candidates would control all five appointments. With cumulative voting, a group gathering as little as 17 percent of the electorate and coordinating on a single candidate is guaranteed to have him elected. With a long historical tradition – it was the voting system electing the Illinois House of Representatives from 1870 to 1982[9] – and a current presence in both local jurisdictions and corporate elections, cumulative voting is emerging as a desirable alternative to the creation of majority-minority single-member districts.

9. It fell in 1982 in a voters-approved constitutional amendment, apparently as stand-by victim of a campaign to reduce the size of the House, after representatives had voted themselves a large and unpopular salary increase.

Advocated by civil rights scholars, most prominently by Lani Guinier (1994), in some instances it has been mandated by the courts as remedy to violations of the Voting Rights Act. Although the unfamiliar voting system is often resisted initially, follow-up studies suggest that it works as expected, leading not only to the election of minority candidates, often for the first time, but substantially increasing the expenditure in public goods in minority neighborhoods.[10]

Storable votes differ from cumulative voting because the two rules apply to different types of elections. Cumulative voting is an instrument of indirect democracy: it is an *electoral system* that applies to the choice of representatives in a single election in which multiple seats are to be filled. It is related to *limited voting* and *single transferable vote*, other semi-proportional systems designed to give voice to minorities. Storable votes are instead an instrument of direct democracy: *a decision-making rule* resolving disagreement over multiple proposals, each of which is presented to voters in a separate election, and each of which can either pass or fail. They are designed to protect minorities in yes/no decisions.

As a result of having different fields of application, the two systems function differently. In an election with five open seats, cumulative voting selects five winners, the five candidates with more votes overall. Storable votes apply to pair-wise choices only, and in each contest select a single winning outcome; the votes the winning outcome receives are compared only to the votes received by its competing alternative. Thus, a well-organized minority that coordinates its votes and has sufficient size can guarantee itself one seat with cumulative voting, but it cannot guarantee itself any victory with storable votes. Because in this latter case all contests are pair-wise, if both minority and majority assign

10. Pildes and Donoghue (1995) provide a fascinating case study of the introduction of cumulative voting in Chilton County, Alabama, taking the reader through initial reactions, parties' strategies, voters' education campaign, and final outcomes. Bowler, Donovan, and Brockington (2003) describe more widely the use of cumulative voting in local elections. The final report of the Illinois Assembly on Political Representation and Alternative Electoral Systems (2001) discusses in detail the experience with cumulative voting in Illinois. The background paper prepared by Richard Briffault for the New Jersey Property Tax Convention Tax Force (2004) is a short and very clear compendium of the U.S. experience with cumulative voting, limited voting, and single transferable vote. There are countless discussions of cumulative voting in the voting literature; three noticeable ones are Dodgson (1884) for its historical value; Cox (1990) for a classical theoretical study; and Gerber et al. (1998) for an experimental analysis.

highest importance to the same proposal and favor different outcomes, the majority will win. And if the minority has concentrated its bonus votes on that one proposal, the majority will win all contests. In the logic of storable votes, such an outcome is in fact desirable: if majority and minority agree on the relative importance of the different proposals, then the majority "should" win, on the strength of its larger size alone. The goal of storable votes is to solve disagreements taking into account intensity of preferences, not to guarantee representation to the minority per se, as in the case of cumulative voting. Minority victories, when they occur, are the by-product of the expression of the intensity of preferences that storable votes make possible.

The application to multiple pair-wise choices, as opposed to a single choice with multiple alternatives, also distinguishes storable votes from other well-known voting rules. *Borda count*, *range* (or *point*) *voting*, *approval voting*, all apply to one election with several alternatives. Each of these voting rules allows voters to rank the different options, with differing amounts of freedom: range voting asks voters to assign any value in a specified range – for example 0 to 9 – to each alternative; Borda count restricts the choices to the ordinal rank of the alternatives; approval voting amounts to assigning a score of either 0 (disapprove) or 1 (approve) to each available choice. In all cases, the most highly ranked alternative overall is chosen. Note that each of these systems in fact reduces to simple majority voting if the choice is pair-wise.[11]

A mechanism very similar to storable votes is proposed independently in Hortala-Vallve (2010), where it is applied to multiple simultaneous pair-wise decisions in small committees.[12] In such a setting, the two

11. With two alternatives only, being asked to assign 0 and 1 points to the two choices (as in simple majority or approval voting), or 1 and 2 (Borda count), or, in fact, 5 and 95, are all equivalent cases. In this latter case, for example, what matters is the 90-point advantage of the preferred alternative. If alternative *A* beats alternative *B* by 9,000 points, it beats it by one hundred votes. The votes could be normalized to 0 and 1 with no effect. In the case of range voting, individuals are free to choose the number of points, and their exact choice of points could matter. But any voting strategy different from assigning the maximum to one's preferred alternative and the minimum to the other is irrational (with the exception of equal scoring or abstention in the case of indifference). Thus, this case, too, reduces to a fixed choice between two specified numbers of points (or abstention) and hence is again equivalent to majority voting. Finally, note that when the choice is pair-wise, the equivalence to simple majority also holds for cumulative voting.

12. See also Hortala-Vallve and Llorente-Saguer (2010).

systems are identical. Once we recognize the possibility of shifting votes across decisions, however, voting may also occur over time. As implied by their name, storable votes highlight the possible time horizon of the voting rule, and with the exception of Chapters 5 and 6, all scenarios studied in this book refer to multiple proposals presented to voters in sequential order. The time horizon could be very short, as in the case of a single meeting, but could also be longer: Chapter 2 is motivated by the example of the board of a central bank, deciding its interest rate policy in consecutive monthly meetings, and suggests the possibility of endowing members with bonus votes valid for a calendar year. The budget of bonus votes creates a link among decisions taken over the course of many months, and the intertemporal dimension of storable votes becomes very visible. The rights of individual voters are safeguarded by granting each voter the same budget of bonus votes and thus treating all identically over the full time horizon; although over each individual decision, after the first, different voters in general will have a different number of votes at their disposal. Storable votes build on what Adam Cox calls the "temporal dimension of voting rights."[13] The concept seems logically unexceptional, but, with the exception of Cox' work, to my knowledge has not been invoked, let alone implemented, elsewhere.

Pildes and Donoghue (1995) report the first puzzled reactions to cumulative voting in Chilton County, Alabama: "[T]he silliest thing. . . " (p. 9) , "I just know it's unconstitutional." (p. 14). The resistance was caused by the very idea of casting multiple votes in a single election, which the public thought *must* violate the principle of one man-one vote. Yet, each voter entered the voting booth with the same number of votes. It seems likely that storable votes, with a conception of voting rights that relies on considering the full time horizon, would encounter even more resistance. Before worrying about public reactions, however, we need to ask whether in fact storable votes *should* be applied in practice. This is the purpose of this book.

Chapter 1 presents the basic intuitions behind storable votes, in the simplest setting and with a single bonus vote. Chapter 2 extends the discussion to decisions taken over time and multiple bonus votes; Chapter 3 studies how storable votes affect outcomes when one group is

---

13. Cox (2007). See also the response by Richard Pildes (2007).

consistently in the minority in all decisions; Chapter 4 analyzes agenda power: how do storable votes function when the committee's chair can choose either the order alone, or both the order and the content of the agenda? All four chapters begin by presenting theoretical results, and proceed to describing laboratory experiments that tested the theory's predictions. Chapter 5 extends the analysis to large electorates, and Chapter 6 describes a field quasi-experiment – a survey matched to actual observed behavior – run during university student elections at Columbia University.

Part I

The Idea

I

The Simple Logic of Storable Votes

Storable votes reflect a simple idea: if you are free to distribute your votes among different proposals, casting more votes on decisions you consider important increases the probability of obtaining your preferred alternative exactly where it matters. A fully rational voting strategy will take into account not only your priorities, but also others' priorities and their expected voting strategies. The final reasoning will be more complex, and future chapters will discuss these aspects in detail. However, it is good to begin by making the central idea as transparent as possible. This chapter describes a very simple scenario in which the logic of the voting scheme appears clearly, strategies that are likely to emerge as rules of thumb in more realistic situations are optimal here, and a number of results can be proved rigorously.

1.1 The Theory

Consider a committee of voters, meeting to decide whether to implement a number of distinct proposals, each of which can pass or fail. The proposals constitute the known, fixed agenda of the meeting, and the committee votes over the proposals sequentially. Think of the committee as the board of a corporation or an assembly of share holders, or think of it as a government body: a city council, a school board, a legislature, an international organization in which members are country representatives, or in fact as any group faced with a series of collective decisions. What is important is that each vote is a simple yes/no vote, and, for now, that the set of proposals is known and fixed before the actual votes are called. Although there are several proposals on the agenda, each stands on its own. There is no aggregate constraint that puts a limit on how many proposals can pass or that ties the approval of a proposal to the approval, or rejection, of another.

1.1.1 Preferences and information

Each member of the committee has a preference over whether any specific proposal should pass or fail and attributes a particular value to the outcome he desires. Thus, each person's preference has two features: the *direction* in which the person wishes the vote to go, and the *intensity* with which the preference is held. The intensity is summarized by the value a person attaches to a proposal. Think of the value as precisely defined: it could be in monetary terms – the amount of money the person is willing to pay to obtain the desired outcome, as opposed to its opposite; or it could be in terms of other goods foregone – for example, the time and effort a person is willing to devote to see his preferred outcome prevail. In either case, each member of the committee is able not only to rank the importance he assigns to the different proposals, but also to state whether one decision is twice as important as another one, three times more important, or only 10 percent more important. In economic-theory terms, the problem is phrased in terms of *cardinal values*: not only the ranking, but also the precise relative values, matter.

At the end of the meeting, the total value accruing to each committee member – the *utility* he derives from the meeting – is the sum of the values he attaches to all proposals that are decided in his preferred direction. Note that a concrete definition of value requires specifying the reference point, which here is the value of winning a proposal *as opposed to losing it*. Thus, by construction, the member receives zero value from outcomes that are opposite to his preferences. If values were defined with respect to an intermediate point – a tie, or possibly the status quo, if the status quo is not one of the two alternatives – the model would involve costs of losing, in addition to benefits from winning. The difference is semantic only. The only variable that matters is the difference in utility between winning and losing – simply called *value* or *intensity* in the first formulation, adopted here, it amounts to the value of winning *plus* the avoided cost of losing in the second.[1]

Every person knows his own preferences over all proposals on the agenda but does not know the preferences of the other committee members. However, everybody knows the statistical properties of these preferences. To keep matters as simple as possible, suppose that the proposals are unrelated, and preferences are independent both across proposals and across individuals: for any given proposal, the direction and the value of one person's preferences carry no information about the direction and the value of another person's, and for any given person, being in favor of one proposal carries no information about the preferred direction of a different proposal, and the value attributed to one proposal carries no information about the value attributed to a different one. Suppose also that each person is equally likely to be in favor of or against any proposal, an assumption that captures two different aspects of the environment. First, before the agenda is specified and concrete proposals are put on the table, no committee member expects to be systematically biased toward a favorable or a negative position. Second, once the proposals are known, each member is unable to predict the preferences of the others, and in the absence of any known bias, estimates that they are most likely to be equally split. Although individuals do not know others' preferences, these regularities are known to all. Finally, individuals know how strong and how dispersed preferences are on average. More precisely, everybody knows the probability distribution from which preferences are drawn, which is

1. Suppose that two proposals are on the table. In the first formulation, you derive, for example, a value of 1 from winning the first proposal rather than losing it and a value of 0.5 from the second (the units per se have no meaning). In the second formulation, you derive a value of 0.5 from winning the first proposal, relative to the status quo, and incur a loss of 0.5 from losing it; for the second proposal, the gain from winning is 0.25, and the loss from losing is 0.25. Clearly, you would rather win both proposals. Suppose that only one can be won. In the second formulation, if you win the first proposal and lose the second, your utility is $(0.5 - 0.25) = 0.25$; if you lose the first and win the second, your utility is $(-0.5 + 0.25) = -0.25$. Hence, you prefer the first scenario to the second because $0.25 > -0.25$, or $0.5 > 0$. This is exactly what the first formulation tells immediately: if only one proposal can be won, you prefer winning the first, because $1 > 0.5$, or $0.5 > 0$. It is true that the number summarizing your total utility is different in the two formulations, but remember that the units per se have no meaning.

the frequency with which a random voter's value is expected to assume different magnitudes.

The statistical properties of the voters' preferences play an important role because they summarize the environment in which the decisions have to be taken – the type of proposals submitted to the committee and the heterogeneity in the members' preferences and priorities. I will return to them below.

1.1.2 The voting rule

The proposals are voted upon sequentially, and each committee member has one regular vote to cast on each proposal. Each member also has one single *bonus vote* that can be cast, in addition to the regular vote, on any proposal. Think of the regular votes as red votes, and of the bonus vote as a single blue vote. In principle, the blue vote need not count exactly as one red vote – it could count more and be equivalent to several red votes, or it could count less, and it would then take multiple blue votes to equalize a single red vote. Whether smaller, equal, or larger, the blue vote is indivisible, and each committee member can cast it on a single proposal of his choice. In more general designs of the voting scheme, the voters will have multiple bonus votes, but, again, it helps intuition to keep matters as simple as possible. The total number of votes cast on each proposal is expressed in terms of regular votes: if the value of the bonus vote is different, the appropriate exchange rate is applied. A proposal passes if there are more votes in favor than against, and it fails in the opposite case. For simplicity, ties are resolved randomly. The outcome and the total number of votes cast on each proposal are known publicly.

The model is designed to ask whether the addition of the bonus vote changes matters, relatively to simple majority voting, and, if so, how. More precisely, imagine a preliminary constitutional stage, preceding the workings of the committee and held in ignorance of the specific agendas that will be voted upon later. The members can choose whether the committee will take decisions according to storable votes or to simple majority. What will they choose?

Box 1.1 The Formal Model. Version 1

Consider a committee of n voters, meeting to decide whether to implement T distinct proposals, $\{P_1, ..P_T\}$, each of which can either pass or fail. The T proposals constitute the known, fixed agenda of the meeting, and the committee votes on the proposals sequentially. Each member i of the committee has preferences over each proposal P_t summarized by a cardinal valuation v_{it}. Valuations v_{it} are independently and identically distributed both across proposals and across individuals according to the distribution $G(\mathrm{v})$ with support $[-1, 1]$, symmetric around 0. A negative valuation means that the voter is against the proposal; a positive valuation means that he is in favor. Call voter i's absolute valuation $v_{it} \equiv |\mathrm{v}_{it}|$ i's *intensity* (or *value*) over proposal P_t. For each proposal P_t, voter i receives utility $u_{it} = v_{it}$ if the decision goes in his preferred direction, and 0 otherwise. Voter i's utility from the entire meeting, U_i, equals $\sum_{t=1}^{T} u_{it}$.

In addition to a regular vote over every proposal, each committee member is given one indivisible bonus vote equivalent to B regular votes, with $B > 0$. Each proposal is decided in the direction that receives more votes; in case of a tie, a coin is flipped. When voting on any proposal, a member knows $\{\mathrm{v}_{i1},..\mathrm{v}_{iT}\}$, his own valuations over all proposals, but does not know others' valuations over any of the proposals. The independence of the valuations and the distribution G from which they are drawn are common knowledge. After voting, the total number of votes cast for and against a proposal is commonly known, and thus so is the number of voters still endowed with bonus votes, a number denoted by l_t. The state of the game at t is summarized by (l_t, t). The focus is on symmetric Perfect Bayesian equilibria in weakly undominated strategies.

Proposition 1.1: Equilibrium. (1) For all T, n, G, and B, there exists an equilibrium in which each voter i casts his bonus vote on P_t if and only if $v_{it} = \max\{v_i\}$. (2) For some T, n, G, and B, no other symmetric equilibrium in weakly undominated strategies exists.

Call Ev the expectation of the absolute valuation, or the expected intensity, and $Ev_{(T)}$ the Tth order statistic among each voter's T absolute valuations, or the expected highest-intensity draw. Finally, call EV_0 ex ante utility with storable votes, and EW_0 ex ante utility with simple majority voting, both evaluated before valuations are drawn, or equivalently before the agenda is specified, but in the knowledge of T, n, G, and B, and of equilibrium strategies. Then:

Proposition 1.2: Efficiency. For all T, n, and G, there exists a range of strictly positive values for B, $\mathcal{B}(n)$, such that for all $B \in \mathcal{B}(n)$: (i) If n is even, $EV_0 > EW_0$. (ii) If n is odd, $EV_0 > EW_0$ if $Ev_{(T)}/Ev > [T(n+1)]/[T(n-1)+2]$.

1.1.3 The voting decision

To evaluate whether storable votes are preferable to majority voting, individuals need to forecast how the bonus vote will be used, by themselves and by others. First, can voters ever benefit from misrepresenting their preferences and voting against their preferred alternative? Second, on which proposal will they cast their bonus vote? The answer to the first question is simple: there is no reason to misrepresent one's preferences. Because the proposals are unrelated, the direction of past votes holds no information about the direction of future votes and thus cannot be used to manipulate others' voting strategies. Voting against one's interest on any given proposal can only reduce the probability of obtaining the preferred outcome. Even if individuals are strategic, they will vote sincerely.

Less clear is when to cast the bonus vote. The choice must depend not only on how intensely a voter feels about the different proposals – the values he attaches to them – but also on the probability that casting the bonus vote will alter the outcome, relative to what it would have been without it – the *pivot probability* of the bonus vote. The pivot probability itself must depend on how others are using their bonus votes. Imagine being one of the committee members, and suppose, for example, that the first proposal is the one you care most about but there are others on the agenda over which you have strong preferences. As the first proposal is voted upon, you may hesitate to cast your bonus vote, on the argument that its impact could be higher on later proposals, when fewer bonus votes are likely to remain in circulation. The reasoning seems plausible, but it is mistaken: it is true that fewer bonus votes will be available to the other voters in future proposals, but there is no reason to expect that more will be cast on the first proposal than on any other. In fact, if every committee member casts the bonus vote on his highest-priority proposal, then he is equally likely to cast it on any of the proposals on the agenda. When the voting decision on the first proposal must be made, all proposals look identical in terms of the expected voting behavior of the other committee members: thus, if the first proposal is the one you care most about, it is by spending your bonus vote on this proposal that you can expect to benefit the most. Of course, once the votes on the first proposal are made public, typically fewer bonus votes will be left. All future proposals are, however, equally likely to receive bonus votes, and again, any voter left with the bonus vote should cast it on the proposal to which he assigns highest value.

The optimal voting strategy is very simple and corresponds to the intuitive rule of thumb of casting the bonus vote on one's highest-priority proposal. It is the only strategy that remains optimal for every voter, regardless of committee size and number of proposals on the agenda. It is also robust, in the sense that in many cases a voter should follow it even if other voters do not. Suppose that some cast their bonus vote randomly, or on their second, or third, or fifth priority. Because any proposal is just as likely to be chosen randomly, or to be someone's second, third, or fifth priority as it is to be somebody's first priority, nothing changes from the perspective of the remaining committee members, and their optimal strategy is unaffected.[2]

Note the good incentive properties: voters reveal their priorities truthfully through their own voting choices, and the bonus vote gives them weight. This a central feature of storable votes and stems directly from the budget constraint – the limited number of bonus votes – and hence from the links among the different proposals created by the budget constraint. The intensities with which preferences over the different proposals are held must be compared, and relative intensities are revealed sincerely and taken into account by the voting rule. In the case of a single bonus vote, what is revealed is the most strongly felt decision; with multiple bonus votes, the information revealed would be richer.

2. The optimal strategy changes only if some of the voters condition their voting choices on the *order* of proposals, as opposed to the intensity of their preference. I will return to this point in Chapter 4.

From the point of view of an individual voter, casting the bonus vote on a given proposal can only increase the probability that the preferred alternative wins. Clearly, using more votes cannot decrease the weight that an individual's preferences receive. The complication is that others are using their bonus votes, too. For example, if everyone casts the bonus vote on the same proposal, then every proposal is decided by simple majority, exactly as if no bonus votes were available. Storable votes make a difference if priorities differ across voters; if they do not, the bonus vote causes no damage, but it does not help, either. Suppose, then, that priorities do differ across voters, and bonus votes are cast on different proposals. In this case, the probability of obtaining one's preferred alternative is higher than with simple majority in the proposal on which the bonus vote is cast, but it is lower in the others: just as the presence of some "regular" voters works to increase the influence of those spending the bonus vote, the presence of "bigger" voters works to reduce the influence of those voters who cast their regular vote only.

To make matters concrete, suppose the bonus vote has the same value as any other vote, and consider two examples: an agenda of three proposals and an agenda of six. With each proposal equally likely to receive bonus votes from the other committee members, a voter's *probability of winning* any of the proposals – the probability of obtaining his preferred alternative – can be read from the Figure 1.1.[3]

The variable on the horizontal axis is the number of voters in the committee. The black dots plot the probability of winning when adding the bonus vote to one's regular vote, and the gray dots when casting the regular vote only, both relative to the corresponding probability with simple majority, when no bonus votes are allowed. Thus, for example, a dot at value 1.1 indicates a 10 percent increase in the probability of winning relative to simple majority voting, and a dot at 0.9 a 10 percent decline. In both figures, all black dots are above 1, and all gray dots are below 1, as expected. When the committee is small, the winning probabilities are very sensitive to odd or even numbers of members, and the dots in the graph "jump" with the addition of a single member. As the size of committee increases, the dots stabilize. In the case of three proposals, at larger committee sizes the probability of winning when

3. All calculations used to derive the figures are in Part II.

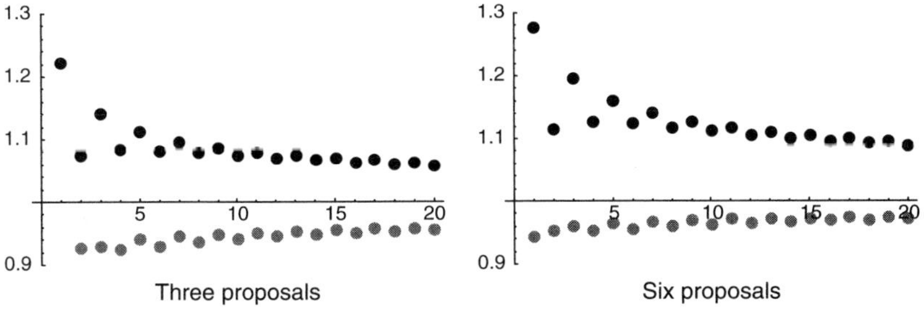

FIGURE 1.1 The effect of the bonus vote on winning probabilities. The horizontal axis is the number of voters. The black dots plot the probability of winning when casting the bonus vote, and the gray dots when not casting the bonus vote, both relative to the probability of winning with simple majority. The bonus vote is equivalent to a regular vote.

using the bonus vote is approximately 5 percent higher than with simple majority, and the probability of winning when not using the bonus vote is approximately 5 percent smaller. The direction of the change does not depend on the number of proposals on the agenda but the magnitude does, as shown by the second figure, with six proposals. As the number of proposals increases, the bonus votes become more dispersed; as a result, casting the bonus vote is more effective, and not casting it less penalizing (always relative to simple majority) than with three proposals. As the size of the committee increases, the probability of winning stabilizes around a 10 percent gain when using the bonus vote and a 3 percent loss when not using it.

The reason why storable votes can be preferable to simple majority voting is that the increase in the probability of winning is achieved over the decision that the voter considers most important, while the decline affects decisions about which the voter feels less strongly. Do storable votes then improve the committee's welfare?

1.1.4 *Welfare*

1.1.4.1 *The welfare criterion*

When we ask whether storable votes are desirable, from the point of view of the voters, the term "desirable" must be made precise. The normative evaluation must be separate from the personal benefit or loss derived in a specific instance. Thus, individuals should form their evaluation *before* the realization of their preferences is known or, equivalently, by referring not to the specific agenda or to the specific outcome of one meeting but to what they expect these to be in a typical meeting governed by the voting rule.[4]

The crucial element from which all other information can be deduced is the probability distribution that describes voters' preferences before uncertainty is resolved. As mentioned earlier, this probability distribution summarizes the environment in which decisions are taken. For example, if the committee's responsibilities are wide, a voter is likely to assign low intensities to most proposals, with few exceptions that matter to the voter greatly: the scenario is summarized by a probability distribution with large probability mass at low value realizations, and small probability mass at high values. If, instead, the committee is very specialized, a voter is likely to find all proposals of similar value, a scenario described by a probability distribution with most mass concentrated in a small interval.

As the Introduction discusses, in principle, the probability distribution of realized values could differ across different voters. In evaluating the group's welfare, however, on what basis can the preferences of one voter be recognized as systematically more intense than the preferences of another? The normative imperative of equal treatment translates into a normalization requiring that all committee members assign the same *average* value to the universe of possible proposals that come under the committee's jurisdiction. A stronger restriction, imposed in most of this book, is that the full probability distributions be identical across voters: it means forcing the voters to adopt an equal scale and to organize the different decisions according to a fixed ranking. Concretely, before the specific agenda is realized, each member expects that a typical proposal submitted to the committee will be of greatest importance to him (say, in the top 10 percent of possible values) with some probability. The model requires that such probability be equal across all members and extends

4. The observation that moral judgment requires a "veil of ignorance" over individuals' own positions in society was originally formalized by Harsanyi (1953, 1955) and recurs in welfare economics and in political philosophers' analyses of justice (most noticeably, Rawls (1971)).

this requirement to each interval of possible values. Imposing the same probability distribution does not amount to imposing the same *realizations* of intensities: *which* decisions will fall into the different intervals and, thus, which specific values will be realized typically will differ across different voters.

The evaluation of the voting rule should then be based on the expectation of future proposals, of their values, and of the voting outcomes that will follow, taking into consideration how voters will use their bonus votes. The expected utility measure that a voter can construct has no interpretation in itself: it is a number whose magnitude depends on the number of proposals and on the arbitrary scaling of the values distribution – whether, for example, the maximum possible value attached to each proposal is normalized to 1 or to 100. Any meaningful reading of the measure must be *relative*: it requires that it be compared to the equivalent measure under a different voting rule or a different decision-making procedure. An obvious possibility is to compare expected utility with storable votes to expected utility with simple majority voting; a still better alternative is to express both relative to expected utility under some ideal decision-making rule, thus being able to evaluate how well the two voting rules work, in some absolute sense.

As in the case of the two voting rules, the optimal decision-making rule specifies whether any future proposal should pass or fail, depending on the future realized preferences of the committee members, cannot discriminate according to the voter's identity, and must be chosen *ex ante*, before the agenda is specified and preferences are known. Under these constraints, the rule that every voter prefers, the rule that maximizes every voter's long-term payoff, is one that for each proposal favors the side with higher total value. A moment of thought makes the intuition clear. A rule that always favors the larger side (simple majority) means that a voter can expect to win more than half of the time. This is certainly better than deciding with a coin toss (in which the voter would expect to win half of the time), and better than a rule that favored the smaller side. It is the rule that maximizes the frequency with which any voter expects to win, but it is still not ideal because it does not recognize that some decisions matter a lot and some do not. A rule that favors the side with higher total value maximizes the total utility of the committee as a whole, and because everyone is identical before preferences are realized, that same rule must maximize the expected utility of any of the voters. Note that, although optimal, the rule cannot be used in practice because it depends on voters' intensity of preferences, a variable that is not observable and that individuals have an incentive to misrepresent: every voter would say that he cares very strongly about all decisions.

If the optimal decision-making rule provides a ceiling, it is also useful to consider a floor on the expected utility that an individual can achieve. In measuring how well a decision rule fares, a plausible floor is expected utility when decisions are made by flipping a coin, ignoring voters' preferences. The difference in expected utility between the ceiling (the optimal rule) and the floor (the equally probable random outcome) is the *available surplus* – the room for improvement over flipping a coin that is available to a decision rule. The measure of welfare most often used in this book is the share of available surplus that a voting rule is expected to appropriate: that is, how much of the improvement that the optimal scheme achieves over flipping a coin can be achieved through storable votes or majority voting.

1.1.4.2 Welfare comparisons

To begin evaluating the welfare properties of storable votes, some concrete examples will help. Even if in practice evaluations are likely to be more qualitative, precise numerical analyses discipline thought and clarify the role of different assumptions. Suppose that the bonus vote is equivalent to a regular vote. Consider first a situation in which voters have very little information, the committee's range of actions is diverse, and, as a result, voters believe that future proposals are equally likely to be of any degree of importance. For both storable votes and simple majority, the two diagrams in Figure 1.2 plot a voter's expected utility before the specific agenda is on the table, for the two cases of three and six proposals, expressed as the share of available surplus. Before the agenda is realized, all voters are identical, and a voter's expected utility summarizes the rule's welfare properties for all voters. A dot in the diagram at 0.9, for example, means that the voting rule is expected to capture 90 percent of the utility improvement of the optimal rule relative to flipping a coin. As in Figure 1.1, the variable on the horizontal axis is the number of voters in the committee. The black dots refer to storable votes, and the gray dots refer to simple majority voting. With storable votes, the figure

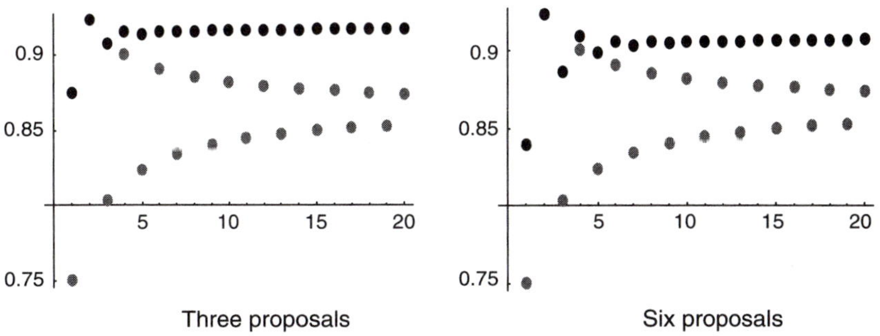

FIGURE 1.2 Expected surplus, as share of maximal surplus. The horizontal axis is the number of voters. The black dots refer to storable votes, the gray dots to simple majority, both as share of the optimal rule. The bonus vote is equivalent to a regular vote. Proposals are equally likely to be of any value.

is constructed under the expectation that all voters cast their bonus vote on their highest-intensity proposal, as indeed is rational.

The number of proposals makes very little difference. In both diagrams, the gray dots corresponding to simple majority voting trace two different curves: a lower curve, when the number of voters is even, and a higher curve, when the number is odd, whereas the black dots tend to be much closer to one another. Indeed, the most striking aspect of the figure is the stability of the storable votes' welfare measure, as opposed to the sensitivity of simple majority to odd or even numbers, especially when there are few voters.

With majority voting, when the number of voters is even and small, the probability of a tie is high, and there is no natural criterion guiding how to make the decision. Here I suppose that either side is chosen with equal probability, but other plausible outcomes (for example, favoring the status quo, if there is one) give very similar results: the voting system is inefficient because the decision criterion cannot reflect how strongly the two different sides feel about the proposal in question. When the number of voters is odd and small, on the other hand, majority voting performs well, because not only is a tie ruled out, but the majority is always so large, relative to the minority – twice as large in the case of three voters, at least 50 percent larger in the case of five – that only rarely would accounting for strength of preferences recommend the opposite outcome. The curve traced by the gray dots when the number of voters is odd lies above the curve traced when the number is even, and the difference is more pronounced when the number is small.

With storable votes, a tie occurs not when the number of *voters* is equal on the two sides, but when the number of *votes* is equal. This is very different: because of the bonus votes, the probability of a tie does not change much, whether the number of voters is odd or even. More than that, because bonus votes are used to express the intensity of voters' preferences, storable votes tend to favor the side that feels more strongly about the issue in question, as the optimal rule does. The figure shows that the two voting schemes are equivalent in committees of three voters (the highest point in both diagrams, where the black and the gray dots are superimposed), but storable votes outperform simple majority for all other committee sizes. Predictably, the difference is larger when the number of voters is even and small.

What happens when the number of proposals on the agenda increases? Both the optimal decision rule and majority voting are unaffected by changes in the number of proposals, because in both cases each decision is taken independently of all others. With storable votes, instead, decisions are tied by the votes' budget constraint: there is a single bonus vote to be cast on only one of the proposals. In this specific example, the relative performance of storable votes is slightly weakened by moving from three to six proposals and eventually stabilizes to a gain over simple majority of approximately 3 percent of possible surplus, as opposed to a gain of approximately 5 percent in the case of three proposals. The conclusion is not general, however. When the number of proposals increases, there are more proposals over which a voter cannot cast the bonus vote and over which his influence is less than with simple majority. But the value he expects to associate with the decision he will care most about increases, too, and so does the gain from having more influence over this one decision. Which of the two effects dominates depends on how large the expected difference in value between the voter's highest priority and all others is, and, thus, on the values' probability distribution, reflecting the committee's responsibilities.

It is probably unrealistic to think that voters can describe fully the nuances of values they expect to attribute to future proposals. A coarse classification, rather than a continuous distribution, seems more likely. Suppose, then, that voters classify proposals into four classes of importance: "not important," "somewhat important," "important," and "very important," with these labels corresponding to a partition of the range of possible intensities into four intervals of equal size. Depending on the type of committee, members assign probabilities to the event that a random future proposal will correspond to each of the four classes. Consider the three examples in Figure 1.3.

The height of each column corresponds to the probability assigned to a typical proposal falling within each class of importance. The gray columns represent the example just discussed, in which voters believe that a typical proposal brought in front of the committee is equally likely to be "not important," "very important" or anything in between. The white columns correspond to a situation in which most decisions are expected to be strongly felt, with an increasing fraction falling into increasingly higher importance: only 5 percent of proposals are considered "not important" and close to 45 percent "very important." Finally, the black columns correspond to the opposite case, in which a full 50 percent of all

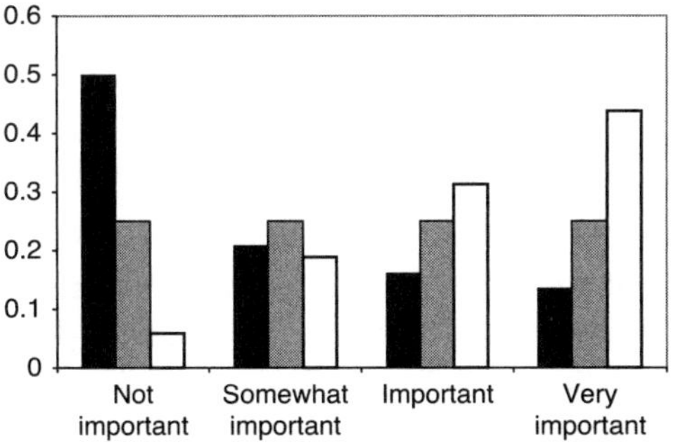

FIGURE 1.3 An example: Three coarse assessments of the probable importance of a random proposal. Each column denotes the probability of ranking a proposal in the corresponding class of importance, for three different distributions of values. The category "not important" corresponds to the lowest 25 percent of values; "somewhat important" to the second lowest quarter; "important" to values in the second highest, and "very important" to values in the highest quarter.*

* The columns are discrete approximations of continuous probability distributions, described by the cumulative distribution function $F(v) = v^b$ with different values of the parameter $b : b = 1/2$ (black columns); $b = 1$ (gray columns) and $b = 2$ (white columns).

future decisions are expected to be "not important," with the expected proportion belonging to each class declining as the attributed importance increases, until only about 10 percent of all proposals are expected to be "very important."

A bonus vote is most valuable when it allows a voter to select the rare proposal that matters to him, in contrast to the great majority that do not – the scenario represented by the black columns. Here, storable votes work particularly well: relative to simple majority, their performance is better than in Figure 1.2 for any number of proposals and all sizes of the committee. With three proposals, for example, the percentage gain over simple majority in the share of available surplus stabilizes at approximately 13 percent, at committee sizes of approximately twenty members or more.

On the other hand, consider a committee whose authority is exercised almost exclusively on matters of real consequence to all members, the scenario represented by the white columns in Figure 1.3. Now, storable votes perform less well because the possibility to increase one's voting power on a single issue, at the cost of reducing it on the others, is less valuable. With three proposals, storable votes continue to compare favorably to simple majority if the number of voters is either even or large enough, but their welfare properties are worse if the number of voters is odd and small. With a committee of three voters, storable votes are associated with a loss in expected welfare of 3 percent, relative to simple majority. As the size of the committee increases, the loss declines, reaching 1 percent for a committee of nine members and eventually becoming a gain of approximately 1 percent when the committee size reaches twenty-five or more.

These results are summarized in the top panels of Figure 1.4 (Figure 1.4a), representing the ratio of expected utility with storable votes to expected utility with simple majority, with three proposals. A dot at a vertical value of 1, for example, indicates that the two voting rules are equivalent. The horizontal axis is the number of voters, and, to keep the figures easy to read, the panel on the left refers to odd numbers; the panel on the right to even numbers. The color of the dots refers to the color of the columns in Figure 1.3.

I have used the example of three proposals to be concrete, but, in general, a committee will evaluate a different number of proposals at

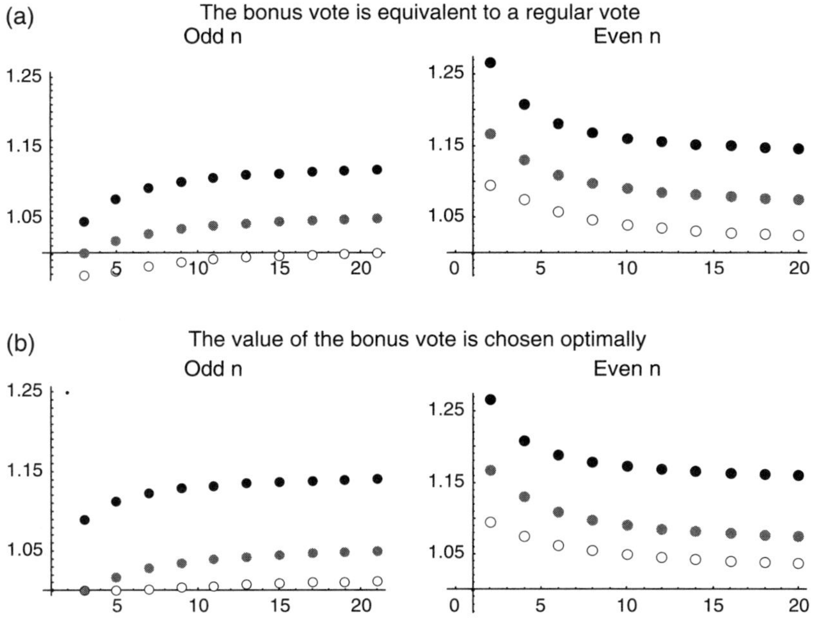

FIGURE 1.4 Expected utility with storable votes, relative to simple majority, for different value distributions. Three proposals. The horizontal axis is the number of voters, odd in the figures on the left, even in the figures on the right. The different colors correspond to the three different value distributions approximated by the columns of matching color in Figure 1.3. In Figure 1.4b, the value of the bonus vote is 2 for the black dots, 1 for the gray dots, and 0.5 for the white dots.

each meeting. The analysis can be extended immediately by considering the probability of each number of proposals. There is no reason why the calculations should not be transparent, and Box 1.2 describes one example in some detail.

Box 1.2 The welfare calculations: An example

Alice, Barbara, Caroline, and Dorothea – A, B, C, and D – form a committee that will meet regularly to vote on several proposals at each session. Consider A's reasoning in evaluating whether storable votes are desirable, relative to majority voting, keeping in mind that the evaluation takes place before any concrete proposal is identified, and the voting rule, if chosen, will be maintained over all future meetings of the committee. If the reasoning seems too sophisticated, read it as a measure of how each of A, B, C, and D would fare on average over many meetings of the committee, under either voting rule. The bonus vote is equivalent to a regular vote.

Consider first a meeting with three proposals. Alice begins by estimating the impact that storable votes will have on her probability of winning any proposal. She knows and takes into account that preferences are not correlated within the group and that, like herself, B, C, and D are equally likely to favor or oppose any proposal. If no bonus votes are allowed, A wins if B, C, and D all agree with her (with probability $(1/2)^3$); if two of the three agree with her (with probability $3(1/2)^3$), or if one of the three agrees with her and A's group wins the tie break (with probability $3(1/2)^3(1/2)$). The total probability of these events is 11/16, or 69 percent. In the presence of bonus votes, A conjectures that each of the other will cast her bonus vote on her most important proposal. With intensities of preferences uncorrelated across the four voters, any proposal has probability 1/3 of being a voter's priority, regardless of how intensely others feel about it. With these elements, A can calculate her probability of winning. Suppose, first, that A casts her bonus vote. If all three others also cast their bonus vote (an event with probability $(1/3)^3$), everyone casts the same number of votes, the scenario is identical to simple majority, and A wins with probability 11/16. If none of the others casts a bonus vote (with probability $(2/3)^3$), A wins if at least one of them agrees with her, an event occurring with probability $1 - (1/2)^3 = 7/8$. The other scenarios can be computed in the same manner: if only one of the others casts her bonus vote (with probability $3(1/3)(2/3)^2$), A wins with probability 3/4, and if two do so (with probability $3(2/3)(1/3)^2$), A again wins with probability 3/4. Thus, A's probability of winning a proposal when casting her bonus vote is as follows: $(2/3)^3(7/8) + (1/3)^3(11/16) + 3(1/3)(2/3)^2(3/4) + 3(2/3)(1/3)^2(3/4)$, or 78.5 percent. Following the same logic, A's probability of winning when *not* casting her bonus vote can be calculated as 64 percent. Thus, relative to simple majority voting, storable votes allow a voter to win her first priority decision more often (an increase of almost 10 percent) but also cause her to win the other two decisions less often (a decrease of 5 percent). Whether the trade-off is advantageous depends on the importance A assigns to her first priority, relative to the other decisions on the table.

Before any concrete agenda is specified, this relative importance must be estimated. Suppose that A estimates that any proposal is equally likely to be of any degree of importance. In different, but equivalent, terms, A estimates that there is a 10 percent chance that she will judge a proposal in the highest 10 percent range of possible importance, a 20 percent chance that she will judge it in the highest 20 percent range, etc. It is not difficult to verify that these beliefs imply that A expects to feel twice as strongly about her first priority proposal than, on average, she will feel about the others. Thus, together the two less important decisions will matter to Alice, on average, as much as the most important one. Since the increase in the probability of winning the latter is almost twice as large as the decrease in the probability of winning the two less important issues, expected utility with storable votes must be higher than expected utility with majority voting.

Assigning specific values to the boundaries of possible intensities yields specific numbers, summarizing the welfare evaluations. The exact numbers differ with different boundaries, but the ratios of expected utilities with different decision-making rules do not. Here, the interval of intensities is normalized as lying between 0 at the minimum and 1 at the maximum. On average, then, each of A, B, C, and D will assign to a random proposal an intensity of 0.5; the most strongly felt of the three proposals has an expected intensity of 0.75 and the weakest an expected intensity of 0.25. Expected utility with simple majority then equals (0.69)(0.5)(3) – the expected utility associated with each proposal is equal, and there are three proposals. Expected utility with storable votes on the other hand is (0.785)(0.75) + (0.64)(0.5) + (0.64)(0.25). The numbers are 1.03 and 1.067: relative to simple majority, storable votes yield a percentage gain in expected utility just below 4 percent, a result that would be unchanged had the normalization been different. If decisions were always resolved in favor of the side with higher total value, expected utility can be calculated to be 1.10. Thus, a committee member expects to obtain, on average, 97 percent of maximum expected utility with storable votes, and slightly below 94 percent with simple majority voting. If decisions are taken randomly, expected utility equals 0.75 – or (1/2)(0.5)(3), because the probability of winning any decision is 1/2. The percentage of available surplus over random decision-making that storable votes are expected to capture is then: (1.067 – 0.75)/(1.10 – 0.75), or 90.8 percent, versus 80.4 percent with majority voting.

It may well be that A, B, C, and D do not know exactly how many proposals will be decided at each meeting. For example, they may guess that there will be between three and ten proposals, but that this will vary across meetings. The same reasoning can be replicated for each case, and an average can be computed. If any number of proposals between three and ten proposals is equally probable, on average, expected utility with storable votes is 2.5 percent higher than with simple majority, and just above 96 percent of expected utility under the most-efficient rule (versus 93.7 percent for simple majority voting). In terms of available surplus, the percentage appropriated on average is 88 percent with storable votes, versus 80.4 percent with simple majority. The decline in the advantage enjoyed by storable votes, relative to majority, depends on the specific distribution of values – the assumption that any proposal is equally likely to be of any degree of importance – and may or may not occur with other distributions.

Once we understand what makes storable votes more or less desirable, we can think of improving the rule. First of all, when a large fraction of proposals are important, a single bonus vote does not allow a voter to represent his full priorities correctly. Why not grant *multiple* bonus votes? This is a question addressed in the next chapter.

Second, the impact of the bonus vote on the probability of winning a decision depends on the bonus vote's value, relative to a regular vote – whether it is worth one regular vote, as supposed so far, or two, or ten, or one-half. The larger its value, the stronger the effects: the larger the increase in the probability of winning the proposal on which the bonus vote is cast, but the larger the decrease in all other proposals.

Thus, ideally, the value of the bonus vote should depend on the relative importance assigned to the highest-priority proposal versus all others. Suppose that the probability of proposals of different importance is represented by the three cases in Figure 1.3. In the case of the black columns, having a bonus vote worth two regular votes, as opposed to one, improves the welfare properties of the voting mechanism, at all committee sizes and for all numbers of proposals: having a "big" bonus vote to cast on the occasional important decision is valuable, and the loss in influence over the other proposals is not very harmful. In the case of the white columns, on the other hand, storable votes perform better if the weight of the bonus vote is *reduced*. If the bonus vote is worth half of a regular vote (that is, if two bonus votes are needed to counter a regular vote), then expected utility with storable votes is always at least as high as with simple majority. Here most decisions are likely to be important, and losing influence over all proposals that are not one's single highest priority is costly. The bottom panels of Figure 1.4 show these results.[5]

The value of the bonus vote is part of the design of the voting scheme – the bonus vote is a special additional vote, and there is nothing particularly artificial in making it different from a regular vote. Is it *always*, however, possible to find a value of the bonus vote such that storable votes outperform simple majority? The answer is "almost always." More precisely, the answer is in Proposition 1.2 of Box 1.1, the main conclusion of the formal analysis. A value of the bonus vote that improves over simple majority is guaranteed to exist if one of the following conditions is satisfied: either the number of voters is even, or it is large enough, or the difference in expected intensity between a voter's highest priority and the average proposal is large enough. The proposition says a bit more: given the distribution of intensities that voters expect to assign to the proposals, it identifies the minimum committee size such that the storable votes scheme can be superior to simple majority voting. For the three examples of Figure 1.3, the only cases for which a strict improvement in expected welfare cannot be guaranteed are committees with three or five voters when most decisions are important (when the probability distribution is described by the white columns).

5. In the intermediate case, in which an equal fraction of all proposals is expected to belong to each class of importance (the gray columns), the bonus vote should be equivalent to a regular vote.

The conclusion, then, is that the welfare properties of storable votes depend on the probability distribution of preference intensities and on the value of the bonus vote, which itself should be chosen according to the distribution of intensities – large if low intensities are more likely, small if high intensities are more likely. This said, in practical applications, setting the bonus vote at the optimal value seems difficult. First, it requires the knowledge, shared by all, of the probability distribution of intensities. Second, in general, the value of the bonus vote should be different for different committees, opening the voting scheme to confusion and manipulation. It seems more reasonable to keep the system as simple, as unambiguous, and as constant as possible. For most of this book, the value of the bonus vote, or bonus votes when more than one is granted, will be kept constant. The numerical examples discussed in this chapter, the intuitions they convey, and the formal results in Box 1.1 all suggest the same lesson: it is prudent to set such a value not too high. The conservative recommendation is that the bonus vote should have a value not larger, and maybe smaller, than a regular vote.

1.2 The Experiment

The theoretical properties of the mechanism are one thing, but the use of the bonus vote in practice may be another. Laboratory experiments provide a controlled environment in which the scenario studied by the theory can be replicated, and deviations in behavior detected. They are the natural first stage in testing a new mechanism and are used extensively throughout this book. With a single bonus vote, a voter's decision problem is simple, and the optimal strategy is very intuitive. The one remaining concern is the possible temptation to hoard the bonus vote and use it disproportionately on later decisions.

Seven experimental sessions were run in 2006 and 2007 in the Center for Experimental Social Science (CESS) at New York University and studied how voters used the bonus vote.[6] Because both the practical organization of the experiment and its structure are common to all

---

6. The experiment was designed, programmed, and run with the help of Raj Advani, Bogachen Celen, and Shuky Ehrenberg.

experiments in the book, I describe them in some detail. Subjects were registered students who enrolled in the experiment by logging into CESS web site, and each of them participated in one experimental session only. After entering the laboratory, the subjects were seated randomly in booths separated by partitions and were assigned ID numbers corresponding to their computer terminals. When everyone was seated, the experimenter read aloud the instructions and answered all questions publicly. Each experimental session consisted of multiple *rounds*, varying in number from a minimum of five to a maximum of twenty. Each round consisted of the same voting game: subjects were matched randomly into committees of either three or four members and voted over three consecutive proposals, casting one regular vote for each proposal and a single bonus vote, which in all sessions had value equal to a regular vote.

Laboratory experiments are designed to control two variables that more than any others are difficult for an outsider to evaluate outside the laboratory: preferences and information. Preferences are not elicited, with the difficulty of evaluating the sincerity of the answers and comparing intensities across subjects; rather, they are induced, in the form of payoffs that are actually earned if the proposals are decided in the direction that the computer specifies for each subject.[7] To avoid adding subjective, and thus unknown, reactions to specific issues, the proposals are kept abstract and are distinguished by a neutral identifier, which was color in this experiment (green, blue, or red) and in the experiments described in other chapters. Information is always communicated publicly, ensuring that every subject not only shares the same information but is aware that everyone else does, too.

At the start of each voting game, each subject was told whether he was in favor of or against each of the three proposals (the direction of his preferences) and how much he would earn if each of the three proposals went in his preferred direction (the intensity of his preferences). For example, a subject would read on his computer monitor, "You are against the Green proposal and will earn 22 points if the Green

7. Factors remain that cannot easily be controlled – the value attached to money, the risk-aversion of specific subjects. They are not problematic in the experiment described here, in which the working assumption is simply that subjects prefer a higher payoff to a lower one, and, thus, everything else equal, prefer to cast more votes on the proposal that is associated with the largest gain.

proposal does not pass; you will earn 0 points if the Green proposal passes," and correspondingly for the other two proposals, typically with different preferred directions and different values. At the end of the experimental session, accumulated points were exchanged into dollars at a preannounced rate, yielding average hourly earnings of approximately $20. Subjects were not told the preferences of the other committee members, but during the instructions period everybody was informed of the statistical process followed by the computer in assigning all preferences: each subject was equally likely to be in favor or against any proposal, and each subject's value was equally likely to be any number between 1 and 100. Thus, any proposal had equal probability of being associated with any admissible value, and a coarse approximation into four classes of importance would look like the gray columns in Figure 1.3.

The order of proposals, announced at the start of each voting game, was chosen randomly by the computer, independently of the proposals' color. After being shown his values, a subject chose whether to cast his bonus vote on the first proposal. The computer screen then showed the number of votes cast by each member of the subject's committee, whether the proposal had passed or not, and the subject's own payoff from the vote on the first proposal (ties were broken randomly by the computer). The committee then proceeded in the same manner to the second proposal, and then to the third and last, when all remaining votes were automatically cast. The vote over the third proposal concluded the voting game, the round. Subjects were then assigned a new budget of votes, and a new round started where three proposals were again voted upon in sequence. Four of the seven experimental sessions included a second treatment, described in Chapter 4, that required that the composition of the committees be kept fixed for the duration of the experiment. Because subjects' values were independent across both proposals and subjects, there should have been neither the incentive nor the possibility of coordinating voting choices, even with fixed committees. To verify that this was indeed the case, two experimental sections (identified as Sections 4 and 5 in Table 1.1) were designed with random rematching of subjects into new committees at the end of each round. The behavior of the subjects in these two sections is indistinguishable from all others. As for all

Table 1.1 Experimental Design

Session	Committees Size	No. of Subjects	Rounds
1	3	12	20
2	3	12	10
3	3	15	10
4	4	12	12
5	4	12	12
6	4	12	8
7	4	16	5

experiments described in the book, a sample of the instructions is in the Appendix.[8]

The experimental design is summarized in Table 1.1.

The results of the experiment were very close to the theory. The 91 subjects played a total of 974 rounds and in each decided which of the three proposals was to receive the bonus vote. In 974 rounds, there were 76 instances in all in which the bonus vote was not cast on the subject's highest value, and of these 76 strategic mistakes, a third (25) were due to only three subjects. Figure 1.5 reports the frequency of strategic mistakes and the corresponding number of subjects. The bins on the horizontal axis are frequencies of errors, as percentages of the total number of rounds in which a subject participated; the vertical axis is the number of subjects who fall into each bin. The figure says that 58 of the 91 subjects, close to two thirds of all subjects, never made any mistake; 12 made mistakes not more than 10 percent of the time; and 13 made mistakes not more than 20 percent of the time.

Did subjects benefit from storable votes? For the two committee sizes used in the experiments, Table 1.2 reports the expected share of available surplus that the theory associates with storable votes and simple majority voting. With the parameters used in the experiment, storable votes are expected to be equivalent to simple majority voting when committees

8. All storable-votes experiments, including those described in later chapters, were programmed with the Multistage Game software package developed jointly between the Social Science Experimental Laboratory (SSEL) at Caltech and the California Social Science Experimental Laboratory (CASSEL) at UCLA. This open-source software can be downloaded from http://software.ssel.caltech.edu/

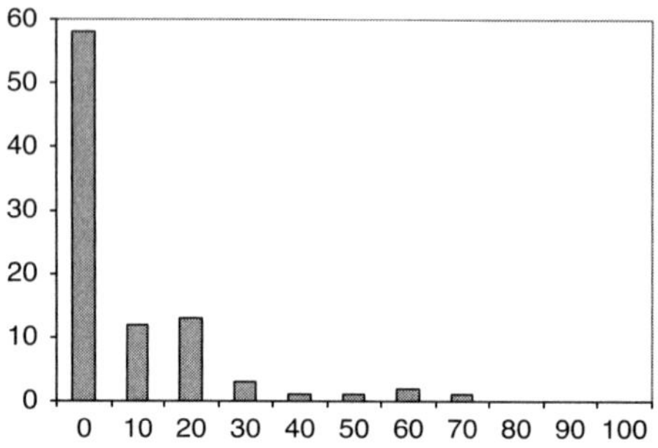

FIGURE 1.5 Experimental results: Individual error rates (91 subjects). The bins on the horizontal axis are percentages of errors over all rounds played; the vertical axis is the number of subjects in each corresponding bin.

Table 1.2 Theoretical Predictions

Committees Size	Surplus SV	Surplus Maj. Voting
3	92.3	92.3
4	90.8	80.4

are composed of three voters and superior when they are composed of four voters.

Figure 1.6 reports realized aggregate experimental earnings in each session and compares them both to the theoretical predictions (Figure 1.6a) and to the earnings that subjects would have had if decisions had been made with simple majority voting (Figure 1.6b). Each dot corresponds to an experimental session; black dots represent three-voter committees, and white dots represent four-voter committees.

Consider first Figure 1.6a. The vertical axis measures aggregate experimental earnings in each session as share of maximum possible total earnings; the horizontal axis measures the share of maximal earnings that subjects would have earned, had they made no strategic mistakes. All measures are calculated using the values assigned to subjects' preferences by the computer in each experimental session. For example, suppose that in a given round the assigned preferences for the Blue proposal in a three-person committee were $\{-27, 91, -32\}$. Then, over that proposal in that round, maximum aggregate earnings were 91 – the side favoring the proposal had higher value than the

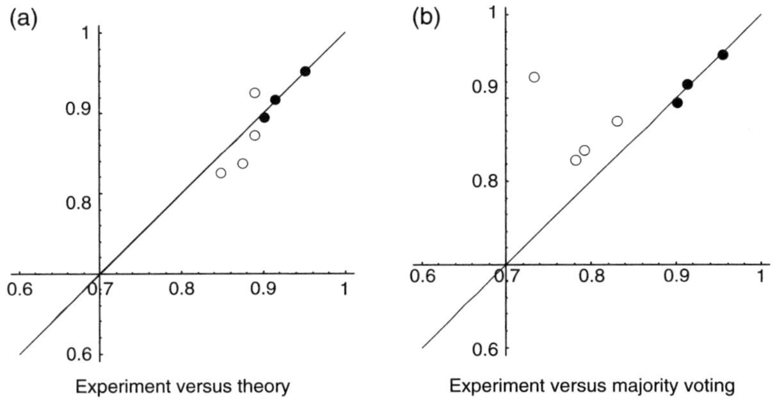

FIGURE 1.6 Experimental surplus, as share of maximal surplus. The vertical axis reports total experimental earnings per session, as share of maximal earnings. The horizontal axis reports the share of maximal earnings that subjects would have earned in each session in the absence of any strategic mistake (Figure 1.6a), or if decisions had been made through simple majority (Figure 1.6b). Black dots are sessions with three-voter committees; white dots with four-voter committees. All earnings are measured as gains over earnings with random decision-making.

side opposing it ($27 + 32 = 59$). Aggregate experimental earnings were the earnings realized in the experiment, in which the winning side was the side casting more votes, including bonus votes. Aggregate earnings in the absence of strategic mistakes would be computed taking into account the subjects' assigned values over the other two proposals, and supposing that each subject cast his bonus vote on the proposal with highest value. In the figure, all earnings are measured as gains over expected earnings when the proposal is decided by flipping a coin ($(1/2)(91) + (1/2)(59) = 75$ for the for the Blue proposal in this example), and thus the measures are immediately comparable to the numbers in Table 1.2.

The vertical axis shows that realized earnings ranged between 82 and 92 percent of maximal earnings for committees of four voters, and between 89 and 95 percent for committee of three voters. As predicted, the share tends to be higher for groups of three voters than for groups of four. The effect of strategic mistakes appears in the vertical distance between each dot and the 45-degree line: by construction, dots on the 45-degree lines are sessions in which the aggregate payoff is exactly as predicted by theory. The three experimental sessions with three-voter committees all yielded aggregate earnings that match almost perfectly those predicted by the theory. For four-voter committees, the results are slightly more variable, reflecting the lower number of rounds and, thus, the higher variability of average intensities and aggregate payoffs, but the distance from the 45-degree line remains small.

As expected from Table 1.2, the difference between the two treatments emerges clearly when experimental earnings are compared to earnings under majority voting. In Figure 1.6b, the vertical axis is again the share of maximal earnings captured in each session, but the horizontal axis reports the corresponding share under majority voting, again with the realized experimental draws – in the example above, aggregate earnings with majority voting would equal 59, since the majority opposes the proposal. As in Figure 1.6a, all earnings are measured as gains over random decision-making, and can be compared to the predictions of Table 1.2. Dots above the 45-degree line indicate experimental sessions in which aggregate earnings were higher than they would have been with majority voting.

As shown in Table 1.2, the theory predicts that three-voter committees should fare equally well under storable votes as under simple majority voting, while four-voter committees should fare better. Indeed, now all four white dots are above the 45-degree line, one particularly so, while the three black dots continue to lie on the 45-degree line. Again, the theoretical predictions are borne out. The disparity in results between the two treatments deserves emphasis: the four-voter committees' results show that storable votes are indeed capable of making a difference.

The experiment was very simple and the positive results not too surprising. They are, however, encouraging. The most basic model of storable votes has not been rejected. The next chapters can begin to enrich it.

1.3 Conclusions

Individuals differ in the strength with which they hold preferences over the alternatives offered to their choice. Any single individual will consider some choices important and some trivial, and different individuals will typically rank the importance they assign to the various options differently. This is true for private goods, and it is the basis of the functioning of markets through prices. It is also true for public decisions, and a voting system that is responsive to the intensity of people's preferences can exploit and mirror this difference, allowing voters to come closer to their preferred outcome when it matters to them most. Storable votes is a voting system with just such a property: by granting a budget of votes to cast freely over a set of decisions, it allows voters to express the intensity of their preferences, exactly as prices do in a market system, and to increase the probability of obtaining the outcome they desire in those decisions in which they are willing to "spend" more of their budget of votes.

This chapter has studied the simplest model of storable votes, in which, in addition to a regular vote for each decision, voters are granted a single extra vote to cast freely over a set of binary decisions, and preferences are not correlated either across voters or across decisions. Each decision is taken according to the majority of votes cast. The single bonus vote reduces the analysis to its essence and clarifies the intuitions on which the system rests. In contrast to simple majority voting, the addition of a single bonus vote is sufficient to stabilize the performance of the voting rule, regardless of whether the number of voters is odd or even. Majority voting performs well when the number of voters is small and odd, but especially if the bonus vote is of value comparable or somewhat smaller to a regular vote, storable votes outperform it for all or almost all numbers of voters. The result is unambiguous if decisions are either equally likely to be considered of any level of importance, or if most decisions are judged to be low priorities, with the occasional outlier that can then benefit from the bonus vote. Confirming the straightforward, intuitive logic behind storable votes, the theoretical predictions were almost exactly verified in a laboratory experiment.

2

Storing Votes over Time

Part of the appeal of storable votes is the possibility to link votes *over time*. In Chapter 1, committee members vote over different proposals sequentially but know their preferences over the full agenda of the meeting and have a single bonus vote. Together, these two features effectively make the problem static – nothing would change if all votes were simultaneous. Storable votes, however, can be applied to situations that are truly dynamic, in which time *does* matter because preferences and alternatives become clearer, and the evolving distribution of available bonus votes among the different individuals, not only their total number, affects behavior.

Think for example of the European Central Bank, whose Governing Council meets each month to decide the bank's interest rate policy, and, for our purposes, think of the choice as binary – either leave the interest rate as is, or change it by an agreed-upon amount in an agreed-upon direction. Suppose that each monthly decision is made according to the majority of votes cast – as indeed stated in the European Central Bank's statute – but that each Council member is given twelve votes on January 1 to spend as desired over the twelve monthly meetings. In a given month, a member who disagrees with the majority view but has hopes of swaying the Council may choose to cast multiple votes in support of his preferred decision, at the cost of abstaining during several other months. Such a choice requires an estimate of future policies, and thus of future economic conditions that cannot be known precisely at the time of voting. What each Council member knows at the European Central Bank, and is assumed known in the model, are the statistical properties followed by the different national economies, including his own, and thus by each country's ideal interest-rate policy. It is on the basis of this incomplete knowledge that each member forms his voting strategy.

In a formulation that is almost equivalent but easier to analyze, committee members can be granted a regular vote for each decision and a stock of bonus votes to distribute freely over time. The natural analogy to granting all votes at the beginning of a voting cycle is to allow for multiple bonus votes. Relative to a single bonus vote, committee members now have a more flexible instrument, but a more difficult problem: they need to choose not only which decisions deserve their bonus votes but also how many votes they want to cumulate over any of the decisions.

The scenario is more complex, and the probability of strategic mistakes higher, but the intuitive sense of what the bonus votes can achieve and how they can be used remains very clear. The contrast makes the game a particularly good object of experimental study: are people actually able to solve the problem optimally? And if they are not, how do storable votes perform then?[1]

2.1 The Theory

The model builds directly on the previous chapter and is described formally in Box 2.1. In brief, a group of individuals votes sequentially over a known number of proposals, each of which can either pass or fail. The proposals are presented to the group over time. Voters have a regular vote to cast over every proposal, plus a stock of bonus votes that can be used freely. Each bonus vote is equivalent to a regular vote. Decisions are taken according to the majority of votes cast, including bonus votes, with ties broken randomly. Individuals' preferences are characterized by the preferred direction of any proposal – up or down – and by the intensity with which such preference is held. When deciding how many votes to cast over a given proposal, a voter knows how many bonus votes each of the other committee members still has available and knows his own preferences over the current proposal. He does not know,

1. The original intertemporal model comes from Casella (2005). This chapter is based on Casella, Gelman, and Palfrey (2006).

however, the preferences of the other committee members or his own preferences over proposals that will be brought to a vote later. The voter knows the statistical properties that both his own and others' preferences satisfy: in particular, preferences are independent both across proposals and across individuals; voters are equally likely to be against or in favor of any proposal, and the known probability distribution of intensities is identical for all voters and identical whether a voter favors or opposes a proposal. As in Chapter 1, the restrictions imposed on the distribution of preferences simplify the analysis, highlight the essence of the voting mechanism, and have the added benefit of making the game easier to grasp for subjects who play it in the laboratory.

What does the theory say about voters' best strategies? As far as the direction of the votes, the answer remains very simple: there is no reason to vote against one's preferred direction, because today's preferred direction holds no information about one's own future preferences and, thus, cannot be used to affect others' voting strategies. The interesting question is the number of votes that each voter should cast. Multiple bonus votes complicate voters' strategic considerations, but there is a precisely defined sense in which the simple rule of casting more votes over one's priorities always holds true. The result, summarized in Proposition 2.1 in Box 2.1, states that *given* the bonus votes held by others and the number of proposals still on the agenda, it is always better for a voter to cast at least as many votes on a decision over which he feels more strongly than on one over which he feels less strongly. The result may seem trivial, but in fact it is essential to the functioning of storable votes: it is this *monotonicity* in the number of votes – the higher the intensity, the larger the number of votes cast – that makes it possible for a voter to express the intensities of his preferences. As this chapter will show, it is this monotonicity, intuitively understood and easily satisfied, that keeps the actual performance of storable votes in the experiments close to their theoretical properties, even in the presence of other strategic mistakes.

It is easy to see why mistakes may occur. A voter is likely to cast more votes on a proposal on which he feels strongly than on one over which his intensity is weak, as theory says he should – for example, he will cast more votes if the intensity of his preference is in the top 10 percent of the intensity scale than if it is in the bottom third. But *how many* more? Suppose he has five bonus votes: should he cast three in the first case and one in the second? Or four and one? Or two and none? The answer must depend on the environment: the number of voters, of proposals, and of bonus votes, and the probability distribution of the voters' preferences. But it must also depend on the state of the game at the moment the voter makes his decision: the number of proposals that remain to be voted upon, and the number of bonus votes still held by each of the other members. Clearly, this decision is a complicated matter, much more so than the choice of where to cast the single bonus vote in Chapter 1. Thus, a voter's best strategy can be thought of in two parts: the intuitive rule of casting more votes, all else equal, on proposals that the voter considers more important, and the detailed, difficult determination of the exact number of votes to cast.

The theoretical predictions cannot be described without referring to the *equilibrium* strategy: the rule followed by each voter, linking the number of votes cast to the environment, one's own preferences, and the state of the game, that generates the voter's highest possible utility when the other voters themselves follow the rule that yields each of them maximal utility, given everybody's correct understanding of the rules followed by the others. In a symmetric equilibrium, as studied in this and the previous chapter, the equilibrium rule is identical for all voters – each of them would respond identically if facing the same state and the same intensity of preferences. Note, however, that the strategy is a *rule*, not a number, and, in general it yields a different number of votes for different intensities and for different stocks of available votes. Thus, two voters following an identical strategy will typically cast a different number of votes. An equilibrium is a behavioral resting point: no amount of observation of others' choices should change behavior. In general, there can be multiple equilibrium strategies: if everyone follows rule *a*, it is optimal to follow rule *a*, but if everyone follows rule *b*, then it becomes optimal to follow rule *b*. With multiple bonus votes, not only is it difficult to identify the equilibrium strategy, but multiple equilibria may exist, further complicating the voters' problem.

What can the theory say about the welfare properties of storable votes in this complex scenario? The intuitions of Chapter 1 continue to hold true here and work through the monotonicity of the voting strategies: by shifting votes towards higher realizations of intensities, a voter tends to increase his expected payoff, relative to simple majority. The effect appears clearly and can be proved rigorously in the transparent case of two voters, for any number of proposals and bonus votes: if the two voters use their optimal strategies, they can expect utility gains, relative to majority voting. In fact, a stronger result holds: *all* monotonic voting strategies lead to expected utility gains, even when the exact number of votes cast is not the optimal one.[2] With more than two voters, matters are more complicated because asymmetric states – states in which voters have different stocks of available votes – multiply. In these states, optimal voting choices differ across voters even when the intensity of their preferences does not, and because a larger number of votes cast need not always correlate with stronger preferences, the link that underpins the expected welfare gains is broken. In all numerical examples I have studied, storable votes lead to welfare gains when most proposals are expected to elicit low intensity of preferences and only a few are associated with high intensity, as the previous chapter discussed, or when the group is not too small – results that continue to seem intuitive, but that with multiple bonus votes are difficult to prove rigorously. What can be shown, as Proposition 2.3 in the box states, is that for any number of voters, of proposals, and of bonus votes there always are monotonic voting rules that lead to higher expected utility than simple majority. Although such rules are desirable from the point of view of the committee as a whole, however, they need not be optimal for an individual voter, who may be able to do better by deviating unilaterally. One question for the experimental analysis, then, is the frequency with which such cooperative strategies are observed.

Box 2.1 The Formal Model. Version 2

Consider a committee of n voters, meeting to decide whether to implement T distinct proposals, $\{P_1, ..P_T\}$, each of which can either pass or fail. The committee votes on the proposals over time. Each member i of the committee has preferences over each proposal P_t

2. The result is proven in Chapter 2 of Part II.

summarized by a cardinal valuation v_{it}. Valuations v_{it} are independently and identically distributed both across proposals and across individuals according to the distribution $G(\mathrm{v})$ with support $[-1, 1]$, symmetric around 0. A negative valuation means that the voter is against the proposal; a positive valuation means that he is in favor. Call voter i's absolute valuation over proposal P_t: $|\mathrm{v}_{it}| \equiv v_{it}$, i's intensity, or value, over P_t and $\boldsymbol{v}_t$ the vector of individuals' intensities, or values, over P_t. For each proposal P_t, voter i receives utility $u_{it} = v_{it}$ if the decision goes in his preferred direction, and 0 otherwise. Voter i's utility from the entire meeting, U_i, equals $\sum_{t=1}^{T} u_{it}$.

In addition to a regular vote over every proposal, each committee member is given a stock of B_0 bonus votes that can be cast in any manner the voter sees fit, where B_0 is an integer, and each bonus vote is equivalent to a regular vote. Each proposal is decided in the direction that receives more votes, including bonus votes; in case of a tie, a coin is flipped. When voting over proposal P_t, a member knows v_{it}, his own valuation over the proposal, but does not know either others' valuations over any of the proposals or his own valuations over proposals that will be voted upon later. The independence of the valuations and the distribution G from which they are drawn are common knowledge, as is the number of bonus votes still available to each voter when proposal P_t is called to a vote, a tuple denoted by $\mathbf{B}_t$.

The set of actions available to individual i voting on proposal P_t is denoted by X_{it} and equals all feasible numbers of votes between 1, the regular vote, and $1 + B_{it}$. The analysis focuses on symmetric Perfect Bayesian equilibria in weakly undominated strategies. It ignores history-dependent strategies and concentrates on strategies such that the number of votes each individual chooses to cast each period, x_{it}, depends only on the individual's intensity of preferences, v_{it}, and on the state of the game at t, that is, on the profile of bonus votes each voter has still available, $\mathbf{B}_t$, and the number of remaining periods, $T - t$. The state of the game is denoted by $(\mathbf{B}_t, t)$, and strategies by $x_{it}(v_{it}, \mathbf{B}_t, t)$. Equilibrium strategies have the following properties:

Proposition 2.1: Monotonicity. Call a strategy *monotonic* if, at a given state, the number of votes cast x_{it} is monotonically increasing in the intensity of preferences v_{it}. For any number of voters n, horizon length T, and state $(\mathbf{B}_t, t)$, *all* best response strategies are monotonic.

Proposition 2.2: Equilibrium. The game has a Perfect Bayesian equilibrium in pure strategies. All equilibrium strategies are monotone cut-point strategies: at any state $(\mathbf{B}_t, t)$ and for any voter i with $B_{it} + 1$ available votes, there exists a set of cut-points $\{c_{i1}(\mathbf{B}_t, t), c_{i2}(\mathbf{B}_t, t), \ldots, \}$, $0 = c_{i0} \leq c_{i1} \leq \ldots \leq c_{iB_{it}+1}$, such that i will cast x votes if and only if $v_{it} \in (c_{ix-1}, c_{ix}]$.

Proposition 2.3: Welfare. Call $EV_0(B_0)$ a voter's ex ante expected utility at time 0, before the realization of any valuation, when votes are storable and each voter has a stock of B_0 bonus votes. Call EW_0 the corresponding utility with simple majority voting. Then: (i) For $n = 2$ and all G, B_0, and $T > 1$, $EV_0(B_0) > EW_0$, with $EV_0(B_0)/EW_0$ monotonically increasing in T. (ii) For all n, G, B_0, and $T > 1$, there exists a monotonic cut-point strategy profile $\mathbf{x}_t^C(\mathbf{v}_t, \mathbf{B}_t, t)$, such that $EV_0^C(B_0) > EW_0$.

2.2 The Experiment

All sessions of the experiment were run either at the Hacker SSEL laboratory at Caltech (CIT) or at the CASSEL laboratory at UCLA, with students recruited from the whole campus through the laboratory web sites, with the only constraint that they could not participate in more than one session. In each session, all subjects were given an initial number of bonus votes equal to the total number of proposals to be decided, in addition to one regular vote for each proposal. There were two main treatment variables: the *number of voters in a group*, n; and the *number of proposals*, and number of bonus votes, T. Overall, there were six different treatments: $n = 2, 3, 6$ for each of two possible numbers of proposals $T = 2, 3$.[3] Table 2.1 summarizes the experimental design.

The methodology of the experiment was described in Chapter 1. I summarize it briefly here, emphasizing where the two experiments differ. Subjects were matched randomly in groups of n each (with $n = 2, 3$ or 6, depending on the session) and given T bonus votes (either two

3. As a check on some of the results, we also ran one UCLA session with two voters and two proposals, but three bonus votes. It will be discussed later.

Table 2.1 Experimental Design

Session	n	T	Subject Pool	Subjects	Rounds
c1	2	2	CIT	10	30
c2	2	2	CIT	10	20
c3	2	3	CIT	10	30
c4	2	3	CIT	8	30
c5	3	2	CIT	12	30
c6	3	3	CIT	9	30
c7	6	2	CIT	12	30
u1	2	2	UCLA	16	30
u2	2	3	UCLA	20	30
u3	3	2	UCLA	21	30
u4	3	3	UCLA	18	30
u5	6	2	UCLA	18	30
u6	6	3	UCLA	18	30

or three, again depending on the session), as opposed to one. The size of the group and the number of proposals and of bonus votes were commonly known. In contrast to the previous experiment, each subject was shown his valuation for the first proposal only and asked to choose how many votes to cast in the first election. For each proposal, valuations were drawn randomly by the computer independently for each subject and could be any integer value between −100 and 100 (excluding 0), with equal probability. After everyone in a group had voted, the computer screen showed to each subject the result of the vote for the group and the number of votes cast by all other group members. Valuations over the second proposal were then drawn, and the session continued in the same fashion. After T proposals, subjects were rematched and a new sequence of T proposals took place – a new round. Each session consisted of 30 rounds. At the end of each session, subjects were paid privately their cumulative values for all proposals resolved in their preferred direction, multiplied by a predetermined exchange rate. Average earnings were about $25 an hour.[4]

4. There were two exceptions to the description in the text: (1) In the first session, *c*1, one subject was mistakenly assigned a valuation of 0. This observation is treated as missing data, and the programming error was corrected in later sessions. (2) Session *c*2 at Caltech had 20 rounds, not 30.

With either two or three proposals, two or three bonus votes, and equally probable values, equilibrium strategies and expected welfare can be calculated for different numbers of voters. They are reproduced in Table 2.2, with the rows corresponding to the experimental treatments in bold. As in the previous chapter, the efficiency of the voting rule is measured in terms of the available surplus that a voter is expected to appropriate. The available surplus is defined by an upper bound, corresponding to expected earnings if each decision is resolved in favor of the side with higher total intensity, and a lower bound, corresponding to expected earnings when the outcome is chosen by flipping a coin. The efficiency of the voting rule is measured by the increase in expected earnings associated with the rule over random decision-making, relative to the maximum possible such increase, expressed in percentage terms.

Table 2.2a reports the theoretical predictions in the case of two successive proposals and two bonus votes. When the second (final) proposal is put up for a vote, all remaining votes are cast; thus, the only strategic decision is how many votes to cast *on the first proposal*, from a minimum of one to a maximum of three. The equilibrium strategy is summarized by the numbers in the second column, indicating the maximum values at which a voter casts one vote (c_1), and two votes (c_2). I call these values *cut-points* and discuss them at length in the rest of the chapter because they summarize all one needs to know about a voter's behavior. In general, the optimal cut-points depend on how many bonus votes the voter holds and how many each of the other members has still available. When voting on the first proposal, everyone has the same number of votes, and the optimal cut-points are identical across all voters. With two proposals and two bonus votes, the choice is between casting one, two, or three votes. Thus, there are only two cut-points. In the case of two voters, for example, the two cut-points coincide at 50, indicating that a voter should cast one vote on the first proposal if his value is below 50 and three votes if it is above. Because the two cut-points coincide, casting two votes, or splitting the bonus votes, is never an equilibrium strategy.

The surplus measure is reported in the third (storable votes) and fourth (majority voting) columns. In the case of two voters, storable votes allow them to appropriate 84 percent of the possible surplus,

Table 2.2 Theory: Strategies and Efficiency

Table 2.2a: Two Proposals, Two Bonus Votes

n	(c_1, c_2)	Surplus SV	Surplus Maj.	Surplus SV^C	(c_1^C, c_2^C)
2	**(50, 50)**	**84.3**	**75.0**	**86.0**	**(33, 66)**
3	**(35, 67)**^{A}	**90.6**^{A}	**92.3**	**94.0**	**(50, 100)**
	(50, 50)^{B}	**89.5**^{B}			
	(0, 100)^{N}	**92.3**^{N}			
4	(44, 56)	87.7	80.5	88.7	(38, 74)
5	(50, 50)^{B}	88.1^{B}	90.1	92.2	(56, 100)
	(0, 100)^{N}	90.1^{N}			
6	**(45, 55)**	**87.6**	**82.2**	**89.5**	**(43, 82)**
7	(50, 50)^{B}	88.1^{B}	89.2	91.5	(58, 100)
	(0, 100)^{N}	89.2^{N}			

Table 2.2b: Three Proposals, Three Bonus Votes

n	$(c_1, c_2, c_3)_{P_1}$	Surplus SV	Surplus Maj.	Surplus SV^C	$(c_1^C, c_2^C, c_3^C)_{P_1}$
2	**(37, 75, 100)**	**88.3**	**75.0**	**89.8**	**(37, 73, 100)**
3	**(47, 66, 84)**^{A}	**89.7**^{A,B,N}	**92.3**	**94.3**	**(48, 87, 100)**
	(48, 66, 84)^{B}				
	(47, 69, 84)^{N}				
4	(49, 64, 83)	88.7	80.5	91.5	(41, 76, 100)
5	(53, 65, 77)*	87.8	90.1	92.9	(56, 100, 100)
6	**(54, 64, 76)**	**87.3**	**82.2**	**91.6**	**(45, 81, 100)**
7	(56, 65, 73)*	86.9	89.2	92.7	(56, 100, 100)

The superscripts A, B, and N identify three different equilibria. The asterisks indicate that although there are multiple equilibria in some of the second period subgames, the differences in first period cut-points and expected welfare disappear when cut-points are discretized. The subscript P_1 in the headings of the second half of the table indicates that the equilibrium cut-points refer to the choice of votes over the first proposal only.
Rows in **bold** correspond to the experimental treatments.

versus 75 percent with majority voting. If voters chose their strategies cooperatively, the expected surplus share would rise to the number in the fifth column, and the strategy would be summarized by the cut-point values reported in the last column (note the superscript C). The term *cooperative* defines the rule of behavior that maximizes the expected surplus, without necessarily being robust to individual deviations. If all voters adopt it, their expected aggregate surplus is as high as possible under the voting rule, but it may be advantageous for a single voter to deviate, adopt a different strategy, and benefit even more while worsening the other members' prospects. With two voters, the cooperative strategy is to cast one vote on the first proposal at values smaller than 33, two votes at values between 33 and 66, and three votes above. This strategy is not an equilibrium, and individual deviations would be profitable, but if the two voters used this rule they could expect to appropriate 86 percent of possible surplus.

Consider the theoretical predictions for the treatments with two proposals and two bonus votes, reported in Table 2.2a. With two voters, the equilibrium is particularly simple. Each voter's best strategy is to concentrate all bonus votes on the proposal with highest value, and because the preference over the second proposal is not known when the first vote takes place, the cut-point is given by the expected intensity, 50. In fact, in this treatment this is the best strategy regardless of what the other voter does, avoiding the need to guess the other's strategy. When the number of voters is even but larger than two, the values' cut-points at which the optimal number of votes changes remain unique. Now, however, they are much less intuitive: with a six-member committee, one of the experimental treatments, a voter should cast one vote on the first proposal for values lower than 45, two votes for values between 45 and 55, and three votes for values higher than 55. The earlier comment on the difficulty of identifying the correct cut-points becomes very clear: why 45 as opposed to, say, 35, or 55 as opposed to, say, 72? In addition, the optimal strategy now depends on the other members' strategy: the cut-points are optimal *given that the other voters are using them, too.* The strategy is an equilibrium but is not any longer an optimal response for any possible strategy adopted by the rest of the committee.

When the number of voters is odd, identifying the best strategy is more complicated still, because the equilibrium is not unique. In the case of three voters, if voters 1 and 2 each cast two votes, the third voter can affect the outcome only if the other two voters have opposing valuations, but then he does so regardless of the number of votes he casts, and this is true in both periods. Thus, always casting two votes ($c_1 = 0$, $c_2 = 100$) is an equilibrium, and the outcome then is identical to simple majority. One can see immediately that the result holds for all odd numbers of voters, if there are two proposals (and two bonus votes). Other equilibria exist too, the more robust being $c_1 = c_2 = 50$ (never cast two votes, and switch from one to three votes at the mean value) which again can be shown to exist for all odd numbers of voters.[5] Note, however, that all equilibrium cut-points, for an even or an odd number of voters, for each equilibrium when more exist, always imply monotonic strategies: it is *always* the case that a voter casts at least as many votes when his value is higher than when it is lower.

With two proposals, there is always an equilibrium such that storable votes yield at least as high expected welfare as majority voting. While the efficiency gain is robust when the number of voters is even, however, it is not when the number is odd and small. As discussed in Chapter 1, the reason is the sensitivity of majority voting to the number of voters, as shown clearly in the third and fourth columns of the table. Majority voting does quite well when the number of voters is odd and small, and the majority is large enough, relative to the minority, that minority victories are rarely efficient. Although not shown in the table, as the number of voters increases, the storable votes mechanism becomes always more efficient than simple majority, whether the number of voters is odd or even. In addition, efficiency is always higher with storable votes than with simple majority if the cut-points are chosen cooperatively. In general, the cooperative strategy has voters casting two votes for a larger range of values than the equilibrium strategy, while casting three votes becomes less likely and never occurs when the number of voters is odd.

Table 2.2b summarizes the theoretical predictions when three successive proposals are considered and voters are given three initial bonus votes. The table reports the equilibrium cut-points for the first proposal only, when voters can cast any number of votes between one and four.[6]

5. In contrast to the two-player case, this strategy is only optimal if the other voters follow it, too. In the table, the different equilibria are identified by the superscripts A, B, and N.

6. As mentioned earlier in the text, when the first proposal is presented for a vote, everybody holds the same number of votes, and the strategy over the first proposal is summarized by a single set of cut-points. When the second proposal is presented, there are many possible profiles of bonus votes still available to the voters, depending on how may votes have been cast over the first proposal. More precisely, there are 4^n different possible profiles, where n is the number of voters, and to each correspond different sets of cut-points for voters holding different numbers of votes. Reporting all equilibrium

As one would expect when the horizon lengthens, the equilibrium cut-points are now strongly asymmetrical, relative to the mean value of 50: voters are always at least twice as likely to use no bonus votes than to use all of them. Still, with the exception of the two-voter case, there is a sizable range of values for which using all bonus votes is an equilibrium, in clear contrast to the cooperative strategy, where casting four votes should never occur.[7]

Increasing the number of proposals has no effect on the expected surplus associated with majority voting: the one-period game repeats itself. It has an effect when votes are storable. With two voters, the expected share of surplus must increase, as stated by Proposition 2.3 in Box 2.1, but in the majority of other treatments, Table 2.2b shows it declining, if only slightly. Predicting whether in general a larger number of proposals should make storable votes more or less desirable is difficult: for example, in a different model in which votes can be accumulated for future use through past abstentions, increasing the number of proposals beyond two is associated with an initial decrease but a subsequent increase in the expected share of surplus.[8] As for the cooperative solution, moving from two to three proposals increases, in all treatments, the share of the efficient surplus that voters can expect to appropriate.

The experimental treatments were chosen according to two criteria. First, the design selected cases with clearly different theoretical predictions, particularly in terms of welfare. Second, it compared simpler treatments, in which optimal strategies are more straightforward, with more complex ones, in which either the larger number of voters or the longer horizon, or both, complicate calculations. The welfare criterion lead to three choices: two-voter treatments, in which storable votes do much better than simple majority; six-voter treatments in which the

---

strategies is then quite confusing. It is also not very useful from the point of view of the experiment, because each of these different states is reached with small probability and thus too infrequently in the experiment to provide interesting tests of the data. The formal analysis of this chapter in Part II has a discussion of the second-proposal strategies for the two-voter case.

7. The cooperative strategy maximizes expected earnings taking into account the whole path of the game. In this specific game, the problem can be solved backward, recognizing that voters will play the appropriate cooperative strategy in any future state (but for the last proposal, when all remaining votes are cast).

8. See Casella (2005). The result refers to three-voter committees.

efficiency differences are less pronounced, and three-voter treatments, in which, again, surplus differences between the two mechanisms are moderate but now go in the opposite direction. As for the complexity of the game, the two-voter, two-proposal case leads to the simplest optimal strategy, while increasing the number of voters from two to three to six increases the difficulty of computing equilibrium strategies. Even more so does increasing the number of proposals: calculating equilibrium strategies in the three-proposal treatments, especially with three and six voters, is objectively difficult.

2.3 The Results

The central question about storable votes is whether the mechanism is indeed able to deliver welfare gains over standard sequential majority voting. The theory suggests it often should, but with multiple bonus votes it predicts a highly strategic behavior that relies on complex calculations. Therefore, the first question posed to the experimental data is whether these gains were actually achieved by the experimental subjects.

2.3.1 Efficiency

How do realized outcomes compare to the theoretical predictions? The short and surprising answer is that realized earnings match the predictions almost perfectly in all treatments, for all group sizes and number of proposals. The theory is highly successful in predicting both the welfare effects of storable votes and the mechanism's sensitivity to environmental parameters. The results are summarized in Figure 2.1.

Figure 2.1a reports realized versus predicted surplus levels in all sessions. As in the similar figure in Chapter 1, the horizontal axis is the surplus share associated with equilibrium earnings – the aggregate earnings that the subjects would have obtained had they all played the equilibrium strategies, given the valuation draws in each experimental session. The vertical axis is the surplus share calculated from realized aggregate earnings in the experiment. There is one data point for each session. Black dots are two-voter committees sessions, gray dots are three-voter committees, and white dots are six-voter committees;

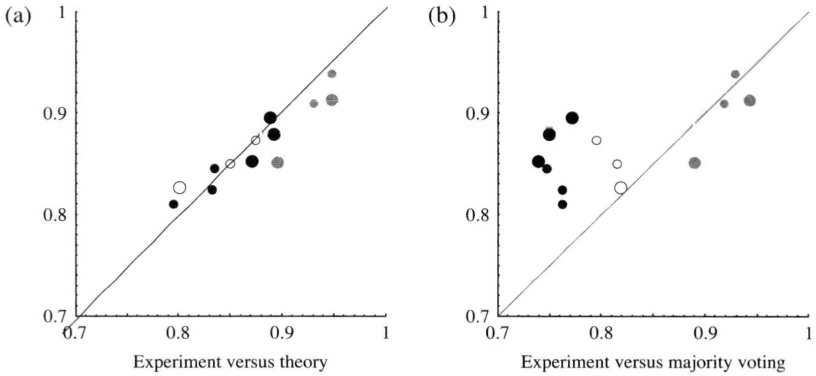

FIGURE 2.1 The vertical axis reports total experimental earnings per session, as share of maximal earnings. The horizontal axis reports the share of total to maximal earnings in each session in the absence of any strategic mistake (Figure 2.1a), or if decisions were made through simple majority (Figure 2.1b). Black dots are two-voter committee sessions; gray dots three-voter committees, and white dots six-voter committees. Smaller dots are two-proposal sessions; larger dots are three-proposals. All earnings are measured as gains over earnings with random decision-making.

smaller dots are two-proposal sessions, and larger dots are three-proposal sessions. Points on the 45-degree line represent sessions in which realized aggregate earnings exactly equal the theoretical prediction, and points above/below the line are sessions with realized earnings above/below what theory predicts. Overall, the experimental data align nicely with the theory, and there is no evidence that the higher complexity of the three-proposal game results in systematically lower earnings. The two subject pools – Caltech and UCLA students – have similar results and are not identified in the figure.[9]

From a practical standpoint, the interesting question is whether storable votes lead to better outcomes than majority voting. Figure 2.1b plots realized aggregate surplus in each experiment, on the vertical axis, versus aggregate surplus if subjects had cast a single vote in all elections, on the horizontal axis, with the realized experimental

9. The strong experimental results are not an artifact of aggregation. Conclusions are unchanged when the analysis is based on committee-level data, as opposed to the full group of subjects participating in each experimental session (see Casella, Gelman, and Palfrey (2006)).

valuations, again distinguishing among treatments according to group size and to number of proposals. Here, too, the experimental results across different treatments match the theoretical predictions: the larger gains from storable votes appear in the two-voter experiments, while the difference between the two voting rules is smaller for six-voter sessions, and smaller still and negative for three-voter sessions. Moving from two to three proposals improves the relative performance of storable votes in the case of two voters, and worsens it in the case of six or three voters. The two-voter experiments show a large range in realized surplus reflecting the empirical variability in the frequency of unanimous preferences, a likely scenario with two voters that directly affects realized earnings. Note that the range in realized surplus is not indicative of erratic behavior since Figure 2.1a shows that, given the actual valuation draws in the individual sessions, earnings are very well predicted by the theory. Storable votes are associated with higher surplus than majority voting in all but three sessions – three of the four sessions with three-voter committees, exactly as theory predicted. On average, the surplus gain from storable votes is 9.5 percent in two-voter sessions, 4 percent with six voters and −2 percent with three voters.

It is then natural to ask: Did the theory predict outcomes so well because individuals adopted the equilibrium strategies?

2.3.2 Individual behavior: Two-proposal sessions

Consider first the two-proposal treatments. The only decision concerns the number of votes to cast on the first proposal: one, the regular vote only; two, the regular vote and one bonus vote; or three, the regular vote and both bonus votes. Each experimental session repeats the voting game 30 times, and thus each subject finds himself deciding how many votes to cast on the first proposal 30 times. Figure 2.2 displays the voting behavior of a sample of subjects from two-proposal sessions. Each graph summarizes the behavior of one subject. The horizontal axis is the value of proposal 1, and the vertical axis the number of votes cast on that proposal. The dots correspond to the 30 rounds of decision/value pairs for that subject.

The figure is organized in three subclasses, according to how strictly a subject followed a monotonic strategy. The first subject at the very

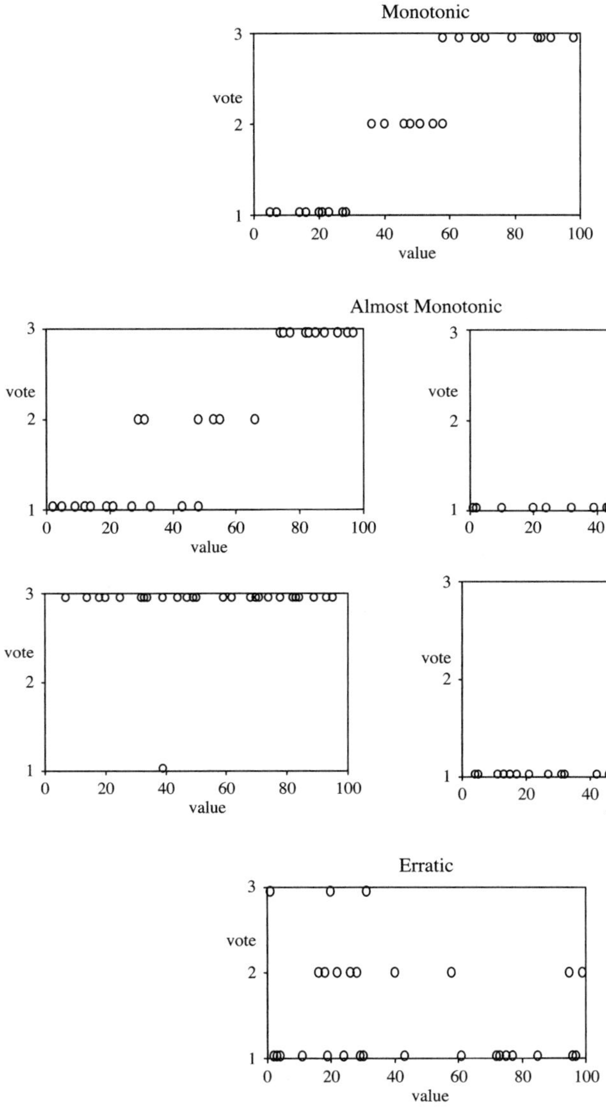

FIGURE 2.2 Number of votes cast on the first proposal. Some example individuals. Each panel corresponds to an individual subject. The horizontal axis is the value of proposal 1, and the vertical axis the number of votes cast on that proposal. The dots correspond to the 30 rounds of decision/value pairs for that subject.

top is perfectly monotonic: the number of votes cast at higher values is *always* at least as large as the number cast at lower values. This behavior is present in the data, but less frequent than the behavior shown in the second subclass, that of subjects who are *almost* perfectly monotonic. In this subclass, the minimum number of voting choices that would have to be changed to achieve perfect monotonicity is very small, one or two in the examples shown here. Almost perfect monotonicity is by far the most common pattern in the data. Finally, the last subject in the figure is a rare example of apparently erratic behavior.

Figure 2.2 illustrates an important point: monotonicity is consistent with a wide range of individual behaviors. The number of votes cast at different values can be constant (see the subject almost always casting three votes), and if not, the value cut-points at which the number of votes changes need not replicate the theoretical equilibrium (casting one vote for values below 50, and three votes for values above 50 is the optimal strategy in this treatment). The most common behavior in the data is followed by the second subject in the figure – one vote is cast at low values, two at intermediate values, and three at high values, with a few monotonicity violations – although the exact cut-points that best described voting patterns differed across subjects. Thus, while monotonicity on the whole is strongly supported by the data, equilibrium behavior is not. A more systematic analysis of the data makes the point more precisely.

2.3.2.1 Monotonicity

Call *errors* for each subject the minimum number of voting decisions that would have to be changed to achieve perfect monotonicity, and *error rate* the fraction of such errors over the 30 voting decisions. Figure 2.3 shows the histograms of all individuals' error rates for each treatment: the vertical axis is the number of subjects with different error rates, and the horizontal axis the error rates organized in progressive bins: 0 to 5 percent, 5 to 10 percent, 10 to 15 percent, etc. As a comparison, the last histogram is obtained from a simulation where each voter casts one, two, or three votes with equal probability at all values (with 21 subjects and 30 rounds).

In the random simulation, only two voters have an error rate (just) below 40 percent; in contrast, in the actual data the number of subjects

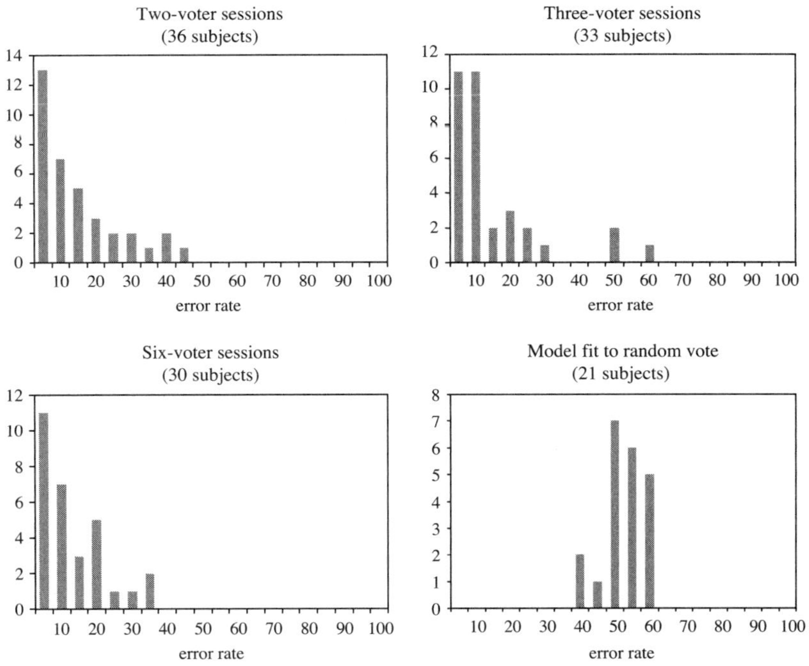

FIGURE 2.3 Individual error rates. Two-proposal treatments. The vertical axis is the number of subjects with different error rates, the horizontal axis is the error rate organized in progressive bins: 0 to 5 percent, 5 to 10, 10 to 15, etc. The last histogram reports the results of a simulation where each voter casts one, two, or three votes with equal probability at all values (with 30 rounds). In all cases, individual cut-points are estimated to minimize each subject's error rate. The scale in each panel is the relative frequency.

with error rates below 40 percent is 35 out of 36 in the two-voter game, 30 out of 33 in the three-voter game, and 30 out of 30 in the six-voter game. In every session, more than half of the subjects had error rates below 10 percent (i.e., zero, one, or two violations of monotonicity out of 30 decisions).

A natural question is whether subjects are learning to employ monotonic strategies as they gain experience. The data for each treatment can be divided into two subsamples – rounds 1–10 and 11–30 – with error-minimizing cut-points calculated separately for each subsample. The percentage of subjects with error rates below 5 percent increases in the later rounds, going from 45 percent to above 60 percent on average over the three treatments, and in all treatments reaching at least 50 percent in the second subsample. Subjects with higher error rates in each treatment show less evidence of learning.

The frequency of errors is a possible measure of monotonicity violations, but so is the *severity* of the errors. A measure of the severity of a monotonicity violation is the distance between the actual number of votes cast and the number that would satisfy monotonicity. It can be calculated for each subject, now using cut-points estimated to minimize such a distance, as opposed to minimizing the subject's error rate. The results are very similar to those obtained when looking at error rates.

2.3.2.2 Cut-points

Figure 2.4 reports estimated cut-points for the three two-proposal treatments. The horizontal axis measures the value at which a subject switches from one to two votes: the first cut-point, c_1; the vertical axis the value at which the subject switches from two to three votes: the second cut-point, c_2. Points on the diagonal correspond to strategies such that the two cut-points coincide (never cast two votes). The cut-points were estimated so as to minimize error rates, and monotonicity is therefore built into their definition and the estimation method. As a result, all estimated cut-points must lie on or above the diagonal. The three corners of the box correspond to weakly monotonic strategies: the axes origin corresponds to "always cast three votes," the top left corner to "always cast two votes," and the top right corner to "always cast one vote." The black symbols refer to Caltech subjects, the gray ones to UCLA; the larger, white circles indicate the equilibrium values corresponding to each treatment. For both subsamples the figure shows large dispersion in the estimated cut-points, and large deviations from equilibrium values: the dots do not appear to concentrate around the white circles, and the three panels seem, on the whole, quite similar to one another.[10]

Table 2.3 below summarizes the median cut-points in each of the two-proposal sessions (a better statistic than the mean, here, because of outliers), together with equilibrium and cooperative cut-points.

10. For some subjects, there are multiple cut-points that minimize the number of monotonicity violations. The figure presents cut-points estimated at the lowest value consistent with minimizing each subject's number of violations.

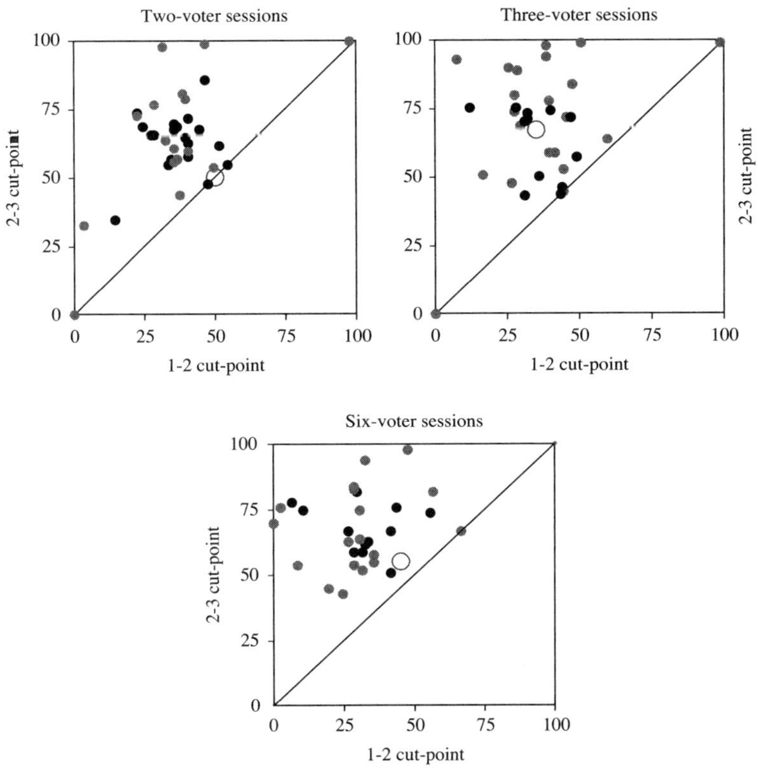

FIGURE 2.4 Individuals' cut-points. Two-proposal treatments. The horizontal axis measures the value at which a subject switches from one to two votes – the first cut-point, and the vertical axis the value at which the subject switches from 2 to 3 votes. Points on the diagonal correspond to strategies such that the two cut-points coincide (never cast two votes). The cut-points are estimated so as to minimize error rates. The black symbols refer to Caltech subjects, the gray ones to UCLA. The white circles indicate the equilibrium cut-points corresponding to each treatment.

The most noticeable feature of the table is the similarity of the observed cut-points across treatments, a similarity that contrasts with both equilibrium and cooperative predictions. The table can suggest strategies approaching cooperation in the case of two voters, or approaching the equilibrium predictions in the case of three (in both cases with some added noise). But when all treatments are observed together, a simple rule of thumb behavior – "cast one vote for intensities in the bottom third of the possible range, two votes for intensities in the second third, and

Table 2.3 Median Cut-points. Two-proposal Sessions

Subject Pool	n	Subjects	Median c_1, c_2	Equil c_1, c_2	Coop c_1, c_2
CIT	2	10	36, 68	50, 50	33, 66
CIT	2	10	38, 58	50, 50	33, 66
UCLA	2	16	37, 62	50, 50	33, 66
CIT	3	12	36, 70	35, 67*	50, 100
UCLA	3	21	38, 73	35, 67*	50, 100
CIT	6	12	32, 66	45, 55	43, 82
UCLA	6	18	30, 65	45, 55	43, 82

* Equilibrium cut-points closest to the observed cut-points.

three votes for intensities in the highest third" – seems a more convincing reading of the data. Such a behavior is a clear deviation from equilibrium, but is monotonic.

The similarity of the cut-points across treatments remains true if we divide the data into early and late trials. The data suggest that learning, if it occurs, is weak: the distance between estimated and equilibrium cut-points tends to decline in the later rounds, but remains large. For example, in the two-voter treatments the distance falls in the late trials for 25 out of 36 subjects, but the median cut-points move only from (33,61) to (36,63) (relative to equilibrium values of (50,50)).

2.3.3 Individual behavior: Three-proposal sessions

When individuals vote over three successive proposals, in the second election the distribution of available bonus votes depends on the voting decisions on the first proposal. But such distribution of bonus votes affects the optimal voting strategy on the second proposal: for given preference intensity, in general the optimal number of votes to cast depends on the number of bonus votes still in circulation, and on how concentrated or diffuse their ownership is. Thus, describing equilibrium strategies in the second election is complicated, and so in fact is describing the data: each realized distribution of available votes constitutes a different state of the game, and each state has to be evaluated separately. I discuss here the data from the first proposal, leaving to Chapter 2 in Part II of the book the analysis of the second proposal in two-member committees, where the number of states remains small enough to be tractable.

The data for the first election recall those obtained in the two-proposal sessions. With very few exceptions, subjects employed monotonic strategies, with a small number of errors, but their strategies were more similar across treatments than theory suggests. Figure 2.5 reports the histograms of the errors (the minimum number of monotonicity violations) in all treatments and, as a comparison, with random voting.[11]

With the exception of only one subject in the three-voter game, all had lower error rates than the minimum observed in the random voting comparison. In all treatments, more than half of all subjects had error rates below 10 percent (with four possible choices, the error rate associated with random behavior tends to 3/4 asymptotically).

Figure 2.6 depicts the aggregate frequency of the different voting choices in the three treatments, as a function of intensity, aggregated over all relevant sessions. The draws of intensity values in the experimental sessions are partitioned into bins with an equal number of sample points in each bin.

Over a large range of values, subjects cast one vote with high probability, while they were clearly reluctant to cast four votes. To some extent, these choices match the theory: for example, as Table 2.2 showed, in two-voter experiments the equilibrium strategy has voters never casting four votes, and in six-voter experiments it has them casting one vote for a majority of possible values. But equilibrium strategies differ across treatments more than the data: in the two-voter treatments, the frequency of casting one vote is too high, and in the six-voter treatments, the frequency of casting four is too low. Because the number of bonus votes equals the number of proposals, adding one proposal means also adding one bonus vote. To disentangle what the chosen strategies owe to the longer horizon alone, an experimental session was run with two proposals, two voters, and three bonus votes. The frequency of the voting choices in the first election of this treatment is presented at the bottom of Figure 2.6. The figure shows clearly that the length of the horizon

11. The random voting data were obtained from a simulation of 18 subjects and 30 rounds.

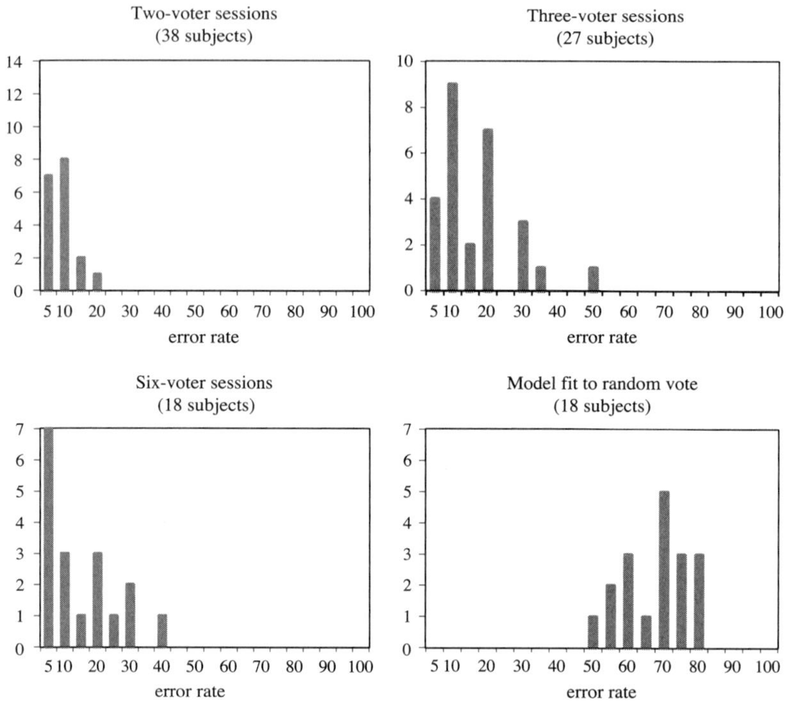

FIGURE 2.5 Individual error rates. Three-proposal treatments. The first proposal. The vertical axis is the number of subjects with different error rates, the horizontal axis is the error rate organized in progressive bins: 0 to 5 percent, 5 to 10, 10 to 15, etc. The last histogram reports the results of a simulation where each voter casts one, two, three, or four votes with equal probability at all values (with 30 rounds). In all cases, individual thresholds are estimated to minimize each subject's error rate. The scale in each panel is the relative frequency.

does matter: as theory suggests, the propensity to cast three and four votes is much higher in the two-proposal session.[12]

In all treatments, the frequencies are not perfectly monotonic – for example, in two-voter, three-proposal sessions, the frequency of one is higher for intensities between 65 and 70 than between 55 and 60. But the apparent violations are not very meaningful: the figure summarizes the *aggregate* features of the data, and cannot be read in

12. The session was run at UCLA with 20 subjects and 30 rounds. The equilibrium strategy is to cast one vote for values smaller or equal to 50, and four votes otherwise.

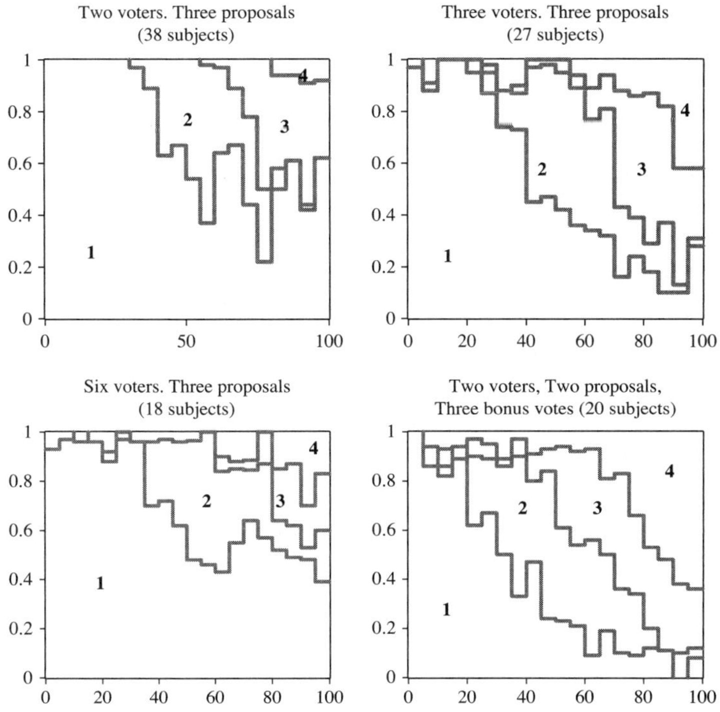

FIGURE 2.6 Empirical votes on the first proposal. Three bonus votes. The vertical axis is the frequency of different voting choices on the first proposal, aggregated over all relevant sessions. Realized experimental value draws are reported on the horizontal axis, divided into different bins, such that each bin has an equal number of sample points.

terms of individual behavior: a subject who always casts three votes, for example, follows a weakly monotonic strategy, but can induce an apparent violation of monotonicity in the figure if he happens not to draw intermediate intensities. Monotonicity violations are individual errors, summarized by Figure 2.5.

2.3.4 Relationship between individual behavior and efficiency

Given the individual behavior shown by the subjects, the efficiency results are surprisingly good. So good, in fact, that one must wonder whether payoffs could be rather insensitive to the strategies played.

To check this possibility, realized experimental earnings can be compared to the payoffs that the subjects would have obtained had they chosen the number of votes randomly, over their feasible alternatives. In every experimental session, earnings would have been lower. Relative to the experimental results, the difference in appropriated surplus goes from a minimum of 9 percent on average in the two-person treatments (with a relatively high frequency of unanimous decisions) to a maximum of 80 percent on average in six-person treatments, where random voting leads to a large number of welfare-reducing minority victories.[13]

The result underscores the importance of monotonicity. Storable votes can lead to efficiency gains because voters can express the intensity of their preferences by casting more votes when their values are higher. Even if the cut-points are incorrect, as long as strategies are mostly monotonic, outcomes reflect the intensity of preferences, and the essence of the mechanism is captured. This is also why the efficiency results for the experiments are not systematically different for the three-proposal treatments: the higher complexity of the equilibrium strategies has limited importance if subjects can approach the equilibrium payoffs by following the simpler criterion of monotonicity.

As mentioned earlier, in the case of two voters the intuition is supported by a formal argument: storable votes lead to expected welfare gains, relative to majority voting, whenever the two voters follow monotonic strategies for *any* arbitrary interior value of the intensity cut-points. But the theory does not say how close to the equilibrium earnings the experimental earnings would be, nor that monotonicity would be sufficient to reap the full welfare potential of storable votes in the more complex experimental treatments. These are observations we draw from the experimental data.

Thus, as long as strategies are monotonic, the loss from not choosing the correct cut-points is small. Figure 2.7 illustrates this point in a graph;

---

13. For reach experimental session, every round – every two or three-proposal game – was simulated 100 times, with subjects playing random strategies (with all remaining votes cast in the last election). In each simulation, earnings were calculated using the valuations actually drawn in the experimental round. To obtain payoffs from random voting in an experimental session, aggregate payoffs were averaged over the 100 simulations of each round, and summed over all rounds.

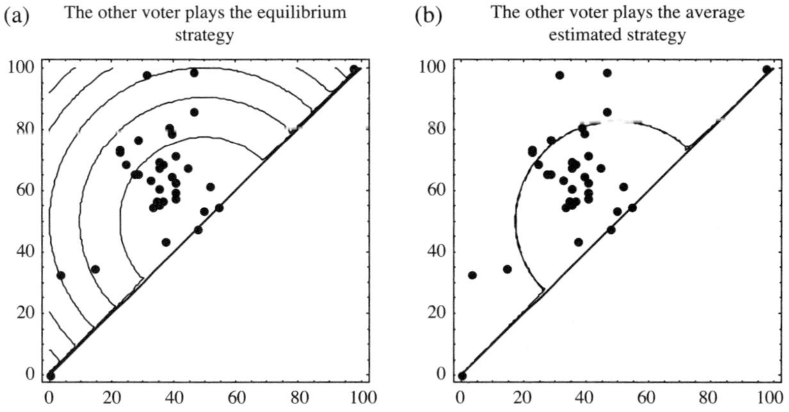

FIGURE 2.7 Isoutility curves. Two voters, two proposals. The horizontal axis reports the first cut-point; the vertical axis the second. The black dots correspond to the estimated cut-points for all subjects in two-voter, two-proposal experimental sessions. The curves are isoutility levels. In Figure 2.7a, each contour is a loss of 7.5 percent of potential utility. In Figure 2.7b, the isoutility curve is drawn at the level of the equilibrium utility.

it is drawn for the most transparent case of two voters and two proposals, but its lessons apply to all treatments. As in Figure 2.4, the horizontal axis is the first intensity cut-point, c_1, the value at which a voter switches from casting one vote to casting two votes; the vertical axis is the second cut-point, c_2, the value at which the voter switches from casting two votes to casting three votes, and the dots are the individual cut-points estimated from the data. The figure depicts individual expected isoutility curves: curves tracing pairs of cut-points along which expected earnings are constant. The equilibrium strategy, and the highest earnings, corresponds to $c_1 = c_2 = 50$, the center of the square.

Figure 2.7a is drawn supposing that the other voter follows the equilibrium strategy. Every isoutility contour, moving away from the center, indicates a loss of 2 percent in expected surplus, reaching down to the 10 percent loss associated with majority voting at the three corners. The figure illustrates one reason why the strategic mistakes found in the data do not affect earnings very much: the area within the first contour is large enough to encompass more than half of all of the data points. However, Figure 2.7a ignores a second possible reason for the high off-equilibrium efficiency of the data: as shown by Table 2.3, the strategies observed in the experiment were, in fact, closer to the optimal cooperative strategies than to the equilibrium. Figure 2.7b reports the individual isoutility curve at the equilibrium level (that is, the curve tracing the pairs of cut-points that would give a voter expected earnings equal to equilibrium earnings) when the other voter adopts the average cut-points estimated in the experimental data. The strategy $c_1 = c_2 = 50$ is always optimal, and thus leads once more to the highest expected payoff, but now the whole region between the isoutility curve and the 45-degree line corresponds to strategies yielding a *higher* expected payoff than the equilibrium level. Two-thirds of the estimated cut-points (25 out of 36) belong to this region.

2.4 Conclusions

The bottom line of the analysis is clear. The welfare gains made possible by storable votes appear robust to deviations from theoretically optimal strategies, as long as voters cast more votes when their intensity is stronger. In the experiment, the conclusion held true across subject pools, across number of proposals, and across the various parametric environments. It is an important conclusion, because equilibrium strategies in this game are difficult to compute: knowing at exactly which cut-point of intensity one should switch from casting two votes to casting three votes, for example, is not trivial, and depends on considerations that are difficult to evaluate precisely in the heat of a voting session. How well, for example, can a voter evaluate the influence that the balance of bonus votes available to other members should have on his voting behavior? But monotone strategies, the simple idea of casting more votes when the decision on the table is more important, are very natural. The inexperienced subjects in the experiment had no difficulty using them almost with no exception. And it is this monotonicity that drives the idea of storable votes: compared to majority voting, storable votes allow voters to shift the probability of obtaining their desired outcome toward those decisions that weigh more in their utility. The experiment described in this chapter was necessarily highly stylized, designed to simplify the subjects' task and to allow a complete description of equilibrium behavior. But monotonicity seems to be a general characteristic of storable votes environments and is likely to apply to richer problems. As long as monotonicity is preserved, the outcomes will reflect intensity of preference – it is hard to imagine how or why the positive welfare results might be reversed.

3

Protecting Minorities without Sacrificing Efficiency

If storable votes can improve aggregate welfare, relative to majority voting, it must be because they make it possible for a minority to win sometimes. In the environments I have discussed so far, all individuals have an equal probability of finding themselves in the minority over any proposal and an equal probability of benefitting from the bonus votes. If bonus votes are a relatively efficient mechanism to protect minorities, however, they acquire special importance when there are some voters for whom the probability of being in the minority is unusually high – when there is what we can call a *systematic minority*. Democratic systems are built, with good reason, on majoritarian principles, but these very principles imply the risk of disenfranchising any group that regularly finds itself on the losing side of public decision-making. What is the value of the right to vote if all decisions are taken as if some specific groups were excluded from participating? Setting limits to the *tyranny of the majority* is one of the fundamental challenges of democratic theory, viewed by political theorists as essential to the legitimacy of a democratic government. The difficulty, of course, is that the two objectives, democracy and protection of minorities, seem inherently contradictory.

The problem is not only one of guaranteeing basic *rights*, and thus it cannot be solved simply through an independent judiciary. It is the subtler problem of representing and taking into account, at least sometimes, minority *preferences*. The argument is more transparent if we push it to the extreme: imagine a society facing a number of public decisions, and suppose that the society is divided in two groups, of different sizes, such that all members of each group always agree among themselves and disagree with the other group. What matters here is that the composition of the two groups is constant: the smaller group is a *systematic* minority.[1] The objectives of both groups are acceptable, according to the norms of the society; both are sanctioned as legitimate by the courts, and there is no higher principle requiring that the preferences of one of the two groups should be ignored. If decisions are made by majority voting over each decision, however, the voice of the minority group is never heard. The outcome is exactly as if the members of this group were not voting. Our instinctive understanding of fairness is violated: shouldn't the minority have its way at least sometimes? The United States Supreme Court has identified these two criteria – cohesive groups voting as blocs, and the majority preventing expression of minority preferences – as defining conditions for "vote dilution," the effective disenfranchising of the minority, and thus as requiring reform of the voting procedure in the jurisdiction.[2] The problem is usually debated in reference to electoral systems, the public's choice of representatives, and constitutes the strongest defense of proportional rules. But it applies with as much strength to direct decision-making. Wouldn't it be preferable to have the minority win with a frequency related to its relative size in the population? Or, better yet, to follow the minority's preferences on those decisions, if they exist, that matter to it a great deal and do not matter much to the majority?

Suppose, for example, that this fictional society was facing three decisions and that the two groups assigned to the decisions different relative importance. The majority favors all proposals, considers passing the first particularly important, and does not put great weight on the third. The minority opposes all proposals and considers blocking the third particularly important, but it does not put great weight on the first. Intuitively, favoring the majority on decisions 1 and 2 but letting the minority block the third proposal, seems a desirable outcome. If the

1. All the argument really needs is that some citizens have a disproportionate probability of belonging to the smaller group, for all decisions.

2. See for example Issacharoff, Karlan, and Pildes (2002), on Section 2 of the Voting Rights Act and on the Court's opinion in Thornburg v. Gingles, 478 U.S. 30, 1986. For a discussion of minorities' right of representation, see the papers in Grofman and Davidson (1992); for a focus on the legal doctrine of voting rights, in their application to groups, see Issacharoff (1995).

two groups do not differ too much in size, many plausible welfare criteria support it. For example, expected welfare calculated under the veil of ignorance, before an individual knew which of the two groups he belongs to, may well be higher if the third decision follows the minority's preferences. If we give weight to the intensity of preferences, the minority should be allowed to win occasionally. Note the distinction between equity and efficiency. The equity problem stems from the existence of a smaller group whose preferences are systematically in the opposite *direction* of the larger group's preferences. The efficiency problem stems from differences in the *strength* of preferences of the two groups.[3]

One may think that in reality an intense minority will prevail over a lukewarm majority because a deal will be struck: some majority members can be persuaded to vote with the minority in exchange for support on a different decision. In the case of a systematic minority, however, this type of agreement will not emerge: if the members of the majority are always winning, they are not interested in making deals. Nor will the solution come from raising the threshold for approval, requiring supermajorities or unanimity. Any threshold higher than the relative size of the larger group will cause *all* proposals to fail, an outcome worse than the result of simple majority voting on both equity and efficiency grounds. What is needed is a mechanism that goes beyond voting issue by issue but that, contrary to log rolling, creates incentives for expressing the intensity of preferences even for members of a stable majority.

It is clear at this point how storable votes can help. By granting a sufficient number of bonus votes, storable votes make it possible for the minority to win sometimes, when the strength of its preferences is high enough to justify spending a large number of votes. But because the majority, too, can use its bonus votes, it is typically in a position to overrule the minority if it cares to do so. Thus, the minority wins when its preferences are strong *and* the majority's preferences are weak, which is exactly when the minority should win on efficiency grounds: fairness and efficiency both improve.

3. Again, nothing fundamental depends on the direction of preferences within each group being *perfectly* correlated or on all members in a group having *identical* intensity of preferences on every issue. All is needed is that preferences be positively correlated within each group.

Note that, because the number of bonus votes is equal among all voters, storable votes treat every voter identically. This is very important: although the mechanism makes it possible for the minority to win occasionally, it does not treat members of the minority more favorably than anybody else, and the process through which a decision is reached is not biased in favor of any individual or group. The lack of bias also implies that the mechanism does not need to be redesigned if the size of the minority changes or if the very existence of a systematic minority comes into doubt – after all, the previous chapters showed that the mechanism is usually desirable even in the absence of a clearly identified minority.[4]

This chapter makes these intuitions precise, again by reducing the problem to a simple model and analyzing it with some rigor. The introduction of a systematic minority complicates the problem because it creates asymmetry between the two groups and poses difficult questions of coordination among members of the same group. The theory gives promising results, but the strategic sophistication it assumes may be unrealistic. Once again, it is important to test how storable votes could be used in practice, and the chapter reports the results of a laboratory experiment, as a first step in that direction.[5]

Before moving to the detailed description of the model, the precise meaning with which the term *minority* is used here must be made clear. A *minority* is a clearly identifiable group characterized by two features: first, a small numerical size, smaller than the majority; second, preferences that are systematically different from the preferences of the majority. Thus, a minority is a *political* minority, which may, but need not, correspond to a minority according to racial, ethnic, religious, or any other type of considerations. In terms of political decisions, what matters are the coherent and idiosyncratic preferences of the group, as opposed to its sense of identity. Although, of course, such preferences may derive from its sense of identity, the preferences themselves are the

4. In principle, of course, it is possible to grant a different number of bonus votes to different individuals. A natural example would be an international committee in which members represent countries with different populations. If it is believed that population size should be reflected in different voting power, representatives of larger countries could be given a larger stock of bonus votes. It is an intriguing application that remains to be studied, and I will return to it in the Conclusions of this book.

5. This chapter is based on Casella, Palfrey, and Riezman (2008).

primitives of the analysis. This also means that there is no prior that the minority is necessarily "deserving." The minority may be a group that has been kept away from the center of power by abuse, discrimination, or historical circumstances, as the discussion has implied so far, but in fact it could just as well be a restricted, privileged group that resists the will of the majority. Specific applications will give content to the identity of the minority and to its claims in terms of fairness. In the more abstract analysis described here, judging the performance of the voting scheme in terms of its efficiency is important not only because we need to know the trade-off between aggregate welfare and minority protection, but also because efficiency is a relatively value-free criterion and ignores the subjective and changing weights assigned to minority interests in different circumstances.[6]

3.1 The Theory

Consider again the scenario studied in the previous chapter: a committee votes successively on a number of proposals, each of which can either pass or fail. Each member of the committee casts a regular vote on all proposals, but in addition is endowed with a stock of bonus votes that can be spent as the member wishes, choosing freely to spread them over several proposals or to cumulate them over one or few proposals. When counting votes, each of these bonus votes is equivalent to a regular vote. Contrary to the previous chapter, however, the committee is now formed by two groups of unequal size whose membership remains constant as the voting proceeds. The two groups always disagree over their preferred outcome for any proposal. For concreteness, suppose that all members of the smaller group prefer to pass all proposals, and all members of the larger group would like to see all proposals fail, but the precise direction of the groups' preferences is irrelevant; what matters is that they are always opposed. To avoid confusion, in this chapter a *group* is a subset of voters who agree on the preferred outcome of the vote and a *committee*

6. It is possible to argue that efficiency may increase when the minority has disproportionate power, even if the intensity of preferences is ignored. Chwe (1999) presents such an argument, based on efficient aggregation of diffuse information when different groups have different biases.

is the full set of all voters. Everyone in the committee knows both the existence and the size of the two groups.

If you are a member of the minority (majority), you favor (oppose) all proposals, but the value you attach to each of them varies. As in the previous models, suppose that the values are independent across different proposal: having strong preferences over today's proposal yields no information about how strongly you will feel over tomorrow's proposal. Each voter learns which specific proposal is on the table, and thus the intensity of his preferences, just before the vote is called. Intensities are also independent across groups, and a voter's knowledge of his intensity of preferences does not give him information about the intensity with which members of the opposite group feel about the proposal. As for members of his own group, different assumptions are both plausible and interesting. The model considers the following two polar cases. If the group is not particularly cohesive, its members may well agree on the desired outcome of the vote but disagree on the importance they assign to it: a voter's intensity of preferences over a given proposal is not informative about how strongly the other members of the voter's own group feel. Call this case B (the *base* case): intensities are distributed independently both across and within groups. Alternatively, a very cohesive or very well-coordinated group may agree (or function as if it agreed) not only on the direction of their preferences but also on their intensity. In the extreme case, all intensities are identical for all members of the group, and when a group member learns which proposal is up for voting, and thus how strongly he feels about it, he also simultaneously knows how strongly all others in his own group also feel. Call this case C (the *correlated* case).

The model is described more formally in Box 3.1.

Box 3.1 The Formal Model. Version 3

Consider a committee of n voters, meeting to decide whether or not to implement T distinct proposals, $\{P_1,..P_T\}$, each of which can either pass or fail. The committee votes on the proposals sequentially. Each member i of the committee has preferences over each proposal

P_t summarized by a cardinal valuation v_{it}. A negative valuation means that the voter is against the proposal; a positive valuation means that he is in favor. For each proposal P_t, voter i receives utility $u_{it} = |v_{it}| = v_{it}$ if the decision goes in his preferred direction, and 0 otherwise. Voter i's utility from the entire meeting, U_i, equals $\sum_{t=1}^{T} u_{it}$.

The committee is composed of two *groups*, the *Majority group* **M**, with M members, and the *Minority group* **m**, with $m < M$ members. The two groups differ systematically in their preferences: members of **m** are in favor of all proposals, and members of **M** are against all proposals. For all t, $v_{it} > 0$ if $i \in \mathbf{m}$, and $v_{it} < 0$ if $i \in \mathbf{M}$. All members of the minority have valuations drawn from a distribution G_m with support $[0, 1]$, identical across proposals, while all members of the majority have valuations drawn from a distribution G_M with support $[-1, 0]$, again identical across proposals. The distributions of valuations are assumed to be symmetric across the two groups so that the distribution of intensities (or values) F_M for all members of the majority group, with support $[0, 1]$, is assumed identical to $G_m(v) = F_m(v)$ and labeled F for both groups. F is common knowledge, as are the existence and size of **M** and **m**.

Intensities are always drawn independently across proposals and across the two groups. Within each group, two polar cases are considered: in case B (the *base* model), intensities are drawn independently for each member of a group; in case C (the *correlated* model), intensities are identical for all members within a group. The correlation of within-group intensities (or lack thereof) is common knowledge, as is the independence of intensities across proposals and groups. Intensities are revealed privately and sequentially before each proposal is put to a vote.

In addition to a regular vote on every proposal, each committee member is given a stock of B_0 bonus votes that can be cast in any manner the voter sees fit. B_0 is an integer and each bonus vote is equivalent to a regular vote. Each proposal is decided in the direction that receives more votes; in case of a tie, a coin is flipped. When proposal P_t is put to a vote, the current endowment of bonus votes for every voter, denoted $\mathbf{B}_t = (B_{1t}, \ldots, B_{nt})$, is common knowledge.

The analysis focuses on symmetric Perfect Bayesian equilibria in weakly undominated strategies. It ignores history-dependent strategies and concentrates on strategies such that the number of votes each individual chooses to cast each period, x_{it}, depends only on the voter's intensity of preferences v_{it} and on the state of the game at t, $(\mathbf{B}_t, t)$. As in the previous models, because the sign of each group's preferences is common knowledge and intensities are independent over time, with weakly undominated strategies the direction of each individual vote is always chosen sincerely: all the minority members' votes are cast in favor of each proposal, and all majority votes are cast against each proposal. Equilibrium strategies have the following properties:

Proposition 3.1: Equilibrium. For any F, B_0, M, m and T, both model B and model C have an equilibrium in monotone cut-point strategies: at any state $(\mathbf{B}_t, t)$ and for any i with $B_{it} + 1$ available votes, there exists a set of cut-points $\{c_{i1}(\mathbf{B}_t, t), c_{i2}(\mathbf{B}_t, t), \ldots, c_{iB_{it}+1}(\mathbf{B}_t, t)\}$, $0 = c_{i0} \leq c_{i1} \leq \ldots \leq c_{iB_{it}+1} = 1$, such that i will cast x votes if and only if $v_{it} \in (c_{ix-1}, c_{ix}]$. In model B, the strategies are individual equilibrium strategies and $i \in \{1, .., n\}$; in model C, the strategies are group strategies and $i \in \{M, m\}$.

Proposition 3.2: Minority victories. In both models B and C: (i) For any F, T, M, and $m > 1$ there is a finite $B_0'(M, m, T)$, such that for all $B_0 > B_0'$ there exist equilibria of the storable votes mechanism where the minority wins some of the time with strictly positive probability. (ii) If $T > M$ and $B_0 > B_0'$, then the minority wins some of the time with strictly positive probability in all equilibria.

As in the previous models, denote by $EV_0(B_0)$ a voter's expected utility from all T proposals before any valuation is realized, and thus before knowing whether he belongs to **M** or to **m** (but taking into account the existence and size of **M** and **m**), when all voters have B_0 initial bonus votes. The equivalent measure under simple majority voting is denoted by EW_0. Then:

Proposition 3.3: Welfare. In model C, for all F, M, and $m > M/2$, there is a finite $\overline{T}(M, m)$ such that if $T < \overline{T}(M, m)$ there exists an integer number B_0 and an equilibrium of the storable votes mechanism for which $EV_0(B_0) > EW_0$.

With simple majority voting, the minority loses all the time, and no proposal ever passes. With storable votes, the minority may win sometimes, but the answer is less clear-cut than one might expect. The main problem is the extent of coordination that the groups, and particularly the minority, succeed in achieving. For example, imagine a situation where two proposals are to be voted upon, and suppose that every voter is endowed with two bonus votes. Regardless of the size of the two groups and of the realizations of the preferences, there is always an equilibrium where the minority always loses: if every other voter, including all minority voters, casts one bonus vote on each proposal, no individual minority voter can deviate and win. The reason is that the majority has always at least one member more than the minority, and thus is always beating the minority by at least two votes (one regular vote and one bonus vote); an individual minority voter can at most shift one bonus vote, which is never enough. This observation holds true regardless of the correlation of intensities within the groups, and does not depend on the number of bonus votes: with B_0 bonus votes, in an equilibrium where all bonus votes are split over the two proposals, the minority always loses by at least $1 + B_0/2$ votes, and any individual voter can at most shift $B_0/2$ – not enough. This said, for the minority at least, the strategy does not seem very plausible: since it is always losing, any deviation from the prescribed strategy has no costs, and minority voters must be aware that their chance of winning comes from cumulating votes. Consider then equilibria where voters' use of the bonus votes is sensitive to the intensity of preferences.

The game is more complicated than in the previous chapter, because the voters' positions are asymmetrical: a minority voter will typically be better off choosing a different strategy from a majority voter because he knows he can count on the support of a smaller group. Still, Proposition 3.1 in Box 3.1 states that equilibria in monotonic strategies of the type discussed in the previous chapter – strategies such that, given the distribution of available votes among all committee members, the number of votes cast is never lower at higher intensity of preferences – continue to exist. When intensities of preferences are independent within each group (case B), monotonicity applies to the number of votes cast by each single voter; when, instead, intensities are perfectly correlated within the group (case C), then monotonicity applies to the total number of votes cast by each group. In this modified fashion, the intuitive principle behind the workings of storable votes continues to hold.[7] And by cumulating votes on more strongly felt issues, the minority can indeed win some of the time. It is necessary, of course, that the number of available bonus votes be large enough to compensate for the difference in group sizes, but if such a condition is satisfied, the intuition that storable votes can help minorities is confirmed by the formal analysis: the minority can win in equilibrium (Proposition 3.2 in Box 3.1). The result differs from establishing that a minority victory is possible for some arbitrary configuration of votes, an observation that follows automatically from the very design of the voting rule. What it says is that a minority victory may happen when every voter, including every majority voter, correctly estimates the voting strategies followed by the others and responds optimally.[8]

Making it possible for the minority to win occasionally favors fairness and representation, but implies that the larger group occasionally loses. In principle, this is problematic for the efficiency properties of the mechanism: there is no uncontentious reason why the preferences of one group should necessarily count more than the preferences of the other, and if, on average, the preferences of members of the two groups have equal intensity, then group size matters and most plausible efficiency criteria will penalize victories by the smaller group. The reason this logic does not apply to storable votes is that, *conditional on the minority winning*, the preferences of the two groups do *not* have equal intensity: by varying the number of votes cast according to the intensity of preferences, the minority tends to win when minority intensities outweigh majority intensities.

The good efficiency properties of voting strategies that respond positively to intensity hold true whether intensities are correlated within each group or not, but efficiency gains are more robust and easier to characterize in the case of perfect correlation, case *C*. Proposition 3.3

---

7. Monotonic strategies include the possibiity of casting the same number of votes for all intensities, but the focus of this chapter is on the subset of monotonic strategies that are strictly responsive to the intensity of preferences.

8. Thus, the result differs, for example, from calculations of minority size thresholds necessary for representation in the literature on cumulative voting or other semi-proportional electoral rules (Briffault (2004), provides a very clear summary). Such calculations can be very useful, but they posit rules of behavior, and in particular a degree of coordination among minority voters, that are not necessarily individually rational.

in Box 3.1 states that if the relative size of the minority is not too small and the number of bonus votes is chosen correctly, then there are equilibria of the mechanism where expected welfare with storable votes is indeed higher than with simple majority voting. As written, the proposition requires that the total number of proposals on which the bonus votes can be cast should be limited (although necessarily at least as large as two), but as Chapter 3 in Part II shows, the threshold can be made arbitrarily large if we allow for fractional, as opposed to integer, numbers of votes. In practice, there have been elections where fractional votes were allowed, and they could be obtained here by allowing for fractional values for the bonus votes.[9] In addition, the conditions identified in the proposition are sufficient conditions only: weaker ones may be all that is needed. Note that although the result does not address explicitly how the minority fares, it is clear that it must be expected to win with some positive probability, because aggregate welfare could not differ from simple majority otherwise. Thus, it is equally clear that the minority must be expected to do better.

As in all other chapters, expected welfare is calculated under the veil of ignorance treating each individual equally before preferences are realized. It is also necessary, then, to estimate the probability that a typical individual will belong to the minority or the majority. In the presence of a systematic minority whose size and composition remain constant over the full set of proposals, the probability of belonging to the minority is assigned once and for all – as opposed to being recalculated for each proposal – and simply equals the relative size of the minority group. The simplest approach, followed here, assumes that the relative size of the two groups is known. Generalizing the model to allow for some uncertainty in the size of the two groups, however, or for some limited flexibility in their membership over different proposals, would not be too difficult and would not change the substance of the analysis.

Stating sufficient conditions for efficiency gains requires identifying equilibrium strategies that are responsive to intensities and still are simple

9. For example, the implementation of cumulative voting for elections in the Illinois House of Representatives allowed for half votes. See the description in Sawyer and MacRae (1962).

enough that expected welfare can be computed and compared for generic parameter values. Without imposing more structure on the problem, this is not easy, particularly in model *B*, in which priorities may differ within each group, and coordination becomes difficult to sustain. If we are willing to sacrifice some generality and consider specific examples, the task is made much easier, and the intuitions behind the formal results appear more clearly.

Consider, then, the following case, which will also be the basis of the experimental design. Suppose that the total number of voters is odd, all intensities are equally probable in a range normalized to run between 0 and 1, there are two consecutive proposals, and each voter is given two bonus votes. When the second proposal comes to a vote, all remaining votes are cast. Thus the only choice a voter needs to make is the number of bonus votes to cast over the first proposal, as a function of his preference intensity. The example has simple equilibria, one of which is particularly intuitive. In model *B*, all voters, whether in the minority or in the majority, spend all bonus votes over the first proposal if the intensity of their preferences is higher than the expected intensity of the second proposal (0.5), and none otherwise. If the majority is more than three times the minority, it always wins, but otherwise the minority wins one of the two proposals with positive probability. In model *C*, in which all members of a group have the same intensity of preferences, it is easier for the majority to ensure itself victory over both proposals: as long as its size is at least 50 percent larger than the minority size, it can do so by dividing all bonus votes equally over the two proposals. If that is not the case, however, the minority wins one proposal with positive probability. In this equilibrium, the minority cumulates all bonus votes on the first proposal if the intensity of preferences is higher than 0.5, and casts none otherwise; the majority follows the same strategy unless the two groups are of very similar size, in which case it casts either one or two bonus votes, in total, even when the intensity of preferences is lower than 0.5 and the remainder if it is higher. The precise strategies and the expected outcomes are discussed in detail in Chapter 3 of Part II. Figure 3.1 summarizes the results. The size of the minority is reported on the horizontal axis, and in the figure the majority is supposed to always have one voter more than the minority.

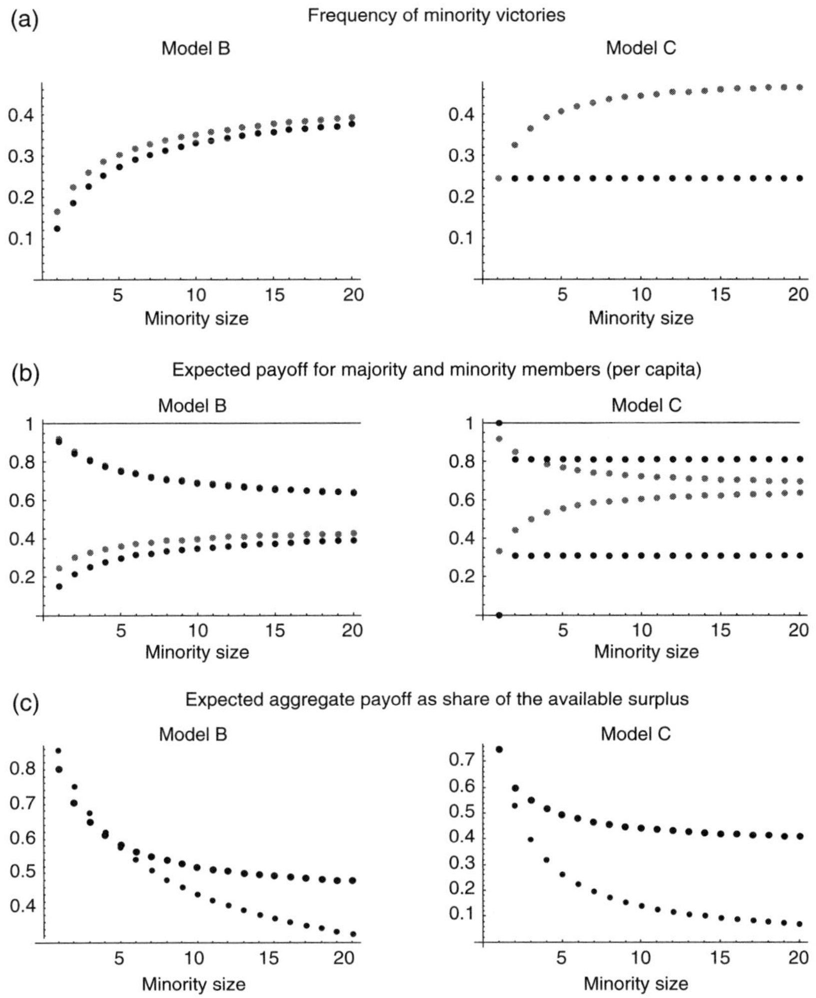

FIGURE 3.1 Two proposals, two bonus votes. All intensity values have equal probability. The majority is one voter larger than the minority. The black dots plot equilibrium payoffs with storable votes; the gray dots efficient payoffs, and the small black dots in Figure 3.1c payoffs with simple majority voting.

The precise difference in the size of the two groups, one in this case, is relatively unimportant. Whatever its value, its importance diminishes as the absolute size of the two groups increases. The qualitative features of the figure hold generally. The figure compares equilibrium and efficient outcomes, in which, as usual, efficiency is identified as the decision-making rule that maximizes the total realized values of the committee (or, equivalently, as resolving each decision in favor of the side with higher total value).

Figure 3.1a shows, for the two polar cases of full and no intensity correlation within the groups, the probability of a minority victory over one of the two proposals with storable votes – the black dots – and in the first best – the gray dots. The minority can never win both proposals because the majority always has a larger total number of votes. As the absolute size of the minority increases, and the numerical difference between the sizes of the two groups remains constant, the relative size of the minority increases. Not surprisingly, in both models this results in an increase in the probability of minority victories. In model *B*, the probability increases smoothly, eventually converging to one-half as the number of voters becomes large and the absolute difference negligible. The efficient frequency of minority victories is slightly higher than the equilibrium frequency, but the difference disappears as both converge to one-half. In model *C*, the change in the probability of minority victories is discontinuous, jumping from zero to one-quarter as the majority becomes unable to overrule the minority over both proposals, and remaining constant at that level. The minority size at which the jump occurs depends on the difference in the size of the two groups. The efficient frequency of minority victories, on the other hand, increases smoothly with the relative size of the minority and is always higher than the equilibrium frequency, again converging to one-half as the difference in the size of the two groups becomes negligible.

Figure 3.1b plots the expected per capita payoff for majority and minority members. With simple majority rule, the respective values are 1 and 0 in both models. With storable votes, unless the majority can ensure itself victory, the expected payoffs of the two groups are closer to each other, although the minority's payoff remains lower than under the most efficient decision rule (the gray dots in Figure 3.1b), eventually converging to the gray dots as the number of voters increases in model *B*, but not in model *C*. In model *C*, equilibrium per capita payoffs remain constant for each group, regardless of the absolute size of the two groups, once the threshold has been passed where the majority always wins.[10] The specific values depend on the shape of the probability distribution of intensities; as described above, the figure represents the case where all intensities are equally likely.

It would be incorrect to conclude that storable votes are a more valuable mechanism when intensities are not correlated within each group, in model *B*, than when they are, in model *C*. Figure 3.1c plots the normalized measure of expected surplus for both models, for both storable votes and simple majority voting, where, as usual, full efficiency is 100 and the surplus from random committee decisions is 0. As the figure shows, when the number of voters is small and the difference in size between the two groups relatively important, the possibility of minority victories in the storable votes mechanism is accompanied by some loss of efficiency in model *B*, but not in model *C*, where efficiency is always at least as high as under simple majority rule. The loss in model *B* is not large, and disappears rapidly as the number of voters and the relative size of the minority increases. For most sizes of the electorate, storable votes allow voters to appropriate a larger share of the total surplus in both models.

In fact, the main difference between the two models is not visible in the figure, but emerges when the two groups become very large. It is interesting in itself, even though it is not immediately relevant to the discussion in this chapter focused on small committees. When intensities are not correlated within each group, in model *B*, as the population becomes very large the law of large numbers guarantees that in both groups the empirical average intensity of preferences over each proposal converges to the mean of the distribution of intensities, 0.5 in this example. If the numerical difference in the size of the two groups is fixed, it becomes irrelevant as the groups become large. The final result is that it does not matter really which group wins: random committee decisions, simple majority voting, and storable votes all converge to first best efficiency, and any efficiency-based argument for protecting the minority disappears. In model *C*, on the other hand, in which the

10. In fact, they remain unchanged for any absolute difference between the two groups, as long as the majority is less than 50 percent larger than the minority.

intensity draws within each group are perfectly correlated, the law of large numbers does not apply. As the number of voters increases, the difference in size between the two groups becomes negligible, and simple majority voting again converges to random choice, but random choice remains inferior to efficient decision-making and to storable votes. In very large populations, only minorities who share not only preferences but also priorities should be protected on efficiency grounds.[11]

3.2 The Experiment

We tested the performance of storable votes in the presence of a systematic minority in a series of experiments run in 2004 and 2005 at Caltech (CIT), UCLA, and Princeton University (PU). All sessions focussed on the specification just discussed: subjects voted on two consecutive proposals and were allocated two bonus votes, in addition to the regular vote they were required to cast on each proposal. With the exception of one session, committees were composed of five voters, divided in two groups of three and two voters with systematically opposed preferences.[12]

The experimental protocol followed closely the experiments described in the previous chapters, and, as in those cases, the subjects were registered students recruited anonymously through the laboratories' web sites. Subjects were matched randomly into committees and within each committee were assigned randomly to the majority or the minority group. Each member of the minority favored all proposals and earned a positive payoff whenever a proposal passed; each member of the majority opposed all proposals and earned a positive payoff whenever a proposal failed. Subjects' potential payoffs correspond to the values, or intensities, of the theoretical discussion, and were drawn by the computer, with equal probability, from all integers in the support [1, 100]. At the beginning of the first round, each subject was shown his value for the first proposal

---

11. It is interesting that the observation, here purely mathematical, echoes Lani Guinier's (1998) implicit claim that representation should be guaranteed to minorities as long as they are cohesive and well-organized.

12. One session had committees of nine voters, each divided in two opposite groups of sizes five and four.

and asked to choose how many votes to cast in the first election. After everyone in a committee had voted, the computer screen showed to each subject the number of votes cast by each of the two groups in the subject's committee, whether the proposal had passed or not, and the subject's own payoff from that election. Values over the second proposal were then drawn, the remaining votes were automatically cast, and the outcome determined.

Values were always drawn independently for majority and minority members, but the correlation within the groups reflected the two models discussed so far: in treatment *B*, each member of each group was assigned a value drawn independently from the specified support; in treatment *C*, all members of the same group in the same committee were assigned the same value (i.e., all majority members in a given committee shared the same value, as did all minority members in a committee). Values were private information, but the statistical process through which they were assigned, including their independence within each group in treatment *B* and their perfect correlation in treatment *C*, were common knowledge.

After the second proposal had been voted upon, subjects were rematched, each was assigned a new budget of bonus votes, and each committee again voted on two consecutive proposals. Experimental sessions consisted of 15 to 30 rounds, each round corresponding to a pair of consecutive proposals and a new match of the experimental subjects into groups and committees. In the rematching, minority members always remained minority members and majority members always remained majority members, but the composition of each group and of each committee was randomly determined. At the end of the experimental session, subjects were paid privately their cumulative valuations for all proposals resolved in their preferred direction, multiplied by a pre-determined exchange rate and complemented by a fixed show-up payment of $10. Average earnings were approximately $17 per experiment for minority subjects and approximately $31 for majority subjects.

In both treatments, theory predicts that minority members should cumulate their bonus votes on a single proposal, on the first proposal if the intensity attached to it is at least 50, and on the second otherwise (the cut-point is 50 because, with the maximum value set to 100, 50 is the expected intensity over the second proposal). The same is true for a majority member in treatment *B*. In treatment *C*, the majority's strategy is less straightforward: the equilibrium has the majority collectively casting five votes on the first proposal if its intensity is below 50, and seven otherwise. Since neither five nor seven is divisible by three – the majority size – there is no simple symmetric individual strategy that produces the equilibrium group vote. Different majority voters must use different strategies, a difficult coordination problem. To see whether the coordination problem affected the results, the design included two further variations of the *C* treatment. In the first variation, called *CChat*, subjects were allowed to chat electronically with other members of their own group before the vote on the first proposal. Voters were instructed not to identify themselves, and the messages were anonymous, but it was possible for the group to coordinate on a preferred group strategy. Everything else in the experiment – the stochastic properties of the value draws, the timing, the random re-matching – followed exactly the *C* treatment, with perfectly correlated values within a group. In the second variation, called *C2*, a single subject represented an entire group: the game was rephrased as taking place between two voters only, with asymmetrical voting power and preferences. Each majority group representative had three indivisible regular votes to cast on each of the two proposals and six bonus votes to cast as desired. Each minority group representative had two indivisible regular votes to spend on each of the two proposals and four bonus votes to cast as desired. Each committee then consisted of one minority and one majority representative. The timing of the game proceeded as described earlier, and after each two-proposal round, group representatives were rematched. Equilibrium group strategies and expected outcomes are identical in the three *C* treatments: *C*, *C2*, and *CChat*.

Table 3.1 reports the equilibrium outcomes predicted by theory with the parameterization used in the experiment.[13]

---

13. As mentioned earlier, other equilibria do exist. In treatments *B* and *C* (but not *C2* and *CChat*), if everybody aways splits the two bonus votes over the two proposals, a voter's best response is to do the same, and the mechanism replicates simple majority voting. In treatments *C*, *C2*, and *CChat*, when the two groups are of size {3, 2}, the majority has other equilibrium strategies that are responsive to intensity, but all are payoff-equivalent and all are monotonic, and they are treated as identical below when reporting the experimental results. All equilibrium strategies satisfy: cast zero, one, or two bonus votes with probabilities p_0, p_1, p_2 if intensity is smaller than 50, and four, five, or six bonus

Table 3.1

Treatment	C	B
Min victories, SV	25	19
Min victories, efficiency	33	22
(Min/Maj) payoff, SV	38	26
(Min/Maj) payoff, efficiency	52	35
Surplus, SV	60	71
Surplus, majority voting	53	75

The first two rows report the expected frequency of minority victories, and the fully efficient frequency, respectively. The third and fourth rows give the expected share of payoffs for minority versus majority members, in equilibrium and with full efficiency respectively. The last two rows describe theoretical gains from storable votes over simple majority rule.

In equilibrium, the minority is expected to win one-quarter of the time in treatment C, and just below one-fifth of the time in treatment B. In both cases, this is less than efficiency recommends, but obviously much more than with simple majority voting when, by definition, the minority always loses. A minority member is expected to have a payoff that is just below 40 percent of a majority member's payoff in treatment C, and just above 25 percent in treatment B; efficiency recommends a larger share in both cases, but again, the payoff is zero with majority voting. In treatment C, storable votes are not only more responsive to minorities but more efficient; in treatment B, with groups of three and two voters, storable votes come with some efficiency losses, but the losses are small in magnitude.

In total, we ran 11 experimental sessions with 167 students. The experimental design is summarized in Table 3.2, where the labels of the individual sessions indicate the treatment. In all sessions the majority was formed by three subjects and the minority by two, with the exception of session b_3 where the number of subjects in each group was five and

votes with probabilities q_0, q_1, q_2 if intensity is larger than 50, where p_2 is at least as large as q_2 and p_1 equals q_1. The strategy described in the text corresponds to $p_0 = p_1 = 0$, and $q_1 = q_2 = 0$.

Table 3.2 Experimental Design

Session	Groups Size	Subject Pool	Subjects	Rounds
*b*1	3,2	CIT	15	30
*b*2	3,2	UCLA	20	30
*b*3	5,4	UCLA	27	30
*c*1	3,2	UCLA	15	30
*c*2	3,2	PU	15	20
*c*3	3,2	PU	10	20
*c*21	3,2	CIT	12	30
*c*22	3,2	UCLA	16	30
*c*23	3,2	PU	12	20
*cchat*1	3,2	PU	10	20
*cchat*2	3,2	PU	15	15

four respectively. Session b_3 serves as a control on the sensitivity of the experimental results to the size of the groups.[14]

3.3 The Results

The experiment had two principal goals. First, do voting outcomes match the theory, and in particular, are minority subjects able to win some of the votes? Are they able to do so without loss of aggregate efficiency? Second, to what extent does voting behavior match the theory? Do subjects still employ monotonic strategies? Or does the complexity of the asymmetrical game result in more fundamental strategic mistakes?

3.3.1 Voting outcomes and efficiency

Figure 3.2 summarizes the experimental outcomes. The diagram on the left of Figure 3.2a reports the frequency of minority victories. The vertical

14. With a committee of size $\{5, 4\}$, the relative size of the minority is larger and its prospects with storable votes are better. In treatment *B*, the expected proportion of minority victories rises to 25 percent (versus 28 under efficiency); the expected share of per capita payoff, relative to a majority member, is 36 percent (versus 45 under efficiency), and the expected share of normalized surplus is 61 percent (versus 62 with simple majority). The equilibrium strategy continues to be to cast all bonus vote on the first proposal for values larger than 50, and none otherwise, for both minority and majority voters.

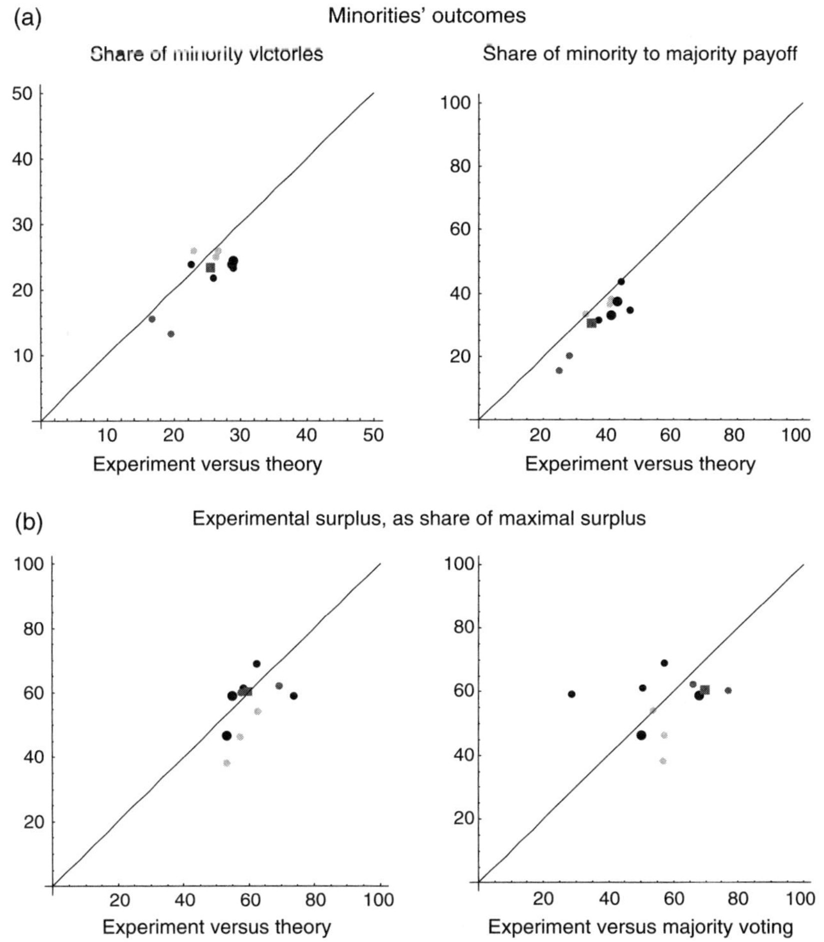

FIGURE 3.2 Experimental outcomes. The vertical axis reports experimental results. In Figure 3.2a, and in the left panel of Figure 3.2b, the horizontal axis reports the equivalent theoretical prediction, in the absence of strategic errors. In the right panel of Figure 3.2b, the horizontal axis reports the aggregate surplus share with majority voting. Black small dots are C sessions; black large dots are CChat sessions; light gray dots are C2 session; dark gray dots are B sessions, and the single dark gray square is the B session with {5,4} groups.

axis is, for each session, the fraction of times the minority prevailed, and the horizontal axis is the fraction of times it would have prevailed if all subjects had played the equilibrium strategy, given the values drawn during the experimental sessions. Different treatments are indicated by different symbols, as described in the figure's legend.

The figure can be read in several ways. The vertical height tells us that the minority won between 20 percent and 25 percent of the time in *C*, *C2*, and *CChat*, with little dispersion among the three treatments; it won less frequently in the *B* sessions (approximately 15 percent of the time) with the exception of the one experiment of size {5, 4} where the minority won approximately 23 percent of the time. Clearly, storable votes help the minority win. The differences across treatments match the theoretical predictions, as is evident from the way the points align along the 45-degree line. The closer to the line a point is, the closer the experiment's results are to the equilibrium predictions. If we estimate a simple regression line, the hypotheses of a unitary slope parameter and a zero constant term cannot be rejected at standard confidence values.[15] On average, the frequency of minority victories in the experiments differs from the equilibrium predictions by 3 percentage points, without clear outliers and without systematic treatment effects.

The diagram on the right of Figure 3.2a plots per capita minority payoff as percentage of per capita majority payoff in the experiment, on the vertical axis, and in equilibrium on the horizontal axis, using the symbols of the previous figure to identify the different experimental sessions. In all *C*, *C2*, and *Cchat* treatments, the relative minority payoff was higher than in any *B* treatments, as predicted by the theory, ranging between 33 percent and 45 percent of the average majority payoff, versus 16 percent to 20 percent in the *B* treatments of size {3, 2} and 30 percent in the *B* treatment of size {5, 4}. Again, the effect of the voting mechanism in raising the minority's payoff was significant. Out of 11 experimental sessions, all but two are below the 45-degree line, suggesting that the minority was unable to fully exploit the opportunity presented by the voting mechanism. But the discrepancy is not large – the average distance from the 45-degree line is 5 percentage points, again

15. The estimated parameters are: 0.76 for the slope (with a standard error of 0.23) and 3.4 for the constant term (with a standard error of 5.8).

without clear outliers or treatment effects, which is small in comparison to the differences across treatments.[16] Again, if we estimate a regression line, we cannot reject the hypotheses of unitary slope and zero constant.[17]

The left hand side of Figure 3.2b plots the normalized total surplus in each session on the vertical axis, against the equilibrium predictions on the horizontal axis, calculated from the actual value draws in the experiment. As usual, points on the 45-degree line indicate a perfect match to the theory. The mean distance from the 45-degree line is 7 percentage points, again with little evidence of outliers, versus a mean equilibrium surplus share of 60 percent. As in the previous figures, we cannot reject a regression line with unitary slope and 0 constant, although the fit is poorer.[18]

The central question is how the efficiency of storable votes compares to the efficiency of simple majority voting. In the diagram on the right of Figure 3.2b, the vertical axis is again the normalized total surplus in each session, now plotted against the equivalent measure with majority voting, calculated from the experimental values. Theory predicts that data from *C*, *C2*, and *CChat* sessions should lie above the 45-degree line, while *B* data should lie below. The prediction is confirmed by the *C* and by the *B* sessions. Surprisingly, it is the "easier" treatments with coordination, *Cchat* and particularly *C2*, that fall short of the prediction. Pooling all *C*, *C2*, and *CChat* data, the mean difference in normalized surplus is +2 percentage points, compared to the theoretical prediction of +7. Pooling all *B* data, the mean difference is approximately −10 percentage points, compared with the theoretical prediction of −4.

Overall, the data can be summarized in three main points. First, storable votes helped minorities substantially, both in terms of the frequency with which minorities won decisions, and in terms of the resulting benefits. Second, the correlation of intensities worked to the advantage of the minority. Third, the efficiency costs associated with the increased

16. A plausible range of values in the right hand side diagram of Figure 3.2a is between 0 (the outcome with simple majority voting) and 100 (the expected outcome with random decision-making). In the left hand side diagram, the corresponding range is between 0 and 50.

17. The estimated parameters are as follows: 1.03 for the slope (with a standard error of 0.19) and −6.2 for the constant term (with a standard error of 7.1).

18. The estimated parameters are as follows: 0.7 for the slope (with a standard error of 0.40), and 14.1 for the constant term (with a standard error of 24.1).

representation of minority interests were small in magnitude. Without correlation, storable votes induced (small) aggregate welfare losses, but with perfectly correlated intensities, storable votes produced (small) welfare gains over simple majority voting.

3.3.2 Voting behavior

Because the monotonicity of voting strategies is the essence of storable votes, it is natural to analyze subjects' behavior in the experiments by studying this property first. Consider first individual behavior in the treatments that did not allow group members to coordinate their strategies (treatments B and C).

3.3.2.1 Individual behavior

As in the previous chapter, a natural measure of monotonicity can be obtained by estimating monotonicity errors and voting cut-points. Recall how these estimates are obtained. For each subject, we have either 20 or 30 pairs of observations, depending on the session (15 pairs for session cchat2). Each pair consists of the subject's value for the first proposal, and the number of votes cast in the first election, either one, two, or three. A perfectly monotone strategy is one for which we can find two cut-points, c_1 and c_2, with c_1 smaller or equal to c_2, such that when the subject's first proposal value was below c_1 the subject cast one vote, when it was above c_2, the subject cast three votes, and when it was between c_1 and c_2, the subject cast two votes. The number of errors is defined as the minimum number of voting choices that must be changed, for each subject, to make the strategy perfectly monotonic, and the estimated cut-points are the pair of cut-points consistent with such monotonic strategy. When multiple cut-points are all consistent with the same number of monotonicity violations, the pair closest to the equilibrium cut-points is selected.

Figure 3.3a presents histograms of individual errors in treatments B and C. The horizontal axis is divided into deciles representing the percentage of errors over the total number of voting decisions, and the vertical axis reports the fraction of subjects who belong to each decile.

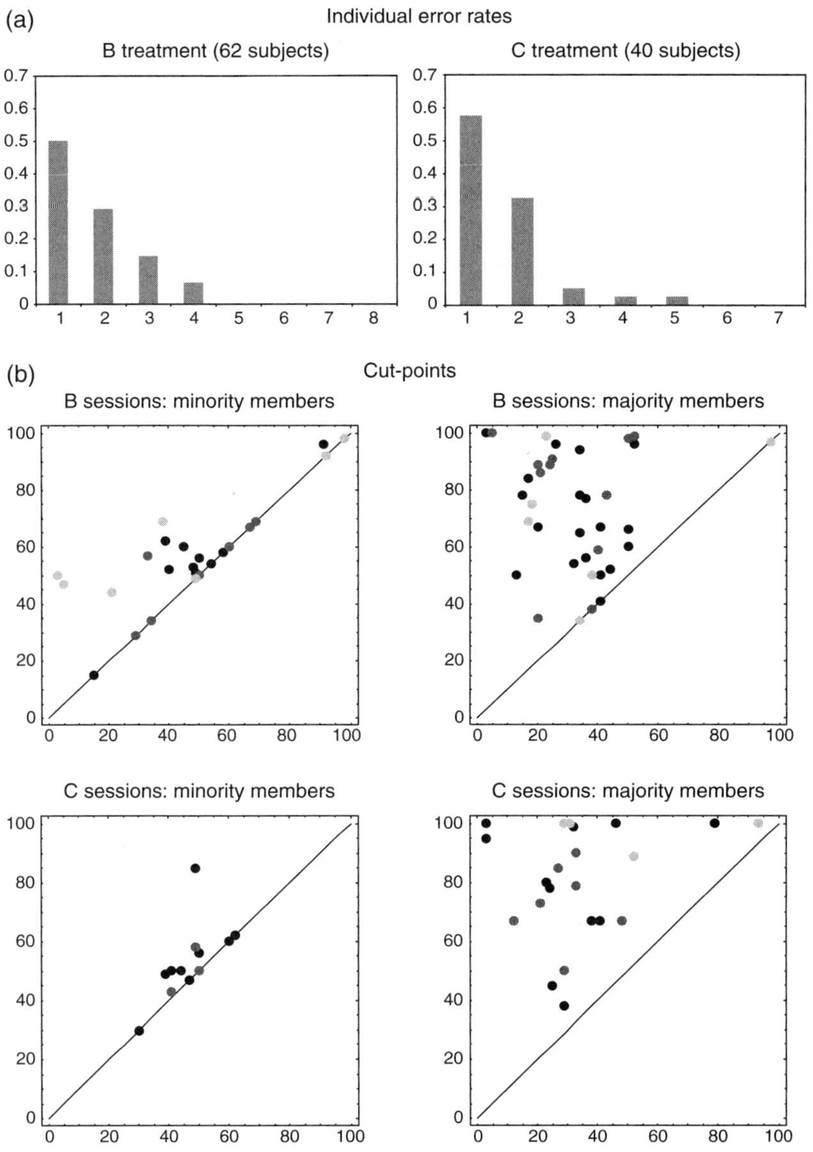

FIGURE 3.3 Individual behavior. In Figure 3.3a, the vertical axis is the percentage of subjects with different error rates, the horizontal axis is the error rate organized in progressive bins: 0 to 5 percent, 5 to 10, 10 to 15, etc. In Figure 3.3b, the horizontal axis measures the value at which a subject switches from one to two votes, and the vertical axis the value at which the subject switches from two to three votes. The cut-points are estimated so as to minimize error rates. Shading corresponds to different error rates: black dots refer to subjects with error rates not larger than 10 percent; dark gray to subjects with error rates between 10 and 20 percent, and light gray to subjects with error rates larger than 20 percent.

In both treatments, at least half of all subjects had error rates smaller or equal to 10 percent (50 percent of the subjects in the *B* treatment and 57 percent in the *C* treatment). As a comparison, in the simulation of random voting reported in the previous chapter, no subjects had violation rates lower or equal to 30 percent and more than half had error rates above 50 percent.[19] Thus, although there is some noise, individual choices indeed tend to be monotonic.

The estimated cut-points for all individual subjects in the *B* and *C* sessions are displayed in Figures 3.3b. As in Figure 2.4 in Chapter 2, each dot represents one subject's estimated pair of cut-points, with c_1 on the horizontal axis and c_2 on the vertical axis. All cut-points lying on the 45-degree line involve no splitting of bonus votes, while moving to the upper left corner of the graph are cut-points that involve more and more splitting of bonus votes, i.e., using one bonus vote in each period for a range of values that increases as one approaches the corner. The upper left corner of the graph, at (0, 100), corresponds to always casting one bonus vote. Cut-points for subjects in the minority group are in the left graph, and cut-points for the subjects in the majority group are in the right graph. The rates of monotonicity errors are indicated by the shading of the dots, with darker shading corresponding to smaller rates.

In the *B* treatments, the equilibrium cut-points for both majority and minority subjects are (50, 50): if everyone played the equilibrium strategies all dots would be on the 45-degree line at 50. In the *C* treatments, (50, 50) remains an equilibrium for individual minority subjects but not for subjects in the majority, whose asymmetrical strategies are contingent on the behavior of the other members of the group and cannot be identified unambiguously in the figure.

Two features of the distribution of cut-points appear in both treatments. First, the minority cut-points do cluster around (50, 50), and on average minority subjects whose cut-points are closer to equilibrium have lower violation rates. Second, bonus votes are much more frequently split by majority voters, with little difference between the two treatments in spite of the different theoretical predictions. Intuitively, majority voters have less to lose from splitting their bonus votes – their larger number

19. See the last histogram in Figure 2.3.

implies that they are guaranteed to always win one of the two decisions, and one single vote more or less plays a smaller role than in the case of the minority. Consider the parameter values used in the experiments and a committee of size (3, 2). The expected loss to a voter deviating from his equilibrium strategy and always casting one bonus vote on each proposal is 15 percent in model *B* and 50 percent in model *C* for a minority voter, versus 4 percent in model *B* and 8 percent in model *C* for a majority voter (relative to the expected equilibrium payoff).[20]

3.3.2.2 Group behavior

The monotonicity of the individual strategies provides only a partial picture. Efficiency requires *group* strategies to be monotonic in the group value. In the *B* treatment, the notion of "group value" is not clearly defined because different subjects within a group have different values. We can, however, check for group monotonicity in the *C* treatment – we can check whether the sum of the votes by members of one group is monotone in their (common) value. If there is heterogeneity in behavior, monotonicity at the individual level need not imply monotonicity at the group level because individuals are continuously rematched. The problem is particularly severe for the majority whose individual equilibrium strategies are asymmetric.[21]

The histograms in the first row of Figure 3.4a illustrate the difficulty that groups had in the *C* treatment. More than 40 percent of the groups had error rates above 20 percent, compared to only 10 percent of individual subjects in the same sessions (see Figure 3.3a). As expected, and as shown by the histogram on the right, most errors are associated with the majority, where more than 60 percent of the groups had more than 20 percent error rates.

---

20. Supposing that all other voters play the equilibrium strategy. In model *C*, the calculations suppose that the individual majority voter's deviation causes the majority group strategy to switch from casting either five or seven votes to always casting six.

21. A group is identified by the label in the experiment (group 1, group 2, etc.), but rematching implies that the composition of each group continues to change. Note that if equilibrium strategies were symmetric, the changing composition of the group would not matter.

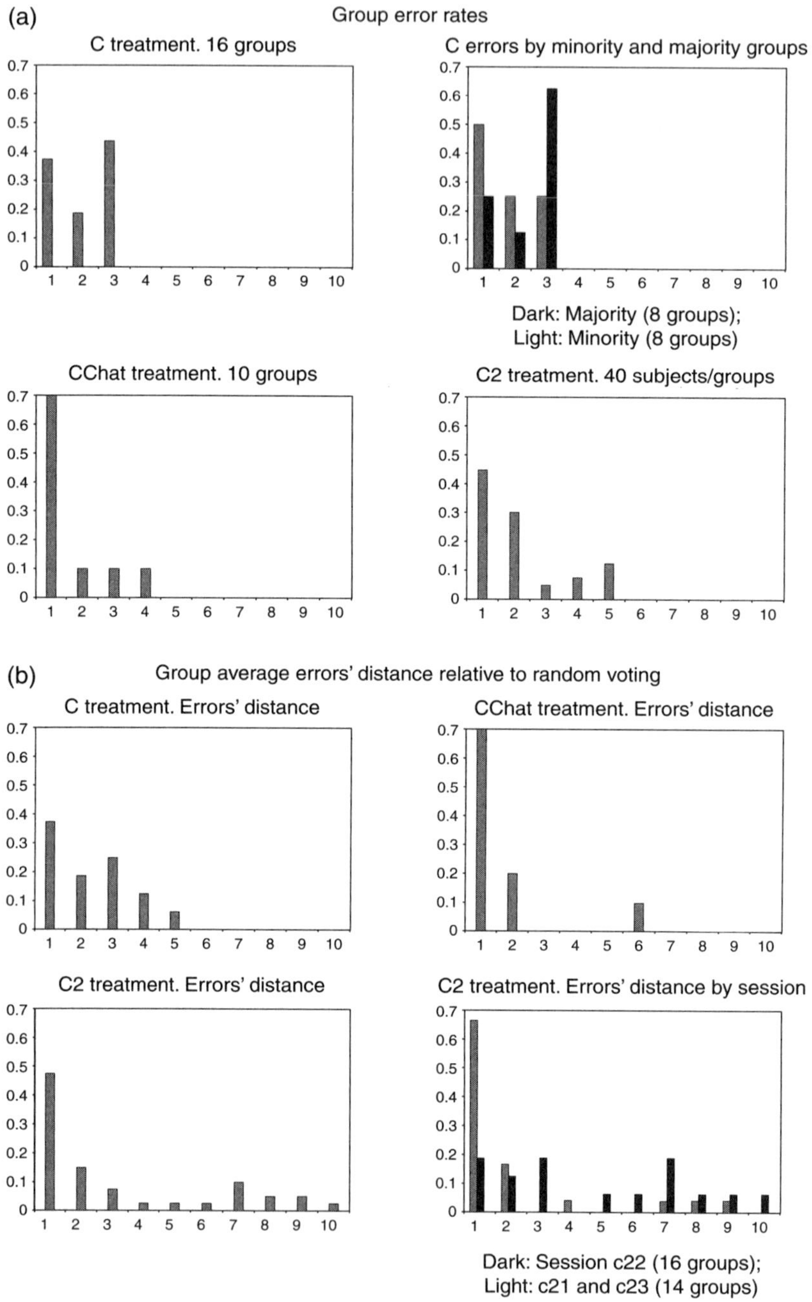

FIGURE 3.4 Group error rates. In Figure 3.4a, the vertical axis is the percentage of subjects with different error rates, the horizontal axis is the error rate organized in progressive bins. In Figure 3.4b, the bins on the horizontal axis correspond to different percentages of the average error distance with random voting; the vertical axis is the percentage of subjects falling into each bin.

A comparison of these results to monotonicity violations in the *C2* and *CChat* treatments allows us to study the role of explicit coordination. According to the histograms in the second row of Figure 3.4, the open communication in *CChat* reduced group violations dramatically: *all* minority groups and two out of five of the majority groups had fewer than 10 percent violations. More surprising is the poor performance of the *C2* treatment, in which perfect coordination is imposed by the experimental design.

These results leave us with a puzzle: if the aggregate group behavior of the experimental subjects in sessions *C* often violates monotonicity, why did the outcomes of these sessions – in terms of minority victories and efficiency – still conform to the theory? Why did these sessions outperform, on average, the *C2* sessions with apparently comparable record of monotonicity violations? The answer comes from the underlying monotonicity of the *individual* behavior in treatment *C*. Intuitively, because individual subjects did cast their votes monotonically, the violations resulting from the uncoordinated aggregation of the votes are numerous, but not large. "Mistaken" (i.e., non-monotonic) voting choices tend to occur just below or just above the cut-point values. To verify this, the histograms in Figure 3.4b summarize the distribution of the average distance of non-monotonic voting choices from the cut-points as percentage of the expected distance if voting choices were random. Both in the experimental data and in the theoretical random case, the cut-points themselves are estimated so as to minimize the average distance.[22] The *CChat* experiments show the greatest consistency: with one outlier, all groups have error distances below 20 percent of the random case. But it is the comparison between the *C* and the *C2* treatments that is particularly revealing: one-fourth of all *C2* groups have error distances that are closer to the purely random case than *any* of the *C* groups. This reflects mostly one outlier session, *c*22, and how much of an outlier *c*22 is made clear in the diagram on the right, in the bottom row of Figure 3.4b. Almost half of all groups in this session have error distances

22. With a very large number of random voting choices, the two cut-points that minimize the expected errors' distance are (50, 50). The frequency of error is two-thirds, with an average distance of 25, yielding an expected distance of 50/3. The corresponding number in the experimental data is, for a given pair of cut-points, the sum of all errors' distances, divided by the number of rounds in the experiment.

that are closer to the purely random case than *any* of the *C* groups, and fewer than one-fifth have distances that are less than 10 percent of the random case, a very different result from the other two *C2* sessions. This explains why the aggregate experimental payoff of session *c22*, in Figure 3.2b, falls short both of the theoretical prediction and of the payoff with simple majority. Why the experimental subjects found the *C2* treatment so difficult is an open question. The problem may come from the larger size of the individual strategy space: each minority voter had five different choices of how many votes to use in the first period (2, 3, 4, 5, 6), and each majority voter had seven different choices (3, 4, 5, 6, 7, 8, 9).

As in the analysis of individual behavior, the monotonicity analysis generates cut-points estimates for each group.[23] Group cut-points are depicted in Figure 3.5, with minority cut-points on the left and majority cut-points on the right. The strategies of each group can be summarized through two cut-points, represented by a dot in the diagrams and equal to (50, 50) in equilibrium for both the minority and the majority.[24]

The first row of diagrams in Figure 3.5 refers to *C* treatments, the second row refers to *C2*, and the last refers to *CChat*. As in Figure 3.3b, darker dots indicate fewer monotonicity violations. The availability of explicit coordination affects the cut-points of the minority groups: none of the estimated cut-points in treatments *C2* and *CChat* lies outside the 45-degree line, as opposed to what we observe in treatment *C*. In accordance with equilibrium, in treatments *C2* and *CChat*, the behavior of all minority groups is best described as casting either two votes (at lower values) or six votes (at higher values), with some dispersion around the equilibrium cut-points (50, 50). The majority's behavior, on the other hand, is best described as splitting the bonus votes for some intermediate range of values. In addition, the light shading of most dots in the majority figures reflects the relatively large number of monotonicity violations

23. The cut-point estimates that minimize the number of monotonicity violations need not be identical to those that minimize the errors' distance. In practice, they differ mostly in the case of those subjects with more random behavior. The substance of the results does not change, and we report here the cut-points that minimize the number of violations, for consistency with the discussion of individual behavior.

24. For the majority groups, all payoff-equivalent strategies are treated as identical – i.e., voting either three, four, or five for values below 50, and voting either seven, eight or nine above 50.

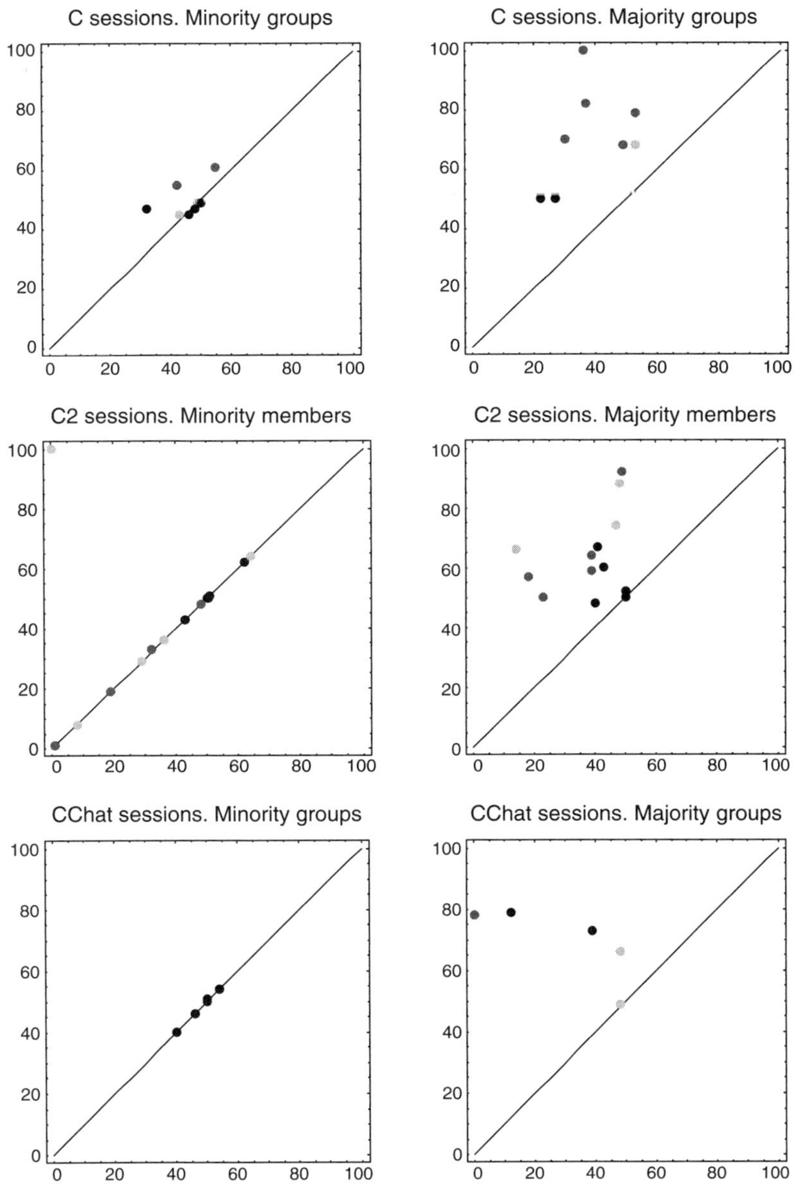

FIGURE 3.5 Group behavior – Group cut-points. In all panels, the horizontal axis measures the value below which a group casts two votes, if minority, or three votes, if majority; the vertical axis the value at which a group moves to casting six votes if minority, or nine votes if majority. Payoff equivalent strategies are treated identically. Cut-points are estimated so as to minimize error rates. Shading corresponds to different error rates: black dots refer to groups with error rates not larger than 10 percent; dark gray to groups with error rates between 10 and 20 percent, and light gray to subjects with error rates larger than 20 percent.

for any estimate of cut-points. Once again, the relatively greater deviation from equilibrium by the majority groups may reflect the relative low cost of such deviations. With a single coordinated strategy, the expected percentage loss to the majority from always splitting the bonus votes is approximately 8 percent when the minority plays the equilibrium strategy.[25] For the minority, on the other hand, splitting the bonus votes can be very costly: a minority always casting four votes *always* loses against a majority casting five votes at values below 50 and seven at values above 50.

3.4 Conclusions

Majoritarian principles are a fundamental ingredient of democratic institutions, but they carry the risk of disenfranchising minority groups. In a well-designed democracy, a judicial system protecting minority rights needs to be complemented by political remedies that ensure the minority a voice through the daily, ordered exercise of political rights. Various remedies have been proposed and are used around the world to guarantee some representation to minorities in the choice of representatives. Much less attention has been given to granting minorities a voice when actual decisions, proposals that can simply pass or fail, are on the table. This chapter has analyzed the potential of storable votes to fulfill such a function. As expected, storable votes allow the minority to cumulate votes on specific issues and to win sometime, but equally important is that they are able to do so without substantial aggregate costs: because the minority wins only if its strength of preferences is high, *and the majority's is low*, the gains in terms of equity have little if any cost in terms of efficiency.

Could storable votes help minorities in practice? Especially in the presence of a systematic minority, the strategic demands put on voters can seem daunting. The experiments described in this chapter, however, suggest that here, too, the simple, intuitive rule of thumb of concentrating votes on more strongly felt issues is sufficient to achieve results that

25. In fact, in this model, the majority's maximin strategy entails splitting the bonus votes. It corresponds to cut-points (25, 100): cast no bonus votes for values below 25, but split the bonus votes for all values above 25.

are very close to what theory predicts when everybody casts their votes optimally. The results of the experiment are clear: even in the presence of some strategic mistakes, the minority succeeded in winning a substantial share of decisions and in achieving non-negligible payoffs, and it did so without compromising, in fact often improving, overall efficiency.

4

Agenda Control

Storable votes allow voters to concentrate their weight on some decisions only. What happens, though, if voters are not sure of the decisions they will be called to vote upon in the future? There are two main sources of uncertainty: future proposals may be unknown – think of a committee with the mandate to decide issues that arise over the length of its tenure – or the proposals may be known, but the preferences of the committee members may be changing over time – think again of the European Central Bank and its monthly meetings, in which preferences over future interest-rate policy depend on the evolving state of each economy. In both cases, the result is that voters cannot evaluate precisely the importance they will assign to a future decision or, indeed, what their preferred outcome will be. Mistakes are unavoidable. Yet, as Chapters 2 and 3 have shown, uncertainty per se does not alter the logic of the analysis. As long as voters can predict their preferences on average, they can still use their expectations to decide their strategy and evaluate the welfare potential of the voting scheme, in the knowledge that sometimes they will overestimate the importance of future decisions and sometimes underestimate it. This is exactly the reasoning the two chapters describe.

The real complication could be different: what happens if one or more committee members *control* the agenda? The order of voting on independent yes/no decisions is irrelevant with majority voting, but not with storable votes. Imagine a committee chair deciding which proposals are to be voted upon. Could the chair choose the sequence of proposals so as to exhaust others' bonus votes and then win an unpopular decision on the strength of his bonus votes? Would this use of storable votes result in welfare losses? Or, on the contrary, is this scenario just what it should be, with all members casting their bonus votes on decisions that matter to them and the minority winning occasionally? Is the welfare comparison to simple majority voting robust to the endogenous determination of the agenda?

They are not simple questions, and to keep matters easily tractable, the chapter returns to the bare-bones model studied in Chapter 1: no voter is more likely to be in the minority than any other, all favor or oppose any proposal with equal probability, and all have a single bonus vote. The only addition is that one of the voters is the committee's chair and chooses the agenda.

Simplifying even further, in the first part of the chapter the chair is bound to the known set of proposals; all he can choose is the *order* in which the proposals are brought to the vote. The extension seems trivial, but it in fact sheds light on what the chair can accomplish by setting the agenda in more general scenarios. This chapter will show that with storable votes, control over the agenda works mostly as a communication device: the chair can use it to communicate to the rest of the committee his priorities and commit to a voting strategy. In practice, when the chair chooses the order of the agenda, the message can be interpreted as a norm: think of committees in which the chair is known always to put on the table his highest-priority decision first, or second, or last; or his least important decision first, or second, or last; and so on.

In the second part of the chapter, the chair controls not only the order but also *which* proposals are brought to the vote. Agenda power allows the chair not only to communicate his relative priorities, but also to make sure that his absolute priorities – the decisions on which he mostly wants a vote – are considered. The other members of the committees face a more difficult problem: as proposals are called for a vote, they ignore whether their priorities will or will not be on the agenda, and it is this uncertainty that mostly affect their voting choices. Predictably, the chair's advantage is larger in this latter scenario. Less predictably, in both parts of the chapter, the welfare comparison to majority voting remains fundamentally unchanged. Relative to the chair, the other committee members lose mostly from not being able to call their own priorities to a vote, a loss that is common to majority voting, too. And when a proposal *is* on the table, the opportunity to signal the strength of one's preferences remains valuable. If the relative importance assigned to one's first priority is sufficiently high, storable votes remain likely to dominate simple majority voting.

As in all previous chapters, the subtleties of the theory are tested with laboratory experiments. The qualitative conclusions are very similar to those discussed in the earlier chapters: the finer theoretical predictions are not confirmed, but the more sophisticated points of strategy do not appear to matter much. Subjects always use their bonus vote to signal the intensity of their preferences, and this behavior, even marred by increasing mistakes as the problem they face becomes increasingly difficult, allows them to obtain rewards that are close to the theoretical predictions, both in their absolute values and in comparison to simple majority voting.

4.1 Controlling the Order of the Agenda

4.1.1 The theory

The set-up is as in Chapter 1, and for convenience is repeated in Box 4.1, with the only difference that one of the voters has the role of committee chair. Very briefly: A committee faces a series of known proposals, each of which can either pass or fail. Voters know their preferences over each proposal, but not the preferences of others. Each voter is equally likely to favor or oppose any proposal, and preferences over one proposal convey no information about either the voter's own preferences over other proposals, or other voters' preferences over the one proposal. Each voter is endowed with one regular vote to cast on each proposal, and a single bonus vote to use freely. The bonus vote can be worth more or less than a regular vote. Every proposal is decided according to the majority of votes cast, with all votes expressed in terms of regular votes: for example, if the bonus vote is worth one-half of a regular vote, then two bonus votes are required to counter one regular vote. The committee has a chair – one of the voters – whose role is to announce, before any voting takes place, the order in which the proposals will be presented to the vote. A voter's strategy is, for all voters including the chair, the choice of the proposal on which to cast the bonus vote, and, for the chair alone, the order in which the votes are called.

Box 4.1 The Formal Model. Version 4.1

A committee of n voters meets to decide whether to implement T distinct, known proposals, $\{P_1, ..P_T\}$, each of which can either pass or fail. The committee votes on the proposals sequentially, and at the start of the meeting one of the members, the *chair* c, announces the order in which all proposals will be brought to a vote.

Each member i of the committee has preferences over each proposal P_t, summarized by a cardinal valuation v_{it}. Valuations v_{it} are independently and identically distributed both across proposals and across individuals according to the distribution $G(\text{v})$ with support $[-1, 1]$, symmetric around 0. A negative valuation means that the voter is against the proposal; a positive valuation that he is in favor. Voter i's absolute valuation $v_{it} \equiv |\text{v}_{it}|$ is i's intensity over proposal P_t. For each proposal P_t, voter i receives utility $u_{it} = v_{it}$ if the decision goes in his preferred direction, and 0 otherwise. Voter i's utility from the entire meeting, U_i, equals $\sum_{t=1}^{T} u_{it}$.

In addition to a regular vote over every proposal, each committee member is given one indivisible bonus vote equivalent to B regular votes. Each proposal is decided in the direction that receives more votes; in case of a tie, a coin is flipped. Before any voting takes place, and before the chair announces the order of the agenda, each committee member knows $\{\text{v}_{i1}, ..\text{v}_{iT}\}$, his own valuations over all proposals, but does not know others' valuations over any of the proposals. The independence of the valuations and the distribution G from which they are drawn are common knowledge, as is the set of voters still endowed with the bonus vote when proposal P_t is called to a vote.

A voter's strategy is, for all voters including the chair, the choice of the proposal on which to cast the bonus vote, and, for the chair alone, the order in which the votes are called. The focus is on quasi-symmetric Perfect Bayesian equilibria in weakly undominated strategies such that all voters who are not the chair play symmetric strategies.

Call P_i^* the proposal to which voter i attaches highest priority: $v_i^* = \max\{\boldsymbol{v}_i\}$. (Hence P_c^* is the proposal to which the chair attaches highest priority: $v_c^* = \max\{\boldsymbol{v}_c\}$). Then:

Proposition 4.1. For all T, n, G, and B, there exists an equilibrium where the chair orders P_c^* in any position on the agenda with equal probability, and every voter i, including the chair, casts his bonus vote on P_i^*.

The equilibrium identified by Proposition 4.1 is identical to the exogenous agenda equilibrium discussed in Chapter 1. Call it the *non-informative* (*NI*) equilibrium, and denote by EV_0^{NI} a voter's ex ante utility in the non-informative equilibrium, before preferences are realized and before the chair's role is assigned. Denote by EW_0 ex ante utility with simple majority voting; Ev the expected intensity, and $Ev_{(T)}$ the expected highest-intensity draw. From Chapter 1, there exists a set of bonus vote values, $\mathcal{B}(n)$, such that if $B \in \mathcal{B}(n)$, $EV_0^{NI} > EW_0$ for all n and T if either n is even, or n is odd and $Ev_{(T)}/Ev > [T(n+1)]/[T(n-1)+2]$ (Proposition 1.2 in Box 1.1 in Chapter 1). Thus, for all T, n, G, and $B \in \mathcal{B}(n)$, there exists an equilibrium with an endogenous order of agenda, such that the welfare comparison to majority voting identified in Chapter 1 carries through identically.

Define an equilibrium *informative* if, after the chair's announcement of the agenda's order, all voters identify the chair's highest-priority proposal with probability higher than $1/T$. A *fully informative* (*FI*) equilibrium is one where the chair's highest-priority proposal is identified with probability 1.

Proposition 4.2. Suppose $T = 2$. (1) For all n, G, and $B \in \mathcal{B}(n)$, there exist two payoff-equivalent fully informative equilibria such that: (i) the chair sets $P_c^* = P_t$, with $t \in \{1, 2\}$, and always casts his bonus vote on P_t; (ii) any other committee member i casts his bonus vote on P_t if and only if $v_{it} \geq \alpha(n, G)v_{is}$, $s \neq t$, with $\alpha(n, G) \geq 1$ and unique. (2) With $T = 2$ and $B \in \mathcal{B}(n)$, there exist G and n, for which no other quasi-symmetric informative equilibrium exists.

Call $P_{i\mathcal{S}}^*$ the proposal to which voter i attaches highest priority among some set of proposals $\mathbf{P}_{\mathcal{S}}$: $v_{i\mathcal{S}}^* = \max\{\boldsymbol{v}_{i\mathcal{S}}\}$, and $P_{i\mathcal{T}-\mathcal{S}}^*$ the proposal to which voter i attaches highest priority among the complement set $\mathbf{P}_{\mathcal{T}-\mathcal{S}}$. The following result gives some insight on the equilibria of the game with an arbitrary number of proposals.

Proposition 4.3. Suppose $n \in \{2, 3, 4\}$ and $B \in \mathcal{B}(n)$. (1) For all G and T there exist T payoff-distinct equilibria such that: (i) the chair selects his S-lowest-intensity proposals, with $S \in \{0, 1, 2, .., T-1\}$, and arranges them, in any order, in the first S positions on the agenda; he orders the remaining $T-S$ proposals with equal probability in each of the last $T-S$ positions; (ii) the chair always casts his bonus vote on P_c^* (and thus never casts it on the first S proposals); (iii) any other committee member $j \neq c$ casts his bonus vote on $P_{jT-\mathcal{S}}^*$ if $v_{jT-\mathcal{S}}^* \geq \alpha(n, G, T, S)v_{j\mathcal{S}}^*$, and on $P_{j\mathcal{S}}^*$ otherwise. For all G, T, and S, $\alpha(n, G, T, S) \geq 1$ and unique. (2) For $n = 3$, these are the only payoff-distinct quasi-symmetric equilibria holding for all G, T, and $B \in \mathcal{B}(n)$.

Note that with $n \in \{2, 3, 4\}$, $B = 1$ belongs to $\mathcal{B}(n)$: the proposition applies to environments where the bonus vote is equivalent to a regular vote.

Call EV_{0c}^S the chair's ex ante utility in the equilibrium identified by Proposition 4.3, for given value of S, before valuations are realized, but after the role of chair has been assigned. Note that $S = 0$ defines the non-informative equilibrium ($EV_{0c}^0 \equiv EV_{0c}^{NI}$), $S = T - 1$ defines the fully informative equilibrium ($EV_{0c}^{T-1} \equiv EV_{0c}^{FI}$), and $S \in \{1, .., T-2\}$ defines informative but not fully-informative equilibria. Then:

Proposition 4.4. In all equilibria described in Propositions 4.2 and 4.3, $EV_{0c}^S \geq EV_{0c}^{NI}$, with $S \in \{1, .., T-1\}$.

The question the model addresses is the possibility that the chair might want to postpone decisions he deems important, waiting for the depletion of others' bonus votes. Is this going to occur, and can it lead to efficiency losses? And, are the efficiency losses magnified in equilibrium, as the other committee members adjust their own strategies?[1]

One answer to the first question comes immediately from Chapter 1. If every voter casts his bonus vote on his highest priority, the chair has no reason to expect that any specific proposal, at any position in the order of the agenda, should receive either more or fewer bonus votes than any other. The position in the order is irrelevant. Thus, the chair can set

1. This section draws on Casella (2011).

the order randomly and simply cast his bonus vote on his own highest priority, correctly expecting others to do the same. Given the discussion in Chapter 1, the observation is not surprising, but it is important here because it sets the stage for the rest of the analysis. It has two direct implications.

First, giving to one committee member the right to set the order of the agenda need not have *any* impact on voting choices and welfare. The results of Chapter 1 can carry over unchanged – the expected welfare gains over simple majority, the importance of the distribution of preferences, the determination of the optimal value of the bonus vote. It is true that the agenda power granted to the chair in this first scenario is very limited: not only is it limited to the order of proposals, but the chair is restricted to announcing the full agenda once and for all at the beginning of the game. Note, however, that the equivalence to Chapter 1 would continue to hold if the chair announced proposals sequentially, after observing how many votes have been cast. The reasoning is unchanged: if voters cast their bonus vote on their highest priority, at any point in time and for any number of remaining bonus votes all future proposals are equally likely targets of bonus votes. The position of a proposal in the agenda continues to be irrelevant. The chair can do no better than setting the order randomly and casting his own bonus vote on his highest priority, a strategy that is correctly guessed by the other voters and supports their own exclusive focus on their own priorities.

The second implication, however, is that this logic also hints at the possibility of a different result. If other voters conditioned their strategy on the position of a proposal in the agenda, it may well be an optimal response to do so, too. For example, if the chair were known to call the decision he considers most important first and to cast on it his bonus vote, the other committee members may prefer to save their own bonus vote for later proposals. And their reluctance to spend the bonus vote on the first proposal encourages the chair to pursue the strategy attributed to him. The central point is that the order the chair assigns to a proposal can work as a communication device: it can convey information about the chair's priorities and use of the bonus vote. In fact, the order of a proposal can *only* work as a communication device. In this set-up, there is no other manner for the chair to exploit his agenda-setting power.[2]

Note that while information about the chair's highest priority can be transmitted credibly, the same is not true for the *direction* of the chair's preferences. The reason is that revealing the direction of one's vote can be counterproductive: it induces allies to refrain from using their bonus votes on the issue, freeing their votes for future use, when their preferences may well differ from the chair's.[3]

Intensity, on the contrary, *can* be revealed. Consider, then, a voter who expects the chair to cast his bonus vote on the first proposal. Competition with others' bonus votes is counterproductive, and the voter has an incentive to keep his bonus vote for use on a later proposal. But what if the first proposal is also his own highest priority? If it is just barely more important than a different proposal, the answer is clear. Otherwise? There must be a threshold, such that if the voter's intensity of preferences over the first proposal is sufficiently stronger than the intensity of his preferences over his second priority, he will not be deterred by the chair's strategy. An example helps. Imagine a committee of three voters, one of whom is chair. Suppose also that the bonus vote is equivalent to a regular vote and that each voter's intensity is equally likely to take any value in some fixed interval. If there are two proposals, then there is an equilibrium in which the chair always orders his most important proposal first and spends on it his bonus vote, and each of the other two committee members casts his bonus vote on the first proposal only if he considers it at least 50 percent more important than the second one. Thus, on average, a voter who is not the chair casts his bonus vote on the

2. Economists refer to situations of this type as "cheap talk" games: a person can give a signal indicating his intentions, but there is no cost involved in the signal. Talking is the most obvious example – a person can say what he intends to do – and talking is cheap. The contrast is to signaling games in which the signal acquires credibility because it is costly: in Michael Spence's famous example, schooling is a credible signal of ability because it requires effort, but less effort the higher the natural ability (Spence (1973)). Cheap talk games were introduced by Crawford and Sobel (1982). In the agenda setting case studied here, the chair can transmit information about his relative priorities over multiple proposals, a multi dimensional cheap talk problem introduced by Battaglini (2002) and bearing some similarities to the model in Chakraborty and Harbaugh (2007). Early applications of cheap talk games to political decision-making are Ordeshook and Palfrey (1988), Austen-Smith (1990), and Palfrey and Rosenthal (1991).

3. The proof of Proposition 4.2 in Part II shows this rigorously.

first proposal only one-third of the time. By following these strategies, all committee members reduce the competition they expect for their bonus vote.

There is nothing special in the first proposal per se. The chair may just as well order the proposal he deems most important second and save for it his bonus vote. If the other voters have learned to read this meaning in the agenda order, they will respond by shifting their own bonus votes toward the first proposal. In the example just described, there is a second equilibrium, a mirror image of the first, in which the chair always casts his bonus vote on the second proposal while the other two voters spend theirs on the first, unless they deem the second proposal at least 50 percent more important to them than the first.

If there are more than two proposals, in principle any position in the agenda can be devoted by the chair to his most important proposal. With an arbitrary number of proposals, the result can be proved rigorously if the committee has two, three, or four members, and the bonus vote is equivalent to a regular vote, conditions that will be satisfied in the experiment described below. In all of these cases, the order of the agenda can communicate perfectly the chair's priority, and the committee achieve what I call the *fully informative* equilibrium. With more than two proposals, however, communication may also be fuzzier. For example, it may be known that the chair's priority is never the first proposal, but that it is equally likely to be any of the others or that it is never the last proposal, or that it is never one of the first two, or the last three, etc. The other committee members respond by shifting their own bonus votes away from the chair's probable priorities, the more so the more confident they are of the chair's intended bonus vote use. Many outcomes are possible, but the main message remains: the only possible function of the agenda order is to communicate the chair's priorities. The communication may allow all committee members to identify the chair's top priority perfectly, or it may restrict the set of proposals to which the chair's priority belongs, or in fact, it may not take place at all and the committee may vote exactly as it would if the order of the agenda were random.

If the chair's control of the agenda has an effect, it is to reduce competition with his bonus vote. This is an equilibrium result: the other voters are not caught unaware by the chair's strategy, nor are they tempted to counter it by cumulating their own votes on the chair's priority. On the contrary, the decision to cast their bonus votes disproportionately on the other proposals is their optimal response. The control of the agenda gives the chair the possibility to commit to a specific voting strategy, and it is in the chair's interest to make this public and in the other members' interest to shift their bonus votes away from the chair's priority.

Is the chair's control of the agenda's order therefore advantageous for all? If no communication occurs, clearly, it makes no difference. If it does make a difference, it must be advantageous for the chair, who succeeds in exerting more influence over his first priority – this is Proposition 4.4 in Box 4.1. The position of committee chair does have value. For the other voters, the result is less clear. On one hand, they compete less with the chair, but on the other, they may use the bonus vote for a proposal that is not their first priority, and they do face the increased competition of the other committee members. The net effect is ambiguous: its sign depends on the parameters of the problem. In some examples, voters who are not chairs lose, relative to the case of an external agenda, and in some examples they gain.

Figure 4.1 shows ex ante expected utility when the chair's most important proposal is identified with certainty, relative to expected utility when no information is conveyed (Figure 4.1a) and when decisions are taken with simple majority voting (Figure 4.1b), for the two cases of three-member and four-member committees. In the figure, the bonus vote is equivalent to a regular vote, and each voter is equally likely to hold preferences of any intensity. The horizontal axis is the number of proposals. Each plot has three series of dots: the two series of gray dots plot individual expected utility for the chair (the upper one) and for a voter who is not chair (the lower one) before the realization of valuations, but after the role of chair has been assigned; the black dots plot expected utility before valuations are realized and before the chair's role position is assigned, with equal probability of being chair.

Figure 4.1a shows that the chair always gains from the transmission of information. In three-member committees, the chair's expected gain is maximal with two proposals and declines monotonically as the number of proposals increases. In four-member committees, the magnitude of the gain is not monotonic in the number of proposals, reaching a maximum at five proposals and declining thereafter. In the examples plotted in the figure, although not in general, a voter who is not the chair expects to

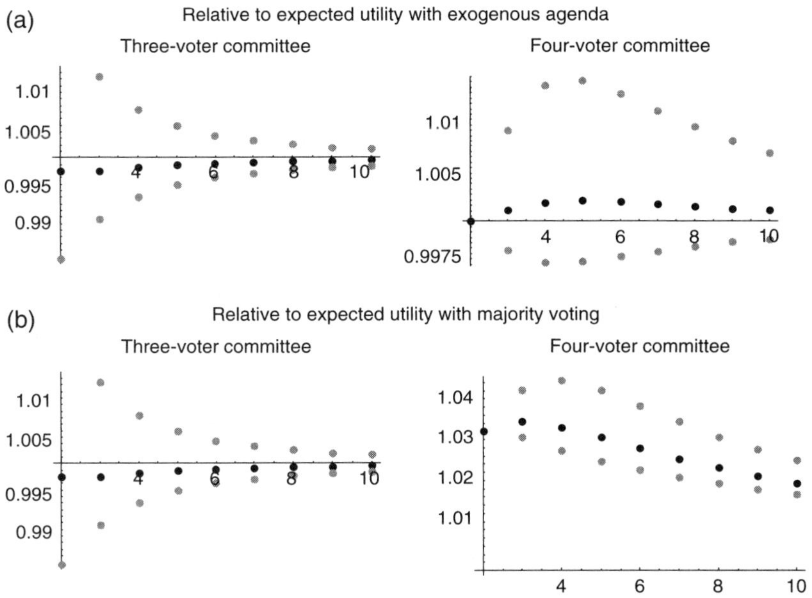

FIGURE 4.1 Expected utility in the fully informative equilibrium as function of the number of proposals. In all panels, the horizontal axis is the number of proposals, the bonus vote is equivalent to a regular vote, and each voter is equally likely to hold preferences of any intensity. The upper gray dots refer to the chair; the lower gray dots to a representative voter who is not the chair, and the black dots to ex ante expected welfare with equal probability of being chair.

fare worse when information is conveyed, with an expected loss that mirrors imperfectly the chair's gain, with opposite sign.[4] Expected utility before the chair's role is assigned combines the expected utility of the chair and of the other voters, and results in a small loss in three-member committees and a small gain in four-member ones. All effects tend to disappear as the number of proposals becomes large, and the probability of competing over the same proposal declines.

Figure 4.1b reports the utility measures as share of the corresponding measures with simple majority voting. In three-voter committees, if agenda control transmits information perfectly, the chair expects

4. In other examples, however, a voter who is not chair may benefit, too, from the transmission of information. One such case is a five-member committee deciding on two proposals, when two bonus votes are required to counter one regular vote.

higher utility than with majority voting, the other voters expect lower utility, and the overall effect is very slightly negative.[5] In four-member committees, every voter expects to fare better than with simple majority.

Whether positive or negative, in Figure 4.1 the overall effects are small. The expected welfare change is at most of the order of 0.2 percent, relative to welfare with exogenous agenda. This is a recurring result of all numerical examples I have studied: regardless of the distribution of intensities, of the value of the bonus vote, and of the numbers of voters and proposals, the welfare impact of identifying the chair's priority was always quantitatively small. Of course, the welfare effect of granting control of the order of proposals to the chair is nil if its possible use in transmitting information is not recognized. All considered, it seems safe to conclude that the theory predicts very little welfare change relative to the case in which the agenda is fixed externally. In particular, the comparison to majority voting discussed in Chapter 1 continues to be a good reference here. What happens in practice, though, is an empirical matter, best left to experimental testing.

4.1.2 Experiment 4.1

The experiment asks two main questions. Are experimental subjects able to identify the subtle potential for communication highlighted by the theory? If they do not, do they adopt voting behaviors that result in sensible declines in efficiency? The use of inexperienced subjects biases the results against the probability of observing optimal strategies, but it lends more weight to the answer to the second question. If the experimental subjects still succeed in using the bonus vote profitably, we can be more confident that this would occur in practical applications, with more experienced voters playing for higher stakes.

All sessions of the experiment were run at CESS at NYU, between November 2006 and May 2008, with enrolled students recruited from the whole campus through the laboratory web site. No subject participated in more than one session.

---

5. When the bonus vote is equivalent to a regular vote and all intensities of preferences are equally probable, in three-voter committees, expected utility with simple majority voting is identical to expected utility with storable votes and no information transmission, for any number of proposals. The left panel of Figure 4.1b replicates exactly the left panel of Figure 4.1a.

Subjects were matched randomly in groups of three members in some sessions and four members in others, and they were asked to vote successively over three proposals, named the *Green*, *Red*, and *Blue* proposals. In addition to one regular vote for each proposal, all subjects were endowed with a single bonus vote, identical in value to the regular votes. Valuations for all three proposals were drawn randomly by the computer, independently for each subject and for each proposal, and they could assume any integer value between −100 and 100 (excluding 0), with equal probability. Before any decision was taken, each subject was shown his valuations over the three proposals, and one group member was chosen by the computer as chair and given the task of deciding the order of proposals. The order was then communicated to the other members of the chair's group. Subjects were then asked to vote on the first proposal, and they could choose whether to cast the bonus vote. After the vote, the computer screen showed whether the proposal had passed and the number of bonus votes still available to the other group members. Voting continued in this fashion up to the third and last proposal, on which all remaining bonus votes were cast automatically. A new round of three proposals was then repeated.

The existence of multiple informative equilibria makes learning particularly difficult, and to allow for it, groups were not rematched but remained unchanged for an entire experimental session. Because valuations were private and drawn independently, even with fixed group membership there was no natural scope for coordination. The same subject acted as chair for a fixed number of rounds, specified in the instructions, and each member of a group acted as chair in turn.

Subjects were paid a fixed show-up fee and their cumulative valuation for all proposals resolved in their preferred direction in five randomly chosen rounds, adjusted by a known exchange rate. Average earnings were approximately $20 an hour.

Table 4.1 reports the experimental design. Sessions 1 to 4 were preceded by several rounds in which the agenda order was decided by the computer and whose results are discussed in Chapter 1. The remaining sessions did not and act as controls.[6]

---

6. Because of a programming error, in session 3, different members within each group were chair for a different and random number of rounds (as opposed to all being

Table 4.1 Experimental Design

The chair controls the order of the agenda.			
Session	n	Subjects	Rounds
1*	3	12	30
2*	3	15	30
3*	4	12	32
4*	4	16	20
5	3	9	18
6	4	12	20

* The session began with several rounds in which the order of the agenda was chosen by the computer. See Chapter 1.

The experiment mirrored closely the theoretical model, and all theoretical results apply here. There are three equilibria with different expected outcomes and payoffs: the *non-informative* equilibrium, equivalent to an externally given order of the agenda; the *fully informative* equilibrium, where the chair always orders his highest-intensity proposal in the same position; and the *partially informative* equilibrium, where the chair orders his highest-intensity proposal either second or third, with equal probability, but always orders his lowest-intensity proposal first. Equilibrium strategies are discussed in detail in Chapter 4 of Part II. Here, I just note that in equilibrium the chair always casts the bonus vote on his highest-priority proposal; voters who are not chair do so if either they do not expect the agenda to convey information about the chair's strategy, or if they do not expect their most important proposal to receive the chair's bonus vote. If neither condition is satisfied, they shift their bonus vote to their second-highest priority, unless the strength of their preferences regarding the two proposals is sufficiently different. The theory allows us to calculate the exact value of the required ratio of intensities.

There is no support in the experimental data for the partially informative equilibrium, and I ignore it in what follows. The expected

---

chair for eight of the thirty-two rounds). The results from the session are effectively indistinguishable from those of the other sessions.

Table 4.2 Equilibrium Expected Earnings

The chair controls the order of the agenda.				
n	Surplus NI	Surplus FI	Surplus Maj.	Chair Gain FI
3	92.3	91.7	92.3	2.2
4	90.8	90.9	80.4	1.1

NI, non-informative equilibrium; FI, fully informative equilibrium.

efficiency of the voting scheme in the two remaining equilibria is reported in Table 4.2. As usual, it is summarized by the expected share of available aggregate surplus appropriated with storable votes, and, for comparison, with simple majority. The last column of the table reports the expected percentage gain to the chair, relative to non-chair committee members, in the fully informative equilibrium. The chair and the other members are not expected to fare differently in the non-informative equilibrium.

With this parameterization, storable votes are either equivalent or slightly inferior to simple majority in three-member committees, depending on the equilibrium, and superior by a 10 percent margin in four-member committees. The chair's expected gain over the other members is just above 2 percent in three-member committees and just above 1 percent in four-member ones.

4.1.3 The results

The strategic behavior of the experimental subjects can be summarized very briefly. The experiment is almost identical to the experiment described in Chapter 1, with the only difference that here the order of the agenda is decided by a chair as opposed to being chosen by the computer. Although the same voting strategies used there remain equilibrium strategies here (corresponding to the non-informative equilibrium), subjects find the presence of the chair confusing, and make more strategic errors, relative to Chapter 1. Nevertheless, the non-informative equilibrium remains the best predictor of the subjects' strategies. The number of errors increases further if voting choices are evaluated against fully informative equilibrium strategies.

As in Chapter 1, I classify as an "error" each round of play (each three-proposal game) in which a subject does not cast the bonus vote on the proposal identified by his equilibrium strategy. In an experimental session, the aggregate error rate is the total number of errors divided by the total number of rounds played by all subjects. Averaging across all sessions, the mean error rate is 10 percent if calculated with respect to non-informative equilibrium strategies and 15 percent with respect to fully informative strategies, a statistically significant difference according to a simple test of proportions.[7] As reference, in Chapter 1 the mean error rate is 8 percent.

The aggregate results are a fair mirror of individual behavior. Figure 4.2 reports histograms of individual error rates: each column represents the fraction of all subjects whose individual error rate, in percentage terms, falls in the corresponding bin. The first bin corresponds to 0 errors; all others are increments of one decile. Relative to non-informative equilibrium strategies, 68 percent of all subjects have error rates below 10 percent; relative to fully informative strategies, the number falls to 45 percent. In statistical terms, the error rates relative to informative strategies stochastically dominate the error rates relative to non-informative strategies: at any frequency of errors, the mass of subjects with errors higher than that frequency is larger when considering informative strategies. In Chapter 1, 77 percent of subjects had error rates below 10 percent.[8]

Why do subjects find this experiment more difficult? One immediate answer is the presence of multiple equilibria. Not only are there different equilibria with different precision of information, but there are multiple fully informative equilibria. Even if the chair's intent to transmit

---

7. At the 5 percent significance level.

8. Voting decisions are made within a group, and if strategic errors within a group are correlated, the independence assumption exploited in comparing aggregate error rates, and the focus on histograms of individual errors are not legitimate. In fact, though, a useful feature of the present game is that individual best response strategies are robust to most strategic errors by other group members. The theoretical prediction is confirmed empirically: a regression of individual errors on errors by other groups members, in each round, cannot reject the hypothesis of no correlation. (See the discussion in Casella (2011)). Being able to maintain the independence of individual error rates allows the use of the largest possible number of data points. The evidence is qualitatively identical at the group level, but with the much smaller sample, the statistical tests lack power.

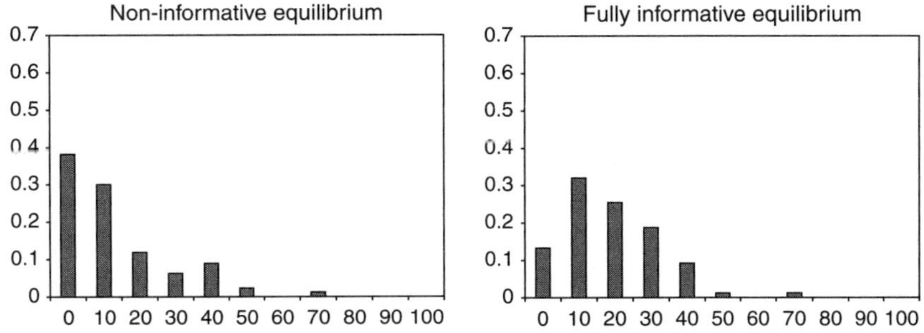

FIGURE 4.2 Individual error rates (74 subjects). The horizontal axis reports the fraction of errors. The first bin corresponds to 0 errors, all remaining bins are 10 percent increments. The vertical axis is the fraction of subjects whose fraction of errors falls into the corresponding bin.

information is understood, will he cast his most important proposal first, second, or third? A priori, nothing distinguishes one particular position as more significant than any other – in economists' terminology, a common language is missing.[9] A second difficulty is still deeper: subjects may well not understand that the order of the agenda is a language at all. The fact that it can be used to communicate relative strength of preferences is far from obvious. The data provide some weak evidence supporting this second explanation: even subjects who routinely order their highest-intensity proposal in the same position when chair, appear not to attribute a strategic role to a proposal's order when not chair.

Having remarked on the higher error rate, however, we should not lose sight of the fact that almost 70 percent of subjects still cast their bonus votes on their highest-priority proposal more than 90 percent of the times. The subtleties of equilibrium play may be lost, but the bonus vote continues to be used to express the intensity of one's preferences. Once again, it is this use of the bonus vote that explains the good performance of storable votes in terms of outcomes and earnings.

Figure 4.3 plots realized aggregate experimental earnings in each session and compares them to the corresponding earnings had subjects

9. Experimental results in cheap talk games are summarized in Crawford (1998). The lack of a common language recalls the experiment in Blume et al. (2001). Blume et al. find that communication does develop, although more slowly in the absence of a common language, and only if the subjects have sufficient experience with the experiment.

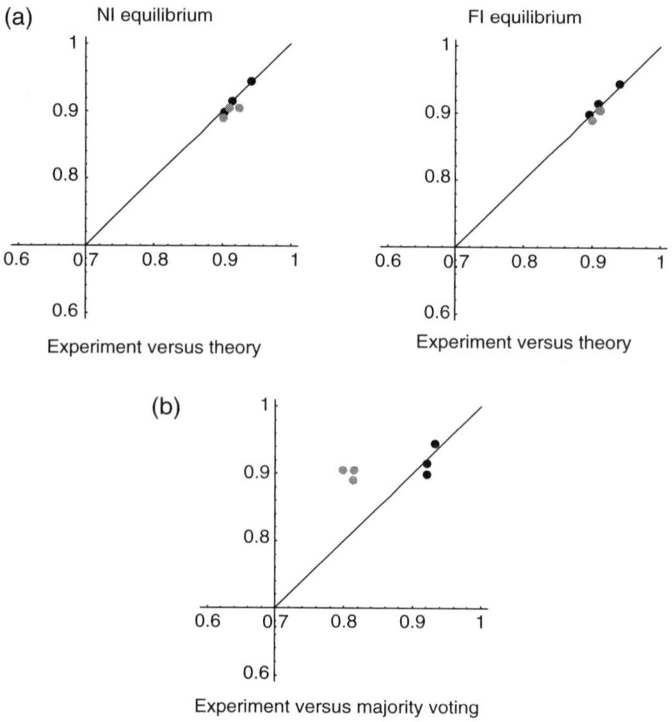

FIGURE 4.3 Experimental surplus, as share of maximal surplus. The vertical axis reports total experimental earnings per session, as share of maximal earnings. The horizontal axis reports the share of total to maximal earnings in each session in the absence of any strategic mistake (Figure 4.3a), or if decisions were made through simple majority (Figure 4.3b). Black dots are three-voter committee sessions; gray dots four-voter committees. All earnings are measured as gains over earnings with random decision-making.

played the equilibrium strategies (Figure 4.3a) or had decisions been made by simple majority (Figure 4.3b). As usual, earnings are expressed as share of the available surplus over random decision-making and are calculated on the basis of the realized experimental draws. Black dots denote experimental sessions with three-member committees, and gray dots sessions with four-member committees. The 45-degree lines make the figure easy to read.

As far as earnings are concerned, the predictive power of the theory is confirmed. Figure 4.3a shows that experimental outcomes replicate the equilibrium results and lie either on or very close to the 45-degree line, and this is true whether evaluated relative to the non-informative or to the informative equilibrium.[10] Because the welfare properties of the two equilibria are very similar, the first conclusion from the experiment is that storable votes do as well, in welfare terms, as they would with an externally fixed agenda. The chair's control of the agenda does not cause a decline in efficiency.

Figure 4.3b shows that aggregate earnings with storable votes are clearly superior to what they would be with majority voting for four-member groups and very similar, possibly just slightly inferior, for three-member groups. The comparison of the experimental results to majority voting is the second conclusion of the experiment. It is important because it adds perspective to the first result. The data make clear that the experimental payoffs *are* sensitive to the voting choices made by the subjects. The floor on subjects' earnings corresponds to their least-profitable strategy, casting the bonus vote on the their lowest-intensity proposal. Given the experimental draws, it would result in a share of aggregate surplus that is 12 percent (for three-member committees) and 20 percent (for four-member committees) lower on average than observed in the data, in both cases significantly below both the equilibrium predictions and the majority voting reference point. A full range of payoffs above this floor but below the majority voting threshold was available to the subjects. By casting the bonus vote on high intensity proposals, subjects were instead able to extract as high a share of surplus as theory predicts in equilibrium.

Finally, did the chair succeed in appropriating a larger share of the surplus, relative to the other subjects? According to the theory, in this experiment an advantage for the chair should exist in the informative equilibria only, and even then the quantitative effect should be small. By isolating the returns to the chair, the sample size is reduced to one-third (when committees have three members) or one-fourth (when committees have four members) of the original size, and the sampling variability trumps the differences in strategies. If we aggregate the data over all sessions in which groups have equal size, in

10. In the plot comparing experimental earnings to the informative equilibrium earnings, the dots indicating sessions 3 and 4 are superimposed and appear as one (the higher of the two gray dots).

four-member committees chairs did better than they would have done in any equilibrium, whether informative or non-informative, and better than with simple majority: the strategic errors favored the chairs. The gain however is always small – averaging over all subjects, relative to a non-chair voter, a chair increased his payoff by between 0.4 and 0.6 percent in all cases. In three-member committees sessions, relative to non-chairs, the chairs did better than they would have done in the non-informative equilibrium but worse than in the informative equilibria and worse than with simple majority. Here, the potentially larger gain available to the chair in the informative equilibrium is compromised by the strategic errors. Again, the quantitative effects are always very small, always smaller than 1 percent. In the experiments, any distributional effect is minor, if it exists at all.

In brief, the theoretical predictions are that the chair's control of the order of the agenda should have little if any effect on the welfare properties of storable votes. This is indeed the conclusion from the experiment: the bonus vote does matter; the chair's control of the agenda does not.

4.2 Controlling the Content of the Agenda

It is true, however, that the agenda power granted to the chair so far is minimal. When we talk of the chair's power, usually we think of the chair controlling not only the order, but also the *content*, of the agenda. How do storable votes perform then?[11]

4.2.1 The theory

Consider the following scenario, in which the model is streamlined even further. The possible agenda consists of four proposals, known to each committee member and assigned by each member values $\{1, 2, 3, 4\}$. Any ranking of the four proposals is equally likely: if we call the proposals P_A, P_B, P_C, and P_D, and write them in order of increasing value, any committee member may order them (P_C, P_B, P_D, P_A), or

11. Solomon Hsiang, Geoff McCarney, and Kyle Gerry all contributed to the work described here.

(P_B, P_A, P_D, P_C), or (P_A, P_B, P_C, P_D), or any other of the twenty-four possible permutations, with equal probability. The realizations of the rankings are independent across committee members. Each member can be in favor or against each proposal, and all possible realizations of preferences for the committee are equally likely, barring unanimity. Each member knows the realization of his own preferences but only the statistical properties of the others' preferences. The voting rule and the objectives of the committee members are as in the first part of the chapter: each member has one regular vote to cast on each proposal and a single bonus vote, equivalent to a regular vote, to cast freely; decisions over each proposal are taken according to the majority of votes cast; and each voter's utility from the meeting is represented by the total value he assigns to proposals decided in his preferred direction. Note that the model assumes implicitly that losing the vote over a proposal is equivalent to not having the proposal brought to a vote at all – the value is normalized to 0 in both cases. Think of each proposal as a choice between two alternatives, a favored initiative that will bring an increase in utility, versus a second initiative that will not. If the proposal does not come to a vote, no initiative is taken.[12]

The central feature of the model is that only three of the four proposals will be voted upon. One of the committee members, the chair, announces the first proposal to be called for a vote, and then sequentially the second and the third, after having observed the votes cast over the previous proposal(s). The set of proposals among which the chair makes his choices is limited by the scope of the committee, or possibly by procedural rules. I suppose here that voters know the set from which proposals are selected and know their own preferences over all of them. I also limit the set to be barely larger than the size of the agenda, a strong simplification but not one that will affect the basic logic of the problem.

The chair has two clear advantages over all other voters: first, he can be sure to put on the agenda the proposals that matter to him most. Second, he faces no uncertainty over the content of the agenda – he

---

12. Thus, positive or negative valuations in the formal model (or the terminology "in favor of" or "against" a proposal in the experiment) are simply short-hand notation for favoring initiative 1 or initiative 2.

chooses the proposals to be called to a vote. Both factors make the chair's position a valuable one, but the first is unrelated to the voting rule, and the second is unrelated to deliberate manipulation of the agenda. For committee members who are not chair, expected welfare is almost identical to what it would be if the agenda were sequential but chosen randomly, for example by a computer, as opposed to a strategic chair. The difference, where it exists, is due to the transmission of information about the chair's priorities and voting strategies that the chair's control of the agenda makes possible. This last effect is identical to what may take place when the chair controls the order of the agenda only, and, as in the examples discussed earlier, remains quantitatively very small. As the analysis will show, the welfare comparison to simple majority is substantively unchanged.

To keep matters as simple as possible, begin by supposing that there are only two voters, one of whom is chair. The two voters have opposite preferences over each proposal but, in general, different priorities. A special feature of the two-voter case is that the decision to cast the bonus vote should be made only by comparing proposals' values, independently of the expected use of the bonus vote by the opponent. There is an option value to holding on to the bonus vote, and it is not difficult to verify that the voter who does not control the agenda will cast it on the first proposal only if its value is 4; on the second proposal if he has not cast it yet and the proposal's value is either 4 or 3, and on the third proposal otherwise.[13] From the point of view of the chair,

13. With a sequential agenda, the problem can be solved backward. If still available, the bonus vote is always cast on the third and last proposal. If available when the second proposal is called to a vote, it is cast if the second proposal's value is either 4, the highest possible value, or 3: two of the four proposals have not been chosen yet, and either is equally likely to be the final one on the agenda, but no expected value can be higher than 3. Moving one step backward, the bonus vote is certainly cast on the first proposal if its value is 4, and certainly not if its value is either 1 or 2, when the voter can be certain of doing better later. If the value is 3, the relevant comparison is to the expected value of the future proposal on which the voter will cast the bonus vote if he refrains from doing so now: 4, if the second proposal's value is 4; 3 if the second proposal's value is 1, taking into account that the bonus vote will then be spent on the third proposal which is equally likely to have value 2 or 4; and 2.5 if the second proposal's value is 2, and, hence, the third proposal's value is either 4 or 1, with equal probability. Thus, if the voter does not cast the bonus vote on the first proposal when this has value 3, he will cast it on a proposal of expected value 3.17 $(1/3(4 + 3 + 2.5))$. It follows that it is better to wait: the voter casts the bonus vote on the first proposal only if it has value 4.

then, the ex ante probability of facing the opponent's bonus vote is 1/4 on the first proposal, 5/12 on the second, and 1/3 on the third. The optimal agenda order minimizes the chair's expected competition with the opponent's bonus vote. Thus, the chair should begin by calling a vote on his highest-intensity proposal, casting on it his bonus vote and then call, in turn, his third and second highest-intensity proposals.

The difficult problem facing the voter who is not chair is the uncertainty over which decisions will be presented in the future, exactly as would happen if the sequential agenda were exogenous (and limited to three of the four proposals); indeed, his expected utility would be identical. It is a different problem from protecting oneself from possible manipulations by the chair. As for the chair, as mentioned earlier, his advantage comes from the ability to call a vote on his most important proposals and to plan the use of the bonus vote without uncertainty over the values of these proposals, not from a scheme intended to reduce the influence of the other voters.

If the voting rule were majority voting, the chair's first advantage would remain, and the chair would continue to fare better than the other committee members. Both voters have higher expected utility with storable votes, because, as usual, the bonus vote allows them to express the intensity of their preferences, even if only imperfectly so in the case of the voter who does not control the agenda.

With more than two voters, the optimal use of the bonus vote depends on the probability with which others are expected to cast it over the different proposals, exactly as discussed in the first part of this chapter. The informative role of the agenda order chosen by the chair appears again: committee members expect the chair to order his highest-priority proposal in a specific position on the agenda and to cast on it his bonus vote. They react by shifting their own bonus vote toward a different proposal, validating the chair's strategy. These considerations, identical to those discussed in the first part of the chapter, lead to the possibility of multiple equilibria, but in all the examples I have studied the impact on the welfare properties of the voting rule is limited. Expected utilities for all voters are almost identical across different equilibria, and for voters who are not chair, expected utilities are almost identical to the case of sequential but exogenous agenda. The agenda order transmits information about the chair's voting strategy, but such information plays a secondary role relative to the uncertainty over which proposals will be called to a vote.

The final result, once again, is that the comparison to majority voting is not affected fundamentally by the endogeneity of the agenda. The logic is unchanged: the chair selects for the agenda the same proposals he would select under majority voting and casts his bonus vote on his highest priority, correctly expressing the intensity of his preferences. The other voters occasionally cast their bonus votes on a proposal that *ex post* is not their highest priority among those on the agenda, but this occurs rarely enough and for differences in intensities small enough that the bonus vote's role in expressing the intensity of preferences is for the most part preserved. The statement is qualified because the possibility of *ex post* mistakes puts some additional restrictions on the range of scenarios for which welfare gains over majority voting can be guaranteed. As in Chapter 1, the necessary condition is a sufficient wedge between the importance assigned to one's highest priority and to the average proposal, but when the chair controls the agenda the required wedge is larger. The condition plays two roles: as in the earlier discussion, it ensures that increasing the probability of winning that one decision matters enough to counter the loss of influence on the other decisions; here, in addition, it affects the optimal strategy, reducing the probability of ex post mistakes. Consider for example a committee of three voters, as discussed in Box 4.2. If the set of values attributed to the four proposals is $\{1, 2, 3, 4\}$, several equilibria exist, all predicting that voters who are not the chair will occasionally cast their bonus vote on a proposal of value 3, without waiting to know the full agenda. In all of these equilibria, a voter who is not chair expects to fare worse with storable votes than with simple majority. If the set of values is $\{1, 2, 3, 6\}$, on the other hand, voters who are not chair never cast their bonus vote on a proposal of value lower than 6, unless it is the last proposal on the agenda. They always expect to fare better than with majority voting. (The chair expects to do better in both scenarios.)[14]

14. With the exception of one of the equilibria with values $\{1, 2, 3, 4\}$.

Box 4.2 The Formal Model. Version 4.2

A committee of n voters meets to decide over three proposals. Each proposal is a choice between two alternatives, one of which will be implemented. At the start of the meeting, it is not known which three proposals will be voted upon, but it is known that they will be chosen by the committee chair from the fixed and known set $\mathbf{P} = \{P_A, P_B, P_C, P_D\}$. The committee votes over the proposals sequentially, and in each election, the vote cast by each member is publicly observable. Call P_t with $t = 1, 2, 3$ the tth proposal called by the chair. The chair announces P_1; after observing the votes and outcome of the first election, the chair announces P_2, and again, after observing the votes and outcome of the second election, the chair chooses the third and last proposal, P_3. In addition to a regular vote on every proposal, each committee member is given one indivisible bonus vote equivalent to a regular vote. As said, each proposal is a choice between two alternatives. The winning alternative is the one receiving more votes, including bonus votes. In case of a tie, a coin is flipped.

Each member i of the committee has preferences over the alternatives presented in each proposal. Call the two alternatives in proposal P_s, $s \in \{A, B, C, D\}$, a_s and b_s. Preferences are summarized by a cardinal valuation v_{is}. A negative valuation means that the voter favors alternative a_s, a positive valuation that he favors alternative b_s. Voter i's absolute valuation $v_{is} \equiv |\mathrm{v}_{is}|$ is i's intensity over proposal P_s. For each proposal P_s brought to a vote, voter i receives utility $u_{is} = v_{is}$ if the decision goes in his preferred direction, and 0 otherwise; the voter receives 0 utility from the proposal that is not brought to a vote.[15] Voter i's utility from the entire meeting, U_i, equals $\sum_{s \in \mathcal{A}} u_{is}$, where $\mathcal{A}$ is the set of proposals on the agenda.

Before any voting takes place, and before the chair announces P_1, each committee member i knows $\{\mathrm{v}_{iA}, .., \mathrm{v}_{iD}\}$, his own valuations over the two alternatives in all four possible proposals, but does not know others' valuations over any of the proposals. It is commonly known, however, that the committee's preferences have the

15. Thus, by assumption, there is always one alternative preferred to the status quo and one alternative equivalent to the status quo. But voters disagree over which alternative is the preferred one.

following properties: (1) *Direction of preferences.* Over any proposal, the committee is never unanimous, but any other of the $2^n - 2$ possible profiles of preferred directions of preferences is equally probable: one voter in favor of alternative a, and all others in favor of alternative b; two voters in favor of alternative a and all others in favor of alternative b; etc. (2) *Intensity of preferences.* Each voter's set of intensities over the four possible proposals is given by $\mathcal{V} = \{1, 2, 3, 4\}$, equal for all voters, but the matching of a given proposal to a specific element of the set – to a specific intensity – is not publicly known. For each voter, any of the 4! possible profiles of intensities is equally probable: if $\mathcal{V}_i$ is the ordered set of voter i's intensities, from P_A to P_D, then $\mathcal{V}_i = (1, 2, 3, 4)$ is as probable as $\mathcal{V}_i = (2, 3, 1, 4)$ or any other permutation. Realizations of intensities are independent across voters.

A voter's strategy is, for all voters including the chair, the choice of the proposal on which to cast the bonus vote, and, for the chair alone, the proposals called and their order. The focus is on quasi-symmetric Perfect Bayesian equilibria in weakly undominated strategies, in which all voters who are not the chair play symmetric strategies. A *non-informative* (*NI*) equilibrium is such that any proposal called to a vote has ex ante equal probability of receiving the chair's bonus vote, regardless of its position on the agenda; a *fully informative* (*FI*) equilibrium is such that the position on the agenda of the proposal receiving the chair's bonus vote is identified ex ante with probability 1.[16]

The chair is chosen randomly among the committee members with equal probability. Call EV_0 ex ante expected utility before preferences are realized and before the chair's role is assigned; call EV_{0i}, $i = c, nc$, voter i's expected utility before preferences are realized, but knowing whether he is chair (c) or not (nc). If the voting rule is simple majority, the corresponding concepts are indicated by EW_0 and EW_{0i}. To separate the importance of a chair controlling the agenda from the uncertainty caused by the sequential voting itself, it is useful to calculate expected utility with a sequential but random agenda, in which every outstanding proposal has equal probability of being called to a vote.

16. *Partially informative* equilibria are possible too, in which the chair's highest priority proposal is identified with probability $\in (1/3, 1)$. Their welfare properties can be predicted from the informative equilibria. An example is discussed in the Appendix.

Such expected utility is denoted by EU_0^X and EU_0^{XM} in the two cases of storable votes and simple majority. For $n \in \{2, 3, 4\}$, the main properties of the model are summarized by the two results that follow.

Result 4.1. Suppose $\mathcal{V} = \{1, 2, 3, 4\}$ and $n \in \{2, 3, 4\}$. Then: (i) There can be no *NI* equilibrium. (ii) There are multiple *FI* equilibria. (iii) In all *FI* equilibria: if $n \in \{2, 4\}$, $EV_{0c} > EW_{0c}$; $EV_{0nc} > EW_{0nc}$, and $EV_0 > EW_0$; if $n = 3$, $EV_{0c} \lesseqgtr EW_{0c}$ depending on the equilibrium; $EV_{0nc} < EW_{0nc}$, and $EV_0 < EW_0$. (iv) For all $n \in \{2, 3, 4\}$, there exists an equilibrium with sequential but random agenda such that in all *FI* equilibria $EV_{0c} > EU_0^X$, $EV_{0nc} \leq EU_0^X$.

The chair benefits from the control of the agenda, relative both to the other members and to a scenario in which the agenda is chosen exogenously. Voters who are not chair are harmed, at least weakly, by the chair's control: their expected utility is lower than with an exogenous agenda. Relative to majority voting, both chair and non-chair members expect to benefit from storable votes with committees of size two and four; with committees of size three, this may continue to hold true for the chair, but the other committee members have higher expected utility with majority voting, and the chair's gain, when it exists, is not sufficient to counter the other members' expected loss.

The comparison between storable votes and simple majority is sensitive to the wedge between the highest and the average intensity:

Result 4.2. Suppose $\mathcal{V} = \{1, 2, 3, 6\}$ and $n \in \{2, 3, 4\}$. Then: (i) There can be no *NI* equilibrium. (ii) There are multiple *FI* equilibria, but all are payoff equivalent. (iii) In all *FI* equilibria, for all $n \in \{2, 3, 4\}$, $EV_{0c} > EW_{0c}$; $EV_{0nc} > EW_{0nc}$ and $EV_0 > EW_0$. (iv) In all *FI* equilibria, for all $n \in \{2, 3, 4\}$, $EV_{0c} > EU_0^X$, $EV_{0nc} \leq EU_0^X$.

4.2.2 Some thoughts about information

If the model proposed here captures the main aspects of the committee's voting problem, the conclusion is that agenda control does not alter deeply the properties of storable votes. Consider, however, how concerns about agenda manipulation are typically phrased: "Could the chair exhaust others' bonus votes by putting on the agenda proposals on which *he knows* their bonus votes would be cast?" Such a behavior, if true, does not imply any particular distortion in voting choices and outcomes, but does presume information about preferences. The assumption is strong, stronger and more problematic, I think, than the assumption maintained throughout the book that preferences are only known in terms of their statistical properties – which direction is expected to be favored, how strong intensities are on average, how correlated preferences are among voters. But it is so tightly linked to concerns about agenda power that it requires a comment here.

If preferences are known, there is no scope for communication of private information, and the chair's control of the agenda can fulfill instead a different function. Because the chair knows the other voters' priorities, and vice versa, he can use the choice of proposals to reward or punish past voting strategies. Consider the following example: the committee is composed of two voters, with opposite preferences, and intensities summarized in the following table:

Table 4.3 Complete Information

An example with two voters.

P	v_c	v_{nc}
P_A	4	4
P_B	3	2
P_C	2	1
P_D	1	3

If intensities were private information, the chair would call, in order, P_A, P_C, and P_B, and both voters would cast their bonus vote on P_A. But when intensities are known, the chair can credibly reward the other voter for not competing with him on P_A by modifying the agenda. After P_A, the chair can call, in order, P_B and P_D: P_C disappears from the agenda. Without cooperation – when both voters cast the bonus vote on P_A, and the agenda is (P_A, P_C, P_B) – all votes are tied, and with a 50 percent chance of winning any vote, the chair's expected utility from the meeting is 4.5, and the other voter's 3.5. With cooperation – when the chair alone casts the bonus vote on P_A, the agenda is (P_A, P_B, P_D), and the other voter casts the bonus vote on P_D – the chair wins the first vote, the other voter wins the third, and the second vote is tied. The chair's expected utility is 5.5, and the other voter's utility is 4. Cooperation can be sustained because a chair who has spent his bonus vote, and faces an opponent who has not, is sure to lose the third election, and thus is indifferent regarding which proposal to call.

The example suggests a number of observations. First, it is indeed true that the chair can use his agenda power to manipulate his opponent's voting choices. But the logic is very different from the concern mentioned earlier: when preferences are known, the rest of the committee will anticipate the chair's choice of agenda. Unless information is asymmetric, and the chair knows more about others' preferences than they know about his, the chair will not be able to "surprise" the committee with an unexpected proposal. Second, in this example the result is a cooperative outcome in which *both* voters benefit from the knowledge of each other's intensities. We could just as well say that the non-chair voter can use his bonus vote to manipulate the chair's choice of agenda. The availability of information here improves the welfare properties of the voting rule. Third, note that in two-member committees, the non-chair voter can always ensure himself at least as much as he would expect to gain with majority rule: for any realization of intensities there is always an equilibrium where the agenda consists of the chair's three highest-intensity proposals, and both voters cast their bonus votes on their highest priority among those three proposals.[17] This equilibrium always weakly improves over majority voting (weakly if both voters consider the same proposal their highest priority among those on the agenda, strongly otherwise). Finally, notice that unless the game is repeated, the cooperative outcome with two voters cannot be supported with simple majority voting, even allowing for the strategic use of abstentions. The voters always have the right to cast a vote, and will do so on the last

17. With two voters, the optimal voting strategy is to cast the bonus vote on one's highest priority on the agenda, regardless of the other voter's use of the bonus vote. The only question is the chair's choice of agenda. If the two voters assign the highest intensity to the same proposal, the agenda strategy described in the text results in a tie over all proposals. The chair could deviate, call first his second priority proposal, cast his bonus vote, and win. Then, however, he will be sure to lose one proposal, and it is not difficult to verify that the deviation is always costly. If the two voters have different priorities, the chair is sure to win his most important proposal but to lose one of the others. Again, it is easy to see that he can never gain by putting on the agenda lower-priority proposals.

proposal, inducing a tie; thus, the chair is never indifferent regarding the choice of the last proposal and cannot commit to an agenda he will find suboptimal.

The observations are intriguing, and it could be that storable votes favor welfare-improving cooperative outcomes more generally, but there are reasons to be cautious. First, the example concerns a two-voter committee, the simplest case to analyze. With more voters, matters become quickly more complex, and the possibility arises of alliances among some but not all of the members. In principle, alliances will concern not only the use of the bonus vote, but also the direction of a committee member's vote. Is such collusion likely, and what effect will it have? In addition, with more than two voters it becomes possible to sustain cooperation with majority rule, and the comparison to majority rule outcomes is much less straightforward.[18] Second, the problem may be better approached as a repeated game: if the committee meets regularly, and both preferences and voting choices can be observed, agreements and implicit trades are likely to develop. Such agreements should be studied both with storable votes and with simple majority.

Staying within the limits of the current model, whether information about preferences is public or not, the chair's control of the content of the agenda complicates further the strategic calculations of the committee members. How did experimental subjects handle the problem?

4.2.3 Experiment 4.2

All sessions of the experiment were run at CESS at NYU, between July 2009 and May 2010, following the recruitment procedures described for the previous experiments. The experiment replicated the model of Box 4.2. Subjects were randomly matched into committees of two, three, or four members, depending on the experimental session, and each committee was faced with four possible proposals, *Red*, *Blue*, *Orange*, and *Green*, only three of which would be voted upon. Each proposal could pass or fail. The computer assigned to each subject a preferred direction for each proposal; unanimity was ruled out, but any

18. If the chair is in the minority over several proposals, he can use the promise to select one over the others as reward for a member who voted with the chair on an earlier proposal.

other profile of preferred directions was chosen by the computer with equal probability. Subjects were also assigned a value for each proposal, representing the number of points the subject earned if the proposal was decided in his preferred direction. Each subject's values for the four proposals were, in increasing order (100, 200, 300, 400), but which value was attached to which proposal was random, with any possible permutation of the four proposals equally likely to be matched to the sequence of values. Subjects earned 0 points for the proposal not brought to a vote.

At the start of each experimental round, the computer randomly selected one member of each committee as chair. After having observed his values, the chair selected and announced the first proposal, and committee members cast their votes. All members were endowed with one vote for each election and a single bonus vote, equivalent to a regular vote. After observing the votes cast in the election and being explicitly reminded of how many bonus votes still remained available, the chair selected the second proposal, and again, after the same information on the second election was conveyed, the chair selected the third and final proposal. This concluded an experimental round. The game was then repeated: groups were randomly rematched, new values and preferred directions assigned, and a new chair randomly selected. At the end of the experimental session, subjects were paid a fixed show-up fee and their cumulative value for all proposals decided in their preferred direction over four randomly chosen rounds, adjusted by a known exchange rate. Average earnings were approximately $23 an hour.

There were two treatment variables: the number of members in a committee: two, three, or four; and the information about preferences: either private – only one own's values and preferred directions were known – or public – all preferences were commonly known. When preferences were private information, the rules through which the computer assigned all preferences were commonly known. When information was public, subjects were identified within each committee by a number that was randomly reassigned after each round. We ran two experimental sessions for each committee size; in one session, the first half of all rounds had private information, and the remainder public information; in the second session, the order was reversed. The theory

Table 4.4 Experimental Design

The chair controls the content of the agenda.					
Session	n	Subjects	Rounds	Sequence*	Max v
1	2	10	20	I-P	400
2	2	10	20	P-I	400
3-chat	2	10	10	P only	400
4	3	15	16	I-P	400
5	3	15	16	P-I	600
6	4	12	16	I-P	400
7	4	12	16	P-I	400

* I, incomplete (private) information; **P**, public information.

predicts that results should be sensitive to the wedge between the maximum and the average value, changing the qualitative comparison to majority voting in three-member committees. To evaluate this prediction, one of the experimental sessions with committees of three members had values {100, 200, 300, 600}. Finally, to explore whether explicit communication helps subjects to cooperate, in one experimental session with public information, members of each committee could exchange unconstrained messages with the rest of the committee (a *chat* treatment, as in the previous chapter).

With private information, the experiment matches the model in Box 4.2 exactly. Its theoretical properties are summarized in Result 1 and Result 2 in the box, and the details of the different equilibria can be found in Chapter 4 in Part II. As in the first half of this chapter, the main purpose of the experiment is to evaluate the welfare properties of storable votes when a chair controls the agenda, compared to the welfare properties of majority voting. Equilibrium expected earnings, as share of the maximum potential surplus over random decision-making and random agenda, are reported in Table 4.5.

The table lends precision to the qualitative statements made earlier. In five of the six cases, storable votes are associated with higher expected aggregate earnings than majority voting. The exception is a committee with three members and values {100, 200, 300, 400}: with three voters and a small wedge between the highest and the average value, only rarely can the minority's value be larger than the majority's, and the minority

Table 4.5 Equilibrium Expected Earnings

The chair controls the content of the agenda.

Private Information

Table 4.5a: Values are {100, 200, 300, 400}

n	Surplus SV	Surplus Maj.	Chair Gain SV	Chair Gain Maj.
2	60	24	19	20
3	80.5	84	22^{E_1}, $25^{E_2,E_3}$	20
4	80.5	71	20^{E_1}, 22^{E_2}, 21^{E_3}	20

The superscripts E_1, E_2, E_3 refer to the three fully informative equilibria that exist with values {100, 200, 300, 400}.[19]

Table 4.5b: Values are {100, 200, 300, 600}

n	Surplus SV	Surplus Maj.	Chair Gain SV	Chair Gain Maj.
2	63	20	29	22
3	75	71.5	25	22
4	76	62	24	22

victories that storable votes make possible are often costly on welfare grounds. With values {100, 200, 300, 600}, efficient minority victories become more likely, and storable votes become preferable to simple majority voting. With both voting rules, the chair expects to earn more than other committee members, but the difference is larger with storable votes, where the chair has a higher probability of winning his highest priority proposal. The chair's advantage is approximately 20 percent with majority voting, constant across committee sizes, and between 20 and 30 percent with storable votes. In both cases, the chair's advantage is, predictably, increasing in the value assigned to the most important proposal.

4.2.4 The results

Precise theoretical predictions concern exclusively the private information treatments. Here too, however, multiple equilibria complicate the

19. See the discussion in Chapter 4 in Part II.

comparison of observed experimental behavior to the theory. There are two experimental treatments for which equilibrium strategies are pinned down uniquely either for the chair or for the other committee members: two-voter committees with values {100, 200, 300, 400}, and three-voter committees with values {100, 200, 300, 600}. For these two treatments, Figure 4.4 reports the observed frequencies with which individual subjects cast their bonus vote on the first and second proposal (the third proposal being the residual). Realized individual frequencies (the empty dots), as well as average and median frequencies (the black symbols), are compared in the figure to the theoretical prediction (in gray).

In all cases, there is significant dispersion in the observed frequencies, a fact to be expected given that each subject has the chance to be chair and non-chair only a small and variable number of times, and the figure includes all rounds, without allowing for learning. Consider first the two-member committee sessions in Figure 4.4a. Here, theory predicts that the chair should always cast the bonus vote on the first proposal. In the experimental data, 8 of 20 subjects match the prediction exactly; over the full sample, both the average and the median frequency of bonus vote use are three to four times higher for the first proposal than for either the second or the third. Individuals who are not chair cannot choose the order of proposals, and the variability in intensity draws arising from the small sample means that the observed frequencies would vary across individuals even if the strategies – the rules establishing when to and not to cast the bonus vote – did not. Average and median frequencies are more informative. In two-member committee sessions, the median frequency matches the equilibrium prediction exactly: half of all subjects were at least twice as likely to cast their bonus vote on a later proposal than on the first. The average frequency, more sensitive to outliers, shows less sensitivity to the order of the proposal than the theory predicts. Average frequencies are effectively indistinguishable across all three proposals.

In the three-member sessions with values {100, 200, 300, 600} (Figure 4.4b), the chair should always call his highest priority proposal either first or second and thus never cast his bonus vote on the third proposal. In the left panel of the figure, the diagonal line running from the upper left corner ("always cast the bonus vote on the second proposal")

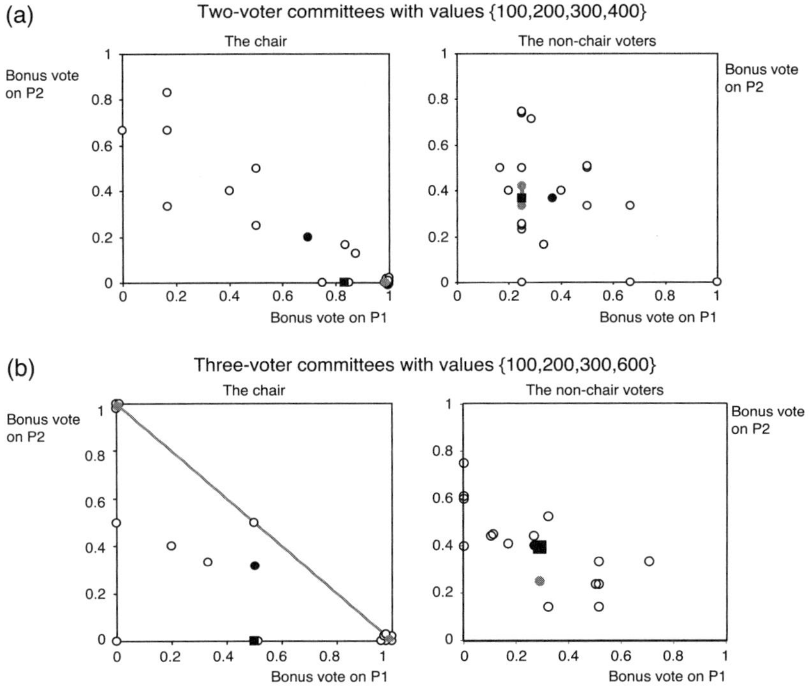

FIGURE 4.4 Experimental strategies when the chair controls the content of the agenda. Private information. Frequency of the bonus vote on the first and the second proposal. In all panels, the horizontal axis is the frequency with which the bonus vote is cast on the first proposal, and the vertical axis is the corresponding frequency for the second proposal, for each subject in the treatment. The panels on the left report subjects' behavior when chair; the panels on the right, when non-chair. Empty dots are individuals' experimental strategies; a black dot is the average and a black square the median of the experimental frequencies; gray is the theoretical prediction, calculated for non-chairs on the basis of the realized proposal values (a gray line traces all multiple equilibria).

to the lower right corner ("always cast it in the first proposal") plots all first- and second-proposal frequencies that sum to 1, all of which are equilibrium strategies for the chair. Dots to the interior of the diagonal line correspond to chairs who cast the bonus vote on the third proposal with positive frequency, contrary to the equilibrium prediction. The theory is perfectly consistent with the behavior of 10 out of 15 subjects: 6 cast the bonus vote always on the first proposal, 3 on the second, and one alternates between the two with equal frequency.

With different and extreme behaviors consistent with the theory, the median and the mean frequencies here are not good measures of the fit of the data to the theory, but they do capture the tendency of the remaining 5 subjects to cast the bonus vote on the third proposal occasionally, and they lie to the interior of the diagonal. In the right panel of Figure 4.4b, the theoretical prediction is that non-chair subjects will always wait for the 600-value proposal, rather than cast the bonus vote on a lower-value one, unless they face the last proposal on the agenda. Thus, the theoretical frequencies should be close to one-fourth for both the first and the second proposals, with some variation due to the small sample variability in the intensity draws. The gray dot in the figure is calculated on the basis of the actual experimental draws. Both the mean and median frequency of bonus votes on the first proposal are almost identical to the equilibrium prediction, but for the second proposal, both mean and median frequency are too high. In fact, all individual dots lie to the outside of the gray dot, suggesting that subjects were less willing to wait for the highest-value proposal than theory predicts.

In the model, individuals are assumed to be risk neutral and in the experimental design they are assumed to maximize their expected earnings. If subjects, or some subjects, in fact are averse to risk, they will prefer to use their bonus vote on a lower-value proposal, rather than wait for the possibility of a future higher value. In this experiment, this is a particular problem, because uncertainty plays a larger role than in the rest of the book, especially for subjects who are not chair. A comparison of the theory, as developed in Box 4.2, to the data is thus a joint test of the maximizing strategies and of risk-neutrality. A less ambitious test is to evaluate deviations from the theory that cannot be explained through attitudes towards risk. Recall that the focus is on treatments with private information only, and consider three possible errors, suboptimal for any attitude towards risk. The first is an agenda error: taking into account that the chair can vary the order of the proposals, the proposal to which he attaches lowest value should not appear on the agenda. Over all experiments, just below three-quarters of all subjects (74 percent) never put on the agenda, when chair, a proposal with value 100. The second is a voting error by the chair: again, because the chair controls both content and order of proposals, he should always cast his bonus vote on his highest priority. Over all experiments, 82 percent of subjects always do so, when chair. Finally, consider a voting error by non-chair subjects: they should never cast their bonus votes on a proposal to which they attach value 100 or 200, unless it is the last proposal on the agenda. Over all experiments, 82 percent of all subjects never do so. The tests are weak, but gross deviations from optimizing behavior are rare.

As in the experiments described in the previous chapters, the theory remains a very good predictor of experimental payoffs. For each experimental session, and considering only rounds with private information, Figure 4.5a plots aggregate experimental earnings, expressed as share of available surplus, on the vertical axis, against the share of surplus that subjects would have appropriated had they all followed equilibrium strategies, on the horizontal axis. This latter variable is calculated assuming that the chair adopted the optimal agenda and using the realized experimental values for the other subjects, given the chair's choice of proposals.[20]

In one experimental session with two-voter committees, subjects did noticeably worse than theory predicts. It is, however, the exception: in all other sessions, aggregate experimental payoffs are extremely close to equilibrium payoffs, given the experimental valuations draws. This means, in particular, that the comparative statics properties are fully satisfied. As predicted by Table 4.5b, the share of appropriated surplus increases monotonically with the number of members in each committee.

Figure 4.5b compares experimental results to subjects' payoffs with simple majority voting. The figure includes the data from the public information rounds in each session, and with public information and majority voting it supposes that the chair's agenda choice maximizes the chair's expected earnings when all others vote sincerely.[21] The close

20. Where there are multiple equilibria with different aggregate payoffs, the numbers differ so little that the figure remains essentially unchanged regardless of which equilibrium is considered. Here, for a maximum value of 400 and three-member committees, the figure selects equilibrium E_1, and for four-member committees, equilibrium E_2 in Tables 4.2a and 4.3a in Part II. The theoretical predictions using expected values, as opposed to the realized experimental draws, are in Table 4.5.

21. There always is such an equilibrium. Each voter casts his vote sincerely, and the chair selects the three proposals with highest expected value, taking into account his probability of winning (one, zero, or one-half, with public information). When multiple proposals have equal expected value for the chair, the figure is contructed selecting the proposal that makes the agenda closest to the experimental agenda.

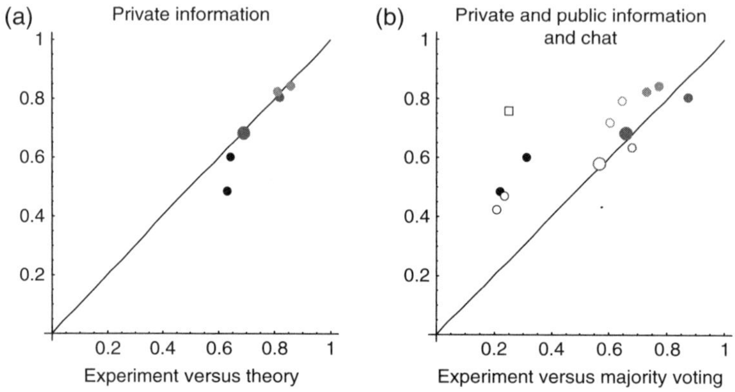

FIGURE 4.5 Experimental surplus, as share of maximal surplus. The chair controls the content of the agenda. The vertical axis reports total experimental earnings, as share of maximal earnings. The horizontal axis reports the share of total to maximal earnings in the absence of strategic mistake (Figure 4.5a), or if decisions were made through simple majority (Figure 4.5b). Each solid (empty) dot corresponds to aggregate earnings in all private (public) information rounds of an experimental session. Black dots denote sessions with committees of two members; dark gray sessions with three members, and light gray with four. The large dark gray symbol is the session with maximal value at 600; the square is the chat treatment.

relationship to the theory's predictions is again very clear: as expected, experimental payoffs are higher than majority voting payoffs in all treatments, with the exception of three-voter committees with a maximum value of 400, a result that holds true with both private and public information. Even in those two cases, the loss in efficiency is not large. Again as expected, the gain from storable votes is largest in two-voter committees, smaller in four-voter committees, smaller still but positive in three-voter committees with a maximum value of 600. An intriguing result is the particularly high experimental payoff in the treatment with explicit communication. While in all other treatments, public information rounds have lower aggregate experimental payoffs than private information rounds, the experimental session with communication (and public information) has much higher realized payoffs than any other two-voter committee session. It may well be that with communication simple majority, too, would have performed better – in two-voter committees, the assumption of no coordination used in constructing the majority payoffs is consistent with purely selfish preferences but may be inappropriate in this case. Looking in more detail at the scope for communication is a natural direction for future work.

Do storable votes magnify the advantage of the agenda setter? This is after all the motivating question of this chapter. Figure 4.6 reports the ratio of the average chair earnings to the average earnings of a non-chair voter in the data, on the vertical axis, plotted against the same variable if decisions were made through majority voting.

Majority voting is not observed, and the comparison here is complicated by the assumption one needs to make about the content of the agenda, in the majority voting counterfactual. As in Figure 4.5, the assumption in Figure 4.6a is that the chair would choose the agenda that maximizes his earnings when all vote sincerely. According to the figure, storable votes reduce the advantage of the chair. All points in the

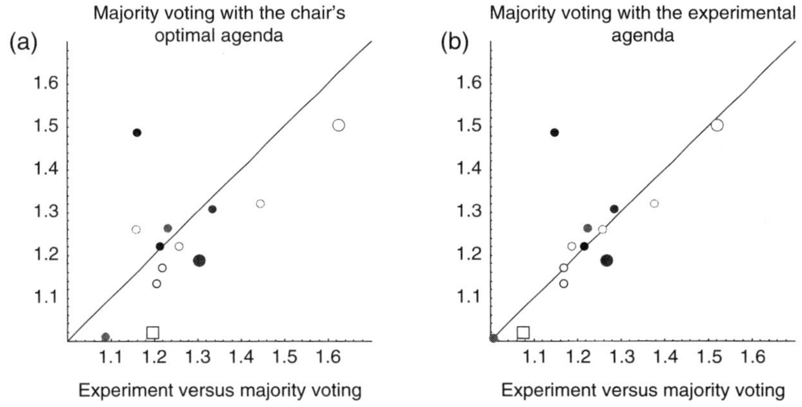

FIGURE 4.6 Relative chair/non-chair earnings. The chair controls the content of the agenda. Private and public information, and chat. The vertical axis reports the ratio of average chair/non-chair experimental earnings. The horizontal axis reports the share of average chair/non-chair earnings if decisions were made through simple majority, with two alternative agendas. Each solid (empty) dot corresponds to average earnings in all private (public) information rounds of one experimental session. Black dots denote sessions with committees of two members; dark gray, sessions with three members, and light gray with four. The large dark gray dot is the session with maximal value at 600; the square is the chat treatment.

figure are above 1 on both axes – in either voting system, the chair has higher earnings than non-chair subjects. But 9 out of 13 data points lie below the diagonal: the chair's relative earnings are higher with majority voting. On the other hand, supposing that the chair makes no strategic mistakes contradicts what is observed in the experiment and biases the numbers toward higher chair earnings with majority voting. Figure 4.6b reports the ratios of average chair to non-chair earnings with the two voting systems, keeping the agenda constant and equal to what observed in the experiment. With the exception of one clear outlier, most points are either on the diagonal or very close to it: in Figure 4.6b, there is no clear difference in the chair's advantage, whether decisions are taken with storable votes or with simple majority. A fair conclusion from the two figures, then, is that there is no evidence that storable votes introduce a new factor in favor of the chair. The chair's advantage comes almost completely from his ability to call a vote on his highest priorities and is independent of the specific voting rule. As in the first part of this chapter, the second aspect of the storable-votes agenda game – the chair's ability to commit to a voting strategy and discourage other voters from competing with him – has very small and variable effects on the other voters' payoffs. It is also very subtle, probably too subtle for the inexperienced subjects in the experiment.

4.3 Conclusions

The possibility of controlling the agenda raises concerns with all voting rules. But because storable votes require voters to foresee the relative importance of issues they will decide in the future, it is natural to wonder whether they are particularly fragile to agenda manipulation. This chapter has studied, theoretically and experimentally, two simplified models that begin to give some structure to the question. It is a difficult question, and the scenarios are very simple – there is a single bonus vote and preferences are independent across all voters and all proposals – but the answers from the two model are very consistent. When the chair controls the order with which proposals are called to a vote, for a given set of proposals on the agenda, he can use the order to convey information about his priorities and commit to a voting strategy. The other voters respond optimally by reducing their competition with the chair, with the result that the chair's influence is increased. The final effect is an increase in the chair's expected utility and a change of ambiguous sign in other voters' utilities. For all committee members, though, including the chair, the effect is quantitatively very small. When the chair controls not only the order, but also the content of the agenda – which of several possible proposals will be called to a vote – the agenda can be used not only to convey information, but also to make sure that the chair's priorities will receive a hearing. This second effect dominates the welfare considerations: it is here that the chair can reap large utility gains, relative to the other members of the committee. It is, however, an effect unrelated to the voting rule, and it is present whether the committee uses storable votes, or simple majority voting, or, indeed, takes decisions with a coin flip. The welfare effects discussed in the previous chapters, when the agenda was fixed, are replicated here with little or no change.

The most unexpected result of the research reported in this chapter is that the chair exploits his agenda control not to surprise other voters, but to *increase* their information about his goals and his voting behavior. It is a result that stems directly from the logic of equilibrium behavior: surprises are difficult to achieve if others can predict that they may occur and arm themselves against them. The chair prefers to commit to a strategy, exploiting the other members' responses to his advantage. Because he commits to using the bonus vote, the others refrain from doing so. One open question is whether the chair would still want to transmit information if he knew more about others' preferences than they know about his. In the models studied here, all committee members are either equally ignorant of others' preferences or, in one treatment of the last experiment, equally well-informed. If the chair is, by virtue of his role, in a privileged position for gathering information, he may know more about others' preferences than they know about his. The asymmetry should increase the chair's advantage, and one may wonder whether storable votes would amplify the effect. It is an interesting question. It is also quite different from the instinctive concerns expressed at the start of this chapter. The formal analysis has structured, qualified, and transformed them.

5

Storable Votes in Large Elections

If storable votes can be useful when decisions are made by small committees, they also have a role to play in large elections. In different political systems, there are various examples of large scale binary elections, but one that is both common to many democracies and of increasing importance is referendums, where I use the term *referendum* to indicate any proposition decided by popular majority voting, whether initiated by the government (referendum in the proper sense) or by the people (properly, an *initiative*). In U.S. states, the number of referendums has increased in every decade since 1970 at an average rate of 70 percent per decade, and in many parts of the world referendums are becoming an established, if not always predictable, tool for decision-making.[1] One example is the European Union, where referendums have the important advantage of lending popular legitimacy to a process of regional integration that has occurred in large part away from direct public scrutiny and voting. Outside the boundaries of a committee, with a reasonably well-defined mandate and known membership, storing votes for use in future ballots may involve too much uncertainty. In many instances, however, referendums are presented to the public in bundles: voters are asked to vote contemporaneously on a number of different proposals.[2] Adding a single bonus vote would then be only a minor modification to

1. Gerber (1999), Matsusaka (2004), the Initiative and Referendum Institute at www.iandrinstitute.org, and the Direct Democracy Institute at www.c2d.ch provide a wealth of information on the history and practice of direct democracy around the world.

2. In many European countries, the practice of bundling referendums is less common when the stakes are high – a mistake, according to the analysis of this chapter.

the current practice and would reproduce, in large elections, the simplest storable votes design. Voters would be asked to cast a regular vote on each of the referendums presented to them and would be granted a bonus vote to cast as desired. This chapter discusses how the basic logic of storable votes extends to large elections and can be expected to improve the functioning of referendums.[3]

The logic is familiar by now: as in small committees, storable votes make it possible for a minority with strong preferences to win occasionally, but only when the majority's intensity of preferences is weak. Typically, the result is an increase in efficiency. The question then is obvious: is there really a need for stronger minority representation in direct democracy? I believe that the answer is positive, both as a matter of principle, and as a matter of practice. The increased reliance on direct democracy strips voters in the minority of the checks and balances of representative democracy. In the legal literature, Cooter (2002), for example, compares "median democracy" (direct democracy) to "bargain democracy" (legislatures) and argues for the practical superiority of the former, while admitting that the latter is "ideally" more efficient. Increasing the protection of minorities through the representation of intense preferences in direct democracy is a step toward higher efficiency. In practice, the need to safeguard minorities, and in particular minorities with little access to financial resources, is the single point of agreement in the often heated debate on initiatives and referendums.[4] Gerber (1999) and Matsusaka (2004) provide exhaustive empirical analyses of direct democracy in U.S. states, where money spent in referendum campaigns is largest and unconstrained. Although their emphasis differs, both authors conclude that there is no evidence that business interests are succeeding at manipulating the process in their favor any more than grass-root citizens' groups. Both books identify the need to protect minorities as the most urgent task in improving the process. According to Gerber (1999), narrow business interests have a comparative advantage in influencing popular votes through financial resources, while grass-root movements have a

3. The chapter is based on Casella and Gelman (2008).

4. See, for example, Broder (2000), with the expressive title *Democracy Derailed*. Opposite views on the promise of direct democracy, held with equal strength, are also common: see for example *The Economist*, Jan. 23, 2003.

comparative advantage in gathering votes. If this logic is correct, storable votes would help to protect resourceless minorities against the power of the majority and reduce the power of money in direct democracy.

5.1 The Theory

A large number of voters are presented with multiple referendums, each of which can either pass or fail. Each voter has a regular vote to cast on each referendums and a single additional bonus vote that can be cast freely. As in Chapters 1 and 4, the value of the bonus vote may differ from the value of a regular vote. All referendums appear on a single ballot, and each voter votes over all of them contemporaneously and contemporaneously to other voters. Individual preferences over each referendums are defined by direction (pro or against) and by intensity, and they are drawn independently across voters from a known distribution. For most of this chapter, the referendums are not related, and preferences across referendums are also drawn independently for each voter. The distributions of preferences may differ across referendums, and, for each referendums, between opponents and supporters. A voter knows his preferences over all referendums but only the statistical properties of other voters' preferences. The model is described formally in Box 5.1.[5]

The large number of voters and the wider class of preference distributions are the defining features of the scenario studied here. As in all other chapters, it remains true that voters cannot gain by voting against their preferences. Thus, voters will vote sincerely, and the only question they need to address is where to cast the bonus vote. In large elections, the strategic calculations dictating the optimal use of the bonus vote are simplified: the exact number of voters, whether such number is odd or even, and the specific shape of the distributions of preferences, all become irrelevant. Asymptotic statistical results pin down the probable effect of voters' actions and are independent of these details. This is a

5. Starting with Ledyard (1984), a large literature has emerged on the effect of voting costs in large elections (for example, Campbell (1999), Krasa and Polborn (2009), Taylor and Yildirim (2010), and Goeree and Großer (2007)). In the model discussed in this chapter, there are no voting costs and everyone votes, an assumption I prefer given our poor understanding of what drives individuals to vote.

particularly welcome feature because the proposals that can be brought to referendums are very diverse and the restrictions imposed so far on the distributions of preferences seem too strong here. The assumption that preferences are identically distributed over all proposals is, in general, unrealistic: many issues put to referendum are typically of interest only to a small minority – the calendar of the hunting season, the decision to grant landmark status to a building, the details of government procedures – while some on the contrary evoke strong feelings from most voters – the draft of a constitution for the European Union, divorce in Italy, same-sex marriage, affirmative action and taxation in U.S. states, and equal rights for women and immigration in Switzerland. If storable votes are to be used in referendums, it must be shown that they can function well when such heterogeneity is taken into account. In addition, assuming that voters are equally likely to favor or oppose any proposal, or that the intensity of preferences is equally distributed among supporters and opponents has sharp implications in large elections. Again, it is important to verify how the voting mechanism behaves when such assumptions are weakened.

The role played by the distribution of preferences in influencing voters' use of the bonus vote, and eventually the welfare properties of the voting scheme, is very intuitive. As in the case of committee voting, when choosing the referendum over which to cast the bonus vote, an individual weighs two considerations. The first is the relative importance the individual assigns to the different referendums. All else equal, it must be best to cast the bonus vote on one's highest priority. The second consideration is the impact of the bonus vote on the pivot probability, the probability that one's own vote changes the outcome. In large elections, such probability is not only very small, but it is also very sensitive to the distribution of preferences. When the number of voters is large and preference realizations are independent across voters, the probability distribution followed by preferences is not only the ex ante probabilistic assessment of other voters' preferences, but also the asymptotic tendency of the ex post aggregate realization of such preferences. Stating that each voter is equally likely to favor or oppose a proposal, for example, implies immediately that with probability very close to one the electorate will be equally split. Thus, assumptions about the distribution of preferences translate closely into realized aggregate voting outcomes and welfare evaluations. These observations will recur because the model is made progressively more general. It is good to begin by the simplest case.

Box 5.1 The Formal Model. Version 5

A large number n of voters are asked to vote, contemporaneously, on a set of $K > 1$ unrelated referendums. Each voter is asked to cast one vote in each referendum, but in addition is given one extra bonus vote that can be cast freely. The bonus vote is worth $B > 0$ regular votes, where B is either an integer or the inverse of an integer and is small relative to $\sqrt{n}$, but otherwise arbitrary. Each referendum is decided in the direction that receives more votes; in case of an exact tie, either side prevails with probability 1/2. Voter i attaches valuation v_{ik} to referendum k. If $\mathrm{v}_{ik} < 0$, i is against the referendum, if $\mathrm{v}_{ik} > 0$, i is in favor of the referendum. For each referendum k, voter i receives utility $u_{ik} = |\mathrm{v}_{ik}| \equiv v_{ik}$ if the decision goes in his preferred direction, and 0 otherwise, where the absolute valuation v_{ik} is called the intensity of voter i's preferences over referendum k. Voter i's utility from the full set of referendums, U_i, equals $\sum_{k=1}^{K} u_{ik}$.

Individual valuations are drawn, independently across individuals and across referendums, from probability distributions $\mathbf{G} \equiv \{G_k(\mathrm{v}), k = 1, .., K\}$, each with full support normalized to $[-1, 1]$. The distributions $\mathbf{G}$ can vary across referendums but are common knowledge. Individual i knows v_{ik}, for all $k = 1, .., K$, but only the probability distributions of the others' valuations and their statistical independence across individuals and referendums. There is no cost of voting.

The analysis focuses on symmetric Bayesian equilibria in undominated strategies where, conditional on their set of valuations, all voters select the same optimal strategy. Since there can be no gain from voting against one's preferences, in these equilibria voters vote sincerely. The only decision is the referendum on which to cast the bonus vote.

With an electorate of size n, denote by EV_{0n} expected utility with the bonus vote ex ante, before the realization of preferences; by EW_{0n} expected ex ante utility with a series of simple majority referendums, and by ER_0 expected ex ante utility with random decision-making (when each proposal is resolved in either direction with probability 1/2).

Define $\omega_n \equiv (EV_{0n} - ER_0)/(EW_{0n} - ER_0)$ as the measure of welfare improvement from the bonus vote, relative to majority voting. Storable votes are said to improve efficiency if there exists an electorate size above which $\omega_n \longrightarrow \omega > 1$.

The core question is how robust is the expected welfare impact of the bonus vote mechanism to different properties of the distributions of valuations. Call *symmetry* of a distribution the lack of systematic differences between supporters and opponents of a referendum: a distribution of valuations is *symmetric* when the corresponding distributions of intensities, for supporters and opponents, are identical. Call *homogeneity* of the distributions the lack of systematic differences across referendums: distributions are *homogeneous* when $G_k(\mathrm{v}) = G(\mathrm{v})$ for all k. Then:

Proposition 5.1 Symmetric homogeneous distributions. Suppose $G_k(\mathrm{v}) = G(\mathrm{v})$ for all k. Then, for any distribution $G(\mathrm{v})$ symmetric around 0 and any number of referendums $K > 1$, there exist $B'(G, K) > 0$ and some n' finite such that for all $n > n'$ and $B < B'$, $\omega_n \rightarrow \omega > 1$.

Proposition 5.2 Symmetric heterogeneous distributions. Suppose $G_{k'}(\mathrm{v}) \neq G_k(\mathrm{v})$ for some or all $k' \neq k$. Then, for any set of distributions $\mathbf{G}$ all symmetric around 0 and any number of referendums $K > 1$, there exist $B''(G, K) > 0$ and some n'' finite such that for all $n > n''$ and $B < B''$, $\omega_n \rightarrow \omega > 1$.

Although storable votes deliver positive percentage gains in expected welfare, relative to simple majority voting, when the distributions of valuations are symmetric and the electorate is very large, the absolute magnitude of the gains must be vanishingly small. With independent preference draws, the sum of the intensity draws must approach the theoretical mean, and the assumption of symmetry imposes equal mean intensity for opponents and supporters of each proposal. Hence, in each referendum the two alternatives are asymptotically welfare equivalent. By implication, asymptotically *any* decision rule is interchangeable. Storable votes can only reward occasional empirical asymmetries, sample deviations from the theoretical distribution whose quantitative importance must disappear as the population becomes large.

The assumption that the distributions **G** are symmetric around 0 has a second strong implication. It states that each voter supports each proposal with known probability equal to 1/2, or equivalently that a large electorate will be equally split with probability very close to 1. Suppose instead that in each referendum the probability of approval is not known ex ante. Before preferences are realized, each voter has probability ψ_k of being in favor of proposal k, and $1 - \psi_k$ of being against, where ψ_k is stochastic and distributed according to some distribution H_ψ defined over the support [0, 1] and symmetric around 1/2. Each realized ψ_k is an independent draw from H_ψ. For both supporters and opponents of each referendum k, intensities are drawn independently across voters and referendums from distributions $\mathbf{F} \equiv \{F_k(v),\ k = 1, .., K\}$, each with full support [0,1]. The model is symmetric ex ante, but *not* ex post, since in general the realized ψ_k's will differ from 1/2 and differ across referendums. Then:

Proposition 5.3 Symmetric homogeneous distributions with stochastic median. Suppose $prob(\mathrm{v}_{ik} > 0) \equiv \psi_k \sim H_\psi$, and $v_{ik} \sim F_k(v) = F(v)$ for all k. Then, for all distributions H_ψ symmetric around 1/2 and all F, and for any number of referendums $K > 1$, there exist some n' finite such that for all $n > n'$, $\omega_n \rightarrow \omega > 1$ for all $B > 0$.

Alternatively, we can maintain the assumption that ψ_k is known and equal to 1/2, but introduce systematic differences in intensities between supporters and opponents of each referendum. Call $\mathbf{F_P} \equiv \{F_{Pk}(v),\ k = 1, .., K\}$, with full support [0, 1], the distributions of intensities of voters in favor of a referendum, and $\mathbf{F_C} \equiv \{F_{Ck}(v),\ k = 1, .., K\}$, with full support [0, 1], the distributions of intensities of voters against a referendum. Suppose $F_{P_k}(v) = F_P(v)$ and $F_{C_k}(v) = F_C(v)$ for all k, and call ϕ_P the ex ante probability of casting the bonus vote in favor of a referendum, and ϕ_C the ex ante probability of casting it against. In equilibrium:

$$\phi_P = \left(\frac{1}{2}\right)^{K-1} \left[\sum_{k=0}^{K-1} \binom{K-1}{k} \int_0^1 F_C(v)^{K-1-k} F_P(v)^k dF_P(v)\right]$$

$$\phi_C = \left(\frac{1}{2}\right)^{K-1} \left[\sum_{k=0}^{K-1} \binom{K-1}{k} \int_0^1 F_C(v)^{K-1-k} F_P(v)^k dF_C(v)\right].$$

Call $E_P(v)$ the expected intensity of a supporter of referendum k, and $E_C(v)$ the expected intensity of an opponent of referendum k. Then:

Proposition 5.4 Asymmetric homogeneous distributions with 0 median. Suppose that for all k, $prob(\mathrm{v}_{ik} > 0) = 1/2$, $v_{ik} \sim F_P(v)$ if $\mathrm{v}_{ik} > 0$, and $v_{ik} \sim F_C(v)$ if $\mathrm{v}_{ik} < 0$, with $E_P(v) > E_C(v)$. For any $B > 0$ and $K > 1$, if $\phi_P > \phi_C$ then there exist some n' finite such that for all $n > n'$, $EV_{0n}/EW_{0n} \rightarrow 1 + [E_P(v) - E_C(v)]/[E_P(v) + E_C(v)] > 1$, and $\omega_n \rightarrow \infty$.

The important assumption is that the two distributions of intensities have different means. Assigning higher mean to the "pro" side comes with no loss of generality: which side has higher mean is irrelevant, and the model can be generalized trivially to allow the side with higher mean to change across proposals. The condition $\phi_P > \phi_C$ is not very transparent. A more intuitive but stronger sufficient condition is first-order stochastic dominance: if $F_P(v)$ first-order stochastically dominates $F_C(v)$, $\phi_P > \phi_C$ and Proposition 5.4 applies.

5.2 Symmetric Scenarios

As in the example just described, suppose, first, that all proposals submitted to referendums are such that a typical voter is equally likely to favor or oppose any of them, and thus, equivalently, that all referendums are expected to be close. Empirically, this is not an unrealistic assumption: studying all ballot propositions in California in the period 1912–89, Matsusaka (1992) concludes that the legislature consistently defers to popular vote on issues that appear particularly contested, i.e., in which the electorate is approximately equally split. There is little political gain in taking responsibility for divisive measures. Now, add the further assumption that nothing systematic distinguishes opponents or supporters of a proposal, neither their mass, as Matsusaka documents, nor the intensity of their preferences. In other words, a random individual is equally likely to be for or against any of the proposals, and the intensity with which he is likely to hold his preferred position is independent of whether he is for or against. Finally, to simplify matters even further, suppose that all referendums have equal salience: voters are as likely to feel strongly about referendum *a* as they are about referendum *b*. If we call a scenario *symmetric* when the statistical properties of preferences are equal for supporters and opponents of each referendum, and *homogeneous* when they are equal across referendums, then this simplest case is both symmetric and homogeneous.

5.2.1 Homogeneous referendums

In such a scenario, from the point of view of a single voter all referendums have equal probability of passing and, indeed, equal probability of passing by any given margin. The expected impact of the bonus vote, small as it may be, is thus equal in all referendums, and the voter's best (and natural) strategy is to cast it on the issue he considers his highest priority.

The question is whether the voter can expect to obtain his preferred outcomes more frequently when granted a bonus vote, taking into account that all others are also using their own bonus votes. Surprisingly, this is a question that can be answered with remarkable precision, even before adding more details on the distributions of preferences. The formal derivations are in Chapter 5 in Part II of the book, but the intuitions are straightforward.

As usual, the bonus vote has two opposite effects: reducing the voter's influence in those referendums in which he casts only his regular vote, and increasing it in the referendum that receives his bonus vote. Both effects are larger the larger is the value of the bonus vote. We are talking of very small magnitudes because with a large number of voters, the probability of being pivotal is very small: in the case we are considering, it is of order $1/\sqrt{n}$, where n is the number of voters, with both simple majority voting and the bonus vote. Still, relative to simple majority, the probability becomes somewhat larger when the bonus vote is cast and somewhat smaller otherwise. A few numbers may help. No matter how small the impact of the bonus vote in these examples, the logic will help to understand later results, when the impact will be larger. Suppose, for example, that there are 10,000 voters and four referendums, and the bonus vote is equivalent to a regular vote. With simple majority, the probability of being pivotal is approximately 1 in 250 in each referendum; with a bonus vote, the probability becomes approximately 1 in 165 when the bonus vote is cast and 1 in 330 when it is not. If the bonus vote is worth two regular votes, the probabilities become 1 in 145 when the voter casts the bonus vote and 1 in 435 when he does not. If the number of voters is one million, and the bonus vote is equivalent to a regular vote, the probabilities become approximately 1 in 2,500 with simple majority, 1 in 1,650 when the bonus vote is cast, and 1 in 3,300 when it is not.[6]

As the number of voters increases, the probability that any single voter affects the final outcome of any referendums approaches zero, and, in the symmetric scenario we are considering here, the share of the electorate favoring each proposal approaches 50 percent. When the number of voters is very large, each proposal passes with probability one-half. This is true with simple majority voting and remains true with the bonus vote. Nor is this result undesirable: in symmetric scenarios, when not only is the electorate equally split, but the strength of preferences is equally distributed among opponents and supporters of each referendum, efficiency is consistent with each side winning with probability one-half. Thus, both storable votes and majority voting converge to the efficient outcome for large enough electorates.[7] In fact, however, so does a coin flip: from a welfare point of view, any outcome is equivalent. In this world, there is no need for voting at all. Two observations follow immediately. First, fully symmetric scenarios are quite special – the analysis will have to be extended to more general cases. Second, particularly in large elections, voting is grounded in needs for legitimacy that the analysis of pivot probabilities does not capture: a coin flip is not perceived as equivalent to voting, even when electorates are indeed very closely split. The impact of the bonus vote on the perceived legitimacy of the voting process is an important question in itself. The unusual voting scheme may be seen as less legitimate than traditional simple majority, or, on the contrary, the increased role of the minority may

6. The formulas are in Chapter 5, in Part II.

7. As mentioned in the Introduction, Ledyard and Palfrey (2002) exploit this logic to identify the threshold of approval that should be set in a simple-majority referendums to obtain asymptotic efficiency, for possibly asymmetric but known distributions of preferences. The idea is simple and clever, but setting different thresholds for different decisions seems politically delicate.

reduce disaffection and increase turn out, as has been argued, for example, in favor of cumulative voting.[8] I do not pursue the question here, but it is an important point that should eventually be addressed.

The welfare comparisons become trivial when the electorate is, strictly speaking, unboundedly large. For any finite electorate, differences in expected welfare exist, even if small, and comparisons can be made. Again, the goal is to build intuition for the results that will follow. With an electorate of finite size, in general, opponents and supporters of a referendum will not be of equal number, even with symmetric distributions of preferences. The probability of being pivotal is always positive, and both storable votes and simple majority do improve over a coin flip. Which of the two performs better depends on the value of the bonus vote – the higher the value of the bonus vote, the larger its impact on the pivot probabilities – and on the difference in the value attributed to one's highest-priority referendum, relative to the others. Not surprisingly, these are the same two factors discussed at length in Chapter 1.

Consider the three panels in Figure 5.1. In all panels, the vertical axis is the percentage increase in expected utility from the bonus vote mechanism, relative to simple majority (for both voting rules, expected utility is expressed as margin over expected utility with random decisions), and all panels are drawn for large electorates.[9] The horizontal axis is the value of the bonus vote, from one-half to five regular votes, in increments of one-half. The different curves correspond to a different number of bundled referendums: two for the black dots, four for the gray dots, and nine for the white dots. What changes across panels is the distribution of preferences: a uniform distribution, in which different intensities are all equally likely, in the first panel; a distribution with higher probability mass at low intensities, in the second; and a distribution with higher probability mass at high intensities in the third. Chapter 1 described these probability distributions in terms of coarse partitions of possible intensities into four intervals, corresponding to the ex ante probability

---

8. See, for example, Bowler, Donovan, and Brockington (2003).

9. All figures in this chapter report asymptotic results. When the electorate is unboundedly large, the *percentage* difference in expected utility between the two voting rules remains a valid criterion, but for both rules the *absolute* improvement over a coin flip approaches 0. I return to this point repeatedly in the text.

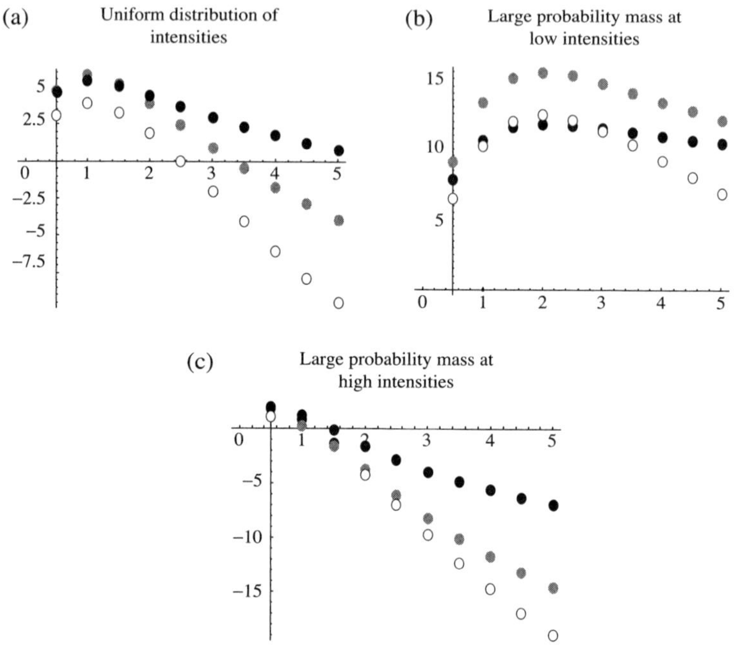

FIGURE 5.1 Percentage gain in expected utility: Storable votes versus majority voting. Large elections. Symmetric and homogeneous scenarios. Expected utility is expressed as margin over expected utility with random decision-making. The horizontal axis is the value of the bonus vote. The three curves in each panel correspond to a different number of bundled referendums: two for the black dots, four for the gray dots, and nine for the white dots. The distribution of intensities is the power distribution whose discrete approximation is represented in Figure 1.3: $F(v) = v^b$. In Figure 5.1a, $b = 1$; in Figure 5.1b, $b = 1/2$; and in Figure 5.1c, $b = 2$. The higher the parameter b the higher the probability mass at high intensities.

of considering a proposal "very important," "important," "somewhat important," and "not important" (see Figure 1.3). As noted there, in the first panel, a random referendum is equally likely to belong to any of the four classes; in the second panel, half of all referendums are expected to be not important and only one in ten is expected to be very important; in the third, on the contrary, close to 45 percent of all referendums are expected to be very important. The expected gain from the bonus vote is largest and most robust in the second panel, where the expected difference in the value of winning the highest-priority referendum, relative to the low mean value attributed to the others, is highest.

Together, the panels make three points. First, in all three panels there are values of the bonus vote for which the bonus vote mechanism outperforms simple majority voting. If the distribution of intensities is uniform, for example, whether the number of referendums is two, four or nine, the result holds as long as the bonus vote is worth less than two-and-half regular votes. In fact, and this is the strong result that can be derived when the electorate is large, there is *always* a range of positive bonus vote values for which the bonus vote mechanism improves over simple majority voting, regardless of the shape of the distribution of intensities or of the number of referendums. This is the claim of Proposition 5.1 in Box 5.1. When the number of voters is small, the analysis is sensitive to the exact number of voters. When the number of voters is large, the results are both simpler and more general. In large electorates, it is possible to calculate easily the optimal value of the bonus vote, a value that guarantees not only the existence of a welfare gain over simple majority but also its maximal size. The exact formula, derived in Chapter 5 in Part II, is so simple that it is worthwhile reporting it here. Call R the ratio of the expected highest intensity to the mean intensity – a ratio that depends on the probability distribution of preferences – and K, the number of referendums. Then the optimal value of the bonus vote equals $K(R-1)/(K-R)$. If the distribution of intensities is uniform, the ratio R equals $2K/(K+1)$ and the formula simplifies to 1, for all values of K: regardless of the number of referendums, the bonus vote should be equivalent to a regular vote. The result is equally straightforward in the cases represented in the other two panels: in the second, the optimal value of the bonus vote is 2; in the third it is 1/2.

In all three panels, a second regularity is that the bonus vote dominates simple majority not only when it is set at its optimal value, but more generally when its value is small. The observation matters for pragmatic reasons: without precise information on the distribution of preferences, a small bonus vote may be a safe enough choice, achieving the conservative goal of "some" welfare gain for a large range of distributions. For example, referring again to the four coarse classes of importance, for any number of bundled referendums, a bonus vote equivalent to half a regular vote yields efficiency gains as long as the frequency with which a typical referendums is considered "very important" is less than 70 percent, and the frequency with which it is considered "not important" is larger than 1 percent.[10]

Finally, Figure 5.1 shows that the welfare effects are sensitive to the number of bundled referendums, as one would expect, but not in easily predictable fashion. An increase in the number of referendums means a larger number of proposals over which the bonus vote is not cast and, thus, over which a voter has less influence. It also means, however, a larger wedge between the expected highest intensity and the mean intensity and, thus, an increase in the expected utility gain in the one referendum on which the bonus vote is cast. The distribution of intensities and the value of the bonus vote determine which of the two effects dominates. In the three panels of Figure 5.1, if the bonus vote is set at its optimal value, the ideal number of bundled referendums is three in the first panel, four in the second, and, taking into account integer constraints, three again in the third. At these optimal values, the expected welfare improvement over randomness due to the bonus vote is, respectively, 6, 15.5, and 2 percent higher than the expected improvement over randomness with simple majority. From a practical point of view, the problem, once again, is how to choose the number of bundled referendums if the distribution of intensities is not known, or if the planner's room for maneuver is limited. Figure 5.1 shows that it is prudent to keep the number low: the fewer the referendums, the less sensitive the outcome to the precise value of the bonus vote.

The conclusions are clean, but the assumptions that make the analysis so simple are strong. One by one, they should be relaxed.

5.2.2 Heterogeneous referendums

The first generalization is straightforward: there are different types of referendums, and some matter mostly to specialized subgroup of voters, while others evoke strong passions more widely. Suppose then that the distributions of preferences differ across types of referendums. Suppose also that for any given type, strong or weak preferences are equally likely

10. The partition is derived from a continuous power distribution $F(v) = v^b$ with parameter b smaller than 4.

between supporters and opponents: some proposals are typically more strongly felt, but this is true regardless of whether an individual is for or against the proposal. Thus, for all proposals, it remains true that there is no systematic difference in the distribution of intensity of supporters and opponents.

The analysis changes only in one dimension: the choice of where to cast the bonus vote should take into account the relative saliency of the different referendums. If a referendum evokes intense preferences, it will receive a large fraction of bonus votes, reducing the marginal impact of one own's bonus vote. It can be preferable to cast the bonus vote in a different referendum, even if it is considered slightly less important. The conclusion echoes one result of Chapter 4, in a different setting. There, a voter refrained from competing with the committee chair; here the competition is with all other voters.

Proposition 5.2 in Box 5.1 states that the result found in the case of homogeneous referendums continues to hold: there are always values of the bonus vote for which storable votes are ex ante preferable to simple majority voting. The conclusion is not surprising. The possibility that some referendums are more salient than others increases the expected dispersion in a voter's intensities of preferences and thus the potential welfare gains associated with the bonus vote.

One possible concern is that, from a practical point of view, the optimal strategy becomes less intuitive, increasing the likelihood of strategic mistakes: the choice of referendum on which to cast the bonus vote depends not only on a direct comparison of the intensity of the voter's preferences but also on the shape of the distribution of intensities in all referendums. Yet, as in the experimental results of the previous chapters, full optimality matters less than using the bonus vote to express the intensity of one's preferences. Expected welfare gains continue to exist if each voter simply casts the bonus vote on the referendum he considers his highest priority.[11] Figure 5.2 describes this result in one

11. The formal result is stated and proved in Chapter 5 in Part II, and, again, the range of admissible bonus vote values must be below an upper threshold that can be identified precisely if the distributions of intensities are known.

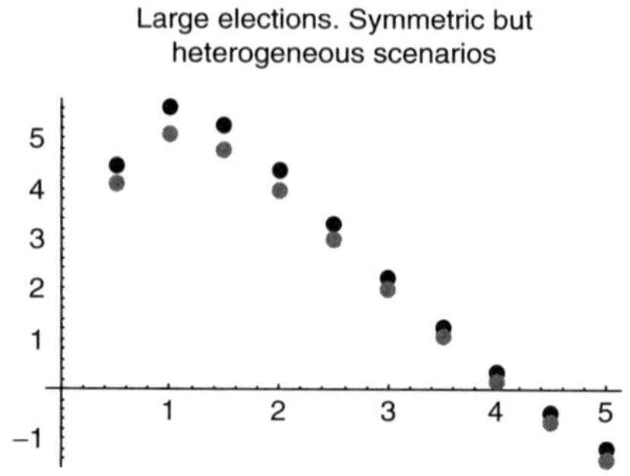

FIGURE 5.2 Percentage gain in expected utility: Storable votes versus majority voting. Large elections. Symmetric but heterogeneous scenarios. Expected utility is expressed as margin over expected utility with random decision-making. The horizontal axis is the value of the bonus vote. The black dots correspond to the equilibrium strategy, the gray dots to casting the bonus vote on the highest priority referendum. There are three referendums, with distributions of intensities given by: $F(v) = v^b$, with $b_1 = 1/2$, $b_2 = 1$, $b_3 = 2$.

specific numerical example. The figure shows the expected welfare gain of the bonus vote mechanism over simple majority when there are three bundled referendums, each associated with a different distribution of intensities. The three distributions correspond to the three panels of Figure 5.1 or, equivalently, to the columns of different shade in Figure 1.3. The horizontal axis is the value of the bonus vote. The black dots correspond to equilibrium strategies, the gray dots to the rule of thumb of casting the bonus vote on the highest-intensity referendum. The welfare measure behaves as we have come to expect: there is an optimal value for the bonus vote – in this case equal to one regular vote – at which the welfare improvement is maximized and reaches approximately 6 percent, and there is an upper threshold for the bonus vote value – in this case equal to four regular votes – that defines the upper boundary of the range that yields welfare improvements. The more important message of the figure is the close proximity of the black and gray dots: if voters cast their bonus vote on their highest valuation, the welfare loss from deviating from the fully optimal strategy is very small.

5.3 Asymmetric Scenarios

In the scenarios studied so far, nothing systematic distinguishes supporters and opponents of any given referendum. The two groups are expected to be of equal size, and the intensity of their preferences has identical statistical properties. As noted earlier, the assumption of symmetry is too powerful in large electorates with independent preferences, in which the actual realization of preferences must approach asymptotically the statistical distribution. Symmetry guarantees that in the limit all decisions are equivalent, and so are all decision rules.

How do storable votes and majority voting compare when the assumption is dropped? The difficult question is how to introduce asymmetries, in ways that capture realistic environments and still are tractable. There are two possible sources of asymmetry: the expected *size* of supporters and opponents in any one referendum, and the expected *intensity* of preferences of the two groups. Both are pinned down by the distribution of preferences of the electorate in that referendum, but it is possible to disentangle them. Ideally, both types of asymmetry should be allowed simultaneously, but the equilibrium analysis becomes quickly too complex. The distinction has some interest because it identifies the sources of strength of the two voting systems: majority voting is designed to handle efficiently the first type of asymmetry – differences in the extent of support; storable votes are designed for the second type – differences in the intensity of support. To keep matters simple enough, I will ignore differences across referendums. Heterogeneity would complicate the analysis, but I see no reason why it should modify the substance of the results.

5.3.1 Asymmetry in the extent of support

With a large electorate and independent and identically distributed preferences across voters, the probability that a typical voter supports a proposal is equivalent to the expected, and asymptotically realized, proportion of "Yes" votes. Suppose, then, that the probability that a voter is in favor of any given referendum takes some value ψ, different from one-half, but known. The intensity of the voter's preferences, on the other hand, has the same probability distribution, regardless of the side the voter prefers. In this scenario, majority voting is efficient: it ensures that the more numerous side will win, and when the majority and the minority are expected to have equally intense preferences, it is the extent of support alone that determines the socially preferable outcome. Storable votes, however, perform equally well: both voting systems select the efficient alternative.[12] If ψ is equal across referendums, or, more precisely, if the expected difference between supporters and opponents is equal across referendums, regardless of its sign, the optimal strategy is again to cast the bonus vote in one's highest-priority referendum. If ψ instead differs across referendums, the optimal strategy is to cast the bonus vote on the referendum expected to be closest. With all voters following this strategy, and, thus, all voters in a given referendum casting the same number of votes, the bonus vote scheme in this latter scenario becomes *identical* to simple majority voting. In either case, the outcome replicates the outcome with simple majority voting, and both voting rules maximize expected welfare.

Note, however, that if the extent of support for a referendum is known and different from one-half, it is difficult to see why the proposal would come to a popular vote. The outcome of the referendum is perfectly predictable, and a legislature that took the issue upon itself would gain the approval of a majority of the electorate. If ψ is different from one-half, then it seems more reasonable to assume that it is not known precisely. Following a model that the literature has proposed and studied in the case of simple majority voting,[13] suppose that ψ is not deterministic but is itself a random variable distributed according to some known probability distribution on the interval between 0 and 1. The assumptions we make about such distribution reflect the voters' beliefs about the popularity of the referendums. To keep the problem

12. With respect to earlier results, the main difference is in the probability of being pivotal. Whether with storable votes or with simple majority, if ψ differs from one-half, in large electorates the probability of being pivotal is of order $1/e^n$, where n is the number of voters, as opposed to being of order $1/\sqrt{n}$ when ψ equals one-half. For example, with 10,000 voters, the pivot probability is of the order of 1 in 100 if the electorate is expected to be equally split, but becomes of the order of 1 in a number with more than 4,000 zeros if ψ differs from one-half. The observation holds for any value of the bonus vote, and for any number of bundled referendums.

13. See, for example, Good and Mayer (1975), Margolis (1977), and Chamberlain and Rothschild (1981). Gelman, Katz, and Tuerlinckx (2002) discuss the implications of a number of alternative models.

tractable, suppose that the probability ψ follows the same distribution for all referendums and that the distribution is symmetric around one-half. Thus, we ignore possible differences across classes of referendums, and suppose that any imbalance in favor of a proposal is just as likely as the same imbalance against it. In this form, the model adds to the richness of an unknown probability of approval the tractability of ex ante symmetry, an important simplifying factor in pinning down voters' strategies with storable votes. In particular, the intuitive strategy of casting the bonus vote in the referendum a voter considers most important remains optimal. Pragmatically, it also remains a likely rule of thumb and a reasonable prediction of voters' behavior. Note that in each referendum, the electorate will *not* be equally divided ex post, even with very large electorates: in each referendum, the expected share of supporters is half the electorate but the probability that it is exactly half the electorate is zero. The contrast is to the models discussed in the previous section in which, with large electorates, the probability that voters are exactly split over each referendums converges to one.

As Chapter 5 in Part II shows, the probabilistic nature of ψ affects the probability that an individual vote may be pivotal. With both majority voting and storable votes, the probability of being pivotal is now of order $1/n$, as opposed to $1/\sqrt{n}$ when ψ is known and equal to one-half. As expected, with storable votes, the probability of being pivotal is lower than with simple majority voting when the regular vote only is cast and higher when both the regular and the bonus vote are cast. Now, however, over the full set of referendums, the relative change in probabilities is always favorable to storable votes. The conclusion is simple and general: if the number of referendums is K, relative to majority voting the improvement in the pivot probability from casting the bonus vote is always $(K - 1)$ times the decline experienced when casting only the regular vote, regardless of the value of the bonus vote and of the number of referendums. And because the bonus vote is cast on the referendum considered most important, the conclusion is *always* an increase in expected welfare. Proposition 5.3 in Box 5.1 states the result formally.

Figure 5.3 shows the percentage gain of the bonus vote mechanism over simple majority when the probability of approval is stochastic. The horizontal axis is the value of the bonus vote, and the three curves in

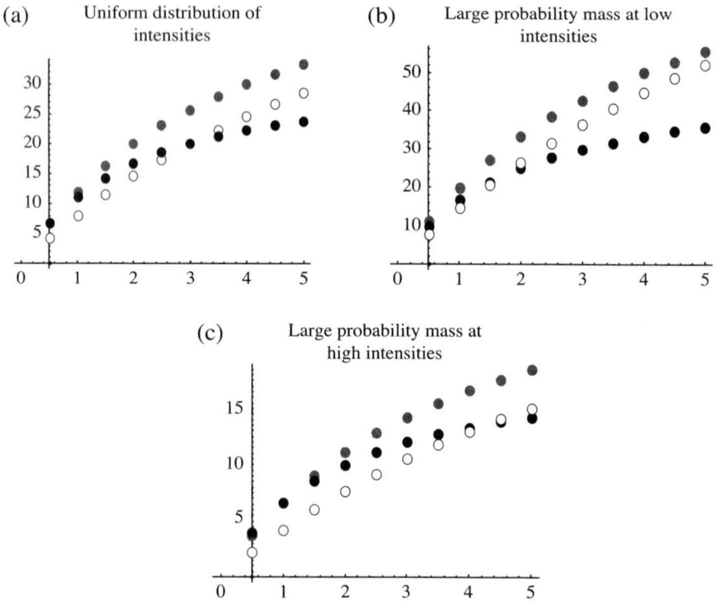

FIGURE 5.3 Percentage gain in expected utility: Storable votes versus majority voting. Large elections. Stochastic probability of support. Expected utility is expressed as margin over expected utility with random decision-making. The horizontal axis is the value of the bonus vote. The three curves in each panel correspond to a different number of referendums: two for black dots, four for gray dots, and nine for white dots. Voters' intensity of preferences is distributed according to $F(v) = v^b$. In Figure 5.3a, $b = 1$; in Figure 5.3b, $b = 1/2$; and in Figure 5.3c, $b = 2$.

each panel correspond to different numbers of referendums: two for the black dots, four for the gray, and nine for the white. The three panels mirror the three panels of Figure 5.1 and reflect different distributions of intensities: uniform in the first panel, mostly concentrated around low values in the second, and mostly concentrated around high values in the third.

Every dot in the figure is above 0: expected welfare is always higher with storable votes than with simple majority. The percentage improvement is highest in the second panel and lowest in the third, but in all panels it remains positive for all values of the bonus vote and for all numbers of referendums considered in the figure. The improvement in expected welfare is larger the larger the value of the bonus vote, eventually converging to the ratio R, the ratio of the expected highest valuation to the mean valuation, when the bonus vote is so large that the regular vote is negligible in comparison. The main lesson from the figure, and from Proposition 5.3, is that allowing for uncertainty in the probability of approval of each referendum improves the relative performance of the bonus vote scheme. Intuitively, the drawback of storable votes is the higher dispersion, and hence the higher uncertainty, in votes cast. When uncertainty is already high, reflecting uncertainty on the split of the electorate, the bonus votes' contribution on this account is minor, and the positive aspects of the voting rule come to dominate the final welfare impact.

5.3.2 Asymmetry in the intensity of support

Recognizing that the probability of support for each referendum should not be treated as known is a good step toward realism. But the need to keep the model tractable imposes a whole series of symmetry constraints, and the model, although allowing realized asymmetries ex post, is fully symmetric before preferences are realized. It is once again the case that random decision-making would behave very well: neither simple majority nor storable votes can improve over it by more than an amount that in absolute terms becomes infinitesimal as the number of voters becomes very large.

The limitation is not in the voting systems, but in the model. The conclusions are very different if the assumption of ex ante symmetry is dropped. Suppose then that in each referendum the intensity of preferences is distributed differently for supporters and opponents, with one side having higher expected intensity. It is important to repeat here what the assumption really entails. Ex ante, before the specific proposals are known and preferences are realized, all individuals are identical, and all draw their valuations, independently from each other and independently across referendums, from the same probability distributions. Ex post, each individual will typically favor some referendums and oppose others. By introducing asymmetries, the model does not posit that, for example, opposition to a referendum "should" count more than support, from a welfare prospective. What it does is drop the restriction that if the electorate were infinitely large, the same percentage of voters on either side of each referendum would rank the issue as belonging to any given percentile of the intensity distribution. An example may help. Suppose that some of the referendums are distributional in nature: if the beneficiaries of the transfer are a small group and the sources of the transfers much more diffuse – think of agricultural subsidies – then it is very likely that supporters of the referendum would feel more strongly about it than opponents, at least on average. But the opposite is possible too: if the beneficiaries are a large group and those supporting the cost are instead few – think of land expropriation for a public project – then it is the opponents who are likely to have more intense preferences. The model does not attribute these preferences normatively, according to some overarching social criterion, but takes them as given. When evaluating welfare, it aggregates preferences *in expectation*, before they are actually realized, knowing that some set of referendums, as yet unspecified, will be on the table, and that supporters and opponents are unlikely to feel equally about them.

Introducing asymmetries inevitably complicates matters, and it is helpful to simplify other parts of the model. Suppose then that the probability of support for each referendum is known, and that the distributions of intensities, although different between the two sides of the electorate in each referendum, are nevertheless identical across referendums.[14] In the language introduced at the beginning of this chapter, this is an asymmetric but homogeneous scenario. Assuming that the distributions of intensities are equal in all referendums guarantees that in equilibrium each voter optimally casts his bonus vote on the highest-priority proposal. The assumption can be dropped if we are willing to take a stance on possible rules of thumb when casting the bonus vote.

In this scenario, the probability of approval, and thus the expected split of the electorate, determines immediately the welfare properties of majority voting. If the side expected to have higher intensity is also the side expected to be more numerous, majority voting is efficient; if the reverse is true, majority voting is inefficient. In the first case it outperforms random decision-making; in the latter case, it underperforms it, but as long as the probability of approval differs from one-half, the outcome with majority voting is predictable with probability very close

14. Which side has higher expected intensity can switch across referendums.

to one even at finite electorate sizes. With storable votes, the efficiency of the mechanism depends in principle both on the expected split of the electorate and on the probability that bonus votes will be cast disproportionately on the side of each referendum preferred by voters with higher expected mean intensity. In all examples I have studied, however, if the expected split of the electorate is different from 1/2, I have been unable to construct equilibria where the first consideration did not dominate. All outcomes with storable votes replicated the outcomes with majority voting.

As noted earlier, the assumption that the division of the electorate is known and different from one-half is difficult to reconcile with the very idea of holding a referendum. Suppose then that the probability of approval equals one-half: a random voter is equally likely to favor or oppose a typical referendum, and a typical referendum is expected to be tied – an assumption that here has the methodological advantage of isolating the role of asymmetries in intensities. Majority voting dominates random decision-making with finite electorates but not asymptotically, where the two rules are equivalent. Storable votes enhance efficiency if voters cast their bonus vote in a referendum in which they side with the part of the electorate with higher mean intensity of preferences. Because they will cast their bonus vote on their highest-priority referendum, the result follows if a voter's highest intensity is expected to be a draw from the distribution with higher mean. This seems plausible enough, but does not follow immediately from the difference in expected intensities; it depends instead on the full shape of the intensity distributions.[15] It can be guaranteed if the distribution with higher mean is also such that probability mass is concentrated toward higher intensities than is the case for the distribution with lower mean. Concretely, suppose once again that the public's intensity of preferences over the different referendums can be identified through a partition into four equally sized intervals of attributed importance. Consider a referendum whose proponents, on average, have

15. Suppose, for example, that the side with higher mean is concentrated in its intensity, while the opposite side is dispersed and bimodal at low and high intensities. With probability increasing in the number of referendums, it is then possible for the bonus votes to be used predominantly by the side with lower mean valuation: the larger the number of draws, the higher the probability that the highest draw will come from the more dispersed distribution.

more intense preferences than opponents. The condition above will be satisfied if there is some monotonicity in the manner in which voters on the two sides are distributed in the four intervals. Among those judging the proposal "very important," the majority should be proponents, and similarly among those considering it either "very important" or "important"; among those judging the proposal "not important" the majority should be opponents, and similarly among those considering it either "not important" or "somewhat important."[16]

The results are summarized formally in Proposition 5.4 in Box 5.1 and proved in Chapter 5 of Part II, and they are qualitatively different from all results derived so far. For any value of the bonus vote, storable votes now dominate majority voting not only at large but finite sizes of the electorate, but also asymptotically. Because each referendum is expected to be won by either side with probability one-half, majority voting converges to random decision-making, and neither is efficient: both ignore intensities of preferences, and thus, in the present case, the asymmetries in intensities. Not so storable votes, which are expected to favor the side of each referendum with higher mean intensity with probability indistinguishable from one. Storable votes are designed to reflect intensities of preferences, and thus asymmetries in these intensities, and they finally come into their own, as a voting rule, in this asymmetric model.

Figure 5.4 shows why the result is important. The figure reports expected utility with storable votes, majority voting, and random decision-making in the case of three referendums, 10,000 voters, and a bonus vote equivalent to a regular vote. In each referendum, the intensity of preferences of opponents and supporters follows the power probability distribution that I have used in all examples, with a power coefficient that differs between the two sides. The higher the coefficient, the more the probability mass is skewed toward high values and the higher the mean intensity.[17] The first panel in the figure pictures the

16. The informal description corresponds to requiring that the distribution with higher mean intensity first-order stochastically dominates the distribution with lower mean intensity.

17. Power distributions with different power coefficients satisfy first-order stochastic dominance: a power distribution with higher coefficient first-order stochastically dominates a distribution with lower coefficient.

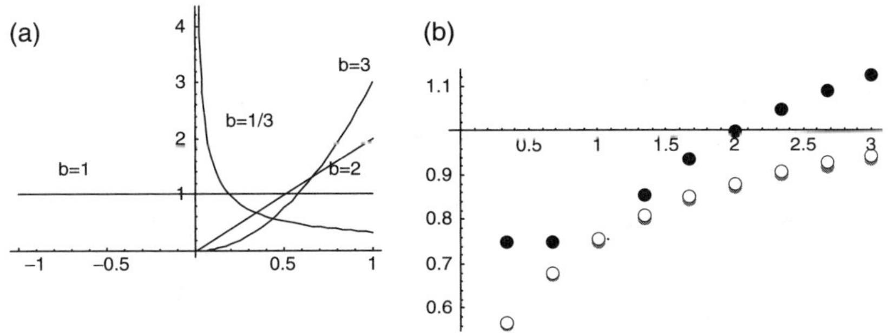

FIGURE 5.4 Expected utility over all referenda, with asymmetric distributions of intensities. In all referendums, voters' intensity of preferences is distributed according to $F(v) = v^b$, but the parameter b differ between supporters and opponents. In the figure, $F(v) = v$ for the opponents, but $F(v) = v^b$; $b\,\varepsilon\{1/3, 2/3, \ldots 3\}$ for supporters. The two distributions are represented in panel (a), where the horizontal axis is the valuation, and negative (positive) valuations correspond to opposing (supporting) the referendum. In panel (b), the vertical axis is expected utility; the horizontal axis is b. The black dots correspond to storable votes, the white dots to majority voting, and the gray dots, barely visible, to random decision-making. There are three referendums, 10,000 voters, and the value of the bonus vote is 1.

distributions. The horizontal axis is the valuation – as usual, positive valuations correspond to supporters of the referendum and negative valuations to opponents. Intensities are absolute valuations, and for both groups take values between 0 and 1. In all three referendums, opponents' intensity of preferences is distributed uniformly (a power coefficient equal to 1), while the distribution of intensity for supporters has a power coefficient varying between 1/3 and 3, in increments of 1/3. The right side of panel (a) represents four cases – a power coefficient equal to 1/3, 1, 2, and 3, out of the nine cases considered in panel (b). Panel (b) reports a voter's ex ante expected utility over the three referendums, as function of the power coefficient of the supporters' distribution, plotted on the horizontal axis. The black dots correspond to storable votes, the white dots to majority voting, and the gray dots, barely visible, to random decision-making.

Two observations are immediate. First, as expected, by effectively guaranteeing that each referendum is decided in favor of the side with more intense preferences, storable votes outperform majority voting, with an expected welfare improvement that is larger the more asymmetric are the two distributions.[18] Second, symmetric scenarios have built our intuition for the functioning of storable votes in large elections, but it is in asymmetric scenarios that storable votes could matter in practice. Consider the result in panel (b) when the power coefficient plotted on the horizontal axis is set to 1, and thus the distributions of intensity are equal on the two sides of each referendum. In the example represented in the figure, the number of voters is 10,000, and it is clear that the asymptotic convergence already bites: the three dots, black, white, and gray are effectively superimposed. The black dot (storable votes) lies just above the white dot (simple majority), itself just above the gray dot (random decision-making), but at the scale of the figure, the differences are hardly visible. The absolute gains are minuscule. The previous figures, referring to scenarios that were always ex ante symmetric, plotted the percentage gain of storable votes over simple majority, with the expected welfare from either voting systems expressed as margin over the expected welfare with random decision-making. In other words, the figures plotted the difference between the black and the white dots, divided by the difference between the white and the gray dots. Scaling by randomness was useful, given the asymptotic convergence of all three measures, but while the figures give a faithful picture of the qualitative impact of storable votes, they do not reveal the small absolute size of the welfare gain. It is possible to argue that the relevant welfare measure should be aggregate – the sum of expected welfare over *all* voters – and thus if the welfare gains approach zero at a speed not faster than the size of the electorate, the asymptotic equivalence of the voting systems in per capita terms does not preclude sizable aggregate gains: if the difference between the dots is multiplied by 10,000, it will appear as quite visible. But the core of the matter remains the intuition behind storable votes. Storable votes are a useful tool if differences in intensity of preferences exist and matter. In large elections, this translates into asymmetric distributions of valuations.

---

18. In the figure, expected utility with storable votes is not sensitive to the power coefficient on the horizontal axis when the coefficient is less than 1. The reason is that, in this case, the referendums are won with probability approaching one by the opposite side, the opponents in the figure, whose distribution of intensity is unchanging. At power coefficients higher than 1, it is, instead, the supporters who carry the referendums, and expected utility does reflect the value of the power coefficient.

When distributions are symmetric, storable votes do not make matters worse and help at the margin, but it is when distributions are asymmetric that storable votes can really be expected to improve upon majority voting.[19]

The scenario discussed here clarifies one point raised earlier only in passing. The welfare result is not an immediate reflection of the probability of being pivotal. Here, the probability of being pivotal is of order $1/\sqrt{n}$ with majority voting, and only of order $1/n$ with storable votes, and yet storable votes are welfare superior. Asymptotically the pivot probability converges to zero in both cases, and faster with storable votes, but the difference in expected welfare remains.

If the pivot probability is so much lower with storable votes, should we expect higher abstention rates? Even if this were the case, the welfare results should be robust: the probability of being pivotal does not depend on the direction of the referendum preferred by the voter, and reversing the welfare results would require disproportionate abstentions by voters with valuations drawn from the distribution with higher expected intensity. This seems implausible enough, and even more so when we keep in mind that voters here vote over several referendums at the same time and are ex ante equally likely to favor or oppose any referendum. It is difficult to rationalize selective abstentions exactly on those referendums that a voter, on average, feels more strongly about.

The restriction imposing the same distributions of valuations, and thus the same extent of asymmetry, in all referendums is unrealistic. How robust are the conclusions if the restriction does not hold? The difficulty is identifying the voters' optimal strategy: as the model is generalized, strategic calculations become much more complex, and optimal strategies, when they can be identified, rely on degrees of information and rationality that voters seem unlikely to possess. If, in fact, voters continue to cast their bonus vote on their highest valuation, the expected outcomes of the referendums and the welfare properties of the bonus vote will remain as described. As long as the distributions of valuations are well-behaved, in the specific sense that the probability that

19. Storable votes could make matters worse, if they favored the side with lower expected intensity of preferences. Examples exist, and one is described in footnote 15, but they are not easy to construct.

a voter's highest intensity is drawn from a specific distribution increases with the distribution's mean, storable votes are expected to increase efficiency, relative to majority voting, and the expected welfare gains do not disappear asymptotically.

5.4 Multiple Bonus Votes

If a single bonus vote can improve the efficiency of referendums, would multiple bonus votes deliver even higher welfare gains? The possibility of choosing the number of bonus votes gives the planner an additional instrument, and in theory, at least, the mechanism can only be superior (if possibly weakly). But the problem becomes substantially more difficult, both for the voters and for the planner, and with the increased complexity comes the increased difficulty of predicting how the bonus votes would actually be used by voters.[20]

Suppose that voters are endowed with multiple bonus votes, and suppose first that the multiple bonus votes can be cumulated freely on any referendum. When considering their optimal strategy, voters need to evaluate any combination of bonus votes over the different referendums – a complicated question on which the theory can make some limited progress. To simplify matters, suppose that the distributions of valuations are identical across referendums and symmetric. Suppose also that each bonus vote is equivalent to a regular vote. Then, for any number of bonus votes, there is always an equilibrium in which all voters cumulate all their bonus votes on their single most important referendum – exactly as if they had a single bonus vote. If the number of bonus votes equals the number of referendums minus one, a plausible choice that rules out the exact replication of simple majority voting, and we concentrate on voters' strategies that are responsive to intensities, this is the *only* equilibrium. When each bonus vote is equivalent to a fraction of the regular vote, the optimal strategy in general depends on the bonus votes' exact value, on their total number, and on the number of referendums, but, again, it is not difficult to find examples in which lumping all bonus votes is optimal (for example, if there are K referendums and each voter is granted

20. The proofs of all statements in this section are in Casella and Gelman (2008).

$K - 1$ bonus votes, each of which is worth $1/K$ regular votes). In all of these cases, the equilibrium with multiple bonus votes is *identical* to the equilibrium with a single bonus vote, although presenting a much more complicated strategic problem. In general, other equilibria are possible too, and other asymmetric scenarios should also be studied. At this point, however, taking into account the high potential for confusion and mistakes and lacking strong theoretical grounds to expect superior outcomes, the argument for multiple cumulative bonus votes is weak.

Suppose, then, that voters are endowed with multiple bonus votes of different values that *cannot* be cumulated. Again, the question is whether possible welfare improvements are worth the increased complication, and again the theory can provide some limited guidance. Suppose that all distributions of valuations are identical across referendums and symmetric. Then with multiple, non-cumulative bonus votes, there is an equilibrium such that each voter casts the bonus vote with the highest value in his highest-priority referendum, the second-highest in the second-ranked referendum, and so on. The optimal values of the bonus votes depend on the shape of the distribution of valuations. For example, if the distribution is uniform, and thus all intensities are equally likely ex ante, the bonus votes' values should be, in order, 0, 1, 2, ... up to $K - 1$, where K is the number of referendums, a particularly intuitive set of values that is exactly equivalent to simply asking voters to rank the referendums.[21] But if the distribution of valuations is not uniform, the optimal values are not particularly intuitive, and the mechanism does not reduce to a simple ordinal ranking.[22] Relative to a single bonus vote, expected welfare gains exist, of a magnitude that depends on the number

21. The result was anticipated by Jackson and Sonnenschein (2007). As described in footnote 6 in the Introduction, the mechanism proposed there asks each individual to announce the intensities attached to a series of unrelated decisions, but with the announcement constrained to mimic the actual distribution of intensities. When the distribution of intensities is uniform, voters are simply asked to rank the decisions: the ranking can be read as fitting the same percentage of decisions into any equal subset of the distribution. The bonus votes mechanism here replicates exactly the Jackson and Sonnenschein proposal. When all distributions of valuations are identical across decisions, the Jackson and Sonnenschein mechanism converges toward full efficiency as the number of decisions becomes unboundedly large. We know little about its properties when the number of decisions is finite and small.

22. For example, with four referendums and a power distribution $F(v) = v^b$, $b = 4$, the values of the bonus votes should be 0, 0.25, 0.41, 0.523.

of referendums and on the shape of the distribution of valuations. In practice, however, it seems a difficult idea to implement without losing trust and legitimacy: because optimal values of the bonus votes depend on the distribution of valuations and on the number of referendums, they would need to change across elections. The question then becomes whether some welfare gains can be obtained either for all values of the bonus votes, or for some specific values, chosen conservatively and kept constant. And are the results robust if the distributions of valuations are asymmetric or heterogeneous, cases for which the theory for now has no answers? These are good questions and deserve study. For now, the simplicity of a single bonus vote recommends it as a safer option.

5.5 Related Referendums

In the entire chapter, I have described the referendums as unrelated, and constrained each voter's valuations to be independent across proposals. Strictly speaking, the menu of referendums is part of the design of the mechanism, and we could demand of the planner that the referendums be unrelated. In practice, however, the assumption is likely to be violated. Does it matter? The answer depends on the form of the violation. If a voter's utility is not separable across referendums – for example, if preferences on a specific referendum depend on the outcome of a different one – then the correct model is not one of K binary decisions, but of a single K-dimensional choice, among 2^K possible alternatives. This is a much more difficult problem, lending itself to the possible pathologies identified by voting theory.[23] However, if the assumption of separable utility can be maintained, the model used so far can be generalized quite simply.

If the referendums are related, the relevant statistical description of a voter's valuations does not take the form of multiple univariate distributions, one for each referendum, but of a single multivariate distribution from which all of the voter's valuations are drawn. If the voters are ex ante identical, this multivariate distribution is also

23. See for example Brams, Kilgour, and Zwicker (1998).

identical across all voters. Suppose then that valuations are statistically dependent across referendums, but remain independent across voters, and the referendums are held simultaneously. The main result in this case is that the previous analysis continues to apply, but needs to be rephrased in terms of the *marginal* distribution of the valuation in each referendums – the distribution obtained, speaking informally, by averaging out the voter's valuations over the other referendums. The difficulty is not the dependence among the voter's valuations per se, but the possible heterogeneity of the marginal distributions, and the complication this heterogeneity creates in identifying the voter's optimal use of the bonus vote. If the marginal distributions are not heterogeneous, however, the analysis is unchanged. Such will be the case, for example, when the pattern of correlation is identical across all referendums.[24] Consider the following example, where I make a distinction between dependence in the *direction* of preferences and dependence in the *intensity* of preferences. Suppose that all referendums concern a single general topic, and the direction of each voter's preferences is perfectly correlated among them: if the voter is in favor of one, then he in favor of all (or, more generally, all signs are perfectly predictable, once one of them is known). Intensities, however, are drawn independently across referendums according to some distribution that is invariant to the sign of the preferences – each individual referendum may be considered by the voter trivial or important, and knowing the intensity over one of them does not help to predict the voter's intensity over a different one. The example assumes perfect correlation in the direction of preferences, and zero correlation in the intensity of preferences, but all that is required is that both types of correlation be symmetric across referendums. In this scenario, marginal distributions of valuations are identical across referendums, and in equilibrium each voter casts the bonus vote on the referendum with highest intensity. The welfare conclusions depend on the shapes of these distributions, but follow the same logic discussed in the rest of the chapter.

---

24. Technically, what we require is that the valuations be *exchangeable* across referendums: random variables are said to be exchangeable if all permutations of their ordering have the same joint probability distribution. In such a case, although the valuations are statistically dependent, the model is fundamentally symmetric: there is nothing to distinguish one referendum from the others.

5.6 Conclusions

Storable votes, or, more precisely, the addition of a bonus vote to a bundle of contemporaneous binary choices, can function well when the number of voters is large. Under plausible scenarios, the result is an expected efficiency gain relative to simple majority. In some environments, the conclusion holds regardless of the value of the bonus vote; in others, the value of the bonus vote should not be too large, an invitation to caution that matches well what common sense also recommends. As in all previous applications, the bonus vote makes it possible for the minority to win at times, but because these victories accompany, on average, high intensity of preferences on the minority side and low intensity on the majority side, the possibility of minority victories increases aggregate expected welfare. When the electorate is large – in fact especially in this case – the scheme remains very intuitive: the equilibrium strategies are simple, the reason for the efficiency gains is transparent, and the modification with respect to existing practices is minor. All that is required is that several referendums be presented to voters simultaneously and that voters be granted a single extra bonus vote.

According to the theory, the scheme is reasonably safe. Examples where storable votes lead to expected welfare losses relative to simple majority exist but are not easy to construct or particularly intuitive. The analysis makes clear, however, that the impact of the bonus vote is closely tied to the shape of the distributions of valuations, distributions on which the theory imposed strong restrictions. What shapes do these distributions assume in reality? What strategies are voters likely to use? Do efficiency gains persist when the distributions of valuations are less stylized than those used in the examples, and when information about them is less precise? These questions are finally empirical, and it is by evaluating storable votes in a real set of elections that answers can slowly be developed. That is the purpose of the next chapter.

6

A Field Test of Storable Votes in Large Elections: Student Elections on the Columbia Campus

All empirical tests presented in this book so far have studied small groups in laboratory settings. In the case of large elections, not only are controlled experiments much more difficult to run, but the main questions left unanswered by the theory have to do with realistic assumptions about preferences and information when these are *not* induced or controlled. A test that comes closer to a field experiment is better suited for what we want to learn.[1]

In spring 2006, we attached a short survey to students' election ballots in two different schools at Columbia University. We selected the subset of elections with two candidates only and asked students to rank the importance assigned to each of these contests and to indicate where they would have cast one additional bonus vote, had one been available. An identifier connected responses and actual voting choices, allowing us to construct distributions of intensities and electoral outcomes, both without and with the bonus vote. Statistical techniques then provided estimates of the bonus vote's probable impact.

To anticipate our results, we find that the bonus vote works well. When minority preferences are particularly intense, the minority wins at least one of the contests with 15 to 30 percent probability, and yet when the minority wins aggregate welfare increases with 85 to 95 percent probability. At the same time, ex post inequality among

1. This chapter is adapted from Casella, Ehrenberg, Gelman, and Shen (2010).

voters falls: the fractions of voters who see either all or none of their preferred candidates being chosen both decline. When majority and minority preferences are equally intense, the effect of the bonus vote is smaller and more variable, but on balance it is still positive.

Student elections are rarely considered worthy of study. They are low-stake contests, measuring students' popularity more than the attractiveness of their electoral platforms, and they take place in a population that is hardly representative of a typical electorate. However, our work is not about extrapolating political tendencies from campus elections. The objective is to study storable votes and their comparison to simple majority voting in realistic large-scale elections in which the distribution of preferences, the information of the voters, and the complexity of the choices *are not controlled by the researchers*. This is the central requirement here. For these purposes, the true determinants of the voters' preferences and the specific choices the voters are making are secondary.

The theory behind this study is described in detail in the previous chapter. I do not repeat it here, but only add that each referendum between two possible outcomes should now be interpreted as an election between two candidates for a given student-government position.

6.1 The Test

6.1.1 The design

Several of Columbia's schools hold elections in the spring, and the student organizations and the deans at the School of General Studies (GS) and Columbia College (CC) agreed to collaborate with us. In each school, voters elected representatives for multiple positions: GS students voted on twenty elections and CC students on twelve. We selected the subset of elections with two candidates or two mutually exclusive party lists only – three elections in GS (Board President, Alumni Representative, and International Representative), and four elections in CC (Executive Board, Senator with Two-Year Term, Senator with One-Year Term, and Academic Affairs Representative).[2]

2. We excluded the elections for class presidents or representatives because they concern different subsets of the electorates. We also excluded two elections in which one of the candidates was accused of irregularities and, in fact, later disqualified.

All voting was electronic, and at the end of the ballot students were invited to participate in our survey. In the GS case, interested students clicked on a link and were redirected to a web page containing the survey. Students' votes and their responses to the survey were matched and saved under anonymous identifiers and were later forwarded to us by the student bodies supervising the elections. In the CC case, the survey was on paper because of logistical difficulties with the voting stations. At the end of their electronic ballot, CC students interested in answering the survey were given a number to be copied at the top of the paper questionnaire. The number allowed us to link their responses to their actual votes, again forwarded to us anonymously after the voting was concluded.

Understandably, the organizers of the elections were concerned with keeping our interference minimal, and the survey had to be short. We asked two sets of questions: first, how much the voter cared about the outcome of each of the elections in our subset, on a scale from 1 (not at all) to 10 (a lot). We call the answer the *score* assigned to each election. Second, we asked in which of these elections the voter would cast a single additional bonus vote in support of his favorite candidate, had one been available. The paper questionnaire for CC is reproduced in the Appendix; the electronic GS questionnaire was identical, with one exception – since it was electronic, and thus faster, we added a question about expected election outcomes.

Prior to the elections, students in both schools were informed about the survey through a school-wide email message and through posters and fliers distributed widely throughout campus. Possible prizes from answering the survey were advertised: respondents from each school took part in a lottery with iPods and $20 gift certificates for Barnes & Noble awarded to the winners.[3]

6.1.2 The data

Out of 1,161 GS students, 476 voted in the GS elections, and 297 of these answered our survey; in the College, 2,057 voted out of a potential

3. The prizes were two iPods and eight gift certificates for the CC lottery (with a potential electorate of 4,073); and one iPod and five gift certificates for the GS lottery (with a potential electorate of 1,161 students).

electorate of 4,073, and 644 answered the survey. After eliminating CC questionnaires that were either unreadable or unmatchable to actual voters, we cleaned the data according to the following criteria: (1) we assigned a score of 0 to any election in which a respondent abstained, a plausible option logically, and the only one available since we could not match the score to a voting choice; (2) we assigned a score of 1 to any election in which a respondent voted but left the ranking blank; and (3) we eliminated from the sample respondents who stated that they would cast the bonus vote in an election in which they in fact abstained, implying that the survey answers were patently untruthful or confused. Because the CC questionnaires were on paper, they lacked the automatic completeness checks that the electronic program forced on the GS students. In particular, nine CC respondents did not indicate where they would have cast the bonus vote. Choosing not to use the bonus vote is a legitimate choice, and we left these respondents in the sample. After cleaning the data, we were left with 276 responses in the GS sample and 502 in the CC sample, or a valid response rate among voters of 58 percent in GS and 24 percent in CC.

Participation in the survey was voluntary, and individuals in our samples appear more engaged in the elections than the rest of the electorate. The data allow us to test the hypothesis that in each school both the rest of the electorate and our sample are random draws from a common population.[4] When we look at abstention rates, the hypothesis is rejected at the 5 percent confidence level for all GS elections and for two of the four CC elections – predictably, individuals who answered the questionnaire have significantly lower abstentions rates. More surprisingly, we also find differences in preferences for candidates. When we look at support for the winning candidate among voters, the hypothesis of random draws from a common population is rejected in the presidential election in the GS sample and in the Academic Affairs election in the CC data. Although the majority candidate does not change, both elections were much closer in our sample than in the full electorate. Statistical techniques would allow us to reweigh the samples to achieve representativeness, but we decided not to do so for two reasons. First, our set of elections is also limited – we selected only elections with

4. The formal test is reported in Table 6.1 in Chapter 6 of Part II.

binary choices – and even with representative samples, the test reported here is not equivalent to adding a bonus vote to the actual Columbia student elections. Second, the biases we see in the data are not predictive of any clear bias in the performance of storable votes, relative to simple majority. It is difficult to see which effect, if any, should result from lower abstention rates. As for the smaller margins of victory, the addition of a bonus vote may result in a higher probability of minority victories, but there is no ground on which to expect either higher or lower welfare. Thus, this chapter should be read as asking not what the impact of the bonus vote would have been in the Columbia elections, but what it would have been in the subset of elections considered, in a population for which the samples of respondents are representatives. Once again, the interest of the study is not in the elections *per se*, but in testing storable votes in a large electorate when voters' preferences, information, and beliefs are not controlled, a condition indeed satisfied here.

6.1.3 The distributions of the scores

Figure 6.1 reports the distributions of the scores assigned by respondents to each election, for both GS (Figure 6.1a), and CC (Figure 6.1b). Scores are labeled positive or negative to distinguish the two candidates the respondent voted for – the sign per se carries no meaning. For ease of reading, in each election we assign positive scores to the candidate commanding a majority in our sample. Consider, for example, the election for Board President in the GS sample, at the top of Figure 6.1a. The scores assigned by Susannah's supporters are plotted on the positive axis, those of Liz's supporters on the negative axis, and the cell at 0, in black, reports abstentions. The histogram says that 23 of Liz's supporters and 31 of Susannah's assigned a score of 10 to the election, 11 of Liz's supporters and 13 of Susannah's assigned it a score of 9, etc. The box next to the histogram summarizes the main data concerning this election. In our sample of 276 students, 142 voters supported Susannah, 129 supported Liz, and 5 abstained; 208 stated that they would have cast the bonus vote in this election, and, attributing the bonus votes according to each respondent's actual candidate choice, Susannah again wins a majority of the bonus votes (110 against 98). Susannah did in fact win the election among all voters, with 241 votes in favor, versus 188 for Liz and 47 abstentions. The box reports also the average score assigned

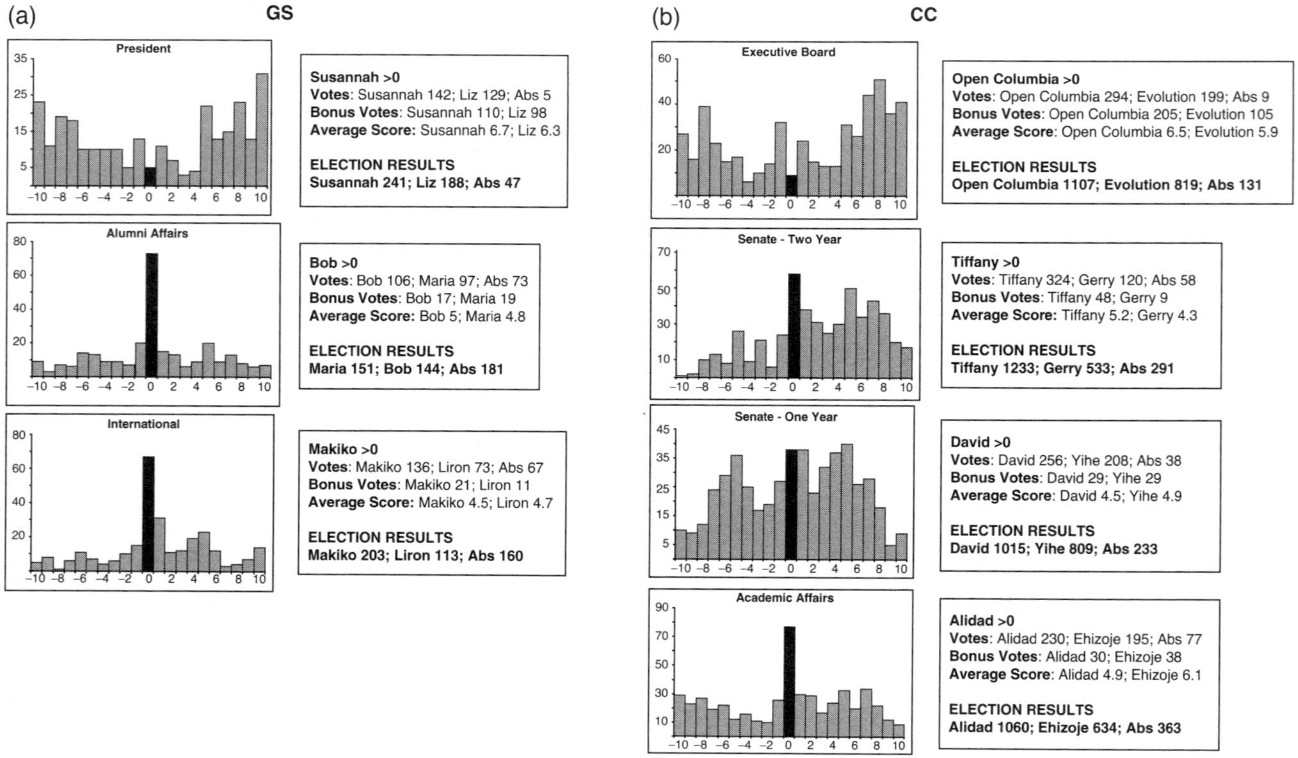

FIGURE 6.1 Histograms of recorded scores.

to the election by the supporters of each candidate: the average score is slightly higher among Susannah's supporters (6.7 versus 6.3 for Liz's supporters).

In the GS sample, the election for President was overwhelmingly the most salient: among respondents who voted at all, abstentions in the President election are less than one-tenth than those of the second best attended election (International), and average scores are approximately 70 percent higher than in the other elections. Two of the three elections (President and Alumni Affairs) were close elections, and in these elections not only is the extent of support similar between the two candidates, but the distributions of voters' scores are also approximately symmetric across the two sides. The third election (International) was quite lopsided. If the elections had been held with bonus votes, none of the outcomes would have changed: in the President and in the International election, the majority winner commands a majority of the bonus votes; it does not in Alumni Affairs, but the difference is small (2 votes), and cannot override the difference in regular votes.

In the CC sample, there is again one election that voters in the sample considered most salient (Executive Board), with both low abstentions and higher average scores, but the difference with respect to the other elections is less pronounced than in GS. The Senate Two-Year election was a landslide, but the others, and in particular Senate One-Year and Academic Affairs, were close elections. The Academic Affairs election, with scores distributed according to the histogram at the bottom of Figure 6.1b, is particularly interesting. Here Alidad won a majority of the votes (230 versus 195 for Ehizoje), but the average score is higher among Ehizoje's supporters (6.1 versus 4.9 for Alidad). The distribution is not symmetric, with the majority of Ehizoje's supporters attributing high importance to the outcome, while the scores given by Alidad's supporters are concentrated in the middle range. Storable votes are designed to address situations of this type, and, not surprisingly, Ehizoje receives approximately 25 percent more bonus votes than Alidad (38 to 30), although the difference of 8 votes would not have been enough to counter the majority advantage. In the CC sample, too, bonus votes would not have changed any of the outcomes.

The scores reflect the importance attached by respondents to the different elections, and they can be interpreted as measures of intensity of preferences. More precisely, and in line with the theoretical model, the scores are read here as proxies for the differential utility that each respondent attaches to having the preferred candidate win that specific election, as opposed to the opponent. The important information is the relative score assigned by each respondent to different contests: it is preferable to have one's favorite candidate win an election rated as a 4 than an election rated as a 2. To give a measurable meaning to intensity of preferences, the scores must be interpreted not only as ordinal but also as cardinal values: using the simplest linear mapping, winning an election rated as a 4 is not only preferable but twice as valuable as winning an election rated as a 2. The distributions of the scores in Figure 6.1 are then the empirical counterpart of the distributions of valuations discussed in the theory.

If the scores measure intensity of preferences, we can construct measures of aggregate welfare in our samples. The most immediate utilitarian measure simply sums all scores over supporters of each candidate and calls *efficient* in any election the victory of the candidate whose supporters have higher aggregate scores. For example, in the Board President election in GS, Susannah's supporters are both more numerous and have higher average scores, guaranteeing a higher aggregate score (954, compared to 810 for Liz's supporters), leading to the conclusion that efficiency favored Susannah's victory.[5]

As welfare measure, the sum of the reported scores has the important advantage of being closest to the questionnaire. The difficulty is that, in general, evaluated over all elections, it will give different weights to different voters, reflecting differences in the total scores that each of them has assigned. The preferences of a voter who rates each election as a 10 will be given ten times the weight of the preferences of a voter who rates all elections as a 1. An alternative is to construct and sum

5. Ignoring the scores assigned by voters on the losing side is equivalent to setting a voter's utility to zero in the case of defeat, the normalization used in all theoretical models discussed in this book. Note, for clarity, that it is a normalization only and has no impact on efficiency rankings. Suppose, for example, that in evaluating the utilitarian measure of welfare we subtracted the scores assigned by all voters on the losing side. Call S_A the aggregate score assigned to the election by supporters of candidate A, and S_B the aggregate score of supporters of candidate B. We would say that A's victory is efficient if $S_A - S_B > S_B - S_A$, or $2S_A > 2S_B$, which is equivalent to $S_A > S_B$, the criterion used here.

normalized scores – scores obtained by constraining all individuals to the same total score. Specifically, the normalized score assigned by an individual to a given election equals his reported score for that election, divided by the sum of the scores assigned by that individual to all elections. Thus, the sum of all normalized scores assigned by an individual always equals 1, and therefore it is constant across individuals, contrary to reported scores. A normalized utilitarian measure of welfare is then the sum of the normalized scores over supporters of each candidate. By construction, total normalized welfare assigns the same weight to each voter.

Which of the two welfare measures is superior is not clear theoretically, because, of course, it could be that the voter who assigns all a score of 10 does indeed care about student elections ten times more than the voter who assigns all a score of 1, relative to a common reference point. It is good, then, to see that the two alternatives are equivalent. Figure 6.2 summarizes the properties of the data, using both reported and normalized scores. The figure reports margins in favor of the majority, in each election, in terms of the number of votes, average scores, and aggregate scores.[6]

Figure 6.2a is based on reported scores, as is Figure 6.1, while Figure 6.2b uses normalized scores. The two sets of figures are not identical, suggesting that the normalization does play some role. Because it accounts for each individual's overall scoring pattern, the normalization in general rescales differently scores from different individuals and, thus, changes both average and total scores. The qualitative conclusions, however, are robust to the choice of reported or normalized scores: if efficiency is measured by higher aggregate scores, the efficient outcome in each election is unambiguous – the dark gray columns always have equal sign in Figures 6.2a and 6.2b. In the GS sample, efficiency always supports the majority choice. In the CC sample, efficiency supports the majority choice in three of the four elections, but the majority's total

6. If $\mathbf{M}$ is the size of the majority, $\mathbf{m}$ the size of the minority, and n the total number of voters, the margin of victory among voters is simply: $(\mathbf{M} - \mathbf{m})/n$. Using s to denote both the reported score in Figure 6.2a and the normalized score in Figure 6.2b, the aggregate score margin in favor of the majority is calculated as follows: $\left(\sum_{i\in M} s_i - \sum_{i\in m} s_i\right) / \sum_{i=1}^{n} s_i$, and the average score margin is: $(\hat{s}_M - \hat{s}_m)/(\hat{s}_M + \hat{s}_m)$, where $\hat{s}_M = (\sum_{i\in M} s_i)/\mathbf{M}$ and $\hat{s}_m = (\sum_{i\in m} s_i)/\mathbf{m}$.

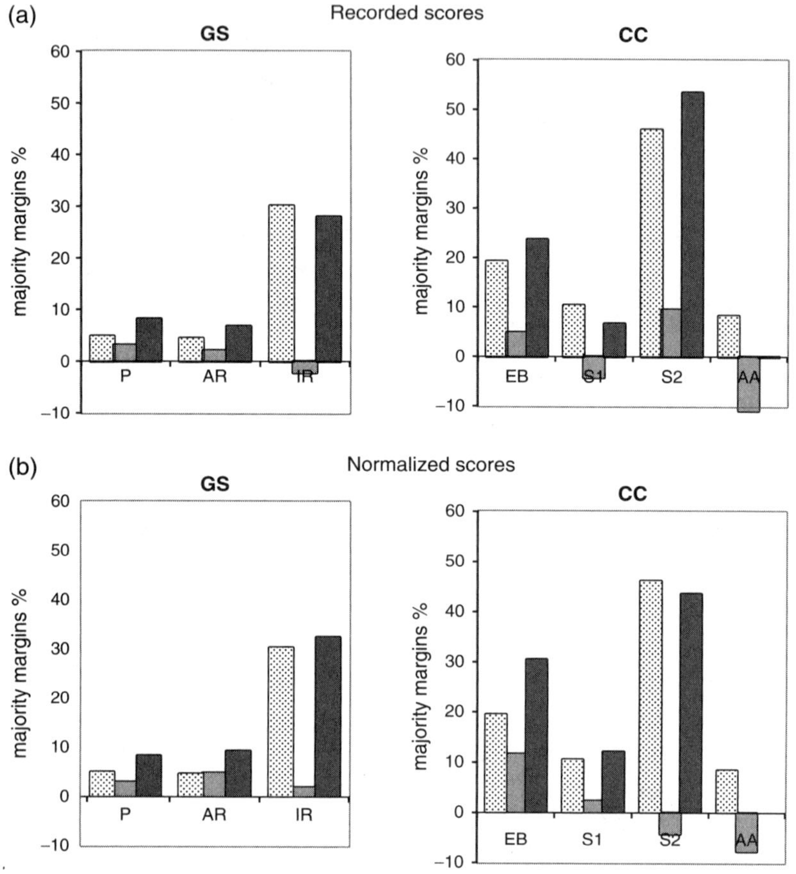

FIGURE 6.2 Margins in favor of the majority, per election, in the samples of respondents. The first series (dotted) is the margin of victory in votes, ignoring the bonus votes. The second series (light gray) is the average intensity margin. The third series (dark gray) is the aggregate score margin.

score margin is slightly negative, albeit with a margin so small as to be undetectable in the figure, in the fourth election (Academic Affairs) where the larger size of the majority is countered by the stronger intensity of preferences of the minority.

6.1.4 The bonus vote decision

In the GS sample, 89 percent of the voters cast their bonus vote in an election to which they assigned their highest score, and 81 percent did so in the CC sample. If voters knew little about all elections and were aware of their lack of information, this would be both the simplest and the optimal strategy. Which other criteria influenced their choice? Figures 6.3a for GS and 6.3b for CC show the relevant data, election by election. Each diagram presents, for all respondents who said they would cast the bonus vote on that specific election, the reported score assigned

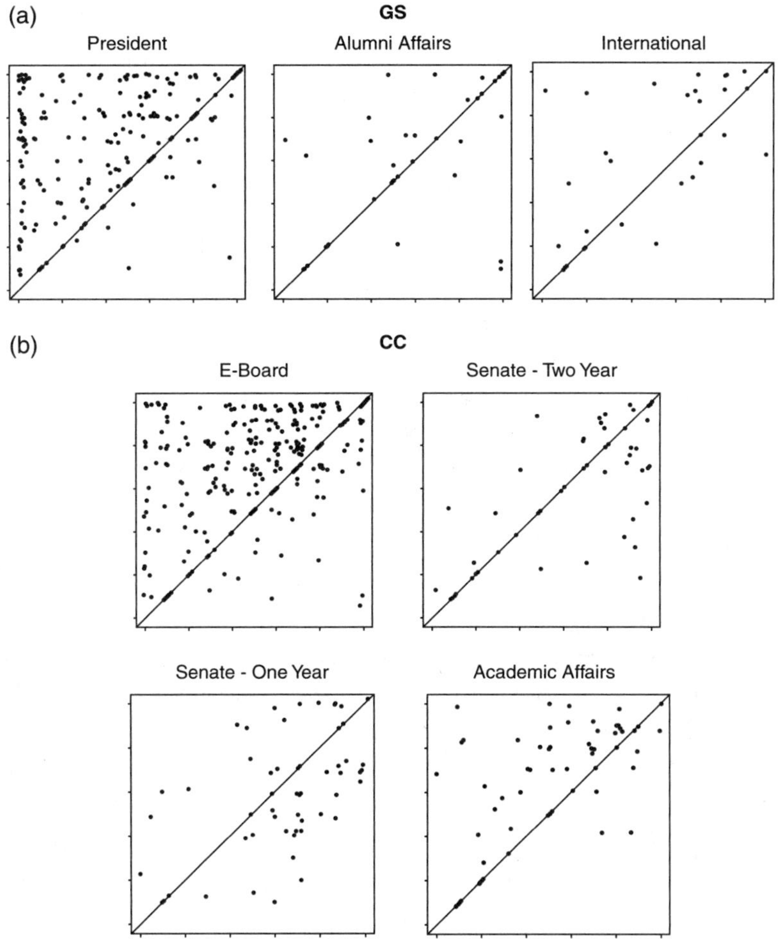

FIGURE 6.3 Relative recorded score of the election receiving the bonus vote. Each point is an individual response. The vertical axis is the recorded score for the election selected for the bonus vote; the horizontal axis is the highest recorded score among all other elections.

to that election on the vertical axis, and to the highest ranked of the other elections on the horizontal axis. If the election selected for the bonus vote is the highest-score election, then the respondent is indicated by a point on or above the 45-degree line; if not, by a point below the 45-degree line. (The only relevant information in the figure is the ordinal ranking of the elections, and reported scores show the difference across elections more clearly. Normalized scores yield a rescaled but otherwise identical figure.)

In each data set, the election with lowest abstention rate and highest average score – the most salient elections: President in GS and Executive Board in CC – received the great majority of the bonus votes, and was also the election most respondents ranked as most important to them. In all elections, some bonus votes came from respondents who ranked a different contest higher. The number of such bonus votes is relatively small in both the GS President election (8 percent) and the CC Executive Board election (12 percent), but less so, in relative terms, in the other contests, reaching 50 percent in the Senate One-Year election in CC. Over the full electorate – and it is the full electorate that a voter would consider when deciding where to cast the bonus vote – Senate One-Year was the closest election in CC. If voters rationally weigh the probability of being pivotal, then this election should command a relatively high number of bonus votes, even with low scores. In the GS data set, on the other hand, the bonus vote choice does not seem to correlate in any transparent manner with the realized margin of victory: the closest election was Alumni Affairs, with a margin of 2 percent, but the fraction of voters who cast the bonus vote in that election while ranking a different one higher is smaller than the fraction in the International election, the most lopsided, with a margin of victory of 28 percent.

According to the theory, the bonus vote choice depends on the *common knowledge* of the distributions of valuations in the electorate at large: everyone knows the distributions of valuations, and everyone knows that everyone else knows, and hence voting patterns can be predicted. But we do not have any evidence that preferences were commonly known. In fact, we have some evidence to the contrary. As mentioned earlier, in the GS questionnaire – electronic and thus faster – we added a question about expected election outcomes. In the election for President, more than 80 percent of the students filling in the questionnaire answered the question, but approximately half of them predicted the wrong winner, and a quarter predicted that she would win by a large margin; in the other two elections, more than half of those filling in the questionnaires chose not to answer the question, in line with the large abstention rate, but among those who did respond, a majority predicted the wrong winner in the Alumni Affairs election, half of them by a large margin, and one-third did so in the International election. These answers may reflect something other than rational calculations of expected outcomes, but cannot be read as support for common knowledge of the distributions of preferences. The lack of information by the voters could explain the anomalies noticed in Figure 6.3.

If preferences were not common knowledge, there is no basis for testing rigorously the strategic behavior predicted by the theory in Chapter 5. In fact, there are two additional reasons to be cautious. First, we do not know the distributions of valuations for the electorate as a whole: it is the choice of the entire electorate that any single voter is trying to influence, but the distributions of valuations we construct from the survey refer to a sample only – the respondents of the survey. Second, when asking where the respondent would cast the bonus vote, the questionnaire did not state explicitly that in the thought experiment all other voters would also be casting a bonus vote. I doubt that answers would have been different otherwise, but cannot exclude it.

Instead of testing the theory, then, it seems more useful to estimate the impact of the bonus vote on outcomes and welfare, checking the robustness of the estimates to different plausible behavioral rules.

6.2 Estimating the Probable Impact of the Bonus Vote

As shown in Figure 6.1 and stated earlier, in the samples no outcome would have changed with the addition of the bonus vote, given how respondents stated they would cast it. However, this is not very informative: because the bonus vote links the outcomes of the bundle of elections over which the voters can choose to use it, there are only two independent data points, one for each school, too few to form an estimate of the bonus vote's probable impact. To obtain such an estimate, ideally we would want to replicate the same elections many times, with many different electorates whose preferences are all drawn from the same underlying distribution. We cannot rerun the elections, but we can approximate such iterations by bootstrapping the data.[7] The objective is to estimate the impact of the bonus vote in a population for which our samples are representative.

The maintained assumption of the bootstrapping exercise is that preferences are independent across individuals, although not necessarily across elections for a single individual. To construct bootstrapping samples, n individuals are sampled *with replacement* from the two data sets, with $n = 276$ for GS and $n = 502$ for CC. Consider, for example, the GS sample: randomly select an individual among the 276 in the data set, and record his actual votes, the scores he assigned to all elections, and his choice of where to cast the bonus vote; then return the individual to the original data set and sample once more; continue the procedure until a new sample – a bootstrap sample – of 276 individuals has been constructed. Because of the replacement, the bootstrap sample will be similar but not identical to the original data: some individuals will appear more than once, and others will be absent. The important point is that because of the random sampling, we can think of both the original sample and the bootstrap sample as representative sets of draws from an underlying original population. Similarly, by sampling with replacement from the original 502 individuals in the CC data set, a bootstrap sample can be constructed for CC. Repeating the procedure 10,000 times, each replication generates a new bootstrap sample, and thus a distribution of preferences over each of the elections and of bonus vote choices for each school. Finally, for each of the 10,000 bootstrap samples for each school, outcomes and measures of welfare can be calculated, simulating what would happen if the elections were held among voters in the sample, either with simple majority voting or with the bonus vote.

With limited confidence in our ability to explain the bonus vote decisions seen in the data, we calculated the results with four different rules governing the use of the bonus vote. Rule A is closest to the data and equals the bonus vote choice actually reported by the individuals sampled in the bootstrapping. It is a plausible but not necessarily correct rule, because the environment differs from the actual elections: outcomes are calculated over voters in the samples only, not in the electorate at large.

7. The classical references are Efron (1979) and Efron and Tibshirani (1993). For a recent treatment, see Davidson and MacKinnon (2006).

Rule B applies to each individual the probabilistic decision rule estimated from the simple statistical model described in Box 6.1 below. In this case, the decision rule reflects the assumptions of a specific model, but, on the positive side, takes into account the change in environment and is adapted to the actual bootstrap sample. Rule C states that every individual casts the bonus vote in the election with highest score (randomizing with equal probability if more than one election has the highest score). It is the simplest, most intuitive rule, and one that would be optimal if voters knew very little about the elections and were aware of their lack of information. Finally, rule D replicates rule C but excludes the two most lopsided elections in each sample, International in GS and Senate Two-Year in CC. It is a correction voters would want to make if landslides were correctly anticipated. Each of the four rules has some argument in its support, but what matters more is the consistency of the results across the different rules.

Given the distributions of valuations in the data, the hypothesis is that storable votes should be approximately equivalent to majority voting in the GS elections, where the distributions are either symmetric between supporters of the two candidates or indicate a landslide, but have more impact and better welfare properties in the CC elections, where one election in particular (Academic Affairs) is both a close election and one to which the minority assigns higher average score. In fact, according to Figure 6.1, the distribution of scores of supporters of the minority candidate almost perfectly first-order stochastically dominates the distribution of scores of the majority candidate, a sufficient condition identified in Chapter 5 for the welfare superiority of storable votes.

The analysis that follows is based on normalized scores, because the constraint of equal welfare weights across voters seems desirable. The results, however, are not sensitive to using either reported or normalized scores (as is to be expected, given Figure 6.2).

Box 6.1 A simple statistical model

The model describes respondents' bonus vote choices through a set of elementary criteria, each of which specifies how to cast the bonus vote. Each respondent's answer, given his scores and the characteristics of the elections he faces, can then be written in terms of the probability of following the different criteria. The model posits four mutually exclusive criteria: (1) cast the bonus vote in the election with highest score; (2) cast the bonus vote in the most salient election; (3) cast the bonus vote in the closest election; (4) some other criterion we ignore, and such that the choice appears fully random. Each criterion is assumed to be followed with some probability, called *pmax* for criterion 1, *psal* for criterion 2, *pclose* for criterion 3 and *prand* for criterion 4. Each respondent's choice can be described through these probabilities. For example, consider a GS voter whose highest score is on the President election, and who indicates that he would cast the bonus vote on that election. According to the model, this behavior occurs with probability $pmax + psal + (1/3)prand$. If the voter assigns the highest score also to a second election, then the probability of the observed behavior becomes $(1/2)pmax + psal + (1/3)prand$, and correspondingly for the other cases. Assuming that respondents' choices are independent, the likelihood of observing the data set is simply the product of the probabilities of all individual choices. The probabilities *pmax*, *psal*, *pclose*, and *prand* can then be estimated immediately through maximum likelihood or Bayesian methods.

We have estimated the probabilities on the two data sets separately, and in both cases maximum likelihood and Bayesian estimation yield identical results, summarized in Table 6.1, with standard errors in parentheses.[8]

In both data sets and with both estimation methods, *psal*, the probability of casting the bonus vote on the most salient election, is relatively large and significantly different from zero. At the same time, *pclose*, the probability of casting the bonus vote on the election with smallest margin of victory, is always small, and in the GS sample is insignificant. Both results are theoretically puzzling: the intensity of one's preferences should be fully captured by the score, and the use of the bonus vote should be higher in close elections. However, the two most salient elections were also reasonably close elections, the second

8. In conducting the Bayesian inference, we assigned uniform prior distributions to each of *pmax*, *psal*, and *pclose* and used the software Bugs (Spiegelhalter et al. (1994), (2002)). The Bayesian approach works well here, because with moderate sample sizes maximum likelihood estimates can be at the boundary of the parameter space. See the discussion in Gelman et al. (2004).

Table 6.1 Estimated Probabilities of Three Behavioral Rules

	GS	CC
pmax	0.55 (0.06)	0.52 (0.04)
psal	0.34 (0.06)	0.30 (0.04)
pclose	0.01 (0.01)	0.04 (0.01)

Standard errors in parentheses.

closest in both data sets, and attracted much more debate and attention prior to voting than any of the others. It is possible that voters chose them disproportionately not because they were salient, but because in fact they knew them to be close contests and had little information about the other elections.

The statistical model provides a synthetic description of the data, and should not be read as a test of the theory. In particular, the probabilities with which the different criteria are followed are treated as exogenous parameters, constant across voters, as opposed to being the expression of each voter's strategy, dependent on the voter's full set of scores, as they would be in a strategic model.

6.2.1 The frequency of minority victories

The first question is the frequency with which, using the bonus vote, at least one of the elections in each set is won by the minority candidate. As shown in Figure 6.4, in the GS bootstrap samples the frequency is stable across the different rules at around 15 percent. In the CC samples, the frequency increases monotonically as we move from rule A to rule D: from 11 to 15 to 23 to 29 percent.

The aggregate number, appropriate because of the linkage across elections imposed by the bonus vote, is the result of different impacts on the specific elections. Tables 6.2a for GS and 6.2b for CC report the frequency with which any individual election is won by the minority, for each bonus vote rule. The last column reports the aggregate frequency depicted in the figure. (In all cases, any sample where either simple majority or the bonus vote resulted in a tie is assigned a weight of one-half.)

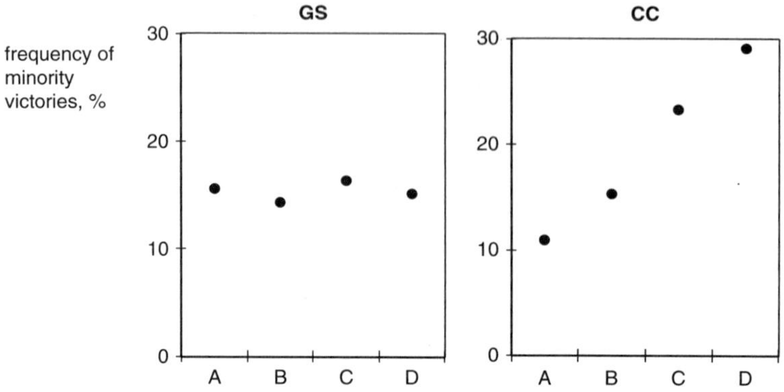

FIGURE 6.4 Percentage frequency of minority victories. Frequency with which at least one election in each set is won by the minority, out of 10,000 bootstrap samples, when voters cast their bonus vote according to each of four different rules.

Table 6.2 Percentage Frequency of Minority Victories in 10,000 Bootstrap Samples

Table 6.2a: GS

	President	Alumni	International	Aggregate
Rule A	5	11	0	16
Rule B	6	9	0	14
Rule C	8	9	0	16
Rule D	7	8	0	15

Table 6.2b: CC

	Exec Board	Senate-Two	Senate-One	Academic	Aggregate
Rule A	0	0	2	9	11
Rule B	0	0	1	14	15
Rule C	0	0	1	23	23
Rule D	0	0	1	28	29

Predictably, the numbers reflect the distributions of preferences over each election. The most lopsided elections (International Representative in GS, and Executive Board and Senate Two-Year in CC) are never won by the minority candidate. The election most susceptible to the impact of the bonus vote is Academic Affairs in CC; moving from rule A to rule D, the number of bonus votes cast on Academic Affairs progressively increases; so does the frequency with which the minority candidate wins, and so does the aggregate frequency.[9] In the GS samples, the impact of the bonus vote reflects mostly how close the different contests are. In the CC samples, again the bonus vote affects exclusively the two closest elections, but the higher intensity of the minority supporters in Academic Affairs plays a clear additional role in tilting the results in the minority's favor when the bonus vote is available.

It is instructive to compare these numbers to the frequency with which a minority victory is efficient, in the different elections. In the GS samples, the frequency is 12 percent for President, 14 percent for Alumni, and 0 for International Representative. In the CC samples, it is 0 for both Executive Board and Senate Two-Year, 1 percent for Senate One-Year, and 40 percent for Academic Affairs. Although still falling short,[10] the bonus vote brings the frequency of minority victories closer to the efficient frequency. Whether minority victories occur in the same samples in which they are in fact efficient will be the question addressed in the next subsection.

The analysis used 10,000 bootstrap samples to guarantee that the experimental error[11] is negligible. As a test, the frequencies in Table 6.2 were recalculated with 20,000 independent bootstrap samples, confirming that all frequencies changed by less than half of 1 percent.

The first conclusion, then, is that in both sets of data and for all rules, although particularly in CC for rules C and D, the bonus vote allows the minority to win with substantial probability.

9. In CC, rule B assigns some bonus votes to the closest election. In estimating the statistical model, we identified as closest the election with the lowest margin of victory in the full electorate. In the bootstrap exercise, we must limit ourselves to the sample. Taking into account the bonus votes, Senate-One Year is the closest election in 26 percent of the bootstrap samples, and Academic Affairs in 72 percent. The remaining 2 percent of bootstrap samples are ambiguous – either election can be closest, depending on how the bonus votes are cast. The ambiguity does not affect the frequencies reported in Table 6.2.

10. With the only exception of rule A in the Senate-One Year election, in the CC samples.

11. The binomial standard error of the observed frequencies due to the finite size of the sample.

6.2.2 The impact of minority victories on aggregate welfare

How costly are minority victories in terms of aggregate welfare? The second result is that minority victories not only are not costly, but, in fact, they typically come with aggregate welfare gains.

In each election, realized welfare is defined as the sum of all (normalized) scores of all voters who supported the winner (in the case of ties, each side is assigned a probability of victory of 50 percent). The relevant unit is again the full set of elections in each school, for each bootstrap sample. Consider all bootstrap samples in which with the bonus vote the minority wins at least one election. In these samples, the presence of minority victories means that the welfare measures differ between simple majority voting and storable votes, and thus can be compared. Among those samples only, the upper panel of Figure 6.5 shows the frequency with which aggregate welfare is higher with the bonus vote than with simple majority voting, and the lower panel shows the mean

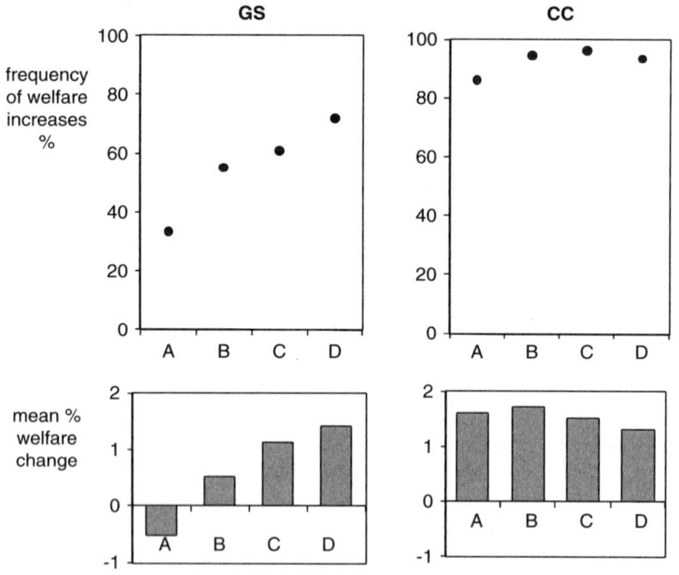

FIGURE 6.5 Welfare impact of the bonus vote. Percentage frequency of aggregate welfare increases and mean percentage welfare change, relative to majority voting, when the minority wins at least one election.

percentage welfare increase, or decrease, obtained by the bonus vote, relative to simple majority.

For all four rules in the CC data and for three of the four in the GS data, the mean effect on welfare is positive. In the CC data, the result is surprisingly sharp: among all bootstrap samples in which the minority wins at least one election, an increase in aggregate welfare occurs from a minimum of 86 percent of the time (rule A) to a maximum of 96 percent (rule C). The minority must be winning when its preferences are more intense than the majority preferences. In the GS data, the mean welfare change is always smaller than in CC, and in one case, when it is smallest, the sign is negative (rule A); with rules B, C, and D, the expected impact is positive, but the frequency with which aggregate welfare rises reaches a maximum at 72 percent (rule D).

In addition to generating the summary results reproduced in Figure 6.5, the bootstrap exercise yields the full distribution of the impact of the bonus vote on aggregate welfare across all bootstrap samples. Figure 6.6 presents the histograms of the percentage difference in aggregate welfare between each of the four bonus vote rules and majority voting in all samples in which, using the bonus vote, the minority wins at least one election in each set. The frequency of positive welfare changes reported in the upper panel of Figure 6.5 corresponds to the positive mass in each of the histograms.

The histograms show clearly the concentration of the probability mass around the positive mean welfare change in the CC samples, while the distribution is more dispersed in the case of GS. The higher variability of the GS results is consistent with approximately symmetric preferences across the two sides in elections affected by the bonus vote. Summary measures of dispersion – standard errors and bootstrap confidence intervals – are obtained easily; they are not reported here because more information can be read from the full distributions. Because the focus is on samples in which the minority wins at least one election, the number of samples analyzed here is between 1,400 and 1,600 for GS and between 1,000 and 3,000 for CC, depending on the bonus vote rule (see Table 6.2). We have compared the results to those obtained from a different set of 10,000 bootstrap samples, confirming that the experimental error remains negligible.

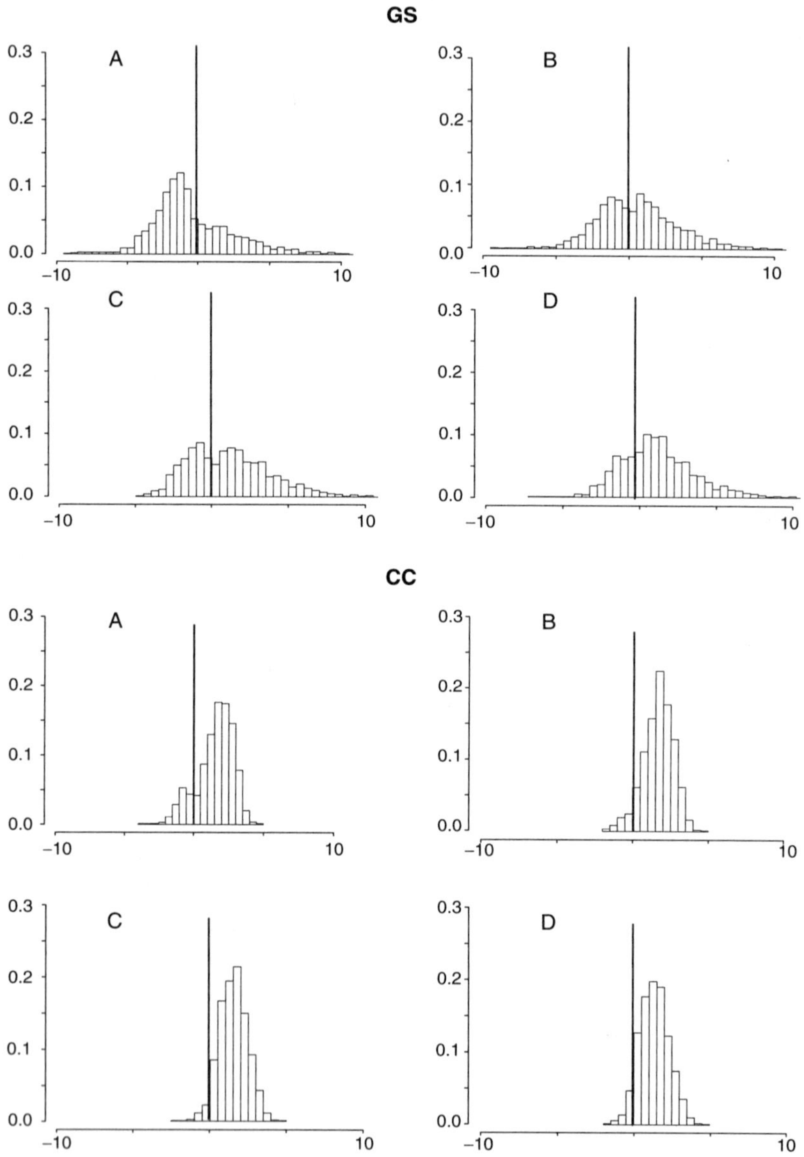

FIGURE 6.6 Distributions of welfare changes, due to the bonus vote. Histograms of percentage welfare differences between the bonus vote scheme and majority voting in all samples where, with the bonus vote, the minority wins at least one election. The vertical axis is the percentage of such samples falling into each bin. The tall vertical line is at 0.

6.2.3 Inequality

Minorities should win occasionally not only because aggregate efficiency is higher when intensity of preferences is recognized, but also because, as argued in Chapter 3, preferences can be correlated across elections, and individuals who find themselves repeatedly on the minority side will feel unrepresented by the political system. If it comes at no cost to aggregate welfare, a more equal distribution of decision-making influence seems desirable in itself. Our data allow us to construct the full distribution of ex post utility – utility after the outcome of the election is decided – across voters in each of the bootstrap samples. In line with the theoretical models, individual utility is defined as the sum of the voter's scores over all elections won by the voter's preferred candidate. The distribution across voters thus captures the different frequencies with which each voter's preferred candidate wins, weighted by the relative importance the voter assigns to the election. Depending on the voting rule, without or with the bonus vote, we obtain two different distributions of voters' ex post utility: one for majority voting and one for storable votes. By comparing the two distributions, it is possible to calculate the impact of the bonus vote on voters' ex post inequality.

Average realized utility distributions are shown in Figure 6.7. The bins on the horizontal axis are ordered in increasing levels of utilities, each bin corresponding to a 5 percent range, from lowest (0) to highest (1).[12] The height of each bin is the fraction of voters with utility falling into the bin, averaged over all samples in which, with the bonus vote, the minority wins at least one election. The black line corresponds to the bonus vote (rule A) and the gray line to simple majority. Here, rule A is fully representative of the results obtained with the other bonus vote rules: the figures are so similar as to appear identical.

The higher polarization of the GS distributions reflects the smaller number of contests (three, as opposed to four in CC) and the overwhelming priority assigned to a single election (President). The impact of the bonus vote on the distribution is hardly detectable in the GS samples, but it is clear in the CC sample, where the frequency of realizations at

12. Maximal utility is 1 because the figure is constructed from normalized scores.

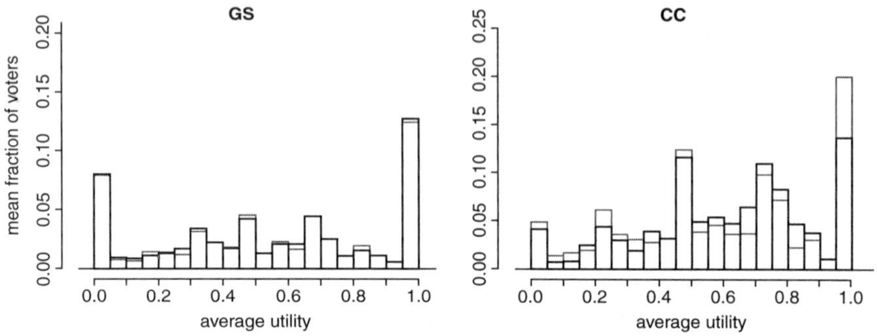

FIGURE 6.7 Realized utility distributions. Simple majority (gray) and bonus vote, rule A (black), averaged over all samples in which the minority wins at least one election.

the two ends of the distribution is reduced in favor of larger probability mass in the center.

The same conclusion can be reached by studying a summary measure of inequality. In studies of income distribution, a standard index of inequality is the Gini coefficient, ranging from 0, for perfect equality, to 1, when all income is concentrated on a single individual. The lower the Gini coefficient, the more equalitarian the distribution.[13] Figure 6.8 reports the impact of the bonus vote on our measure of voters' political inequality as measured by the Gini coefficient. In the CC data, inequality declines unambiguously: over all bootstrap samples in which the bonus vote allows the minority to win at least one election, inequality declines from a minimum of 90 percent of the samples (rule A) to a maximum of 98 percent (rule D). Across all bonus vote rules, the mean percentage decrease in the Gini coefficient is 12 to 13 percent. In the GS data, on the other hand, the bonus vote's effect on inequality is of inconsistent

13. The Gini coefficient is defined as twice the area between the 45-degree line and the curve plotting the cumulative distribution of income, with individuals ordered from lowest to highest income. The horizontal axis is the fraction of individuals, from 0 to 1, and the vertical axis is the fraction of total income, again ranging between 0 and 1. In a world of perfect equality, aggregate income increases at the same constant rate as each additional individual is counted; the curve matches exactly the 45-degree line, and the Gini coefficient is 0. At the other extreme, in a world in which all income is in the hands of a single person, aggregate income remains at 0 until this very last person is added; the curve remains at 0, until jumping to 1 with the last individual, and the Gini coefficient equals $2(0.5) = 1$.

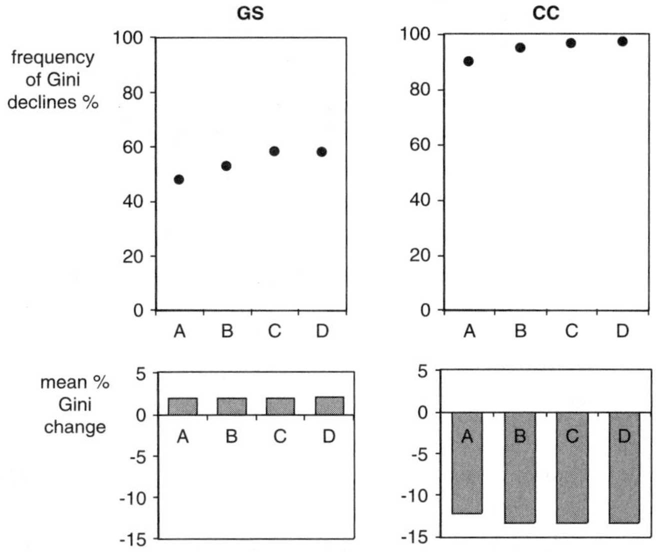

FIGURE 6.8 Impact of the bonus vote on voters' equality of representation. Percentage frequency of more equalitarian distributions of realized utility, and mean percentage decline in the Gini coefficient, relative to majority voting, when the minority wins at least one election.

sign and small magnitude. The Gini coefficient declines barely more than 50 percent of the time with rules B, C, and D, and barely less with rule A. The effects are quantitatively small: the mean percentage change in the coefficient is an increase of 2 percent.

The different results reflect the different roles of the bonus vote in the two data sets. In the GS data, the elections affected by the bonus vote (President and Alumni Affairs) are particularly close, with little difference in volume and intensity of support between the two candidates. The side benefiting from the bonus vote is not consistent across bootstrap samples, and, thus, the average impact of the bonus vote on equality of representation is small and similarly non consistent. In the CC data, on the other hand, the main role of the bonus vote is to overthrow the majority victory in the Academic Affairs election, on the strength of the more intense minority preferences. The distribution of preferences is sufficiently asymmetric to ensure that in the bootstrap samples the bonus vote consistently helps the same candidate. Since the final result is a positive, sizable improvement in equality, it must be that voters on the minority side in the Academic Affairs election are also disproportionately on the minority side in the other elections.[14]

6.3 Conclusions

As anticipated at the beginning of this chapter, in the student elections data we collected, storable votes perform well. When the margins of victory are small, they allow the minority to win occasionally, with no substantive effects on welfare and inequality if the two sides have preferences of similar intensity but with improvements in both if minority preferences are particularly intense. When the margins of victory are large, the bonus vote, predictably, has no impact. The qualitative evidence is quite strong: in the overwhelming majority of cases, if the bonus vote affects the outcome, it is associated with an improvement in welfare. The quantitative effect on welfare is difficult to judge, because there is no natural measure against which changes of a given magnitude can be evaluated, but a recurring regularity is that gains in welfare are not only much more frequent, but they are also consistently larger than the occasional declines. On the basis of this test, and in line with the spirit of the book, storable votes have both the potential to improve welfare and a certain robustness. As in the laboratory experiments, here, too, when conditions are not controlled and the environment faced by the voters is noisier and more confusing, their impact seems in line with the theory. As the theory has stressed, storable votes succeed in increasing equality of representation without costs, and in fact with gains, to efficiency. This remains, in my opinion, their most important function.

In large elections, storable votes should be tested in higher-stake contests, particularly in referendums, to which they are particularly well-suited. Using a new voting system in real elections is, appropriately,

14. The precise numbers reflected in Figure 6.8 are reported in Part II, together with 95 percent confidence intervals. An alternative measure of inequality – the ratio of the average utility of individuals at the bottom 20 percent of the utility distribution to average utility – yields identical conclusions, and is also reported in Part II.

difficult to do, and assembling an experimental data set rich enough to evaluate the system's performance statistically is probably impossible.[15] Survey methods, coupled with bootstrap resampling, are a more practical route. One of the goals of this chapter is also to suggest that the bootstrap methodology is ready to be exploited, easily and cheaply.

15. Laslier and Straeten (2008), for example, report on a very well-designed survey on the possible impact of approval voting on the French 2002 presidential elections. The study is fascinating but makes clear the difficulties associated with collecting new data on high-stakes real elections. Even as a survey, it would be neither easy nor cheap to duplicate.

7

Conclusions

Each chapter of this book has discussed reasons, both theoretical and empirical, to consider storable votes a promising idea. The theoretical models are very stark because the decision problem they analyze is complex even in simple circumstances. Yet they play a central role: they give us a basic understanding of storable votes and shape the hypotheses tested in the experiments. As argued in the Preface to this book, it is the slow and meticulous thinking required by the theory that brings unsuspected results to the surface: the different welfare costs of minority victories when the minority is or is not cohesive, the role of agenda control in transmitting information, and the surprisingly simple and robust results on the superiority of storable votes in referendums. The tightly controlled laboratory experiments fulfill their function, too. Not only do they allow rigorous tests of the theory, but they also provide direct evidence on the small welfare cost of subjects' strategic mistakes. This is something that only experiments can do convincingly. The theory can characterize the implications of equilibrium behavior but is much less well-suited to predicting the welfare costs of strategic errors. The problem, of course, is that we do not know *which* strategic mistakes individuals will make. In comparing two alternative rules, some small deviations from equilibrium behavior could be sufficient to reverse the rules' welfare ranking; or conversely, as in this book, apparently large mistakes – casting the "wrong" number of votes – can have negligible effects on welfare because a deeper logic is obeyed – here, monotonicity, or casting more votes at higher preference intensities. Finally, the study of the Columbia student elections provided the first step toward a test of storable votes in a setting in which preferences and information are not controlled or manipulated by the experimenter.

Each chapter concluded by discussing unanswered questions that require more thought and more testing. If the Hippocratic oath applies to institutional reform as much as it applies to human care – and how could it not? – then storable votes demand more study. Having built our intuition, the environments studied need to be generalized. How do storable votes perform when voters' information does not conform to the assumptions made in this book? When individuals know each others' preferences, for example, as may be true of small groups that meet regularly? When, on the contrary, information on others' preferences or on future proposals is so imprecise as to be unreliable? Or when information is asymmetric, and the committee chair alone knows others' preferences? How do storable votes perform when preferences are correlated over time or across proposals, as would in fact be the case in the Central Bank application that was mentioned more than once? How do they perform when the rules are slightly changed – for example, when voters are told the votes tally for each election but not the full distribution of remaining bonus votes among all other committee members, or when bonus votes expire and can be replenished over time? Most of these modifications lead to much more complicated models than those discussed here. However, the real problem is not the researcher's ability to solve complex models; it is the voters' likely behavior in a complicated strategic environment. Having acquired a basic understanding of storable votes' logic, I think that the promising direction lies less in identifying the voters' theoretically optimal strategy than in evaluating the robustness of the outcomes to different plausible rules of behavior. As in the study of the students' elections, we should posit multiple, simple rules of thumb describing individuals' voting behavior and analyze them in environments of increasing complexity. Computer simulations can illustrate the outcomes of different behaviors and compare the results to the simpler strategic environment of majority voting.

At the same time, we should begin to think of storable votes in concrete applications. The most immediate is to simultaneous referendums, where storable votes could be applied simply by adding a bonus vote to existing ballots. Here, too, the existing results should be complemented by computer simulations with richer, less stylized preference structures and by serious thoughts about the possible manipulation of the slate of proposals.[1]

Storable votes can also be studied in other contexts, in particular in situations in which the simplicity and ease of majority voting runs counter to the institution's desire to protect the minority. A prominent example is international organizations, where the absence of external enforcement makes the protection of minority interests necessary to the very existence of the organization. Countries fear external constraints on their sovereignty and demand disproportionate influence on common decisions. This holds true for politically and economically strong countries – think of the United States' jealously guarded veto power in the International Monetary Fund, or the United Kingdom's consistently maintained opt-out clauses in the European Union – and for weaker ones, for which acknowledged gains from participation mix awkwardly with concerns about foreign interference – think of the disputes about voting weights in the European Union or the hurdles of World Trade Organization negotiations. In addition, the entry of new members and the changing political influence of growing countries require constant renegotiation of all members' decision-making weights. The tension here is that while vetoes and disputes over voting rights are causes of inertia and nontransparent bargaining, countries simply would not enter the organization without such protections.

Consider, for example, the European Union, governed since December 2009 by the Treaty of Lisbon. The treaty was born of the failed attempt at an EU constitution, and its objective remains to help the development of an EU political identity and reduce national obstacles to common decision-making. To this end, it eliminates a number of national vetoes and, starting in 2014, reforms qualified majority thresholds, from the existing Byzantine system of voting weights to a more transparent double-majority requirement (55 percent of the member states representing at least 65 percent of the population in

1. Whether storable votes would make control of the agenda in large elections a larger or smaller problem is not clear. With storable votes, manipulating the agenda effectively requires identifying groups with common interests across different issues and maintaining the cohesion of the groups, in an environment where voting is anonymous.

the Union). The reform has been accompanied by a lively debate about expected changes in individual countries' voting power and about the influence of the double-majority system on the prospects for the possible future accession of Turkey, a very populous country. It is clear that the wish to streamline decision-making procedures is coexisting only with some difficulty with the necessary protection of national sovereignty, and that such protection will continue to be object of renegotiation as the membership and the responsibilities of the Union change over time.[2]

The difficulty exists not only in expanding organizations but also when the membership is constant but political and economic realities change, and countries' international influence rises and falls through the years. The International Monetary Fund and the Security Council of the United Nations are classic examples in which changes in the world's political and economic landscape have led to recurring calls for governance reform.

Voting weights alone do not determine decision-making power, an observation that is particularly appropriate to the elaborate rules of international organisms.[3] Yet, all else equal, such power can only increase with an increase in weights, whose added symbolic meaning should not be discounted in world politics. If we use voting weights as shorthand for influence in international organizations, we have easy examples of

2. National vetoes are preserved in the areas of taxation, social protection and workers' rights, foreign policy, and defense. It is sometimes stated that voting rights in international organizations are of minor importance because decisions are de facto taken by consensus. But the negotiating power of different national representatives is strongly affected by their ability to see through or bloc decisions: whether or not unanimity is recorded at the voting stage, the selection and content of the measures brought to the vote reflect relative national power, including voting power. Presumably, disputes about voting rights would not take place unless countries considered them important.

3. Even ignoring deeper political realities and alliances, voting power is not identified by the number of votes a member holds, but by the full distribution of votes, together with the majority threshold. For example, consider countries A, B, and C holding 40, 20, and 40 votes, respectively, and suppose that the majority threshold is 50 percent, or 50 votes. Country B holds half as many votes as the other countries, but has in fact identical power: exactly as A and C, it loses a decision only if both of the others agree. Now suppose country D is admitted with 20 votes. The 50 percent threshold means that 60 votes are now required for approval. Together, the two large countries A and C can bloc any decision, but the small countries B and D, either together or in alliance with one large country, never can. The relative power of country B has declined. B would demand that voting weigths be renegotiated. Kirman and Widgren (1995) provides a clear discussion of voting power indexes (as applied to the European Union).

existing imbalances in favor of Western countries. In October 2010, the combined voting shares of China and India in the International Monetary Fund were closely comparable to the combined voting shares of Belgium and the Netherlands. At the end of that month, the twenty largest economies agreed in principle to a reallocation of voting shares toward underrepresented countries and toward China in particular. The implementation of the reform, however, is postponed to 2012, and the United States and Europe (if Europe acts collectively) will maintain their veto power. In the Security Council, the five permanent members holding veto power – the victorious allies of the Second World War: the United States, Russia, China, the UK, and France–have remained unchanged since the creation of the United Nations. Several plans for reform have been presented and debated over the years, and the existing powers have endorsed the permanent membership of one or another prominent candidate. Yet no reform has been enacted so far, and the sclerosis of the Security Council permanent membership has fed doubts about the relevance and legitimacy of the United Nations.[4]

Storable votes are not going to resolve all trade-offs over cooperation and sovereignty in the EU, the IMF, or the UN Security Council. But they do add one way of thinking about possible solutions. Conceptually, they lie between vetoes and majority voting, and they allow countries to cast "bigger" votes on questions they consider priorities. Over essential matters – war and peace, defense, foreign policy – vetoes seem inescapable, and probably appropriate. For more routine decisions, a well-designed system of storable votes can mitigate the workings of simple majority.

4. The G20 have agreed to a reform of the IMF that will double the IMF's quotas, which determine voting rights, and make China its third largest member, after the U.S. and Japan. China, India, and Brazil will all rank among the ten largest members, and Europe will renounce two of its seats on the 24-member Executive Board. (See: "G20 agrees historic reform of IMF," *Financial Times*, October 23, 2010, but also "Accord on IMF board masks lack of progress," *Financial Times*, October 25, 2010.) In the Security Council, four countries–Japan, Germany, India, and Brazil–have been identified as priority candidates for an expansion of the permanent seats. (For recent U.S. and UK endorsements of seats for India and Brazil, see "Obama calls for top India role at UN," *Financial Times*, November 8, 2010, and "UK backs Brazil bid for UN security council seat," *Financial Times*, November 9, 2010.) There has also been call for an African presence among permanent members, and some debate about allocating permanent seats generally not to countries but to geographical regions.

For example, as the European Union progresses hesitantly toward a more federal structure, the underlying ethical issue is the balance between the representation of individual countries and the representation of the Union's citizens, according to some principle approaching one-person, one-vote. A system of storable votes could be designed to address this tension: each member country could be granted an equal number of regular votes, while the number of bonus votes would give weight to the country's population. The double-majority requirement in the Treaty of Lisbon affects negatively the relative representation of citizens of middle-sized countries – countries too small to count for much in achieving the majority threshold in terms of total population and too big to benefit from the equal country weights when counting a majority of all member countries. With storable votes, this seems unlikely to happen, because different countries would be expected to use their bonus votes over different decisions. The design is flexible: depending on the ratio of regular to bonus votes, population size can be given more or less relevance.

In other applications, the criteria could be different. For instance, in the IMF, countries' voting weights are linked to membership quotas, stressing the connection between voting power and economic power. Bonus votes could be proportional to a country's income, while regular votes, equal for all, would guarantee some voice to poorer countries. My goal here is not to recommend a specific set of criteria or a specific number of votes, but to suggest that storable votes provide room to take these considerations into account. The hope is that by allowing for the explicit weighing of multiple criteria, storable votes may move institutions toward more transparent rules, favoring both the institutions' legitimacy and their evolution. Of course, more work is needed to see how such designs might operate. The analysis in this book has treated all voters equally: how large can asymmetries in bonus votes be while still preserving the desirable properties of the system? How can different designs best be implemented in practice?

If the indisputable privileges of national sovereignty must be protected in international organizations, federal institutions may be more immediate grounds for storable votes. Here, disparities in economic conditions are limited, and a superior entity providing enforcement exists – the federal government and its courts. The classical question is the stronger protection of minorities that is demanded of a federal system – whether a minority of dissenting states or regions, or a minority of the population living in less densely populated areas. The contradictions inherent in providing such protection are well demonstrated by the current debate on the reform of the U.S. Senate. After dilatory tactics became more common at the end of the nineteenth century, the Senate introduced rules allowing a supermajority of Senate members – currently 60 out of 100 – to demand that debate on a measure be closed, and the measure brought to a vote. While the use of a filibuster – the threat to hold up a vote by prolonging debate – was relatively rare up to the end of the 1980, it has now become an acceptable weapon of party politics, de facto raising the majority threshold to 60 percent. The result has been the increased difficulty of passing legislation.[5] There are numerous proposals for reform: for example, reducing the supermajority threshold in successive attempts at ending debate; making the threshold depend on whether either the minority or the majority position is bipartisan; requiring the physical presence of 41 opposing senators to prevent a vote; or allowing the majority to force the vote as long as there is no active discussion on the floor. All proposals seek a compromise between favoring debate on the majority's proposals and protecting the minority, on one hand, and still subjecting most decisions to simple majority rule, on the other. All proposals also seem arbitrary, shaped by familiarity with the institution's rules and norms but lacking an organizing principle beyond expediency. Together with plausible rules ensuring sufficient time for studying and debating bills, a well-crafted system of storable votes would allow the minority to prevail occasionally, at the cost of accepting certain defeat on other decisions. In the strongly partisan atmosphere of

5. The average per-congress number of motions to end debate in the Senate in the five congresses from 1980 to 1989 was 41, versus 131 in the last two congresses (2007–2008, and 2009-October 2010) ((http://www.senate.gov/pagelayout/reference/cloture_motions/clotureCounts.htm). Political scientists have estimated that in the 1960s approximately 8 percent of major Senate bills were targets of filibusters, as opposed to 70 percent in the years 2000–2010 ("The Rise of the Filibuster: An Interview with Barbara Sinclair," December 26, 2009, in Ezra Klein's blog on *The Washington Post* web site: http://voices.washingtonpost.com/ezra-klein/2009/12/the_right_of_the_filibuster_an.html.) Binder and Smith (1997), and Koger (2010) present more data and discussion. Ezra Klein's blog has been very active in the filibuster debate, as have been other blogs, for example *Politico.com*, and *themonkeycage.org*.

the U.S. Senate, the scenario would approach the systematic minority model studied in Chapter 3. Clearly, the storable votes scheme would need to be carefully designed. The possibility of manipulating the agenda here becomes central: could the majority deplete the minority's stock of bonus votes by submitting more bills? Or should bonus votes accrue with each new bill, as opposed to being granted once for all at the start of the legislative period? Could the majority counter a defeat by repackaging the same controversial provisions in a new bill? Or are there plausible procedural rules that would prevent this strategy?

Again, storable votes cannot be proposed at this stage as the solution to the Senate's deadlock. Their intuitive appeal is strong, however; their theory is well-founded, and tests of the first models have all been very positive. Storable votes can be proposed as a possible component to the search for a solution. It is too early to say how storable votes should be designed when embodied in specific existing institutions. It is not too early to propose and discuss the principle behind them: the possibility of using voters' own knowledge about their priorities to induce them to express truthfully the intensity of their preferences, and in so doing allowing the minority to win occasionally, with little cost to aggregate decision-making and while treating everyone equally. Work is needed to see how this principle can best be realized in different applications. It is the hope of this book that such work will be encouraged by the results presented here.

Part 2

The Proofs

I

The Simple Logic of Storable Votes

1.1 The Formal Model—Version 1

Consider a committee of n voters, meeting to decide whether to implement T distinct proposals, $\{P_1, ..P_T\}$, each of which can either pass or fail. The T proposals constitute the known, fixed agenda of the meeting, and the committee votes on the proposals sequentially. Each member i of the committee has preferences over each proposal P_t summarized by a cardinal valuation v_{it}. Valuations v_{it} are independently and identically distributed both across proposals and across individuals according to the distribution $G(\mathrm{v})$ with support $[-1, 1]$, symmetric around 0. A negative valuation means that the voter is against the proposal; a positive valuation means that he is in favor. Call voter i's absolute valuation $v_{it} \equiv |\mathrm{v}_{it}|$ i's *intensity* (or *value*) over proposal P_t. For each proposal P_t, voter i receives utility $u_{it} = v_{it}$ if the decision goes in his preferred direction, and 0 otherwise. Voter i's utility from the entire meeting, U_i, equals $\sum_{t=1}^{T} u_{it}$.

In addition to a regular vote over every proposal, each committee member is given one indivisible bonus vote equivalent to B regular votes, with $B > 0$. Each proposal is decided in the direction that receives more votes; in case of a tie, a coin is flipped. When voting on any proposal, a member knows $\{\mathrm{v}_{i1}, ..\mathrm{v}_{iT}\}$, his own valuations over all proposals, but does not know others' valuations over any of the proposals. The independence of the valuations and the distribution G from which they are drawn are common knowledge. After voting, the total number of votes cast for and against a proposal is commonly known, and thus so is the number of voters still endowed with bonus votes, a number denoted by l_t. The state of the game at t is summarized by (l_t, t). The focus is on symmetric Perfect Bayesian equilibria in weakly undominated strategies.

Proposition 1.1 Equilibrium. (1) For all T, n , G, and B, there exists an equilibrium in which each voter i casts his bonus vote on P_t, if and only if $v_{it} = \max\{v_i\}$. (2) For some T, n, G, and B, no other symmetric equilibrium in weakly undominated strategies exists.

Call Ev the expectation of the absolute valuation, or the expected intensity, and $Ev_{(T)}$ the Tth order statistic among each voter's T absolute valuations, or the expected highest-intensity draw. Finally, call EV_0 ex ante utility with storable votes, and EW_0 ex ante utility with simple majority voting, both evaluated before valuations are drawn, or, equivalently, before the agenda is specified, but in the knowledge of T, n, G, and B, and of equilibrium strategies. Then:

Proposition 1.2 Efficiency. For all T, n, and G, there exists a range of strictly positive values for B, $\mathcal{B}(n)$, such that for all $B \in \mathcal{B}(n)$: (i) If n is even, $EV_0 > EW_0$. (ii) If n is odd, $EV_0 > EW_0$ if $Ev_{(T)}/Ev > [T(n+1)]/[T(n-1)+2]$.

1.2 Proof of Proposition 1.1

The two results in the proposition are proved sequentially. (1) To verify that the strategies described are an equilibrium, consider i's problem at any time t, when i still holds the bonus vote. Voter i must decide whether to cast the bonus vote on P_t or wait for a future proposal P_{t+k}, $k \in \{1, .., T-t\}$. Recall that $l_t - 1$ is the number of voters other than i left with the bonus vote at t. Call p_{Bs} (p_{1s}) the probability of obtaining the desired outcome when casting $1+B$ (1) votes on proposal P_s, and π_s the probability that a voter holding the bonus vote and other than i casts the bonus vote on proposal P_s. Given the symmetry of G around zero, at any s the probability of obtaining the desired outcome when casting the bonus vote depends exclusively on the number of other voters who also cast the bonus vote. Thus:

$$p_{Bt}^{t} = \sum_{j=0}^{l_t-1} \binom{l_t - 1}{j} (\pi_t^t)^j (1 - \pi_t^t)^{l_t-1-j} p_B(j),$$

where the superscript t indicates the time at which the probability is evaluated, and $p_B(j)$ is the probability of obtaining the desired outcome when j other voters cast the bonus vote and the remaining $n - 1 - j$ do not. In the candidate equilibrium $\pi_t^t = 1/(T - t + 1)$. Thus:

$$p_{Bt}^{t} = \sum_{j=0}^{l_t-1} \binom{l_t - 1}{j} \left(\frac{1}{T - t + 1}\right)^j \left(\frac{T - t}{T - t + 1}\right)^{l_t-1-j} p_B(j). \quad (1.1)$$

Similarly, evaluated at t, the probability of obtaining the desired outcome when casting the bonus vote at $t + k$ is given by:

$$p_{Bt+k}^{t} = \sum_{j=0}^{l_t-1} \binom{l_t - 1}{j} \left[\prod_{s=0}^{k-1} (1 - \pi_{t+s}^t)\pi_{t+k}^t\right]^j \times \left[1 - \prod_{s=0}^{k-1} (1 - \pi_{t+s}^t)\pi_{t+k}^t\right]^{l_t-1-j} p_B(j). \quad (1.2)$$

But in the candidate equilibrium $\pi_{t+s}^t = 1/(T - t - s + 1)$. The probabilities in the square brackets of equation (1.2) simplify, and we obtain:

$$p_{Bt+k}^{t} = \sum_{j=0}^{l_t-1} \binom{l_t - 1}{j} \left(\frac{1}{T - t + 1}\right)^j \left(\frac{T - t}{T - t + 1}\right)^{l_t-1-j} p_B(j) = p_{Bt}^t. \quad (1.3)$$

Following the same logic, we can show $p_{1t}^t = p_{1t+k}^t$. At time t voter i decides whether to cast the bonus vote on P_t or P_{t+k} by evaluating the difference in expected utility from the two actions: $Eu_i(P_t) - Eu_i(P_{t+k}) = v_t(p_{Bt}^t - p_{1t}^t) - v_{t+k}(p_{Bt+k}^t - p_{1t+k}^t) = (p_B^t - p_1^t)(v_t - v_{t+k})$. Since $p_B^t \geq p_1^t$, casting the bonus vote on P_t if $v_t > v_{t+k}$ for all $k \in \{1, .., T - t\}$ is a best response strategy for i at all t: the candidate equilibrium is indeed an equilibrium.

(2) To establish part (2), note first that the strategy described in (1) is a best response for *all* other voters' strategies that result in $p^t_{Bs} = p^t_B$ and $p^t_{1s} = p^t_1$ for all s. But with iid valuations, all strategies that depend exclusively on relative intensities have this property. Thus, no strategy of the type: "cast the bonus vote on the kth-highest intensity with probability π_k" can be an equilibrium unless $k = 1$ and $\pi_k = 1$. If another equilibrium exists, it must involve strategies such that voters differentiate among the proposals on the basis of their order. For the purposes of the proposition, it is sufficient to show that no such equilibrium exists for specific values of n, T, and B. Suppose, for example, $n = 3$ and $B = 1$, and consider a candidate equilibrium where all voters but i cast the bonus vote on some proposal P_r with probability $\pi^1_r = q_r$. With no loss of generality, suppose $q_r > 1/T$. There must then exist at least one proposal P_s for which $\pi^1_s = q_s < 1/T$. With $n = 3$ and $B = 1$, $p^1_{1t} = 3/4 - [q_t(1 - q_t)]/4$, and $p^1_{Bt} = 3/4 + [(1 - q_t)^2]/8$. Voter i's best response is to cast the bonus vote on P_r over P_t if $v_r/v_t > (p^1_{Bt} - p^1_{1t})/(p^1_{Br} - p^1_{1r})$ for all t, and, similarly, on P_s over P_t if $v_s/v_t > (p^1_{Bt} - p^1_{1t})/(p^1_{Bs} - p^1_{1s})$ for all t. It is easy to verify that if $q_r > q_s$, $(p^1_{Br} - p^1_{1r}) < (p^1_{Bs} - p^1_{1s})$. Thus, if voter i plays his best response strategy, he must be expected to cast the bonus vote on P_r with some probability $\pi^1_{ri} < \pi^1_{si}$, contradicting the initial conjecture. No symmetric equilibrium exists for $q_r \neq 1/T$ for any r. ■

1.3 Proof of Proposition 1.2

By part (1) of Proposition 1.1, $p_{Bt} = p_B$ and $p_{1t} = p_1$ for all t, and:

$$EV_0 = p_B Ev_{(T)} + p_1 \sum_{s=1}^{T-1} Ev_{(s)} = (p_B - p_1)Ev_{(T)} + Tp_1 Ev. \qquad (1.4)$$

With simple majority, ex ante utility EW_0 is given by:

$$EW_0 = TpEv, \qquad (1.5)$$

where p is the probability of obtaining one's desired outcome when every voter casts a single vote. With n even:

$$p = \sum_{z=n/2}^{n-1} \left[\binom{n-1}{z} \left(\frac{1}{2}\right)^{n-1} \right] + \binom{n-1}{\frac{n}{2}-1} \left(\frac{1}{2}\right)^{n-1} \frac{1}{2}$$

and with n odd:

$$p = \sum_{z=(n-1)/2}^{n-1} \left[\binom{n-1}{z} \left(\frac{1}{2}\right)^{n-1} \right].$$

The probabilities p_B and p_1 in (1.4) depend on the value of the bonus vote. The proof proceeds by verifying the proposition at the smallest value of the bonus vote for which the voting mechanism differs from simple majority voting, and thus $p_B \neq p \neq p_1$.

(1) Consider first the case of n even. Any positive value of the bonus vote, no matter how small, affects the outcome with positive probability: there is always a positive probability that the voters are exactly split and that one more voter on one side than on the other casts the bonus vote. Consider then a value of the bonus vote small enough that as long as the two groups are not equally split, the bonus votes cannot modify the outcome. This threshold is defined by the condition that a minority of size $n/2 - 1$ casting all bonus votes does not win over a majority of size $n/2 + 1$ casting no bonus votes, or:

$$\left(\frac{n}{2} - 1\right)(1 + B) < \left(\frac{n}{2} + 1\right) \Longleftrightarrow B < \frac{4}{n-2}.$$

We can now derive p_B and p_1 for all values of $B \in (0, 4/(n-2))$. The only difference with respect to simple majority voting can arise when the voters are split into groups of equal size. In this case, simple majority yields a tie, but the existence of the bonus vote creates many possible configurations of voting choices for which one side strictly wins. Consider the problem from the point of view of voter i. It turns out to be simpler to isolate a second voter j on the opposite side of i. Whenever voter j casts the same number of votes as i, the probability that i's side wins equals the probability that j's side wins, and the expected deviations from simple majority cancel out. The relevant cases are those where i and j cast a different number of votes. In calculating p_B then, the deviation from p occurs when j does not cast the bonus vote. Call M_i the number of voters on i's side who vote $1 + B$, ignoring i, and similarly M_j the number of voters on j's side who vote $1 + B$, ignoring j. It is immediate that i's side wins if $M_i > M_j - 1$. Similarly, i's side ties if $M_i = M_j - 1$, and loses if $M_i < M_j - 1$. Thus:

$$p_B = p + \left(\frac{1}{2}\right)^{n-1} \binom{n-1}{n/2} \left(\frac{T-1}{T}\right) \times \left[\frac{1}{2} prob(M_i > M_j - 1) - \frac{1}{2} prob(M_i < M_j - 1)\right].$$

where $(T-1)/T$ is the probability that voter j casts a single vote, and the probabilities inside the square brackets are multiplied by $(1/2)$ because, absent the bonus vote, the relevant events would result in a tie. But $prob(M_i > M_j - 1) = prob(M_i = M_j) + prob(M_i > M_j)$, and $prob(M_i < M_j - 1) = prob(M_i < M_j) - prob(M_i = M_j - 1)$. And since $prob(M_i > M_j) = prob(M_i < M_j)$, we can write:

$$p_B = p + \left(\frac{1}{2}\right)^{n} \binom{n-1}{n/2} \left(\frac{T-1}{T}\right) \times \left[prob(M_i = M_j) + prob(M_i = M_j - 1)\right]. \tag{1.6}$$

Similarly,

$$p_1 = p - \left(\frac{1}{2}\right)^{n} \binom{n-1}{n/2} \left(\frac{1}{T}\right) \left[prob(M_i = M_j) + prob(M_i = M_j + 1)\right]. \tag{1.7}$$

The problem is symmetric, and thus $prob(M_i = M_j - 1) = prob(M_j = M_i - 1)$: the expressions in square brackets in (1.6) and (1.7) are identical. Call them C. We can now write:

$$p_B - p_1 = \left(\frac{1}{2}\right)^{n} \binom{n-1}{n/2} C \tag{1.8}$$

$$p - p_1 = \left(\frac{1}{2}\right)^{n} \binom{n-1}{n/2} \left(\frac{1}{T}\right) C. \tag{1.9}$$

We know from (1.4) that:

$$EV_0 > EW_0 \iff Ev_{(T)}(p_B - p_1) > TEv(p - p_1). \tag{1.10}$$

Substituting (1.8) and (1.9), we obtain:

$$EV_0 > EW_0 \Longleftrightarrow Ev_{(T)} > TEv\left(\frac{1}{T}\right) \text{ or } Ev_{(T)} > Ev,$$

which is always satisfied. We can conclude that if n is even, ex ante efficiency strictly improves over simple majority voting for all values of $B \in (0, 4/(n-2))$. Note that if $n = 2$, the value of the bonus vote is unconstrained.

(2) Consider now the case of n odd. With n odd, there are strictly positive values of the bonus vote that never alter the voting outcome from what it would be with simple majority. These are values such that when the voters are divided into two groups with opposite preferences of sizes as similar as possible ($(n-1)/2$ on one side, and $(n-1)/2 + 1$ on the other), the minority loses even when all voters on the minority side cast their bonus vote, and none of the voters on the majority side does so. Or:

$$\left(\frac{n-1}{2}\right)(1+B) < \left(\frac{n-1}{2}+1\right) \Leftrightarrow B < \frac{2}{n-1}.$$

For all $B < 2/(n-1)$ and n odd, then trivially $EV_0 \equiv EW_0$.[1] Suppose then $B \geq 2/(n-1)$, but suppose also that the bonus vote is small enough not to matter in any other possible configuration of votes. The next smallest threshold is given by a value of B such that when the two groups with opposite preferences are of sizes $(n-1)/2$, and $(n-1)/2 + 1$, and none of the majority voters uses the bonus vote while all but one of the minority voters do so, the result is a tie. That is,

$$\left(\frac{n-1}{2}\right)(1+B) - B = \frac{n+1}{2} \Leftrightarrow B = \frac{2}{n-3}.$$

Suppose then $B \in [2/(n-1), 2/(n-3)]$. From the point of view of voter i, when casting the bonus vote the probability of obtaining the desired outcome differs from the simple majority case only if he finds

---

1. A simple example makes the point clearly. Suppose $n = 3$. Then for all $B < 1$, a voter can win only if at least one of the other two voters agrees with him, exactly as in the case of simple majority voting.

himself in a minority of size $(n-1)/2$ and all of the voters on his side cast the bonus vote, while none of the majority voters do so. Or:

$$p_B = p + \left(\frac{1}{2}\right)^{n-1+I_{tie}} \binom{n-1}{(n+1)/2} \left(\frac{1}{T}\right)^{(n-3)/2} \left(\frac{T-1}{T}\right)^{(n+1)/2}, \tag{1.11}$$

where $I_{tie} = 1$ if $B = 2/(n-1)$, and 0 if $B \in (2/(n-1), 2/(n-3))$.

Similarly, when casting a single vote, the difference with respect to simple majority comes from the possibility of losing, even when belonging to the majority, if all minority voters cast the bonus vote and none of the majority voters do so:

$$p_1 = p - \left(\frac{1}{2}\right)^{n-1+I_{tie}} \binom{n-1}{(n-1)/2} \left(\frac{1}{T}\right)^{(n-1)/2} \left(\frac{T-1}{T}\right)^{(n-1)/2}, \tag{1.12}$$

where the difference in the binomial terms in (1.11) and (1.12) reflects the different size of the two groups, and the fact that p_B in (1.11) is calculated supposing that voter i is in the minority group, and p_1 in (1.12) supposing i is in the majority. Hence:

$$p_B - p_1 = \left(\frac{1}{2}\right)^{n-1+I_{tie}} \left(\frac{1}{T}\right)^{(n-1)/2} \left(\frac{T-1}{T}\right)^{(n-1)/2} \times \left[\binom{n-1}{(n+1)/2}(T-1) + \binom{n-1}{(n-1)/2}\right]. \tag{1.13}$$

Substituting (1.12) and (1.13) in (1.10):

$$EV_0 > EW_0 \Longleftrightarrow D\left[Ev_{(T)}\left(\frac{T(n-1)+2}{n+1}\right) - TEv\right] > 0,$$

where:

$$D \equiv \left(\frac{1}{2}\right)^{n-1+I_{tie}} \left(\frac{1}{T}\right)^{(n-1)/2} \left(\frac{T-1}{T}\right)^{(n-1)/2} \binom{n-1}{(n-1)/2} > 0.$$

Or:

$$EV_0 - EW_0 > 0 \Longleftrightarrow \frac{Ev_{(T)}}{Ev} > \frac{T(n+1)}{T(n-1)+2}.$$

This is the condition in Proposition 1.2. ■

1.4 Construction of the Figures in Chapter 1

1.4.1 (a) Derivation of p_1, p_B for arbitrary B

Consider the problem from the point of view of voter i. The expected voting behavior of the other voters is identical over all proposals. Consider then a proposal P, and call π the ex ante probability that any voter casts the bonus vote on that proposal (where in equilibrium $\pi = 1/T$). Call J the number of other voters who cast their bonus votes. Excluding i, the total number of votes cast in the election is $n - 1 + BJ$. Call M_i (m_i) the number of voters on i's side who vote $1 + B$ (1) over P, and thus $m_i + (1 + B)M_i$ the total number of votes on i's side, ignoring i, and $n - 1 + BJ - m_i - (1 + B)M_i$ the total number of votes on the opposite side. If voter i casts only his regular vote, for any M_i and J, voter i's side wins strictly if: $m_i + (1 + B)M_i + 1 > n - 1 + BJ - m_i - (1 + B)M_i$, or $m_i > [n + B(J - 2M_i)]/2 - 1 - M_i$; and ties if $m_i = [n + B(J - 2M_i)]/2 - 1 - M_i$. Taking into account that for generic n, J, and B, $[n + B(J - 2M_i)]/2$ need not be an integer, we can write:

$$p_1 = \sum_{J=0}^{n-1} \binom{n-1}{J} \sum_{M_i=0}^{J} \binom{J}{M_i} \left[\sum_{m_i=k}^{n-1-J} \binom{n-1-J}{m_i} + \frac{I_I}{2} \binom{n-1-J}{\widetilde{k}} \right] \times \pi^J (1-\pi)^{n-1-J} (1/2)^{n-1}, \tag{1.14}$$

with:

$$k \equiv I^{-}\left[\frac{n + B(J - 2M_i)}{2}\right] - M_i$$

where $I^{-}[x]$ is the largest integer smaller than x;

$$\widetilde{k} \equiv \frac{n + B(J - 2M_i)}{2} - 1 - M_i,$$

$$I_I = \begin{cases} 1 \text{ if } \widetilde{k} \text{ is an integer} \\ 0 \text{ otherwise} \end{cases}.$$

If voter i casts his bonus vote, then for any M_i and J, voter i's side wins strictly if: $m_i + (1 + B)M_i + 1 + B > n - 1 + BJ - m_i - (1 + B)M_i$, or

$m_i > [n + B(J - 1 - 2M_i)]/2 - 1 - M_i$; and ties if $m_i = [n + B(J - 1 - 2M_i)]/2 - 1 - M_i$. We can write:

$$p_B = \sum_{J=0}^{n-1} \binom{n-1}{J} \sum_{M_i=0}^{J} \binom{J}{M_i} \left[\sum_{m_i=k_B}^{n-1-J} \binom{n-1-J}{m_i} + \frac{I_I}{2} \binom{n-1-J}{\widetilde{k}_B} \right]$$
$$\times \pi^J (1-\pi)^{n-1-J} (1/2)^{n-1}, \qquad (1.15)$$

with:

$$k_B \equiv I^- \left[\frac{n + B(J - 1 - 2M_i)}{2} \right] - M_i,$$

where, again, $I[x]$ is the largest integer smaller than x;

$$\widetilde{k}_B \equiv \frac{n + B(J - 1 - 2M_i)}{2} - 1 - M_i;$$

$$I_I = \begin{cases} 1 \text{ if } \widetilde{k}_B \text{ is an integer} \\ 0 \text{ otherwise} \end{cases}.$$

1.4.2 Efficiency

The efficient mechanism resolves each election in favor of the side with higher aggregate intensity. Consider for example the case $n = 2$. For each proposal, half of the time the two voters agree, and each expects utility equal to his expected intensity Ev. Half of the time they disagree, and in the efficient resolution a voter wins only if his intensity is higher than the other voter's. If v is distributed according to distribution function F, with density f, for each proposal the expected utility from the efficient allocation is:

$$EV_0^*(2) = \frac{1}{2} Ev + \frac{1}{2} \left(\int_0^1 \int_{v_j}^1 v_i f(v_i) dv_i f(v_j) dv_j \right). \qquad (1.16)$$

The logic remains identical for an arbitrary number of voters n, although the expression becomes cumbersome as all possible partitions of the group into two sides with opposite preferences must be taken into account.

If F is uniform over [0, 1], however, the expression can be simplified, and expected first best efficiency is given by:

$$EV_0^* = (1/2)^{n-1}\left[1/2 + \sum_{k=0}^{n-2}\binom{n-1}{k}\left(\int_0^k (1/2)h(n-1,x)dx + \int_k^{k+1}\int_{x-k}^1 vdvh(n-1,x)dx\right)\right], \quad (1.17)$$

where $h(n-1, x)$ is the density function of a sum of $n-1$ independent variables, each distributed according to F, or:

$$h(n-1,x) = \sum_{k=0}^{n-1}(-1)^k\binom{n-1}{k}(x-k)^{n-2}Sign[x-k]\frac{1}{2(n-2)!} \quad (1.18)$$

In contrast to storable votes, the expected efficient payoff has no temporal dimension: given independent and identical distributions of intensities, expected utility under efficiency is the same for all proposals. The expected utility from a sequence of T proposals is simply the sum of T one-proposal expected utilities.

2

Storing Votes over Time

2.1 The Formal Model—Version 2

Consider a committee of n voters, meeting to decide whether to implement T distinct proposals, $\{P_1, ..P_T\}$, each of which can either pass or fail. The committee votes on the proposals over time. Each member i of the committee has preferences over each proposal P_t summarized by a cardinal valuation v_{it}. Valuations v_{it} are independently and identically distributed both across proposals and across individuals according to the distribution $G(\mathrm{v})$ with support $[-1, 1]$, symmetric around 0. A negative valuation means that the voter is against the proposal; a positive valuation means that he is in favor. Call voter i's absolute valuation over proposal P_t: $|\mathrm{v}_{it}| \equiv v_{it}$, i's intensity, or value, over P_t and $\boldsymbol{v}_t$ the vector of individuals' intensities, or values, over P_t. For each proposal P_t, voter i receives utility $u_{it} = v_{it}$ if the decision goes in his preferred direction, and 0 otherwise. Voter i's utility from the entire meeting, U_i, equals $\sum_{t=1}^{T} u_{it}$.

In addition to a regular vote over every proposal, each committee member is given a stock of B_0 bonus votes that can be cast in any manner the voter sees fit, where B_0 is an integer, and each bonus vote is equivalent to a regular vote. Each proposal is decided in the direction that receives more votes, including bonus votes; in case of a tie, a coin is flipped. When voting on proposal P_t, a member knows v_{it}, his own valuation over the proposal, but does not know either others' valuations over any of the proposals or his own valuations over proposals that will be voted upon later. The independence of the valuations and the distribution G from which they are drawn are common knowledge, as is the number of bonus votes still available to each voter when proposal P_t is called to a vote, a tuple denoted by $\mathbf{B}_t$.

The set of actions available to individual i voting on proposal P_t is denoted by X_{it} and equals all feasible numbers of votes between 1, the regular vote, and $1 + B_{it}$. The analysis focuses on symmetric Perfect Bayesian equilibria in weakly undominated strategies. It ignores history-dependent strategies and concentrates on strategies such that the number of votes each individual chooses to cast each period, x_{it}, depends only on the individual's intensity of preferences, v_{it}, and on the state of the game at t, that is, on the profile of bonus votes each voter has still available, $\mathbf{B}_t$, and the number of remaining periods, $T - t$. The state of the game is denoted by $(\mathbf{B}_t, t)$, and strategies by $x_{it}(v_{it}, \mathbf{B}_t, t)$. Equilibrium strategies have the following properties:

Proposition 2.1 Monotonicity. Call a strategy *monotonic* if, at a given state, the number of votes cast x_{it} is monotonically increasing in the intensity of preferences v_{it}. For any number of voters n, horizon length T, and state $(\mathbf{B}_t, t)$, all best-response strategies are monotonic.

Proposition 2.2 Equilibrium. The game has a Perfect Bayesian equilibrium in pure strategies. All equilibrium strategies are monotone cut-point strategies: at any state $(\mathbf{B}_t, t)$ and for any voter i with $B_{it} + 1$ available votes, there exists a set of cut-points $\{c_{i1}(\mathbf{B}_t, t), c_{i2}(\mathbf{B}_t, t), \ldots, \}$, $0 = c_{i0} \leq c_{i1} \leq \ldots \leq c_{iB_{it}+1} = 1$, such that i will cast x votes if and only if $v_{it} \in (c_{ix-1}, c_{ix}]$.

Proposition 2.3 Welfare. Call $EV_0(B_0)$ a voter's ex ante expected utility at time 0, before the realization of any valuation, when votes are storable and each voter has a stock of B_0 bonus votes. Call EW_0 the corresponding utility with simple majority voting. Then: (i) For $n = 2$ and all G, B_0, and $T > 1$, $EV_0(B_0) > EW_0$, with $EV_0(B_0)/EW_0$ monotonically increasing in T. (ii) For all n, G, B_0, and $T > 1$, there exists a monotonic cut-point strategy profile $\mathbf{x}_t^C(\boldsymbol{v}_t, \mathbf{B}_t, t)$ such that $EV_0^C(B_0) > EW_0$.

2.2 Proof of Proposition 2.1

Call $p_{xt} \equiv p(x, \mathbf{B}_t, t)$ the probability that i obtains the desired decision over proposal P_t when casting x votes at state $(\mathbf{B}_t, t)$. For any number of voters n, distribution of bonus votes $\mathbf{B}_t$, and time t, p_{xt} must be monotonically (if possibly weakly) increasing in x. Call $EU_{it}(v_{it}, x, \mathbf{B}_t, t)$ voter i's expected utility at t when casting x votes on the current proposal P_t, to which he attributes value v_{it}. Call $EV_{it}(\mathbf{B}_t, t)$ the voter's expected utility before the realization of his preferences. Thus: $EU_{it} = v_{it}p_{xt} + EV_{it+1}(B_{it+1}, \mathbf{B}_{-it+1}, t+1)$, where $B_{it+1} = B_{it} - x + 1$. Call x' (x'') the number of votes cast by i when $v_{it} = v'$ (v''), with $v' > v''$. By definition of best response, the following two inequalities must hold:

$$v'p_{x't} + EV_{it+1}(B_{it} - x' + 1, \mathbf{B}_{-it+1}, t+1) \geq v'p_{x''t} + EV_{it+1}(B_{it} - x'' + 1, \mathbf{B}_{-it+1}, t+1) \tag{2.1}$$

$$v''p_{x''t} + EV_{it+1}(B_{it} - x'' + 1, \mathbf{B}_{-it+1}, t+1) \geq v''p_{x't} + EV_{it+1}(B_{it} - x' + 1, \mathbf{B}_{-it+1}, t+1). \tag{2.2}$$

Adding (2.1) and (2.2) yields:

$$(v' - v'')(p_{x't} - p_{x''t}) \geq 0. \tag{2.3}$$

If both (2.1) and (2.2) hold with equality, (2.3) implies $p_{x't} = p_{x''t}$, and thus, by (2.1) or (2.2), $EV_{it+1}(B_{it} - x'' + 1, \mathbf{B}_{-it+1}, t+1) = EV_{it+1}(B_{it} - x' + 1, \mathbf{B}_{-it+1}, t+1)$. The two strategies x' and x'' are fully equivalent at state ($\mathbf{B}_t$, t), and the choice between them is arbitrary.[1] By convention, then, suppose voter i selects the same number of votes in both cases: $x' = x''$. If at least one of (2.1) or (2.2) holds with strict inequality, then (2.3) is a strict inequality, too. With $v' > v''$, and p_{xt} monotonically increasing in x, (2.3) then implies $x' > x''$. ■

2.3 Proof of Proposition 2.2

The proof in Casella (2005) shows that the game satisfies the conditions required by Milgrom and Weber (1985) for existence of an equilibrium in

1. For example: suppose $n = 2$, $B_{it} = 3$, $B_{jt} = 0$, $t = T - 1$. Voter i is indifferent between casting one or two bonus votes at $T - 1$: in both cases, he wins both remaining proposals with probability one. The choice is irrelevant. I suppose that in such cases of indifference, the choice does not depend on the intensity of preferences.

distributional strategies. Hence an equilibrium exists, and all equilibrium strategies are indistinguishable from pure strategies. Because all best response strategies are monotonic, by Proposition 2.1, and because the intensities' distribution is continuous and the set of strategies – the possible numbers of votes – is finite, equilibrium strategies must be monotone cut-point strategies, as described in the proposition.

If $v_{it} = c_{ix-1}$, a voter is indifferent between casting x or $x - 1$ votes. When the distribution of valuations G is continuous, the probability of $v_{it} = c_{ix-1}$ is 0, and how the indifference is resolved carries no weight. In the experiment, the distribution of valuations is not continuous, and both strategies are classified as equilibrium strategies.

2.4 Proof of Proposition 2.3

We begin with claim (i). Call $Eg_i(\mathbf{B}_t, t)$ the expected one-period utility to voter i in state $(\mathbf{B}_t, t)$ before the realization of his preferences. Hence $EV_{it}(\mathbf{B}_t, t) = Eg_i(\mathbf{B}_t, t) + EV_{it+1}(\mathbf{B}_{t+1}, t+1)$. The logic of the proof is to break down the ex ante expected value of the game into the one-period expected utilities associated with all possible states. If the state is symmetric ($B_{it} = B_{jt}$), it can be shown that the one-period expected utility cannot be lower with storable votes than with simple majority voting; if the state is asymmetrical ($B_{it} \neq B_{jt}$) the result holds on average, for the sum of the one-period utilities in the two mirror-image asymmetrical states. Starting from a symmetric initial endowment of votes, the probability of reaching either of the two mirror-image asymmetrical states must be identical; hence, this is sufficient to establish the result.

Denote by $(\mathbf{B}_t^s, t)$ $((\mathbf{B}_t^a, t))$ any symmetric (asymmetrical) state at t. For simplicity, I drop the subscript i in symmetric states, to emphasize that in such states $Eg_i(\mathbf{B}_t^s, t) = Eg_j(\mathbf{B}_t^s, t)$, and $EV_{it}(\mathbf{B}_t^s, t) = EV_{jt}(\mathbf{B}_t^s, t)$. Also for simplicity, $EV_0(B_0, 0)$ is denoted more concisely by $EV_0(B_0)$. Denote by $F(v)$, with support $[0, 1]$, the probability distribution of intensity v: $F(\cdot)$ can be derived from the distribution of valuations $G(\cdot)$, with $F(z) = 2G(z) - 1$. Finally, denote by Ew a voter's expected one-period utility with simple majority, before the realization of his preferences: $Ew = (3/4)Ev$. Recall that EW_t is defined as a voter's ex ante expected utility at time t, over all remaining $T - t$ periods, with simple majority, before the realization of his preferences. Hence $EW_t = (T - t)Ew = (T - t)(3/4)Ev$. We can prove that in equilibrium $EV_0(\mathbf{B}_0^s) > EW_0$ for all $T > 1$ by showing that the following two lemmas hold:

Lemma 2.1.

(i) $Eg_i(\mathbf{B}_t, t) + Eg_j(\mathbf{B}_t, t) \geq 2Ew$ for all $\mathbf{B}_t$, t
(ii) $Eg(\mathbf{B}_{T-1}^s, T-1) > Ew$ for all $\mathbf{B}_{T-1}^s > 0$.

Lemma 2.2. Suppose the following inequalities hold at $t+1$:

(i) $EV_{it+1}(\mathbf{B}_{t+1}, t+1) + EV_{jt+1}(\mathbf{B}_{t+1}, t+1) \geq 2EW_{t+1}$
(ii) $EV_{t+1}(\mathbf{B}_{t+1}^s, t+1) > EW_{t+1}$.

Then they must hold at t.

Given monotone cut-point strategies, in symmetric states:

$$Eg_i(\mathbf{B}_t^s, t) = (1/4)\left[\int_0^{c_1(\mathbf{B}_t^s,t)} vdF(v)(2 + F(c_1(\mathbf{B}_t^s, t))) + \int_{c_1(\mathbf{B}_t^s,t)}^{c_2(\mathbf{B}_t^s,t)} vdF(v)(2 + F(c_1(\mathbf{B}_t^s, t)) + F(c_2(\mathbf{B}_t^s, t))) + \cdots \cdots + \int_{c_{k-1}(\mathbf{B}_t^s,t)}^{1} vdF(v)(3 + F(c_{k-1}(\mathbf{B}_t^s, t)))\right], \tag{2.4}$$

where $0 \leq c_x(\mathbf{B}_t^s, t) \leq c_{x+1}(\mathbf{B}_t^s, t) \leq 1$ for all t. In asymmetrical states:

$$Eg_i(\mathbf{B}_t^a, t) + Eg_j(\mathbf{B}_t^a, t) = (1/4)\left[\int_0^{\alpha_1(\mathbf{B}_t^a,t)} vdF(v)\,(2 + F(\beta_1(\mathbf{B}_t^a, t))) + \int_{\alpha_1(\mathbf{B}_t^a,t)}^{\alpha_2(\mathbf{B}_t^a,t)} vdF(v)\,(2 + F(\beta_1(\mathbf{B}_t^a, t)) + F(\beta_2(\mathbf{B}_t^a, t))) + \cdots + \int_{\alpha_{B_{it}}(\mathbf{B}_t^a,t)}^{1} vdF(v)\,\big(2 + F(\beta_{k-1}(\mathbf{B}_t^a, t)) + F(\beta_k(\mathbf{B}_t^a, t))\big) + \right. \tag{2.5}$$

$$+ \int_0^{\beta_1(\mathbf{B}_t^a, t)} v dF(v) \, (2 + F(\alpha_1(\mathbf{B}_t^a, t)))$$

$$\left. + \int_{\beta_{B_{it}}(\mathbf{B}_t^a, t)}^{\beta_{B_{it}+1}(\mathbf{B}_t^a, t)} v dF(v) \left(3 + F(\alpha_{k-1}(\mathbf{B}_t^a, t))\right) + \int_{\beta_{B_{it}+1}(\mathbf{B}_t^a, t)}^{1} 4v dF(v) \right],$$

where $\mathbf{B}_t^a = \{B_{it}, B_{jt}\}$, $B_{it} < B_{jt}$, and $0 \leq \alpha_x(\mathbf{B}_t^s, t) \leq \alpha_{x+1}(\mathbf{B}_t^s, t) \leq 1$ ($0 \leq \beta_x(\mathbf{B}_t^s, t) \leq \beta_{x+1}(\mathbf{B}_t^s, t) \leq 1$) are the equilibrium cut-points for voter i (j). Note that for all $t < T$ it is always weakly dominant for voter j to cast fewer than $B_{it} + 3$ votes.

Lemma 2.1 can then be proved by manipulating equations (2.4) and (2.5), exactly as in Casella (2005); Lemma 2.2 is identical to Lemma 2 in Casella (2005) and is proved there. Once the two lemmas are established, the result follows immediately: because all votes are cast at T, $EV_{iT}(\mathbf{B}_T, T) + EV_{jT}(\mathbf{B}_T, T) = 2Ew$ for all $\mathbf{B}_T$; hence in all symmetric equilibria at $T-1$, $EV_{T-1}(\mathbf{B}_{T-1}^s, T-1) = Eg(\mathbf{B}_{T-1}^s, T-1) + Ew > EW_{T-1}$ for all $\mathbf{B}_{T-1}^s > 0$, by Lemma 2.1; but then by Lemma 2.2, the inequalities hold at all previous times t, and in particular $EV_0(\mathbf{B}_0^s) > EW_0$ for all $\mathbf{B}_0^s > 0$, and all $T > 1$. The two lemmas also imply that $EV_0(\mathbf{B}_0^s)/EW_0$ cannot be decreasing in T: intuitively, a longer horizon corresponds to a larger number of nodes in the game tree, all of which are associated with expected one-period utilities for the pair of voters that are not smaller than the expected utilities with majority voting.

The proofs of the two lemmas rely on the monotonicity of the cut-points and on a notion of symmetry – the two voters choosing the same cut-points at the same state. But the proof does not rely on the specific cut-points equilibrium values. The implication is that if the symmetry condition is satisfied, any rule of thumb that results in monotonic cut-points yields expected welfare gains, relative to majority voting, for each voter. If symmetry is not satisfied but monotonicity is, then the expected utilities associated with any state are given by equation (2.5) with the small amendment that cut-points need to be included for all feasible number of votes. The first part of Lemma 2.1 still follows, with the result that the aggregate expected value of the game, for the two voters taken together, cannot be lower than the aggregate expected value with majority voting.

We can now prove claim (ii). Consider the following strategy. At any t up to $T-2$, each voter casts only a regular vote; at $T-2$ each casts $B_0 - 1$ bonus votes in addition to the regular vote. Since every individual is casting the same number of votes, the game is identical to simple majority voting, with identical expected welfare up to $T-1$. Consider now the last two periods, which each voter enters with 1 bonus vote. In period $T-1$, call α a cut-point such that each voter spends his bonus vote if and only if his intensity over proposal P_{T-1} is above α; in period T all remaining votes are cast. Call such a strategy C, and denote by $EV_{T-1}^{C}(\alpha)$ a voter's expected utility over the two last periods, when following strategy C. Thus:

$$EV_{T-1}^{C}(\alpha) = \int_0^{\alpha} v dF(v) p_{1T-1}^{C} + \int_{\alpha}^{1} v dF(v) p_{2T-1}^{C} + \int_0^1 v dF(v)[F(\alpha) p_{2T}^{C} + (1 - F(\alpha)) p_{1T}^{C}]. \tag{2.6}$$

Recall that p_{xt} is the probability of obtaining the desired outcome at t when casting x votes. Here, it is calculated taking into account that all other voters follow strategy C – hence the superscript C. If $\alpha = 0$, all voters cast their bonus vote at $T-1$ and have only their regular vote at T. The whole game is then identical to majority voting. I show here that there always exist values of $\alpha > 0$ such that $EV_{T-1}^{C}(\alpha) > EW_{T-1}$ and hence $EV_0^C > EW_0$.

Consider the derivative of (2.6) with respect to α, evaluated at $\alpha = 0$:

$$\left(\frac{\partial EV_{T-1}(\alpha)}{\partial \alpha}\right)_{\alpha=0} = \int_0^1 v dF(v) \times \left[\left(\frac{\partial p_{2T-1}^{C}}{\partial \alpha}\right)_{\alpha=0} + f(0)(p_{2T}^{C}|_{\alpha=0} - p_{1T}^{C}|_{\alpha=0}) + \left(\frac{\partial p_{1T}^{C}}{\partial \alpha}\right)_{\alpha=0}\right]. \tag{2.7}$$

Begin with the case of n even. Call $p(n)$ the probability of winning when everybody casts the same number of votes, and consider p_{2T-1}^{C} – voter i's probability of winning at $T-1$ when casting 2 votes. If everybody casts 2 votes, i's probability of winning is $p(n)$; if one voter casts a single vote, i's probability of winning differs from $p(n)$ only if $n/2$ voters disagree with his preference – in this case, i wins if the "single voter" is on the other side and loses if he is on i's side, whereas the result is always a tie when everyone casts the same number of votes. Thus:

$$p^C_{2T-1|n\ even} = [1 - F(\alpha)]^{n-1} p(n) + (n-1)F(\alpha)[1 - F(\alpha)]^{n-2} \quad (2.8)$$
$$\times \left[p(n) - (1/2)^n \binom{n-2}{\frac{n}{2}} + (1/2)^n \binom{n-2}{\frac{n}{2}-1} \right] + F(\alpha)^2[.....].$$

The last term in (2.8) refers to scenarios in which at least 2 voters cast a single vote, and because all terms in (2.7) must be evaluated at $\alpha = 0$, will be set to 0 after differentiation.

Consider now the problem at T, where the probability of casting 2 votes equals the probability of having cast 1 vote at $T - 1$. If everybody casts 1 vote, i's probability of winning is again $p(n)$; if one voter casts 2 votes, i's probability of winning differs from $p(n)$ only if $n/2$ voters disagree with his preference – in this case, i loses if the "double voter" is on the other side and wins if he is on i's side. Therefore:

$$p^C_{1T|n\ even} = [1 - F(\alpha)]^{n-1} p(n) + (n-1)F(\alpha)[1 - F(\alpha)]^{n-2} \quad (2.9)$$
$$\times \left[p(n) + (1/2)^n \binom{n-2}{\frac{n}{2}} - (1/2)^n \binom{n-2}{\frac{n}{2}-1} \right] + F(\alpha)^2[.....].$$

It follows that:

$$\left(\frac{\partial p^C_{2T-1}}{\partial \alpha} \right)_{\substack{\alpha=0 \\ n\ even}} = -\left(\frac{\partial p^C_{1T}}{\partial \alpha} \right)_{\substack{\alpha=0 \\ n\ even}}.$$

Thus (2.7) must be strictly positive if $p^C_{2T} - p^C_{1T}$ is strictly positive, when everyone else casts 1 vote. With n even, the condition is satisfied: by casting 2 votes, i can resolve in his favor all decisions that would have resulted in ties:

$$\left(p^C_{2T} - p^C_{1T}\right)_{\substack{\alpha=0 \\ n\ even}} = (1/2)^n \binom{n-1}{\frac{n}{2}} > 0. \quad (2.10)$$

Thus (2.7) must be strictly positive: since $EV^C_{T-1}(\alpha) = EW_{T-1}$ at $\alpha = 0$, there exists some positive α such that $EV^C_{T-1}(\alpha) > EW_{T-1}$, and thus $EV^C_0 > EW_0$ for all $T > 1$, establishing the result.

Consider now n odd. When casting 2 votes at $T-1$, if everyone else but at most one of the other voters is also casting 2 votes, i's probability of achieving his desired outcome cannot differ from simple majority. If the other voters are split equally, $(n-1)/2$ on either side, i can always tilt the vote by casting 2 votes. If $(n+1)/2$ are on the opposing side, and all but at most one of them are casting 2 votes, i's side will lose, even if the 1-vote voter is on the opposing side:

$$p^C_{2T-1|n\ odd} = [1-F(\alpha)]^{n-1}p(n) + (n-1)F(\alpha)[1-F(\alpha)]^{n-2}p(n) + F(\alpha)^2[.....]. \quad (2.11)$$

When casting 1 vote at T, if a single other voter casts 2 votes, i's probability of obtaining his desired outcome can differ from the equivalent probability with majority voting only if $(n+1)/2$ voters are on the opposing side, but the voter casting 2 votes is on his side:

$$p^C_{1T|n\ odd} = [1-F(\alpha)]^{n-1}p(n) + + (n-1)F(\alpha)[1-F(\alpha)]^{n-2}\left(p(n) + (1/2)^n\binom{n-2}{\frac{n+1}{2}}\right) + F(\alpha)^2[.....], \quad (2.12)$$

where the binomial term differs from 0 only if $n > 3$. Therefore,

$$\left(\frac{\partial p^C_{2T-1}}{\partial \alpha}\right)_{\substack{\alpha=0\\ n\ odd}} = 0,$$
$$\left(\frac{\partial p^C_{1T}}{\partial \alpha}\right)_{\substack{\alpha=0\\ n\ odd}} = f(0)(n-1)(1/2)^n\binom{n-2}{\frac{n+1}{2}}. \quad (2.13)$$

Finally, when everybody else casts 1 vote, i's probability of winning can be increased by casting 2 votes, as opposed to 1, only if the side that shares i's preference is exactly one voter short. By casting 2 votes, voter i can induce a tie. Thus:

$$p^C_{2T} - p^C_{1T}{}_{\substack{\alpha=0\\ n\ odd}} = (1/2)^n\binom{n-1}{\frac{n+1}{2}} > 0\ \forall n\ odd. \quad (2.14)$$

We can again conclude that (2.7) must be strictly positive: with n odd, as with n even, there must exist some positive α such that

$EV^C_{T-1}(\alpha) > EW_{T-1}$and thus $EV^C_0 > EW_0$ for all $T > 1$, establishing the result. ■

2.5 Three-proposal Games: The Second Election for the Two-voter Game

Table T2.1 describes voter *i*'s equilibrium strategies in the second election, as function of the bonus votes remaining to the two voters.

Table T2.1 Voter *i*'s Equilibrium Cut-points ($n = 2$, $T = 3$, $t = 2$, $B_0 = 3$)

	$B_{jt} = 0$	$B_{jt} = 1$	$B_{jt} = 2$	$B_{jt} = 3$
$B_{it} = 1$	(50)	(50)	(44)	(50)
$B_{it} = 2$	(0, 100)	(22, 89)	(50, 50)	(40, 60)
$B_{it} = 3$	(0, 0, 100), (0, 100, 100)	(0, 50, 100)	(34, 51, 75)	(50, 50, 50)

There are 12 relevant states (and 4 additional trivial states, where *i* has no bonus votes left and always casts 1 vote). The total number of votes available equals the bonus votes still on hand plus 1; hence, for example, in the first row of Table T2.1, voter *i* has 2 votes available. The row says that *i* should cast 1 vote for valuations lower than 50, and 2 votes for valuations above 50 if the other player *j* has 0, 1, or 3 bonus votes left, and should use a cut-point of 44 if *j* has 2 bonus votes left. (Recall that subjects are told how many bonus votes remain available to the others.)

The equilibrium is very intuitive in the case of symmetric states: in these cases, the subgame is identical to the two-proposal game, and the dominant strategy is to cast a single vote for valuations below the mean, and all available votes for valuations above the mean. But equilibrium strategies are much less intuitive in asymmetrical states, with one exception: when *j* has no bonus votes left and *i* has at least 2 – the last two rows of the first column – *i* can be sure to win both this election and the next by spreading bonus votes: *i* should use at least 1 bonus vote in each election for any valuation. Voter *i*'s dominant strategy is straightforward in these two states, but checking it in the data is complicated by a predictable small-sample problem: in the three-proposal, two-voter treatment, 38 subjects, each playing 30 rounds, generated a total of 1140 data points for each stage of the voting game, but there are only 34 realizations of the two states that are of interest here: $(\{2, 0\}, t = 2)$ and $(\{3, 0\}, t = 2)$. In 8 of these 34 realizations, subjects did not play their dominant strategy. There was no difference in the frequency of mistakes across populations (5/21 at Caltech and 3/13 at UCLA), but, as would be the case with random errors, a higher frequency for the first state as opposed to the second (6/18 vs. 2/16).

Best response strategies must be monotonic for any state of the game, and thus monotonicity should continue to characterize voting choices in the second election. Again, however, monotonicity should be checked for each state and each subject, and the sample size is a problem. Table T2.1 suggests one instance in which the difficulty can be mitigated. As noted earlier, when a voter holds 1 bonus vote, the optimal strategy is insensitive to the number of bonus votes held by the other player (with one exception: a valuation between 44 and 50 and an opponent with 2 bonus votes). We can then aggregate all 1-bonus vote states for each voter (paying attention to the possibility of the exception above). Out of a total of 38 subjects, 36 have more than a single realization in which they face the second election holding 1 bonus vote; for these 36, the number of such realizations per subject goes from a minimum of 2 to a maximum of 12, with a median and mean of 6. In only 2 of the 36 subjects do we observe any monotonicity violation: an error rate of 2/12 in one case, and of 1/9 in the second. (In the whole sample, there are two valuations between 44 and 50 with the other player holding 2 bonus votes, and neither induces a violation of monotonicity). If we aggregate the data over all subjects, ignoring their heterogeneity, the error rate increases but still reaches only 25/240. (The aggregate error rate excludes one observation in which the other player holds 2 bonus votes and the monotonicity violation follows from the equilibrium strategy.) Thus, even keeping in mind that there are now only two possible alternatives, the data in these specific states appear to support monotonicity.

The multiplicity of possible states allows a new question: do subjects condition their strategies on the budget of votes held by the others? Theory says they should, as Table T2.1 makes clear. Consider, for example, the last row in the table, with voter i holding 3 bonus votes:

if the other player holds 1 bonus vote, *i* should cast either 2 or 3 votes, with a cut-point of 50; but if the other player holds 3 bonus votes, then *i* should cast either 1 or 4 votes, again with a cut-point of 50. What do the data show?

Aggregating the sample over all subjects and minimizing the number of monotonicity violations, the estimated cut-points are (10, 74, 100) for the first state and (36, 63, 91) for the second (with the cut-points at the lowest value compatible with minimizing nonmonotonicities). Once again, the experimental cut-points do not match the theoretical values, but share some features predicted by the theory. In the first state, subjects never cast 4 votes, as theory dictates, and very rarely cast 1, although the cut-point at which they switch between 2 and 3 votes is too high. In the second state, they did cast 1 and 4 votes, as they should in equilibrium, but they also cast 2 and 3 votes with comparable cumulative frequency, contrary to the theoretical prediction.

3

Protecting Minorities without Sacrificing Efficiency

3.1 The Formal Model—Version 3

Consider a committee of n voters, meeting to decide whether or not to implement T distinct proposals $\{P_1, ..P_T\}$, each of which can either pass or fail. The committee votes on the proposals sequentially. Each member i of the committee has preferences over each proposal P_t summarized by a cardinal valuation v_{it}. A negative valuation means that the voter is against the proposal; a positive valuation means that he is in favor. For each proposal P_t, voter i receives utility $u_{it} = |\mathrm{v}_{it}| = v_{it}$ if the decision goes in his preferred direction, and 0 otherwise. Voter i's utility from the entire meeting, U_i, equals $\sum_{t=1}^{T} u_{it}$.

The committee is composed of two *groups*, the *Majority group* **M**, with M members, and the *Minority group* **m**, with $m < M$ members. The two groups differ systematically in their preferences: members of **m** are in favor of all proposals, and members of **M** are against all proposals. For all t, $\mathrm{v}_{it} > 0$ if $i \in \mathbf{m}$, and $\mathrm{v}_{it} < 0$ if $i \in \mathbf{M}$. All members of the minority have valuations drawn from a distribution G_m with support $[0, 1]$, identical across proposals, while all members of the majority have valuations drawn from a distribution G_M with support $[-1, 0]$, again identical across proposals. The distributions of valuations are assumed to be symmetric across the two groups, so that the distribution of intensities (or values) $F_M(v)$ for all members of the majority group, with support $[0, 1]$, is assumed identical to $G_m(v) = F_m(v)$ and labeled F for both groups. F is common knowledge, as are the existence and size of **M** and **m**.

Intensities are always drawn independently across proposals and across the two groups. Within each group, two polar cases are considered: in case B (the *base* model), intensities are drawn independently for each member of a group; in case C (the *correlated* model), intensities are identical for all members within a group. The correlation of within-group intensities (or lack thereof) is common knowledge, as is the independence of intensities across proposals and groups. Intensities are revealed privately and sequentially before each proposal is put to a vote.

In addition to a regular vote on every proposal, each committee member is given a stock of B_0 bonus votes that can be cast in any manner the voter sees fit. B_0 is an integer and each bonus vote is equivalent to a regular vote. Each proposal is decided in the direction that receives more votes; in case of a tie, a coin is flipped. When proposal P_t is put to a vote, the current endowment of bonus votes for every voter, denoted $\mathbf{B}_t = (B_{1t}, \ldots, B_{nt})$, is common knowledge.

The analysis focuses on symmetric Perfect Bayesian equilibria in weakly undominated strategies. It ignores history-dependent strategies and concentrates on strategies such that the number of votes each individual chooses to cast each period, x_{it}, depends only on the voter's intensity of preferences v_{it}, and on the state of the game at t $(\mathbf{B}_t, t)$.

As in the previous models, because the sign of each group's preferences is common knowledge and intensities are independent over time, with weakly undominated strategies the direction of each individual vote is always chosen sincerely: all the minority members' votes are cast in favor of each proposal, and all majority votes are cast against each proposal. Equilibrium strategies have the following properties:

Proposition 3.1 Equilibrium. For any F, B_0, M, m and T, both model B and model C have an equilibrium in monotone cut-point strategies: at any state $(\mathbf{B}_t, t)$ and for any i with $B_{it} + 1$ available votes, there exists a set of cut-points $\{c_{i1}(\mathbf{B}_t, t), c_{i2}(\mathbf{B}_t, t), \ldots, c_{iB_{it}+1}(\mathbf{B}_t, t)\}$, $0 = c_{i0} \leq c_{i1} \leq \ldots \leq c_{iB_{it}+1} = 1$, such that i will cast x votes if and only if $v_{it} \in (c_{ix-1}, c_{ix}]$. In model B, the strategies are individual equilibrium strategies and $i \in \{1, .., n\}$; in model C, the strategies are group strategies and $i \in \{M, m\}$.

Proposition 3.2 Minority victories. In both models B and C: (i) For any F, T, M, and $m > 1$ there is a finite $B_0'(M, m, T)$, such that for all $B_0 > B_0'$

there exist equilibria of the storable votes mechanism where the minority wins some of the time with strictly positive probability. (ii) If $T > M$ and $B_0 > B_0'$, then the minority wins some of the time with strictly positive probability in all equilibria.

As in the previous models, denote by $EV_0(B_0)$ a voter's expected utility from all T proposals before any valuation is realized, and thus before knowing whether he belongs to **M** or to **m** (but taking into account the existence and size of **M** and **m**), when all voters have B_0 initial bonus votes. The equivalent measure under simple majority voting is denoted by EW_0. Then:

Proposition 3.3 Welfare. In model C, for all F, M and $m > M/2$, there is a finite $\overline{T}(M, m)$ such that if $T < \overline{T}(M, m)$ there exists an integer number B_0 and an equilibrium of the storable votes mechanism for which $EV_0(B_0) > EW_0$.

3.2 Proof of Proposition 3.1

When characterizing the equilibria of the model, the correlation of intensities within each group in model C can be a source of complications. But matters can be simplified by a simple observation. Call $C2$ the following two-player storable votes game. Voter M has M regular votes each period and a stock of MB_0 bonus votes; his valuation for each proposal is $M\mathrm{v}_{Mt}$, where v_{Mt} is independently drawn from the distribution function G_M with support $[-1, 0]$. Voter m has m regular votes each period and a stock of mB_0 bonus votes; his valuation for each proposal is $m\mathrm{v}_{mt}$ where v_{mt} is independently drawn from the distribution function G_m with support $[0, 1]$. Then the following result holds:

Lemma 3.1. If game $C2$ has an equilibrium, then the game described by model C also has an equilibrium. In addition, call $x^*_{Mt}(v_M, \mathbf{B}_t, t)$ and $x^*_{mt}(v_m, \mathbf{B}_t, t)$ the equilibrium strategies of voter M and voter m in game $C2$, and $\{x^*_{it}(v_i, \mathbf{B}_t, t)\}$ the equilibrium strategies in C. If $C2$ has an equilibrium, then there exist equilibrium strategies of model C

such that $\sum_{i\in m} x^*_{it}(v_i, \mathbf{B}_t, t) = x^*_{mt}(v_m, \mathbf{B}_t, t)$ and $\sum_{i\in M} x^*_{it}(v_i, \mathbf{B}_t, t) = x^*_{Mt}(v_M, \mathbf{B}_t, t)$.

Proof of Lemma 3.1. Suppose that $x^*_{Mt}(v_M, \mathbf{B}_t, t)$ and $x^*_{mt}(v_m, \mathbf{B}_t, t)$ exist. Consider candidate equilibrium strategies $\{x'_{it}(v_i, \mathbf{B}_t, t)\}$ for model C, where $\sum_{i\in m} x'_{it}(v_i, \mathbf{B}_t, t) = x^*_{mt}(v_m, \mathbf{B}_t, t)$ and $\sum_{i\in M} x'_{it}(v_i, \mathbf{B}_t, t) = x^*_{Mt}(v_M, \mathbf{B}_t, t)$. Because preferences between the two groups are always opposed, at any state only the aggregate voting choice of the opposite group affects voters' payoffs. In addition, because in model C preferences within each group are always perfectly correlated, by definition $\{x'_{it}(v_i, \mathbf{B}_t, t)\}$, $i \in m$ maximize the expected payoff of each individual minority member, given $x^*_{Mt}(v_M, \mathbf{B}_t, t)$ (and similarly for $\{x'_{it}(v_i, \mathbf{B}_t, t)\}$, $i \in M$, given $x^*_{mt}(v_m, \mathbf{B}_t, t)$). It follows that no individual deviation from the prescribed strategies can be profitable and $\{x'_{it}(v_i, \mathbf{B}_t, t)\}$ must be equilibrium strategies. Note that in general, the equilibrium will not be unique: any permutation of individual strategies that leaves the aggregate vote for the group unchanged, at given state, is an equilibrium. ■

Lemma 3.1 makes a simple point. In model C, voters' interests within each group are perfectly aligned; if there is an equilibrium where each group coordinates its strategy so as to maximize the group's payoff, given the aggregate strategy of the other group, then no individual voter can gain from deviating.[1] In the n-person game described by model C, call equilibrium *group strategies* the equilibrium individual strategies of the two-voter game $C2$.

Proposition 3.1 can now be proven:

(i) *Existence of equilibrium in pure strategies.* The arguments in Casella (2005), establishing the existence of an equilibrium in pure strategies, require the independence of individual types, conditional on a publicly observed variable. Here, the publicly observed information is each voter's membership in one of the two groups, and hence the support of the distribution from which valuations are drawn. Conditional on public

1. This is the logic exploited by McLennan (1998) to show that whenever "sincere" voting is efficient in common value decision problems, then it must be a Nash equilibrium.

information on the support of each distribution, individual valuations are independent in case B. Hence, an equilibrium in pure strategies exists for model B. Conditional on the same public information, valuations are also independent in model $C2$. Again, an equilibrium in pure strategies exists. But since such an equilibrium must be an equilibrium of the n-voter C game, it follows that an equilibrium in pure strategies of the n-voter C game exists. ■

(ii) *Monotonicity of the equilibrium strategies.* As in the previous chapters, call a strategy *monotonic* if, at a given state, the number of votes cast is monotonically increasing in the intensity of preferences v_{it}. Chapter 2 in Part II shows that at any given state, all individual best response strategies must be monotonic when members of each group do not play correlated strategies. Thus, the argument applies immediately to equilibria of model B. It also applies to model $C2$, and hence to group strategies, as opposed to individual strategies, in the equilibrium we focus on in the n-voter C game. If, at any given state, all best response strategies must be monotonic and an equilibrium exists, it follows that equilibrium strategies must be monotonic. Because there is a continuum of types and a finite set of strategies, then monotonic equilibrium strategies must take the form of monotone cut-point strategies. ■

3.3 Proof of Proposition 3.2

We begin by proving the second part of the proposition. Consider any candidate equilibrium such that the minority is expected to lose with probability 1 over each decision. A minority member cannot be worse off by cumulating all his bonus votes on one decision. Over all decisions, there must be at least one on which with positive probability the majority casts no more than MB_0/T bonus votes, and since the minority can never cast fewer than m total votes, a deviating minority member can always find a decision such that with positive probability the difference in votes cast is at most $M(1 + B_0/T) - m$. Thus, with positive probability the outcome of that decision changes and deviation is profitable if $M(1 + B_0/T) \leq m + B_0$, or $B_0(1 - M/T) \geq M - m$. This condition requires $T > M$, and in this case becomes $B_0 \geq T(M - m)/(T - M)$. For all M and m, the condition is sufficient and applies to both models B and C. Since we know by Proposition 3.1 that an equilibrium exists for arbitrary F, T, M, and m, it must be that if $T > M$, and $B_0 \geq T(M - m)/(T - M)$ the minority is expected to win sometime with strictly positive probability in all equilibria. We now prove the first part of the theorem. Suppose $T \leq M$. Consider the following candidate equilibrium: at time $t = 1$, $x_{i1} = 1 + B_0$ for $i \in \mathbf{m}$ and $x_{j1} = 1$ for $j \in \mathbf{M}$; at all other other times $t \neq 1$, $x_{it} = 1$ and $x_{jt} = 1 + B_0/(T - 1)$. If $m(1 + B_0) > M$ or $B_0 > (M - m)/m$ the minority always wins the first vote, while the majority always wins all other votes. No individual minority member can gain from deviation, for all possible realizations of his valuations, if $m + B_0 < M[1 + B_0/(T - 1)]$, or $B_0[1 - M/(T - 1)] < M - m$, a condition always satisfied when $T \leq M$. No majority member can gain from deviating, again for all possible realizations of his valuations, if $m(1 + B_0) > M + B_0$ or $B_0 > (M - m)/(m - 1)$, a threshold that is finite for all $m > 1$. Thus, if $T \leq M$, $m > 1$, and $B_0 > (M - m)/(m - 1)$, the strategies described are an equilibrium, and the minority always wins the first vote. ■

3.4 Proof of Proposition 3.3

Consider the following strategies. Over the first $T - 2$ proposals, each minority member always casts only the regular vote; each majority member casts $1 + b$ votes, with $b \geq 0$. At $T - 1$, each minority member casts only his regular vote if $v_m < \alpha$, for a fixed $\alpha > 0$, and all bonus votes otherwise; each majority members casts $1 + b$ votes if $v_M < \alpha$ and $1 + h$ otherwise, with $h \geq 0$, and $b + h + (T - 2)b = B_0$. In the last election, all remaining votes are cast.

The proof proceeds in two steps. Step (i) shows that for all M and $m \geq 2$ there exist non-negative values of B_0, b, h, and T for which such strategies are equilibrium strategies, and the minority wins at $T - 1$ if $(v_{mT-1} > \alpha, v_{MT-1} < \alpha)$, and at T if $(v_{mT-1} < \alpha, v_{MT-1} > \alpha)$, but it always loses otherwise. Call $B_0'(M, m, b)$ a non-negative value of B_0 that supports such an equilibrium. Step (ii) then shows that in this equilibrium $EV_0(B_0') > EW_0$ if $m > M/2$. Because the theorem requires $m > M/2$, it cannot apply to $m = 1$.

(i) If:

$$m(1 + B_0) > M(1 + b), \tag{3.1}$$

the minority wins at $T - 1$ and loses at T if $(v_{mT-1} > \alpha, v_{MT-1} < \alpha)$, and it loses at $T - 1$ and wins at T if $(v_{mT-1} < \alpha, v_{MT-1} > \alpha)$. If in addition:

$$M(1 + h) > m(1 + B_0), \tag{3.2}$$

the minority loses at both $T - 1$ and T for all other realizations of intensities. Any unilateral deviation by a minority voter is ruled out if:

$$m + B_0 < M(1 + b). \tag{3.3}$$

Similarly, any unilateral deviation by a majority voter is ruled out if:

$$M + (M - 1)b + B_0 < m(1 + B_0). \tag{3.4}$$

If there exist values of B_0, b, h, and T for which these four inequalities are satisfied simultaneously, and the budget constraint $b + h + (T - 2)b = B_0$ holds, then the strategies are an equilibrium, delivering the outcomes described above. The budget constraint requires $b < B_0$, and it is then the case that (3.4) implies (3.1). Hence, substituting the budget constraint in (3.2), three conditions must be satisfied:

$$T < 1 + \frac{(B_0 + 1)(M - m)}{Mb} \tag{3.2'}$$

$$B_0 < (M - m) + Mb \tag{3.3'}$$

$$B_0 > \frac{M - m}{m - 1} + \frac{M - 1}{m - 1}b. \tag{3.4'}$$

If integer constraints are ignored, then for all $m \geq 2$ the right hand side of (3.3') is larger than the right hand side of (3.4') for all $b > 0$, and thus for any M, $m \geq 2$, and $b > 0$ there exists some value $B_0'(M, m, b) > 0$ that satisfies both (3.3') and (3.4'). Note that $B_0'(M, m, b)$ is bounded above $(M - m)/(m - 1)$ and thus does not converge to 0 even if b does so. Hence, with b arbitrarily small, T can be arbitrarily large, and

$(2(M-m)/(m-1), 2M-m)$, the equilibrium can be supported for any positive finite T. If integer constraints are not ignored, in general they impose an upper bound on T, $\overline{T}$, which depends on M and m. The following observations are implied immediately by (3.2'), (3.3'), and (3.4'): (a) if $m > 2$, then for all $M > m$, there is an equilibrium with $b = 1$, B_0' integer $\in ((2M-m-1)/(m-1), 2M-m)$, and $\overline{T}(M,m) > 2$; (b) if $m = 2$, then the only relevant case satisfying the constraint $M < 2m$ is $M = 3$. For $m = 2$ and $M = 3$, there is an equilibrium with $b = 2$, $B_0' = 6$ and $\overline{T} = 13/6 > 2$.

(ii) In any equilibrium of this type, $EV_0(B_0') > EW_0$ if and only if:

$$F(\alpha)\left[M\int_0^\alpha vdF(v)+F(\alpha)M\int_0^1 vdF(v)\right]$$
$$+[1-F(\alpha)]\left[M\int_\alpha^1 vdF(v)+[1-F(\alpha)]M\int_0^1 vdF(v)\right]$$
$$+F(\alpha)\left[M\int_\alpha^1 vdF(v)+[1-F(\alpha)]m\int_0^1 vdF(v)\right]$$
$$+F(\alpha)\left[m\int_\alpha^1 vdF(v)+[1-F(\alpha)]M\int_0^1 vdF(v)\right]>2M\int_0^1 vdF(v).$$

Simplifying:

$$F(\alpha)[MF(\alpha)+m(1-F(\alpha))]\int_0^1 vdF(v) \qquad (3.5)$$
$$+[mF(\alpha)+M(1-F(\alpha))]\int_\alpha^1 vdF(v)>M\int_0^1 vdF(v).$$

Note that the left hand side simplifies to $M\int_0^1 vdF(v)$ when evaluated at $\alpha = 0$ because at $\alpha = 0$ the majority always wins (and thus $EV_0 = EW_0$). Taking the derivative of (3.5) with respect to α and evaluating it at $\alpha = 0$:

$$\left.\frac{\partial(EV_0(B_0')-EW_0)}{\partial\alpha}\right|_{\alpha=0}=f(0)\int_0^1 vdF(v)(2m-M)>0\Leftrightarrow m>M/2.$$

Thus, if $m > M/2$ there exists a cut-point $\alpha > 0$ such that the strategies described above lead to higher ex ante welfare than simple majority voting. ■

3.5 Derivation and Discussion of Figure 3.1

Equilibrium strategies and outcomes for the example described in the text and illustrated in Figure 3.1 are summarized in the following lemmas:

Lemma 3.2. Suppose n odd; F uniform, and $T = B_0 = 2$. Then:

In model B:

a. There is an equilibrium such that: $x_{i1} = 1$ if $v_{i1} < 0.5$ and $x_{i1} = 3$ if $v_{i1} > 0.5$ for all i.

In such an equilibrium:

b. If $M > 3m$, the majority always wins, but for all $M < 3m$ the minority wins one of the two proposals with probability $\sum_{s=k}^{m}\left[\sum_{r=0}^{m-s}\binom{M}{r}\binom{m}{r+s}2^{-n}\right] > 0$ where $k \equiv (M - m + 1)/2$. Ex ante, each of the two proposals has the same probability of a minority victory.

c. If $M > 3m$, storable votes are identical to simple majority voting, and $EV_0 = EW_0$. If $M < 3m$, there exist m', m'', and M' with $m'' > m'$, such that $EV_0(m', M') < EW_0(m', M')$ but $EV_0(m'', M') > EW_0(m'', M')$.

In model C:

a. There is an equilibrium such that the minority's strategy is: $x_{m1} = m$ if $v_{m1} < 0.5$, and $x_{m1} = 3m$ if $v_{m1} > 0.5$. The majority's strategy is: if $2M > 3m$, $x_{M1} = 2M$ for all v_{M1}; if $2M \leq 3m$, $x_{M1} = \max\{M, m + 3\}$ if $v_{M1} < 0.5$ and $x_{M1} = \min\{3M, 4M - (m + 3)\}$ if $v_{M1} > 0.5$.

In such an equilibrium:

b. If $2M > 3m$, the majority always wins, but for all $2M \leq 3m$, the minority wins one of the two proposals with probability 0.25. Ex ante, each of the two proposals has the same probability of a minority victory.

c. Storable votes are always ex ante weakly superior to simple majority voting: $EV_0 = EW_0$ if $2M > 3m$, and $EV_0 > EW_0$ if $2M \leq 3m$.

Proof of Lemma 3.2.

Model *B.*

(a) *Equilibrium.* To verify that the strategy described is an equilibrium, consider the best response for voter i. If i casts x_{i1} votes on the first proposal, his expected utility over the whole game is as follows: $EU_i|x_{i1} = v_{i1} prob(W_1|x_{i1}) + E(v) prob(W_2|4 - x_{i1})$, where $prob(W_t|x_{it})$ is i's probability of obtaining the desired outcome in period t, conditional on casting x_{it} votes. Since $(n - 1)$ is an even number, and every other voter is casting either 1 or 3 votes, the difference in votes between the two sides, excluding i, must be even for both proposals. Thus, when i considers the choice between casting 3, 2, or 1 votes, the only case in which the choice matters is a difference of 2 votes in his side's disfavor, either over proposal 1 or proposal 2. With F uniform, $Ev = 0.5$. Hence:

$$EU_i|3 > EU_i|2 \Leftrightarrow v_{i1}[prob(\Delta x_{1-i} = 2)] > 0.5[prob(\Delta x_{2-i} = 2)]$$

$$EU_i|2 > EU_i|1 \Leftrightarrow v_{i1}[prob(\Delta x_{1-i} = 2)] > 0.5[prob(\Delta x_{2-i} = 2)],$$

(where Δx_{t-i} indicates the number of votes by which i's side is losing over proposal P_t, absent i's vote). With F uniform, in the candidate equilibrium the probability of any other voter casting 1 or 3 votes is identical, implying: $prob(\Delta x_{1-i} = 2) = prob(\Delta x_{2-i} = 2)$. Thus i's best response is to cast 1 vote if $v_{i1} < 0.5$ and 3 votes if $v_{i1} > 0.5$; the conclusion holds for all i, and the strategy is indeed an equilibrium. If $M > 3m$, $prob(\Delta x_{1-i} = 2) = prob(\Delta x_{2-i} = 2) = 0$, and the number of votes cast is irrelevant.

(b) *Frequency of minority victories.* Write the majority size as $M = m + 2k - 1$, with $k \geq 1$ (recall that n is odd). The minority wins the first vote if there are at least k more intensities above 0.5 among the minority than the majority. With F uniform, the probability of this event is given by the formula in the lemma. The minority wins the second vote if there are at least k more intensities below 0.5 over the first proposal among the minority than the majority, an event that again, with F uniform, has the probability given in the lemma. Note that the two events are mutually exclusive and that the probability can be positive only if $k \leq m$, implying that the majority always wins if $M > 3m$.

(c) *Expected equilibrium payoff.* With n odd and the equilibrium strategies described above, the difference in votes cast by the two groups is always an even number. In addition, F uniform guarantees that the probability of any given difference in votes is equal over the two proposals. Call EV_{i0}^{B} the expected payoff of voter i in model B before any valuation is realized. If $prob(W_M|x)$ is the probability of obtaining the desired outcome for $i \in M$, conditional on casting x votes, then, given F uniform, the ex ante expected payoff of a majority member is as follows:

$$EV_{i0}^{B} = (3/8)prob(W_M|1) + (5/8)prob(W_M|3) \qquad \forall i \in M,$$

where $prob(W_M|1) = prob(x_{M-i} \geq x_m)$ and $prob(W_M|3) = prob(x_{M-i} \geq x_m - 2)$. Recall that $M = m + 2k - 1$. Given the equilibrium strategies, F uniform, and the independence of the valuation draws, if we call "high" an intensity above 0.5, then $prob(x_{M-i} \geq x_m)$ equals the probability that the number of high draws in the minority group is at most $k - 1$ larger than in the majority group, excluding voter i:

$$prob(W_M|1) = 1 - \sum_{s=k}^{m}\left[\sum_{r=0}^{m-s}\binom{M-1}{r}\binom{m}{r+s}\right]2^{-(M-1+m)},$$

Similarly, $prob(x_{M-i} \geq x_m - 2)$ equals the probability that the number of high draws in the minority group is at most k larger than for the majority group, excluding voter i:

$$prob(W_M|3) = 1 - \sum_{s=k+1}^{m}\left[\sum_{r=0}^{m-s}\binom{M-1}{r}\binom{m}{r+s}\right]2^{-(M-1+m)}.$$

Analogous calculations yield the ex ante expected payoff of a minority member:

$$EV_{j0}^{B} = (3/8)prob(W_m|1) + (5/8)prob(W_m|3) \qquad \forall j \in m,$$

where:

$$prob(W_m|1) = \sum_{s=k}^{m-1}\left[\sum_{r=0}^{m-s-1}\binom{M}{r}\binom{m-1}{r+s}\right]2^{-(M+m-1)},$$

and

$$prob(W_m|3) = \sum_{s=k-1}^{m-1}\left[\sum_{r=0}^{m-s-1}\binom{M}{r}\binom{m-1}{r+s}\right]2^{-(M+m-1)}.$$

Ex ante aggregate expected payoff in equilibrium is then: $EV_0^B = M(EV_{i0}^B) + m(EV_{j0}^B)$, $i \in M, j \in m$. The expressions can be simplified slightly, and after some manipulations we derive:

$$EV_0^B > EW_0 = M \iff \frac{5}{8}\frac{(M+m)}{\left(\frac{3m-M-1}{2}\right)!\left(\frac{3M-m-1}{2}\right)!} >$$

$$> \sum_{s=k}^{m}\frac{M}{(m-s)!(M-1+s)!} - \sum_{s=k}^{m-1}\frac{m}{(m-s-1)!(M+s)!},$$

where $k = (M - m + 1)/2$. It is then simple to verify that for all $M = 3m - 1$ (i.e. $k = m$) or $M = 3m - 3$ (i.e. $k = m - 1$), $EV_0^B < EW_0$. At the same time, for M large enough it is not difficult to find values of $m = M - 1$ ($k = 1$) such that $EV_0^B > EW_0$, and to generate examples that satisfy the statement in the lemma. $M' = 8$, $m' = 3$ and $m'' = 7$ is one such example; $M' = 6$, $m' = 3$ and $m'' = 5$ is another.

Model *C*.

(a) *Equilibrium*. If $2M > 3m$, by setting $x_{M1} = 2M$ for all v_{M1} the majority can guarantee itself victory over both proposals. All minority strategies are equivalent, including $x_{m1} = m$ if $v_{m1} < 0.5$ and $x_{m1} = 3m$ if $v_{m1} > 0.5$. No deviation can be profitable for a member of either group, and the strategies are an equilibrium. Suppose then $2M \leq 3m$. When $x_m = m$, the minority always loses ($m < \max\{M, m + 3\} < \min\{3M, 4M - (m + 3)\}$). The only possible deviation for a minority member is to cast 2 or 3 votes when $x_{m-i} = m - 1$, but $m + 2 < \max\{M, m + 3\} < \min\{3M, 4M - (m + 3)\}$: the deviation cannot be profitable. The majority always wins when casting $\min\{3M, 4M - (m + 3)\}$ votes, but loses when $x_M = \max\{M, m + 3\}$ if $x_m = 3m$. A majority member casting either 0 or 1 bonus vote when $v_{M1} < 0.5$ could deviate and cast one additional bonus vote, but the deviation cannot be profitable: with $m > 2$ and $2M \leq 3m$,

$\max\{M+1, m+4\} < 3m$; with $m = 2$, $2M \leq 3m$ can only be satisfied if $M = 3$; in this case $\max\{M+1, m+4\} = 3m$, but the possibility of inducing a tie when $v_{M1} < 0.5$ comes at the cost of a future victory, when $Ev = 0.5$ – a net loss in expected utility. If $v_{M1} > 0.5$, a majority member casting 1 or 2 bonus votes could deviate to casting one fewer. But the logic applies identically: with $2M \leq 3m$, either the deviation makes no difference, or, if $m = 2$ and $M = 3$, the deviation entails a net loss in expected utility. Similarly, a majority member casting 0 bonus votes when $v_{M1} < 0.5$ could deviate and cast 2 additional bonus votes. But the deviation cannot be profitable: with $2M \leq 3m$, either $\max\{M+2, m+5\} < 3m$ and $\min\{3M-2, 4M-(m+5)\} > 3m$, in which case the outcomes are unchanged; or $\max\{M+2, m+5\} > 3m$ and $\min\{3M-2, 4M-(m+5)\} < 3m$, in which case the certainty of winning the second proposal, with $Ev = 0.5$, is traded for the certainty of winning with $v_{M1} < 0.5$ – a net loss in expected utility. The same logic rules out deviating from 2 to 0 bonus votes when $v_{M1} > 0.5$. Hence, $x_{m1} = m$ if $v_{m1} < 0.5$ and $x_{m1} = 3m$ if $v_{m1} > 0.5$; and $x_{M1} = \max\{M, m+3\}$ if $v_{M1} < 0.5$ and $x_{M1} = \min\{3M, 4M-(m+3)\}$ if $v_{M1} > 0.5$ are equilibrium strategies.

(b) *Frequency of minority victories.* If $2M \leq 3m$, the minority wins the first vote if ($v_{m1} > 0.5$ and $v_{M1} < 0.5$) and the second if ($v_{m1} < 0.5$ and $v_{M1} > 0.5$) – given F uniform, it wins each vote with probability 0.25.

(c) *Expected equilibrium payoff.* If $2M > 3m$, the majority always wins, and the expected aggregate payoff over the two proposals equals M. If $2M \leq 3m$, the expected aggregate payoff equals: $(1/4)(M/4 + M/2) + (1/4)(3M/4 + M/2) + (1/4)(3M/4 + m/2) + (1/4)(3m/4 + M/2) = (13M + 5m)/16$ (where the first term is the expected payoff over the two proposals when ($v_{m1} < 0.5$ and $v_{M1} < 0.5$), the second when ($v_{m1} > 0.5$ and $v_{M1} > 0.5$), the third when ($v_{m1} < 0.5$ and $v_{M1} > 0.5$), and the fourth when ($v_{m1} > 0.5$ and $v_{M1} < 0.5$) – all events with probability 1/4). With simple majority voting, the majority always wins, and over the two proposals $EW_0 = M$ for all M, m. In this storable votes equilibrium, $EV_0^C = M$ if $2M > 3m$, but $EV_0^C = (13M + 5m)/16 > M$ for all $2M \leq 3m$, establishing the result in the lemma. ■

Note that both model B and C have multiple equilibria. In both models there is an equilibrium where every voter cast 2 votes each period, and the majority always wins. In model C, the equilibrium described in the text can be supported for all $3m - 2 > M$ (even if $2M > 3m$), and mixed strategy equilibria are also possible (one of these is discussed in footnote 13, in Chapter 3 of Part I, the case $M = 3$ and $m = 2$). Both the figure and the derivations below reflect only the equilibrium described in Lemma 3.2.

Construction of Figure 3.1.

Model B.

(a) *Efficient frequency of minority victories.* According to the efficiency criterion, the minority should win whenever the sum of its valuations is larger than the sum of the majority's valuations. Call y (z) the sum of m (M) independent random variables, each distributed Uniformly over $[0, 1]$. The efficient frequency of minority victories is then given by $\int_0^m \left(\int_z^m h(m, y)dy\right) h(M, z)dz$ where:

$$h(m, y) = \frac{1}{2(m-1)!} \sum_{s=0}^{m} (-1)^s \binom{m}{s} (y - s)^{m-1} sign(y - s), \qquad (3.6)$$

(and correspondingly for $h(M, z)$).

(b) *Expected aggregate payoff under first best efficiency.* For each proposal, the ex ante efficient aggregate payoff EU^*_{0B} is easily derived, given (3.6):

$$EU^*_{0B} = \int_0^m \left(\int_z^m yh(m, y)dy\right) h(M, z)dz + \int_0^m \left(\int_y^M zh(M, z)dz\right) h(m, y)dy. \qquad (3.7)$$

Over the two proposals, the ex ante efficient payoff EV^*_{0B} is $2EU^*_{0B}$. The first term in (3.7) corresponds to the efficient expected payoff for the minority group, and the second for the majority group. The corresponding per capita values (multiplied by 2) are plotted in Figure 3.1b.

(c) *Random choice.* If each group has a fifty percent chance of winning any vote, given $Ev = 1/2$, the aggregate expected payoff is $1/2(M/2) + 1/2(m/2)$, over each proposal, or $(M + m)/2$ for the two-proposal game.

Model C

(a) *Efficient frequency of minority victories.* Given the perfect correlation of valuations within each group, the efficient frequency of minority victories is given by $prob(Mv_M < mv_m) = \int_0^1 \int_0^{(m/M)v_m} dv_M dv_m = m/(2M)$.

(b) *Expected aggregate payoff under first best efficiency.* In model C we can represent the total valuation of the minority (majority) group by a random variable y (z), Uniformly distributed over $[0, m]$ ($[0, M]$). The efficient aggregate expected payoff, per proposal, is given by:

$$EU_{0C}^{*} = \int_0^m \left(\int_z^m \frac{y}{m} dy \right) \frac{1}{M} dx + \int_0^m \left(\int_y^M \frac{z}{M} dz \right) \frac{1}{m} dy = \frac{m^2 + 3M^2}{6M}. \tag{3.8}$$

Over the two proposals, the ex ante efficient payoff is $2EU_{0C}^{*}$. The first term in (3.8) corresponds to the efficient expected payoff for the minority group ($m^2/(3M)$), and the second for the majority group ($(3M^2 - m^2)/6M$). The corresponding per capita values (multiplied by 2) are plotted in Figure 3.1b.

4

Agenda Control

4.1 The Formal Model—Version 4.1

A committee of n voters meets to decide whether to implement T distinct, known proposals, $\{P_1, ..P_T\}$, each of which can either pass or fail. The committee votes on the proposals sequentially, and at the start of the meeting one of the members, the *chair* c, announces the order in which all proposals will be brought to a vote.

Each member i of the committee has preferences over each proposal P_t, summarized by a cardinal valuation v_{it}. Valuations v_{it} are independently and identically distributed both across proposals and across individuals according to the distribution $G(\mathrm{v})$ with support $[-1, 1]$, symmetric around 0. A negative valuation means that the voter is against the proposal; a positive valuation that he is in favor. Voter i's absolute valuation $v_{it} \equiv |\mathrm{v}_{it}|$ is i's intensity over proposal P_t. For each proposal P_t, voter i receives utility $u_{it} = v_{it}$ if the decision goes in his preferred direction, and 0 otherwise. Voter i's utility from the entire meeting, U_i, equals $\sum_{t=1}^{T} u_{it}$.

In addition to a regular vote over every proposal, each committee member is given one indivisible bonus vote equivalent to B regular votes. Each proposal is decided in the direction that receives more votes; in case of a tie, a coin is flipped. Before any voting takes place, and before the chair announces the order of the agenda, each committee member knows $\{\mathrm{v}_{i1}, ..\mathrm{v}_{iT}\}$, his own valuations over all proposals, but does not know others' valuations over any of the proposals. The independence of the valuations and the distribution G from which they are drawn are common knowledge, as is the set of voters still endowed with the bonus vote when proposal P_t is called to a vote.

A voter's strategy is, for all voters including the chair, the choice of the proposal on which to cast the bonus vote, and, for the chair alone, the order in which the votes are called. The focus is on quasi-symmetric Perfect Bayesian equilibria in weakly undominated strategies such that all voters who are not the chair play symmetric strategies.

Call P_i^* the proposal to which voter i attaches highest priority: $v_i^* = \max\{\boldsymbol{v}_i\}$. (Hence P_c^* is the proposal to which the chair attaches highest priority: $v_c^* = \max\{\boldsymbol{v}_c\}$). Then:

Proposition 4.1. For all T, n, G, and B, there exists an equilibrium where the chair orders P_c^* in any position on the agenda with equal probability, and every voter i, including the chair, casts his bonus vote on P_i^*.

The equilibrium identified by Proposition 4.1 is identical to the exogenous agenda equilibrium discussed in Chapter 1. Call it the *non-informative* (*NI*) equilibrium, and denote by EV_0^{NI} a voter's ex ante utility in the non-informative equilibrium before preferences are realized and before the chair's role is assigned. Denote by EW_0 ex ante utility with simple majority voting; Ev the expected intensity, and $Ev_{(T)}$ the expected highest-intensity draw. From Chapter 1, there exists a set of bonus vote values, $\mathcal{B}(n)$, such that if $B \in \mathcal{B}(n)$, $EV_0^{NI} > EW_0$ for all n and T if either n is even, or n is odd and $Ev_{(T)}/Ev > [T(n+1)]/[T(n-1)+2]$ (Proposition 1.2 in Box 1.1 in Chapter 1). Thus, for all T, n, G, and $B \in \mathcal{B}(n)$, there exists an equilibrium with an endogenous order of agenda, such that the welfare comparison to majority voting identified in Chapter 1 carries through identically.

Define an equilibrium *informative* if, after the chair's announcement of the agenda's order, all voters identify the chair's highest-priority proposal with probability higher than $1/T$. A *fully informative* (*FI*) equilibrium is one where the chair's highest-priority proposal is identified with probability 1.

Proposition 4.2. Suppose $T = 2$. (1) For all n, G, and $B \in \mathcal{B}(n)$, there exist two payoff-equivalent fully informative equilibria such that: (i) the chair sets $P_c^* = P_t$, with $t \in \{1, 2\}$, and always casts his bonus vote on P_t; (ii) any other committee member i casts his bonus vote on P_t if and only if $v_{it} \geq \alpha(n, G)v_{is}$, $s \neq t$, with $\alpha(n, G) \geq 1$ and unique. (2) With $T = 2$

and $B \in \mathcal{B}(n)$, there exist G and n, for which no other quasi-symmetric informative equilibrium exists.

Call $P^*_{i\mathcal{S}}$ the proposal to which voter i attaches highest priority among some set of proposals $\mathbf{P}_{\mathcal{S}}$: $v^*_{i\mathcal{S}} = \max\{\boldsymbol{v}_{i\mathcal{S}}\}$, and $P^*_{i\mathcal{T}-\mathcal{S}}$ the proposal to which voter i attaches highest priority among the complement set $\mathbf{P}_{\mathcal{T}-\mathcal{S}}$. The following result gives some insight on the equilibria of the game with an arbitrary number of proposals.

Proposition 4.3. Suppose $n \in \{2, 3, 4\}$ and $B \in \mathcal{B}(n)$. (1) For all G and T there exist T payoff-distinct equilibria such that: (i) the chair selects his S-lowest-intensity proposals, with $S \in \{0, 1, 2, .., T-1\}$, and arranges them, in any order, in the first S positions on the agenda; he orders the remaining $T-S$ proposals with equal probability in each of the last $T-S$ positions; (ii) the chair always casts his bonus vote on P^*_c (and thus never casts it on the first S proposals); (iii) any other committee member $j \neq c$ casts his bonus vote on $P^*_{j\mathcal{T}-\mathcal{S}}$ if $v^*_{j\mathcal{T}-\mathcal{S}} \geq \alpha(n, G, T, S)v^*_{j\mathcal{S}}$, and on $P^*_{j\mathcal{S}}$ otherwise. For all G, T, and S, $\alpha(n, G, T, S) \geq 1$ and unique. (2) For $n = 3$, these are the only payoff-distinct quasi-symmetric equilibria holding for all G, T, and $B \in \mathcal{B}(n)$.

Note that with $n \in \{2, 3, 4\}$, $B = 1$ belongs to $\mathcal{B}(n)$: the proposition applies to environments where the bonus vote is equivalent to a regular vote.

Call EV^S_{0c} the chair's ex ante utility in the equilibrium identified by Proposition 4.3, for given value of S, before valuations are realized, but after the role of chair has been assigned. Note that $S = 0$ defines the non-informative equilibrium ($EV^0_{0c} \equiv EV^{NI}_{0c}$), $S = T-1$ defines the fully informative equilibrium ($EV^{T-1}_{0c} \equiv EV^{FI}_{0c}$), and $S \in \{1, .., T-2\}$ defines informative but not fully-informative equilibria. Then:

Proposition 4.4. In all equilibria described in Propositions 4.2 and 4.3, $EV^S_{0c} \geq EV^{NI}_{0c}$, with $S \in \{1, .., T-1\}$.

4.2 Proof of Proposition 4.1

See the proof of Proposition 1.1 in Chapter 1. In this equilibrium, the probability that a voter endowed with his bonus vote at t will cast it over any of the remaining proposals is constant. From the point of view of a different committee member, then, the only criterion for casting the bonus vote is the intensity of his own preferences. The reasoning of Chapter 1 continues to apply, identically, when the order of proposals is endogenous. If the proposer chooses randomly, no information about his voting strategy is conveyed; casting the bonus vote on their highest priority proposal remains a best response for all other voters, guaranteeing that a random choice is itself a best response for the proposer. The endogeneity of the proposals' order has no impact on expected outcomes.

4.3 Proof of Proposition 4.2

We begin by proving claim (1) in the proposition. Consider first the candidate equilibrium where $P_c^* = P_1$. Recall that each voter i, including the chair, decides whether to cast the bonus vote on P_1 or P_2 by evaluating the difference in expected utility from the two actions: $Eu_i(P_1) - Eu_i(P_2) = v_{i1}(p_{iB1} - p_{i11}) - v_{i2}(p_{iB2} - p_{i12})$, where all probabilities are evaluated at the time of the first decision, and p_{Bs} (p_{1s}) is the probability of obtaining the desired outcome when casting $1 + B$ (1) votes on P_s. Any voter's best response strategy is to cast the bonus vote on P_1 if and only if:

$$\frac{v_{i1}}{v_{i2}} \geq \frac{p_{iB2} - p_{i12}}{p_{iB1} - p_{i11}}, \tag{4.1}$$

where $i = c$ if the voter is the chair, and I ignore the subscript otherwise.

Restricting the value of the bonus vote to $B \in \mathcal{B}(n)$ allows us to calculate (4.1) and establish its properties.

(a) Suppose first that n is even. The derivation of the relevant probabilities proceeds as in the proof of Proposition 1.2 in Chapter 1. Consider first the problem for a voter i who is not the chair, and begin by deriving p_{B1}, the probability of winning P_1 when casting the bonus vote. Recall that $B \in \mathcal{B}(n) \iff B < 4/(n-2)$, implying that the bonus vote can make a difference only if the two groups on opposite sides of any proposal are of equal size. With probability $1/2$, the chair is against i and the chair's bonus vote cancels i's. Thus, $p_{B1}|(c \text{ against } i) = p$, where p is the probability of winning P_1, or any other proposal, under simple majority. With probability 1/2, the chair is on i's side. In this case, consider two voters on the opposite side, whom I call j and z. If both cast their bonus votes, from i's point of view the probability of winning P_1 is again identical to simple majority voting. If either one or both do not cast their bonus vote, however, then the probability is higher. As in Chapter 1, call π_t the probability that a voter other than i, still endowed with his bonus vote, casts it over proposal P_t. Working through the different scenarios, we can derive:

$$p_{B1} = p + \left(\frac{1}{2}\right)^{n-1} \binom{n-2}{n/2} (1-\pi_1) \times \left[A_{11} + \frac{(1+\pi_1)}{2} A_{01} + \frac{(1-\pi_1)}{2} A_{21}\right],$$

where A_{0t}, A_{1t}, and A_{2t} are defined as:

$$A_{0t} \equiv prob(M_{it} = M_{jt}) = \sum_{M=0}^{n/2-2} \binom{n/2-2}{M} \binom{n/2-2}{M} \times \pi_t^{2M} (1-\pi_t)^{n-4-2M}$$

$$A_{1t} \equiv prob(M_{it} = M_{jt} + 1) = \sum_{M=0}^{n/2-3} \binom{n/2-2}{M} \binom{n/2-2}{M+1} \times \pi_t^{2M+1} (1-\pi_t)^{n-5-2M}$$

$$A_{2t} \equiv prob(M_{it} = M_{jt} + 2) = \sum_{M=0}^{n/2-4} \binom{n/2-2}{M} \binom{n/2-2}{M+2} \times \pi_t^{2M+2} (1-\pi_t)^{n-6-2M},$$

and M_{it} (M_{jt}) is defined as the number of voters on i's (j's) side, up to a maximum of $n/2 - 2$ who cast the bonus vote on P_t. The maximum is $n/2 - 2$ because we always exclude voter i and account separately for the chair, and for voters j and z. The details are cumbersome, but not difficult, and we obtain:

$$p_{B1}-p_{11}=\left(\frac{1}{2}\right)^{n-1}\left\{\binom{n-2}{n/2}\left[(A_{11}+A_{01})+(A_{21}-A_{01})\right.\right.$$
$$\left.\left.\times\ (1-\pi_1)^2\right]+\binom{n-2}{n/2-1}\left[(A_{11}+A_{01})+(A_{21}-A_{01})\pi_1(1-\pi_1)\right]\right\}. \tag{4.2}$$

When deriving $p_{B2} - p_{12}$, on the other hand, voter i knows that the chair will not cast the bonus vote, and the expression will not be exactly symmetric to (4.2). Again the details are somewhat cumbersome, but the logic straightforward. The expression is as follows:

$$p_{B2} - p_{12} = \left(\frac{1}{2}\right)^{n-1}\left\{\binom{n-2}{n/2}\left[(A_{12} + A_{02}) + (A_{22} - A_{02})\,\pi_2^2\right]\right.$$
$$\left.+\binom{n-2}{n/2-1}\left[(A_{12} + A_{02}) + (A_{22} - A_{02})\,\pi_2(1 - \pi_2)\right]\right\}. \tag{4.3}$$

With $T = 2$, $\pi_1 = 1 - \pi_2$, and simple manipulations show that for all π_1, $A_{11} = A_{12}$; $A_{01} = A_{02}$, and $A_{21} = A_{22}$. It follows that $p_{B1} - p_{11} = p_{B2} - p_{12}$. A voter i who is not the chair should cast the bonus vote on P_1 if and only if $v_{i1} \geq v_{i2}$. Hence $\alpha(n, G) = 1$, and $\pi_1 = 1/2$.

Consider now the chair's problem. Given $\pi_1 = 1/2 = \pi_2$, the chair's best response is simply to cast his bonus vote on the proposal to which he attaches highest valuation. Thus, if $v_{c1} \geq v_{c2}$, always casting the bonus vote on P_1 is indeed supported as an equilibrium strategy.

But we also know from Proposition 1.1 that with $\pi_1 = 1/2 = \pi_2$, from the point of view of the chair the order of proposals is irrelevant, and choosing P_1 such that $v_{c1} \geq v_{c2}$ is consistent with the chair's best response.

We can conclude that if $B \in \mathcal{B}(n)$, n is even, and $T = 2$, there is indeed an equilibrium such that $v_{c1} \geq v_{c2}$, $x_{c1} = 1 + B$, and $x_1 = 1 + B$ if and only if $v_1 \geq v_2$, or equivalently $\alpha(n, G) = 1$ for all G. The equilibrium is fully informative because it is common knowledge that the chair always orders his higher-priority proposal first.

(b) Suppose now that n is odd. Again, consider first the problem for a voter i who is not the chair. Recall that $B \in \mathcal{B}(n) = [2/(n-1), 2/(n-3))$, implying that the bonus vote makes a difference over simple majority only when the groups on opposite sides of a proposal differ in size by a single voter; all minority voters cast the bonus vote, and none of the majority does. In the candidate equilibrium, the chair always casts his bonus vote on P_1. Thus, i's probability of winning the first proposal when casting the bonus vote differs from the probability of winning with simple majority voting only if the chair is on i's side and so are $(n-1)/2-2$ other voters, all of whom cast their bonus vote, while none of the others do. That is,

$$p_{B1} = p + \left(\frac{1}{2}\right)^{n-1+I_{tie}} \binom{n-2}{(n+1)/2} \pi_1^{(n-5)/2}(1-\pi_1)^{(n+1)/2}, \qquad (4.4)$$

where $I_{tie} = 1$ if $B = 2/(n-1)$, and 0 if $B \in (2/(n-1), 2/(n-3))$. The same logic allows us to derive p_{11}, p_{B2}, and p_{12}, and we obtain:

$$p_{B1} - p_{11} = \left(\frac{1}{2}\right)^{n-1+I_{tie}} \pi_1^{(n-5)/2}(1-\pi_1)^{(n-1)/2} \times \left[\binom{n-2}{(n+1)/2}(1-\pi_1) + \binom{n-2}{(n-1)/2}\pi_1\right], \qquad (4.5)$$

and:

$$p_{B2} - p_{12} = \left(\frac{1}{2}\right)^{n-1+I_{tie}} \binom{n-2}{(n-1)/2} \left[\pi_2(1-\pi_2)\right]^{(n-3)/2}, \qquad (4.6)$$

In the candidate equilibrium $\pi_1 \in (0, 1)$ and the ratio of (4.6) to (4.5) is well defined. Expanding the binomial terms and simplifying, we can write:

$$\frac{p_{B2} - p_{12}}{p_{B1} - p_{11}} = \left[\frac{\pi_2(1-\pi_2)}{\pi_1(1-\pi_1)}\right]^{(n-3)/2} \left(\frac{\pi_1}{1-\pi_1}\right)\left(\frac{n+1}{n-3+4\pi_1}\right), \qquad (4.7)$$

Taking into account that $\pi_1 = 1 - \pi_2$, (4.7) simplifies to:

$$\frac{p_{B2} - p_{12}}{p_{B1} - p_{11}} = \left(\frac{\pi_1}{1-\pi_1}\right)\left(\frac{n+1}{n-3+4\pi_1}\right) \equiv \beta(\pi_1).$$

Voter i's best response strategy is to cast the bonus vote on P_1 if $v_{i1} \geq \beta(\pi_1)v_{i2}$. Given $\pi_{c1} = 1$, a symmetric best response by all voters who are not the chair amounts to finding a value of π_1 that solves

$\pi_1 = prob(v_1 \geq \beta(\pi_1)v_2)$. Call F the cumulative distribution function of intensity v. Then,

$$\pi_1 = \int_0^1 F\left(\frac{v}{\beta(\pi_1)}\right) dF(v). \tag{4.8}$$

With v_1 and v_2 independent and distributed according to F, the strategy described in Proposition 4.2 is a symmetric best response if and only if, for all n and G (and thus F), there exists a solution to (4.8) at some $\widetilde{\pi}_1 \in (0, 1/2]$. For given n and G, call the right hand side of (4.8) $\varphi(\pi_1)$. The function $\varphi(\pi_1)$ is continuous in π_1 and for all $n \geq 3$, $\partial\beta(\pi_1)/\partial\pi_1 > 0$, implying that $\partial\varphi(\pi_1)/\partial\pi_1 \leq 0$, but $\lim_{\pi_1 \to 0} \beta(\pi_1) = 0$, and hence $\lim_{\pi_1 \to 0} \varphi(\pi_1) = 1$, while $\beta(1/2) = (n+1)/(n-1) > 1$ for all finite n, and hence $\varphi(1/2) < 1/2$. Thus, there exists a unique $\widetilde{\pi}_1 \in (0, 1/2)$ such that $\widetilde{\pi}_1 = \varphi(\widetilde{\pi}_1)$, or equivalently a unique $\alpha(n, G) > 1$: the statement in the proposition is verified.

Consider now the chair's problem. The logic is unchanged. From the chair's point of view, $p_{cBt} \neq p$ only if the chair is in a minority of size $(n-1)/2$, all of whose members cast their bonus vote while none of the others do. That is,

$$p_{cBt} = p + \left(\frac{1}{2}\right)^{n-1+I_{tie}} \binom{n-1}{(n+1)/2} \pi_t^{(n-3)/2}(1-\pi_t)^{(n+1)/2} \quad t = 1, 2. \tag{4.9}$$

Similarly, $p_{c1t} \neq p$ only if the chair is in a majority of size $(n+1)/2$, none of whose members cast their bonus vote, while all of the others do:

$$p_{c1t} = p - \left(\frac{1}{2}\right)^{n-1+I_{tie}} \binom{n-1}{(n-1)/2} \pi_t^{(n-1)/2}(1-\pi_t)^{(n-1)/2} \quad t = 1, 2. \tag{4.10}$$

Thus:

$$p_{cBt} - p_{c1t} = \left(\frac{1}{2}\right)^{n-1+I_{tie}} \pi_t^{(n-1)/2}(1-\pi_t)^{(n-1)/2} \times \left[\binom{n-1}{(n+1)/2}\left(\frac{1-\pi_t}{\pi_t}\right) + \binom{n-1}{(n-1)/2}\right],$$

with $t = 1, 2$. If $\pi_1 \in (0, 1)$ we can write:

$$\frac{p_{cB2} - p_{c12}}{p_{cB1} - p_{c11}} = \left[\frac{\pi_2(1 - \pi_2)}{\pi_1(1 - \pi_1)}\right]^{(n-1)/2} \left(\frac{\pi_1}{\pi_2}\right)\left(\frac{n - 1 + 2\pi_2}{n - 1 + 2\pi_1}\right).$$

or, again taking into account that $\pi_1 = 1 - \pi_2$ and simplifying:

$$\frac{p_{cB2} - p_{c12}}{p_{cB1} - p_{c11}} = \left(\frac{\pi_1}{1 - \pi_1}\right)\left(\frac{n + 1 - 2\pi_1}{n - 1 + 2\pi_1}\right). \tag{4.11}$$

The right hand side of (4.11) is strictly increasing in π_1 and equals 1 at $\pi_1 = 1/2$; thus, $(p_{cB2} - p_{c12})/(p_{cB1} - p_{c11}) < 1$ for all $\pi_1 < 1/2$. It follows that if $v_{c1} \geq v_{c2}$, $x_{c1} = 1 + B$ is indeed the chair's best response strategy.

Finally, given $\pi_1 < 1/2$, could the chair gain by changing the order of proposals? Two deviations need to be ruled out. The chair could choose P_1 such that $v_{c1} < v_{c2}$ and (i) cast the bonus vote on P_2, or (ii) still cast the bonus vote on P_1. Call $v_c^* \equiv \max\{v_{c1}, v_{c2}\}$ and $\underline{v_c} \equiv \min\{v_{c1}, v_{c2}\}$. The first deviation is ruled out if: $p_{cB1}v_c^* + p_{c12}\underline{v_c} \geq p_{c11}\underline{v_c} + p_{cB2}v_c^*$, or $v_c^*(p_{cB1} - p_{cB2}) \geq \underline{v_c}(p_{c11} - p_{c12})$. Given $v_c^* \geq \underline{v_c}$ and $p_{cB1} > p_{c11}$, $p_{cB2} > p_{c12}$, a sufficient condition is then $(p_{cB1} - p_{c11}) \geq (p_{cB2} - p_{c12})$, which we know satisfied for all $\pi_1 < 1/2$: the deviation cannot be profitable. The second deviation is ruled out if: $p_{cB1}v_c^* + p_{c12}\underline{v_c} \geq p_{cB1}\underline{v_c} + p_{c12}v_c^*$, or $v_c^*(p_{cB1} - p_{c12}) \geq \underline{v_c}(p_{cB1} - p_{c12})$, or $p_{cB1} - p_{c12} \geq 0$. This can be verified immediately from (4.9) and (4.10) above; again, the deviation cannot be profitable.

We can conclude that if $B \in \mathcal{B}(n)$ and $T = 2$, for both n odd and n even the strategies described in the proposition with $t = 1$ are indeed equilibrium strategies. With $T = 2$, the two positions, $t = 1$ and $t = 2$ are completely symmetric, and the proof can be applied identically to the proposal ordered in position 2, P_2. The two equilibria are mirror images of each other, and they are payoff equivalent.

We can now proceed to proving claim (2). The proposition states that no other quasi-symmetric informative equilibria exist for all n and G. We need to rule out partially informative equilibria in which the chair sets his highest priority proposal as P_1 (or P_2) with some probability $\in (1/2, 1)$. With $T = 2$, such equilibria do indeed exist when

n is even. Suppose, instead, $n = 3$, and consider candidate informative equilibria such that $\pi_{c1} \in (1/2, 1]$. Taking into account $\pi_2 = 1 - \pi_1$ and $\pi_{c2} = 1 - \pi_{c1}$:

$$p_{B1} - p_{11} = (1 - \pi_1 \pi_{c1})(1/2)^{2+I_{tie}}$$

$$p_{B2} - p_{12} = (\pi_{c1} + \pi_1 - \pi_1 \pi_{c1})(1/2)^{2+I_{tie}},$$

where $I_{tie} = 1$ if $B = 1$, and 0 if $B > 1$. If $\pi_{c1} + \pi_1 > 1$, then $p_{B2} - p_{12} > p_{B1} - p_{11}$, implying $\pi_1 < 1/2$.

But we showed above that if $\pi_1 < 1/2$, the chair's best response is to choose P_1 such that $v_{c1} \geq v_{c2}$ and always cast the bonus vote on P_1. The only symmetric best response for the other voters, then, is to cast the bonus vote on P_1 if and only if $v_1 \geq \alpha(3, G)v_2$, an event that occurs with probability $\tilde{\pi}_1 \in (0, 1/2)$, the equilibrium strategy characterized earlier. If $\pi_{c1} + \pi_1 \leq 1$, then $p_{B2} - p_{12} \leq p_{B1} - p_{11}$, implying $\pi_1 \geq 1/2$. But in this candidate scenario $\pi_{c1} > 1/2$, and thus $\pi_{c1} + \pi_1 > 1$, a contradiction. Identical reasoning rules out any informative equilibrium with $\pi_{c2} \in (1/2, 1]$ that would differ from the second equilibrium characterized in the proposition. ■

The focus of the analysis and the definition of informative equilibria stress the possibility of transmitting information on the chair's priorities. Could the order of proposals be used to transmit information about the chair's *direction* of preferences, as opposed to the chair's *intensity* of preferences? With $T = 2$, could there be an equilibrium such that if there is at least one proposal the chair favors, it will be ordered first, and if there is at least one proposal the chair opposes, it will be ordered last? Call d_t the probability that the chair favors P_t. Is there an equilibrium where $d_1 > 1/2$ and $d_2 < 1/2$? The answer is that no such equilibrium can exist for all n. Intuitively, transmitting information about one's priorities can encourage allies to withdraw their bonus vote, relative to voters with opposite preferences, reducing the chair's probability of winning the current proposal. Because preferences are independent across proposals and voters, no future benefit can accrue to the chair from the reallocation of available bonus votes among the other voters. Suppose, for example, $n = 3$, and call i and j non chair voters such that $v_{i1} > 0$

and $v_{j1} < 0$. Then,

$$p_{iB1} - p_{i11} = [1 - \pi_1 - d_1(1 - 2\pi_1 + \pi_1\pi_{c1})](1/2)^{1+I_{tie}}$$

$$p_{jB1} - p_{j11} = [1 - \pi_1 - (1 - d_1)(1 - 2\pi_1 + \pi_1\pi_{c1})](1/2)^{1+I_{tie}}.$$

If $d_1 > 1/2$, $(p_{iB1} - p_{i11}) < (p_{jB1} - p_{j11})$. Hence, the threshold value of v_1/v_2 that induces a voter to cast the bonus vote on P_1 is higher if the voter agrees with the chair. As a result, the chair would be better off lying. The argument extends unchanged to $T > 2$, and the possibility of equilibria of this type is not discussed further.

4.4 Proof of Proposition 4.3

The two claims in the proposition are proved in order. (1) If $n = 2$, the equilibria in the proposition hold with $\alpha(G, T, S)|_{n=2} = 1$ for all G, T, and S. The proof is immediate, and I only sketch its logic here. When $n = 2$, casting the bonus vote on one's highest valuation is a dominant strategy, for any G and for any T and S: the increase in the pivot probability associated with the use of the bonus vote is exactly identical, whether one's opponent casts the bonus vote or not. Thus, whether the agenda's order is informative or not has no effect on the strategy of the voter who is not the chair. Similarly, the chair can choose to transmit information through the agenda setting, or not to, with no effect on his own voting strategy. Welfare is identical to the exogenous agenda case.

Consider then $n \in \{3, 4\}$. For $S = 0$, the equilibrium falls under Proposition 4.1; for $T = 2$, and $S = 1$, the equilibrium falls under Proposition 4.2. Consider then $S > 0$ and $T > 2$. Call $\mathbf{P}_S$ the set of S proposals ordered by the chair in the first S positions of the agenda, and $\mathbf{P}_{T-S}$ the set of $T - S$ proposals ordered in the last $T - S$ positions. The proof is logically identical to the proof of Proposition 4.2.

(a) Suppose first $n = 4$. Consider the best response strategy for voter i, who is not the chair. Voter i casts the bonus vote on proposal P_t over proposal P_s if the ratio v_{it}/v_{is} is larger than:

$$\frac{p_{Bs} - p_{1s}}{p_{Bt} - p_{1t}} = \frac{3 - \pi_s(2 - \pi_s) - \pi_{cs}(1 - 2\pi_s)}{3 - \pi_t(2 - \pi_t) - \pi_{ct}(1 - 2\pi_t)}, \tag{4.12}$$

where the right hand side of (4.12) is derived taking into account $B \in \mathcal{B}(4)$, as in the proof of Proposition 4.2 (but allowing π_c to differ from 0 or 1). If P_s and $P_t \in \mathbf{P}_{\mathcal{S}}$, then in the candidate equilibrium $\pi_{ct} = \pi_{cs} = 0$, and π_t, the probability that another non-chair voter in the four-person committee casts his bonus vote on P_t, must equal $prob(v_{jt} = v^*_{j\mathcal{S}})prob(v^*_{j\mathcal{S}} > (1/\alpha)v^*_{j\mathcal{T}-\mathcal{S}}) = (1/S)prob(v^*_{j\mathcal{S}} > (1/\alpha)v^*_{j\mathcal{T}-\mathcal{S}}) = \pi_s$. Thus, the ratio on the right hand side of (4.12) is equal to 1, and i will cast his bonus vote on P_t, as opposed to P_s, only if $v_{it} > v_{is}$: among all proposals in $\mathbf{P}_{\mathcal{S}}$, the only candidate for i's bonus vote is the highest-intensity proposal in the set, $P^*_{i\mathcal{S}}$. Similarly, if P_s and $P_t \in \mathbf{P}_{\mathcal{T}-\mathcal{S}}$, then in the candidate equilibrium $\pi_{ct} = \pi_{cs} = 1/(T - S)$, and $\pi_t = prob(v_{jt} = v^*_{j\mathcal{T}-\mathcal{S}})prob(v^*_{j\mathcal{T}-\mathcal{S}} > \alpha v^*_{j\mathcal{S}}) = 1/(T-S)prob(v^*_{j\mathcal{T}-\mathcal{S}} > \alpha v^*_{j\mathcal{S}}) = \pi_s$. Again, the ratio on the right hand side of (4.12) equals 1, and among all proposals in $\mathbf{P}_{\mathcal{T}-\mathcal{S}}$, the only candidate for i's bonus vote is the highest-intensity proposal in the set, $P^*_{i\mathcal{T}-\mathcal{S}}$. Suppose, then, $P_t = P^*_{i\mathcal{T}-\mathcal{S}}$ and $P_s = P^*_{i\mathcal{S}}$ (note that this case is only relevant if $S > 0$). The ratio in (4.12) becomes:

$$\frac{p_{Bs} - p_{1s}}{p_{Bt} - p_{1t}} = \frac{3 + \pi_s^2 - 2\pi_s}{3 - \pi_t(2 - \pi_t) - (1 - 2\pi_t)/(T - S)}, \qquad (4.12')$$

where $\pi_s = (1/S)[1 - \pi_t(T - S)]$. We can write the right hand side of (4.12′) as some function $\gamma(\pi_t)$. Voter i's best response is to cast his bonus vote on $P^*_{i\mathcal{T}-\mathcal{S}}$ if and only if $v^*_{i\mathcal{T}-\mathcal{S}} \geq \gamma(\pi_t)v^*_{i\mathcal{S}}$. Thus, in a quasi-symmetric equilibrium π_t, the probability that a non-chair voter in the committee casts his bonus vote on P_t, must equal $prob(v_{jt} = v^*_{j\mathcal{T}-\mathcal{S}})prob(v^*_{j\mathcal{T}-\mathcal{S}} > \gamma(\pi_t)v^*_{j\mathcal{S}})$. Or:

$$\pi_t = \int_0^1 \left[F\left(\frac{v}{\gamma(\pi_t)}\right)\right]^S [F(v)]^{T-S-1}\, dF(v) \equiv \psi(\pi_t). \qquad (4.13)$$

Both γ and ψ are continuous in π_t. Note that $\gamma(0) \in (0, 3/2)$ for all $S < T$, and hence $\psi(0) > 0$; while $\gamma(\pi_t)|_{\pi_t=1/T} > 1$ for all $T > 2$, and hence $\psi(\pi_t)|_{\pi_t=1/T} < 1/T$. It follows that (4.13) must have a solution at some $\tilde{\pi}_t < 1/T$ at which $\gamma(\tilde{\pi}_t) = \alpha(4, G, T, S) > 1$. In addition, for all $S < T - 1$, γ is strictly increasing in π_t, for all $\pi_t \in [0, 1/(T - S)]$, and thus ψ must be strictly decreasing, and $\tilde{\pi}_t$ must be unique. If $S = T - 1$, $\lim_{\pi_t \to 1/(T-S)} \gamma(\pi_t) = 1$, and hence $\lim_{\pi_1 \to 1/(T-S)} \psi(\pi_t) = 1/T$;

but $\partial\gamma/\partial\pi_t$ has a unique root, a maximum, at some $\pi_t' < 1/T$ (and thus ψ has a unique minimum at π_t'), implying that equation (4.13) again has a unique solution: $\alpha(4, G, T, S)$ is unique. Finally, notice that for all $\gamma(\widetilde{\pi}_t) > 1$, $\psi(\widetilde{\pi}_t)$ must be lower the higher is S, and thus for given G and T, $\widetilde{\pi}_t$ must be lower the higher is S. The highest admissible value of S is $S = T - 1$ or $T - S = 1$– the fully informative equilibrium: $\widetilde{\pi}_t$ is monotonically lower the more informative is the equilibrium.

Consider now the chair's problem. Given the order of the proposals and the other voters' posited strategies, the only possible targets for the chair's bonus vote are his highest-intensity proposals in the two sets, $P^*_{c\mathcal{T}-\mathcal{S}}$ and $P^*_{c\mathcal{S}}$ (because in all comparisons between proposals P_s and P_t in the same set, whether $\mathbf{P}_{\mathcal{S}}$ or $\mathbf{P}_{\mathcal{T}-\mathcal{S}}$, $\pi_t = \pi_s$ and thus $(p_{cBs} - p_{c1s})/(p_{cBt} - p_{c1t}) = 1$). Suppose then $P_t = P^*_{i\mathcal{T}-\mathcal{S}}$ and $P_s = P^*_{i\mathcal{S}}$, and recall that in the candidate equilibrium $v^*_{c\mathcal{T}-\mathcal{S}} \geq v^*_{c\mathcal{S}}$. With $B \in \mathcal{B}(4)$ and $n = 4$:

$$\frac{p_{cBs} - p_{c1s}}{p_{cBt} - p_{c1t}} = \left(\frac{1 - \pi_s(1 - \pi_s)}{1 - \pi_t(1 - \pi_t)}\right),$$

an expression smaller than 1 for all $\pi_s > \pi_t$. (Note that with $T > 2$ and $S > 0$, $\pi_s < 1/2$, and $\pi_t < 1/2$). Thus, if $v^*_{c\mathcal{T}-\mathcal{S}} \geq v^*_{c\mathcal{S}}$, it is indeed optimal for the chair to cast his bonus vote on $P^*_{i\mathcal{T}-\mathcal{S}}$. Can the chair do better by deviating in the order of the proposals? As in the proof of Proposition 4.2, two possible deviations must be considered. First, the chair could order his highest-intensity proposal in the first S positions on the agenda and cast on it his bonus vote. Second, the chair could order his highest-intensity proposal in the first S positions but cast his bonus vote on $P^*_{c\mathcal{T}-\mathcal{S}}$. Using the index t to refer to a proposal in $\mathbf{P}_{\mathcal{T}-\mathcal{S}}$ and the index s to refer to a proposal in $\mathbf{P}_{\mathcal{S}}$, the first deviation is ruled out if $v^*_c(p_{cBt} - p_{cBs}) > v_c(p_{c1t} - p_{c1s})$ for all $v_c \leq v^*_c$. A sufficient condition then is $(p_{cBt} - p_{c1t}) > (p_{cBs} - p_{c1s})$, which we know satisfied for all $\pi_s > \pi_t$. The first deviation cannot be profitable. The second deviation is ruled out if $v^*_c(p_{cBt} - p_{c1s}) > v_c(p_{cBt} - p_{c1s})$ for all $v_c \leq v^*_c$. A sufficient condition then is $p_{cBt} > p_{c1s}$. It is not difficult to verify that $p_{cBt} > p$, while $p_{c1s} < p$, implying that the second deviation cannot be profitable either.

Finally, Proposition 4.3 states that the chair will order his S-lowest-intensity proposals in the first S positions of the agenda. Because the bonus vote is spent on v^*_c, the stated ordering is indeed a best response for the chair if $p_{c1t} > p_{c1s}$, which again is immediately verified, given $\pi_t < \pi_s < 1/2$.

(b) Suppose now $n = 3$. The logic proceeds identically. Again, consider the best response strategy for voter i, who is not the chair. Voter i casts the bonus vote on proposal P_t over proposal P_s if the ratio v_{it}/v_{is} is larger than:

$$\frac{p_{Bs} - p_{1s}}{p_{Bt} - p_{1t}} = \frac{1 - \pi_s \pi_{cs}}{1 - \pi_t \pi_{ct}}, \tag{4.14}$$

where the right hand side of (4.14) is derived taking into account $B \in \mathcal{B}(3)$. If P_s and $P_t \in \mathbf{P}_{\mathcal{S}}$, or if P_s and $P_t \in \mathbf{P}_{\mathcal{T}-\mathcal{S}}$, in the candidate equilibrium, the ratio on the right hand side of (4.14) equals 1: only $P^*_{i\mathcal{S}}$ and $P^*_{i\mathcal{T}-\mathcal{S}}$ are candidates for i's bonus vote. Suppose, then, $P_t = P^*_{i\mathcal{T}-\mathcal{S}}$ and $P_s = P^*_{i\mathcal{S}}$ (and $S > 0$). The ratio in (4.14) becomes:

$$\frac{p_{Bs} - p_{1s}}{p_{Bt} - p_{1t}} = \frac{1}{1 - \pi_t/(T - S)}. \tag{4.14'}$$

Call the right hand side of (4.14′) $\delta(\pi_t)$. Voter i's best response is to cast the bonus vote on P_t if and only if $v^*_{i\mathcal{T}-\mathcal{S}} \geq \delta(\pi_t) v^*_{i\mathcal{S}}$. Thus, $\pi_t = prob(v_{jt} = v^*_{j\mathcal{T}-\mathcal{S}}) prob(v^*_{j\mathcal{T}-\mathcal{S}} > \delta(\pi_t) v^*_{j\mathcal{S}})$. In a quasi-symmetric equilibrium, π_t must solve:

$$\pi_t = \int_0^1 \left[F\left(\frac{v}{\delta(\pi_t)} \right) \right]^S [F(v)]^{T-S-1} \, dF(v) \equiv \zeta(\pi_t).$$

Both δ and ζ are continuous in π_t. Note that $\lim_{\pi_t \to >0} \delta(\pi_t) = 1$, and hence $\lim_{\pi_t \to >0} \zeta(\pi_t) = 1/T > 0$; while $\delta(\pi_t)|_{\pi_1 = 1/T} > 1$ for all finite T, and hence $\zeta(\pi_t)|_{\pi_t = 1/T} < 1/T$. In addition, δ is everywhere increasing in π_t, and thus ζ is everywhere decreasing in π_t. It follows that ζ must have a unique solution at some $\tilde{\pi}_t \in (0, 1/T)$. Thus, $\delta(\pi_t)|_{\pi_t = \tilde{\pi}_t} \equiv \alpha(3, G, T, S) > 1$ for all G, T, S, with $S > 0$. Note that for all $\delta(\tilde{\pi}_t) > 1$, $\zeta(\tilde{\pi}_t)$ must be lower the higher is S, and thus, for given G and T, $\tilde{\pi}_t$ must be lower the higher is S. As in the case of $n = 4$, $\tilde{\pi}_t$ is monotonically lower the more informative is the equilibrium.

Consider now the chair's problem. As argued earlier, given the order of the proposals and the other voters' posited strategies, the only possible targets for the chair's bonus vote are his highest-intensity proposals in the two sets, $P^*_{c\mathcal{T}-\mathcal{S}}$ and $P^*_{c\mathcal{S}}$. Suppose then $P_t = P^*_{c\mathcal{T}-\mathcal{S}}$ and $P_s = P^*_{c\mathcal{S}}$, and recall that in the candidate equilibrium $v^*_{c\mathcal{T}-\mathcal{S}} \geq v^*_{c\mathcal{S}}$. With $B \in \mathcal{B}(3)$ and $n = 3$:

$$\frac{p_{cBs} - p_{c1s}}{p_{cBt} - p_{c1t}} = \left(\frac{1 - \pi_s^2}{1 - \pi_t^2}\right),$$

an expression smaller than 1 for all $\pi_s > \pi_t$. Thus, with $v^*_{c\mathcal{T}-\mathcal{S}} \geq v^*_{c\mathcal{S}}$, it is indeed optimal for the chair to cast his bonus vote on $P^*_{c\mathcal{T}-\mathcal{S}}$. Can the chair do better by deviating in the order of the proposals? Once again, two deviations must be considered: (1) The chair could order his highest-intensity proposal in the first S positions on the agenda, and cast on it his bonus vote; (2) the chair could order his highest-intensity proposal in the first S positions but cast his bonus vote on $P^*_{c\mathcal{T}-\mathcal{S}}$. Using the index t to refer to a proposal in $\mathbf{P}_{\mathcal{T}-\mathcal{S}}$ and the index s to refer to a proposal in $\mathbf{P}_{\mathcal{S}}$, the first deviation is ruled out if $v_c^*(p_{cBt} - p_{cBs}) > v_c(p_{c1t} - p_{c1s})$ for all $v_c \leq v_c^*$. A sufficient condition, then, is $(p_{cBt} - p_{c1t}) > (p_{cBs} - p_{c1s})$, a condition we know satisfied for all $\pi_t < \pi_s$. The first deviation cannot be profitable. The second deviation is ruled out if $v_c^*(p_{cBt} - p_{c1s}) > v_c(p_{cBt} - p_{c1s})$ for all $v_c \leq v_c^*$. A sufficient condition, then, is $p_{cBt} > p_{c1s}$. But as in the case of $n = 4$, $p_{cBt} > p$, while $p_{c1s} < p$, implying that the second deviation cannot be profitable either.

Finally, Proposition 4.3 states that the chair will order his S-lowest-intensity proposals in the first S positions of the agenda. Because the bonus vote is spent on v_c^*, the stated ordering is indeed a best response for the chair if $p_{c1t} > p_{c1s}$, which again is immediately verified with $\pi_t < \pi_s < 1/2$ for all $T > 2$.

We now need to prove claim (2) in the proposition. In the equilibria characterized by the proposition: (i) If the chair randomizes over P_c^*'s position in the agenda, he randomizes with equal probabilities. To show that this must be true, consider proposals in positions r and t, and suppose $\pi_{cr} > \pi_{ct} > 0$. With $n = 3$, voter i who is not chair prefers to cast his bonus vote on P_r relative to some other proposal P_s if $v_{ir}/v_{is} \geq (1 - \pi_s\pi_{cs})/(1 - \pi_r\pi_{cr})$, and similarly for P_t. It then follows immediately that any quasi-symmetric equilibrium where $\pi_{cr} > \pi_{ct}$ must have $\pi_r < \pi_t$. For the chair, this implies $(p_{cBr} - p_{c1r}) > (p_{cBt} - p_{c1t})$: in any realization in which the chair orders P_c^* as P_t, he can do strictly better by exchanging P_t and P_r, and thus ordering P_c^* as P_r and casting his bonus vote on P_r.

If $\pi_{cr} > \pi_{ct}$, then $\pi_{ct} = 0$. Thus $\pi_{cr} > \pi_{ct} > 0$ cannot be supported in equilibrium. (In fact, the same argument holds for $n = 4$ if $T > 2$).

(ii) Given the chair's strategy, the only candidates for non-chair voter i's bonus vote are proposals $P^*_{i\mathcal{S}}$ and $P^*_{i\mathcal{T}-\mathcal{S}}$. To show that this must be true, again consider the ratio $(p_{Br} - p_{1r})/(p_{Bt} - p_{1t})$. When both P_r and P_t belong to $\mathbf{P}_{\mathcal{S}}$, $\pi_{cr} = \pi_{ct} = 0$; therefore with $n = 3$, $(p_{Br} - p_{1r})/(p_{Bt} - p_{1t}) = 1$, and i's best response is to cast the bonus vote on P_r rather than P_t if and only if $v_{ir} > v_{it}$. The conclusion follows. When both P_r and P_t belong to $\mathbf{P}_{\mathcal{T}-\mathcal{S}}$, $\pi_{cr} = \pi_{ct} = 1/(T - S)$. Suppose $\pi_r > \pi_t$; then $(p_{Br} - p_{1r})/(p_{Bt} - p_{1t}) < 1$, and voter i's best response results in casting the bonus vote on P_t more frequently than on P_r: any quasi-symmetric equilibrium requires $\pi_r = \pi_t$, and thus $(p_{Br} - p_{1r})/(p_{Bt} - p_{1t}) = 1$, and the conclusion follows. Thus, for $n = 3$, the only payoff-distinct informative equilibria are the ones described in the proposition, and claim (2) is established.

4.5 Proof of Proposition 4.4

In all informative equilibria, $S > 0$, and:

$$EV^S_{0c} = (p_{cBt} - p_{c1t})Ev_{(T)} + \sum_{r=1}^{S} Ev_{(r)}(p_{c1s} - p_{c1t}) + TEvp_{c1t}, \qquad (4.15)$$

where the index t refers to a proposal in $\mathbf{P}_{\mathcal{T}-\mathcal{S}}$ and the index s refers to a proposal in $\mathbf{P}_{\mathcal{S}}$. The probabilities take into account the voting strategies of the other committee members and are derived above in the proofs to Propositions 4.2 and 4.3. Propositions 4.2 and 4.3 imply $\pi_t \leq 1/T$ and $\pi_s = [1 - (T - S)\pi_t]/S \geq 1/T$. If $\pi_t = 1/T$, then $\pi_s = 1/T$, $p_{c1s} = p_{c1t}$ and $EV^S_{0c} = EV^{NI}_{0c}$. Thus, the proof of the proposition amounts to showing that EV^S_{0c} is declining in π_t for all $\pi_t \in [\underline{\pi_t}, 1/T]$ where $\underline{\pi_t}$ is the lower bound on possible equilibrium values of π_t. Because π_t and the probabilities p_{cBt}, p_{c1t}, and p_{c1s} depend on n, T, S, and B, the different cases need to be studied separately. The proof is tedious but straightforward.

(i) Consider first the equilibria described in Proposition 4.2, where $T = 2$ and $S = 1$. Equation (4.15) can be rewritten as:

$$EV_{0c}^{1} = (p_{cB1} - p_{c12})Ev_{(2)} + 2p_{c12}Ev. \tag{4.16}$$

As shown in the proof of Proposition 4.2, if n is even, $\alpha(n, G, S) = 1$, or correspondingly $\pi_1 = 1/2$. Thus $EV_{0c}^{1} = EV_{0c}^{0}$ for all n even. Consider then n odd. Substitute p_{cB1} and p_{c12} in (4.16) from (4.9) and (4.10), taking into account that $\pi_2 = 1 - \pi_1$. Differentiating with respect to π_1, we obtain:

$$\frac{\partial EV_{0c}^{1}}{\partial \pi_1} < 0 \Longleftrightarrow Ev_{(2)}\left(\frac{n-3}{2} - (n-3)\pi_1 - 2\pi_1^2\right) < Ev(n+1)\pi_1(1-2\pi_1). \tag{4.17}$$

Note that the proof of Proposition 4.2 establishes a lower bound $\underline{\pi_1}$ on π_1, where $\underline{\pi_1}$ is the solution to $\beta(\underline{\pi_1}) = 1$ (and thus $\varphi(\underline{\pi_1}) = 1/2$). Solving $\beta(\underline{\pi_1}) = 1$, we find:

$$\underline{\pi_1} = \frac{1}{4}\left[3 - n + \sqrt{(n-3)(n+1)}\right].$$

It is not difficult to verify that the left hand side of (4.17) is negative as long as $\pi_1 > \underline{\pi_1}$. Hence,

$$\frac{\partial EV_{0c}^{1}}{\partial \pi_1} < 0 \Longleftrightarrow \frac{Ev_{(2)}}{Ev} > \frac{2(n+1)\pi_1(2\pi_1 - 1)}{4\pi_1^2 + 2(n-3)\pi_1 - (n-3)},$$

a ratio that is smaller than 1 for all $\pi_1 \in [\frac{n-1-\sqrt{n+1}}{2n}, \frac{n-1+\sqrt{n+1}}{2n}]$. But $\frac{n-1-\sqrt{n+1}}{2n} < \underline{\pi_1}$ and $\frac{n-1+\sqrt{n+1}}{2n} > 1/2$, and in equilibrium $\widetilde{\pi}_1 \in (\underline{\pi_1}, 1/2)$. Hence, in equilibrium $\frac{\partial EV_c^S}{\partial \pi_1} < 0$, and thus $EV_{0c}^{1}(\widetilde{\pi}_1) > EV_{0c}^{1}|_{\pi_1=1/2} = EV_{0c}^{0}$.

(ii) Consider now the equilibria described in Proposition 4.3, where $T > 2$, $n \in \{2, 3, 4\}$, and $B \in \mathcal{B}(n)$. With $n = 2$, $\alpha(G, T, S) = 1$ for all G, T, and S. Thus trivially $EV_{0c}^{S} = EV_{0c}^{0}$ for all S. With $n = 3$ and $B \in \mathcal{B}(n)$:

$$p_{cBt} - p_{c1t} = \left(\frac{1}{2}\right)^{1+I_{tie}} \left(\frac{(1-\pi_t)^2}{2} + \pi_t(1-\pi_t)\right)$$

$$p_{c1s} - p_{c1t} = \left(\frac{1}{2}\right)^{1+I_{tie}} [\pi_t(1-\pi_t) - \pi_s(1-\pi_s)]$$

$$p_{c1t} = (3/4) - \left(\frac{1}{2}\right)^{1+I_{tie}} \pi_t(1-\pi_t),$$

and recall that $\pi_s = [1-(T-S)\pi_t]/S$. Differentiating (4.15) with respect to π_t, we obtain:

$$\frac{\partial EV_{0c}^{S}}{\partial \pi_t} = \left(\frac{1}{2}\right)^{1+I_{tie}} \frac{1}{S^2}\Bigg[-Ev_{(T)}\pi_t S^2 + Ev(2\pi_t - 1)S^2 T + \sum_{r=1}^{S} Ev_{(r)}[S(2+T-4\pi_t T) + 2T(\pi_t T - 1)]\Bigg]. \qquad (4.18)$$

It is not difficult to verify that $\partial^2 EV_{0c}^{S}/\partial\pi_t^2 > 0$, and thus (4.18) is maximal at $\pi_t = 1/T$. But,

$$\left.\frac{\partial EV_{0c}^{S}}{\partial \pi_t}\right|_{\pi_t=1/T} = -\left(\frac{1}{2}\right)^{1+I_{tie}} \frac{1}{ST}\Bigg[SEv_{(T)} + T(T-2) \times \left(SEv - \sum_{r=1}^{S} Ev_{(r)}\right)\Bigg] < 0,$$

(because $SEv > \sum_{r=1}^{S} Ev_{(r)}$), and thus (4.18) is negative for all $\pi_t \in [0, 1/T]$. Notice that although we know that π_t is smaller the higher is S, the observation does not imply that (4.15) must be higher the higher is S because at higher S, the number of terms in the summation increases, and $(p_{c1s} - p_{c1t}) < 0$ for all $\pi_t < 1/T$.

Suppose now $n = 4$. With $n = 4$ and $B \in \mathcal{B}(n)$:

$$p_{cBt} - p_{c1t} = \frac{3}{16}[1 - \pi_t(1 - \pi_t)]$$

$$p_{c1s} - p_{c1t} = \frac{3}{16}\pi_t[1 - \pi_t(1 - \pi_t)] - \frac{3}{16}\pi_s[1 - \pi_s(1 - \pi_s)]$$

$$p_{c1t} = (11/16) - \frac{3}{16}\pi_t[1 - \pi_t(1 - \pi_t)].$$

Differentiating (4.15) with respect to π_t, we obtain:

$$\frac{\partial EV_{0c}^S}{\partial \pi_t} = \frac{1}{16}\Bigg[-3Ev_{(T)}(1 - 2\pi_t) - 3TEv(1 - 2\pi_t + 3\pi_t^2) + \frac{1}{S^3}\sum_{r=1}^{S} Ev_{(r)}A(\pi_t)\Bigg], \quad (4.19)$$

where:

$$A(\pi_t) \equiv 9T(1 - \pi_t T)^2 + 3S(1 - \pi_t T)(9\pi_t T - 3 - 2T) + 3S^2[2 + T - \pi_t(6 + 4T - 9\pi_t T)].$$

If $A(\pi_t) < 0$, then $\partial EV_{0c}^S/\partial \pi_t < 0$ and the proof is concluded. If $A(\pi_t) > 0$, then $\partial EV_c^S/\partial \pi_t$ is increasing in $\sum_{r=1}^{S} Ev_{(r)}$. But $\sum_{r=1}^{S} Ev_{(r)} < SEv$, and thus $\partial EV_{0c}^S/\partial \pi_t$ must be negative if:

$$-3Ev_{(T)}(1 - 2\pi_t) - Ev[3T(1 - 2\pi_t + 3\pi_t^2) - \frac{1}{S^2}A(\pi_t)] < 0.$$

Manipulating this expression, we obtain $3T(1 - 2\pi_t + 3\pi_t^2) - \frac{1}{S^2}A(\pi_t) > 0 \iff 3 - 2S - 3\pi_t(T - 2S) < 0$. It is not difficult to see that the condition must be satisfied for all $S > 1$. When $S = 1$, the condition requires $\pi_t > 1/(3T - 6)$. But if $S = 1$, $\underline{\pi_t} = 1/(1 + \sqrt{1 + T(T-1)}) > 1/(3T - 6)$ for all $T > 3$. The only remaining case is then $S = 1$, $T = 3$. But it is then immediate to verify that for $S = 1$, $T = 3$, $\partial EV_{0c}^S/\partial \pi_t < 0$ for all $\pi_t > 0.131$, a condition that must be satisfied for all $\pi_t \in [\underline{\pi_t}, 1/T]$ since $\underline{\pi_t} = 1/(1 + \sqrt{7}) = 0.274$. Thus (4.19) must be always negative for all $\pi_t \in [\underline{\pi_t}, 1/T]$, and the proof is concluded. ■

4.6 Equilibria: Experiment 4.1

In the experiment, there are five equilibria in all, only three of which result in different payoffs. The existence of the NI and PI (partially informative) equilibria, and of the FI equilibrium in which the chair orders P_c^* as the third proposal follows from Proposition 4.3. There exist two additional payoff-equivalent FI equilibria in which P_c^* is ordered second and first. The FI equilibrium in which P_c^* is ordered second mirrors the payoff-equivalent equilibrium in which P_c^* is ordered third – voting choices over the last proposal are residual, and the chair cannot affect any non-chair strategy by deviating off equilibrium and not casting the bonus vote on P_2. The FI equilibrium in which P_c^* is ordered first does require the specification of off-equilibrium beliefs that can support it as a sequential equilibrium. Plausible beliefs $\pi_{c2} = \pi_{c3} = 1/2$, were the chair to deviate and not cast the bonus vote on P_1, are sufficient for the purpose: they guarantee $\pi_2 > \pi_1$ and thus support the chair's equilibrium strategy.

Showing that with the experimental parameterization no other equilibrium exists is more cumbersome but again builds on arguments used in the proofs to the propositions. For $n = 3$, Proposition 1.1 in Chapter 1 shows that no other NI equilibrium exists; the proof of Proposition 4.3 shows that in the PI equilibrium, the chair must randomize the order of P_c^* over positions $\{T - S, .., T\}$ with equal probability, and that in all equilibria the only candidates for non-chair voter i's bonus vote are proposals $P_{i\mathcal{S}}^*$ and $P_{i\mathcal{T}-\mathcal{S}}^*$. When $T = 3$, all results hold true for $n = 4$, and because the proofs follow the identical logic, I do not repeat them here. These results establish that no other payoff-distinct quasi-symmetric informative equilibrium exists, that the NI equilibrium is unique, and that all FI equilibria are as described. To establish that the list of equilibria in the text is exhaustive, then, one result is missing: we need to show that with $T = 3$ and $n \in \{3, 4\}$, the PI equilibrium remains unique when we allow for payoff-equivalent equilibria. This is the purpose of the following lemma:

Lemma 4.1. With $T = 3$ and $n \in \{3, 4\}$, there is a unique PI equilibrium, and in such equilibrium the chair orders his lowest-intensity proposal as P_1: $\mathbf{P}_{\mathcal{T}-\mathcal{S}} = \{P_2, P_3\}$.

Proof of Lemma 4.1. Suppose, to the contrary, that $\mathbf{P}_{\mathcal{T}-\mathcal{S}} = \{P_1, P_3\}$: the chair orders his lowest-intensity proposal as P_2, and casts his bonus vote with equal probability on P_1 and P_3: $\pi_{c1} = \pi_{c3} = 1/2; \pi_{c2} = 0$. If such an equilibrium exists, a non-chair voter must cast his bonus vote either on P_2 or on $P^*_{\mathcal{T}-\mathcal{S}}$, which is equally likely to be P_1 or P_3. Hence, with $n = 3$, and following (4.14′): $\pi_1 = prob(v_{i1} = \max\{v_{i1}, v_{i3}\})prob(\max\{v_{i1}, v_{i3}\} > (2v_{i2})/(2 - \pi_1))$. But if the chair's bonus vote is not cast on P_1, then, under the candidate strategy, it must be cast on P_3 with probability 1. Non-chair voters will then cast their bonus vote on P_3 with probability $\pi^n_3 = prob(v_{i3} = \max\{v_{i1}, v_{i3}\})prob(\max\{v_{i1}, v_{i3}\} > v_{i2}/(1 - \pi^n_3))$, where the superscript n indicates that the probability has been updated after the chair failed to cast his bonus vote on P_1.

But then $\pi^n_3 < \pi_1$ (in the uniform parameterization used in the experiment, $\pi^n_3 = 1/4$ and $\pi_1 = 2/7$): the chair can gain from deviating and always ordering P^*_c as P_3, and the scenario cannot be an equilibrium. With $n = 4$, the relevant probabilities are given by (4.12′), but the logic is identical (in the uniform parameterization, $\pi^n_3 = 0.274$ and $\pi_1 = 0.307$). Finally, the same logic also establishes that there cannot be an equilibrium with $\mathbf{P}_{\mathcal{T}-\mathcal{S}} = \{P_1, P_2\}$. ■

Equilibrium strategies are reported in Table T4.1. As in Propositions 4.2 and 4.3, the table summarizes the equilibrium strategy through a value α indicating the minimum required wedge between the intensity of the proposal receiving the bonus vote and the second-highest intensity, distinguishing, where necessary, between α_c, the chair's α, and α_{nc}, for the other voters. In particular, $\alpha_c = 1$ always, but α_{nc} depends on the equilibrium. In the NI equilibrium, $\alpha_{nc} = 1$. In the PI and FI equilibria, Proposition 4.3 states that non-chair voters cast their bonus vote on $P^*_{jT-\mathcal{S}}$ if $v^*_{jT-\mathcal{S}} \geq \alpha v^*_{j\mathcal{S}}$, and on $P^*_{j\mathcal{S}}$ otherwise, for some equilibrium value $\alpha > 1$. I denote such a strategy by the notation $\alpha_{nc} = (1, \alpha)$.

Table T4.1 Equilibrium Strategies Three proposals, G uniform, $B = 1$.

n	α_c	α^{NI}_{nc}	α^{PI}_{nc}	α^{FI}_{nc}
3	1	1	(1,1.17)	(1,1.26)
4	1	1	(1,1.05)	(1,1.16)

When evaluating the experimental strategies, it is important to specify how the multiplicity of equilibria is handled. Note for example that the fully informative ordering strategy does not require that a chair always orders his highest-intensity proposal in the *same* position over the multiple repetitions: *any* sequence of ordering, if understood by the other voters, is consistent with a FI equilibrium. In addition, the chair may well alternate freely among all equilibria. The multiplicity of equilibria in the one-match, three-proposal game translates into a much larger multiplicity over the multiple matches played by each chair. In the text, I describe the experimental data in terms of deviations from the following equilibria. First, the non-informative equilibrium (*NI*): all chairs' orderings are always interpreted as random. If the chair's ordering is interpreted as random, any actual ordering by the chair is a best response. Second, the fully informative equilibrium (*FI*): any ordering by the chair is correctly understood as fully informative by the other voters. Again, no ordering decision by the chair can ever be interpreted as a strategic mistake, but once the ordering strategy of the chair is given, the other subjects' equilibrium behavior is pinned down uniquely. In Casella (2008) I discuss also an intermediate scenario: a chair's ordering is interpreted as random unless the chair always casts his most intense proposal in the same position, in which case it is understood as informative (*FI*/*NI*). Strategic mistakes in this latter case are higher than in the uninformative equilibrium, and lower than in the informative one. The substantive results are unchanged.

4.7 The Formal Model—Version 4.2

A committee of n voters meets to decide over three proposals. Each proposal is a choice between two alternatives, one of which will be implemented. At the start of the meeting, it is not known which three proposals will be voted upon, but it is known that they will be chosen by the committee chair from the fixed and known set $\mathbf{P} = \{P_A, P_B, P_C, P_D\}$. The committee votes on the proposals sequentially, and in each election, the vote cast by each member is publicly observable. Call P_t with $t = 1, 2, 3$ the tth proposal called by the chair. The chair announces P_1; after observing the votes and outcome of the first election, the chair announces P_2, and again, after observing the votes and outcome of the second election, the chair chooses the third and last proposal, P_3. In addition to a regular vote on every proposal, each committee member is given one indivisible bonus vote equivalent to a regular vote. As said, each proposal is a choice between two alternatives. The winning alternative is the one receiving more votes, including bonus votes. In case of a tie, a coin is flipped.

Each member i of the committee has preferences over the alternatives presented in each proposal. Call the two alternatives in proposal P_s, $s \in \{A, B, C, D\}$, a_s and b_s. Preferences are summarized by a cardinal valuation v_{is}. A negative valuation means that the voter favors alternative a_s, a positive valuation that he favors alternative b_s. Voter i's absolute valuation $v_{is} \equiv |\mathrm{v}_{is}|$ is i's intensity over proposal P_s. For each proposal P_s brought to a vote, voter i receives utility $u_{is} = v_{is}$ if the decision goes in his preferred direction, and 0 otherwise; the voter receives 0 utility from the proposal that is not brought to a vote. Voter i's utility from the entire meeting, U_i, equals $\sum_{s \in \mathcal{A}} u_{is}$, where $\mathcal{A}$ is the set of proposals on the agenda.

Before any voting takes place, and before the chair announces P_1, each committee member i knows $\{\mathrm{v}_{iA}, .., \mathrm{v}_{iD}\}$, his own valuations over the two alternatives in all four possible proposals, but does not know others' valuations over any of the proposals. It is commonly known, however, that the committee's preferences have the following properties: (1) *Direction of preferences*. Over any proposal, the committee is never unanimous, but any other of the $2^n - 2$ possible profiles of preferred directions of preferences is equally probable: one voter in favor of alternative a, and all others in favor of alternative b; two voters in favor of alternative a and all others in favor of alternative b; etc. (2) *Intensity of preferences*. Each voter's set of intensities over the four possible proposals is given by $\mathcal{V} = \{1, 2, 3, 4\}$, equal for all voters, but the matching of a given proposal to a specific element of the set – to a specific intensity – is not publicly known. For each voter, any of the 4! possible profiles of intensities is equally probable: if $\mathcal{V}_i$ is the ordered set of voter i's intensities, from P_A to P_D, then $\mathcal{V}_i = (1, 2, 3, 4)$ is as probable as $\mathcal{V}_i = (2, 3, 1, 4)$ or any other permutation. Realizations of intensities are independent across voters.

A voter's strategy is, for all voters including the chair, the choice of the proposal on which to cast the bonus vote, and, for the chair alone, the proposals called and their order. The focus is on quasi-symmetric Perfect Bayesian equilibria in weakly undominated strategies, in which all voters who are not the chair playing symmetric strategies. A *non-informative* (*NI*) equilibrium is such that any proposal called to a vote has ex ante equal probability of receiving the chair's bonus vote, regardless of its position on the agenda; a *fully informative* (*FI*) equilibrium is such that the position on the agenda of the proposal receiving the chair's bonus vote is identified ex ante with probability 1.

The chair is chosen randomly among the committee members with equal probability. Call EV_0 ex ante expected utility before preferences are realized and before the chair's role is assigned; call EV_{0i}, $i = c, nc$, voter i's expected utility before preferences are realized, but knowing whether he is chair (c) or not (nc). If the voting rule is simple majority, the corresponding concepts are indicated by EW_0 and EW_{0i}. To separate the importance of a chair controlling the agenda from the uncertainty caused by the sequential voting itself, it is useful to calculate expected utility with a sequential but random agenda, in which every outstanding proposal has equal probability of being called to a vote. Such expected utility is denoted by EU_0^X and EU_0^{XM} in the two cases of storable votes and simple majority. For $n \in \{2, 3, 4\}$, the main properties of the model are summarized by the two results that follow.

Result 4.1. Suppose $\mathcal{V} = \{1, 2, 3, 4\}$ and $n \in \{2, 3, 4\}$. Then: (i) There can be no *NI* equilibrium. (ii) There are multiple *FI* equilibria. (iii) In all *FI* equilibria: if $n \in \{2, 4\}$, $EV_{0c} > EW_{0c}$; $EV_{0nc} > EW_{0nc}$, and $EV_0 > EW_0$; if $n = 3$, $EV_{0c} \lesseqgtr EW_{0c}$ depending on the equilibrium; $EV_{0nc} < EW_{0nc}$, and $EV_0 < EW_0$. (iv) For all $n \in \{2, 3, 4\}$, there exists an equilibrium with sequential but random agenda such that in all *FI* equilibria $EV_{0c} > EU_0^X$, $EV_{0nc} \leq EU_0^X$.

The chair benefits from the control of the agenda, relative both to the other members and to a scenario in which the agenda is chosen exogenously. Voters who are not chair are harmed, at least weakly, by the chair's control: their expected utility is lower than with a random agenda. Relative to majority voting, both chair and nonchair members expect to benefit from storable votes with committees of size two and four; with committees of size three, this may continue to hold true for the chair, but the other committee members have higher expected utility with majority voting, and the chair's gain, when it exists, is not sufficient to counter the other members' expected losses.

The comparison between storable votes and simple majority is sensitive to the wedge between the highest and the average intensity:

Result 4.2. Suppose $\mathcal{V} = \{1, 2, 3, 6\}$ and $n \in \{2, 3, 4\}$. Then: (i) There can be no *NI* equilibrium. (ii) There are multiple *FI* equilibria, but all are payoff equivalent. (iii) In all *FI* equilibria, for all $n \in \{2, 3, 4\}$, $EV_{0c} > EW_{0c}$; $EV_{0nc} > EW_{0nc}$ and $EV_0 > EW_0$; (iv) In all *FI* equilibria, for all $n \in \{2, 3, 4\}$, $EV_{0c} > EU_0^X$, $EV_{0nc} \leq EU_0^X$.

4.8 Proof of Result 4.1

(i) Call π_{it} the probability that voter i casts the bonus vote on P_t, where the index $i = c$ will indicate the chair, and, for clarity, $i = nc$ will indicate a voter who is not chair. In a non-informative equilibrium, $\pi_{ct} = 1/3$ for $t = 1, 2, 3$. Suppose first $\pi_{nct} = 1/3$ for $t = 1, 2, 3$. Then, for a voter who is not chair, $(p_{ncB1} - p_{nc11}) = (p_{ncB2} - p_{nc12}) = (p_{ncB3} - p_{nc13})$, and the voter decides on which proposal to cast the bonus vote on the basis of intensities only. If still available, the bonus vote is always cast on P_3; if available when P_2 is called, the bonus vote is cast if $v_{nc2} \geq E_2(v_{nc3})$ where $E_2(\cdot)$ indicates the expectation taken at the time of the second vote; when P_1 is called, the bonus vote is cast if $v_{nc1} \geq E_1(\max[v_{nc2}, E_2(v_{nc3})])$. With $\mathcal{V} = \{1, 2, 3, 4\}$, this implies casting the bonus vote on P_1 if $v_{nc1} = 4$; on P_2 if either $v_{nc2} = 4$, or $v_{nc2} = 3$ and $v_{nc1} = 2$, or, with probability $\sigma_{23} \in [0, 1]$, if $v_{nc2} = 3$ and $v_{nc1} = 1$; and on P_3 otherwise.

But then $\pi_{nc1} = 1/4$, $\pi_{nc2} = (4 + \sigma_{23})/12$, and $\pi_{nc3} = (5 - \sigma_{23})/12$, contradicting $\pi_{nct} = 1/3$ for $t = 1, 2, 3$. Thus, if a non-informative equilibrium exists, it cannot be with $\pi_{nc1} = \pi_{nc2} = \pi_{nc3}$. There must exist at least one t and one $t' \in \{1, 2, 3\}$ such that $\pi_{nct} < \pi_{nct'}$. Consider now the chair's problem. Given $p_{cBt} \geq p_{c1t} \geq 0$ for all t and π_{it}, the chair selects the three proposals to which he attributes values $\{4, 3, 2\}$ and casts the bonus vote on P_c^* with value 4, but he must also decide the order in which the three proposals are called. In a noninformative equilibrium, the chair must be indifferent between calling P_c^* at t or t', or, for $v \in \{2, 3\}$:

$$p_{cBt}4 + p_{c1t'}v = p_{cBt'}4 + p_{c1t}v,$$

or $(p_{cBt} - p_{cBt'})4 = (p_{c1t} - p_{c1t'})v$. If $n = 2$, $p_{cBt} = 1 - \pi_{nct}/2$, and $p_{c1t} = (1/2)(1 - \pi_{nct})$; if $n = 3$, $p_{cBt} = 2/3 + (1/6)(1 - \pi_{nct})^2$, and $p_{c1t} = (1/3)[2 - \pi_{nct} + (\pi_{nct})^2]$; in both cases, $(p_{cBt} - p_{cBt'}) > (p_{c1t} - p_{c1t'})$ for all $\pi_{nct} < \pi_{nct'}$, and indifference must be violated. If $n = 4$, $p_{cBt} = (3/14)[4 - 2\pi_{nct} + 2(\pi_{nct})^2 - (\pi_{nct})^3]$, and $p_{c1t} = (3/7)[1 + (1/2)(1 - \pi_{nct})(1 + (\pi_{nct})^2)]$; it is easy to verify that for $v \in \{2, 3\}$ again indifference cannot hold for any $\pi_{nct} < \pi_{nct'}$ such that $\pi_{nct} + \pi_{nct'} \leq 1$. Thus, a non-informative equilibrium cannot exist.

(ii)-(iv). 1. Suppose first $n = 2$. In this case, $(p_{iBt} - p_{i1t}) = 1/2$ for all t, $i = c, nc$, regardless of the other member's vote, implying that the bonus vote decision is made exclusively on the basis of intensities. (Note that $(p_{cBt} - p_{c1t}) = 1/2$ for all t does *not* imply that the chair is indifferent about the order of the agenda). Hence, $\pi_{nc1} = 1/4$, $\pi_{nc2} = (4 + \sigma_{23})/12$, and $\pi_{nc3} = (5 - \sigma_{23})/12$. Call $\mathcal{T}_c$ the sequence of the chair's intensities over the proposals he calls to a vote, ordered by time. By the reasoning of point (i) above, $\mathcal{T}_c = (4, 2, 3)$ if $\sigma_{23} > 1/2$, $\mathcal{T}_c = (4, 3, 2)$ if $\sigma_{23} < 1/2$, and the chair is indifferent between the two orderings if $\sigma_{23} = 1/2$. The chair always casts his bonus vote on P_1, or $\pi_{c1} = 1$, $\pi_{c2} = 0 = \pi_{c3}$. Expected utilities can then be calculated immediately. If the agenda is exogenous, $EU_0^X = 4.27$; $EU_0^{XM} = 3.75$. If the agenda is endogenous, with majority voting: $EW_{0c} = 4.5$, $EW_{0nc} = 3.75$, $EW_0 = 4.125$; with storable votes: $EV_{0nc} = 4.27$, $EV_{0c} = 5.042 + \sigma_{23}/24$, and $EV_0 = 4.656 + 0.02\sigma_{23}$ with $\sigma_{23} \in [1/2, 1]$, or $EV_{0c} \in [5.06, 5.08]$ and $EV_0 \in [4.67, 4.68]$. Notice that $\sigma_{23} \in [1/2, 1]$ is sufficient to span the whole range of expected utilities for the chair, because for $\sigma_{23} \in [0, 1/2]$ the chair inverts the order of the last two proposals, achieving identical utilities to those reported here. EV_{0c} and EV_0 are higher the more predictable is the non-chair voter's strategy, and thus the more frequently optimal the chair's order of the proposals. All the inequalities in (ii)-(iv) are verified.

2. Suppose now $n = 3$. In this case, $(p_{ncBt} - p_{nc1t}) = (1/6)(1 - \pi_{nct}\pi_{ct})$ and $(p_{cBt} - p_{c1t}) = (1/6)[1 - (\pi_{nct})^2]$. Consider a candidate equilibrium with $\pi_{c1} = 1, \pi_{c2} = 0 = \pi_{c3}$. Consider first the non-chair's choices. With $\pi_{c1} = 1$, $(p_{ncB1} - p_{nc11}) = (1/6)(1 - \pi_{nc1})$ and $(p_{ncBt} - p_{nc1t}) = (1/6)$

for $t = 2, 3$. If an equilibrium exists, it cannot be that $\pi_{nc1} = 0$, because in such a case $(p_{ncBt} - p_{nc1t})$ is constant for all t, the choice of when to cast the bonus vote depends on intensities only, and from the arguments in (i) above, a non-chair will then cast his bonus vote on P_1 if $v_{nc1} = 4$, contradicting $\pi_{nc1} = 0$. But if $\pi_{nc1} > 0$, then $(p_{ncB1} - p_{nc11}) < (p_{ncBt} - p_{nc1t})$ for $t = 2, 3$, and again from the arguments in (i) a non-chair will not spend his bonus vote on P_1 if $v_{nc1} \in \{1, 2, 3\}$. Thus, the only candidate equilibrium is the following: for the chair, $\pi_{c1} = 1$, and $\pi_{c2} = 0 = \pi_{c3}$; for non-chair voters, $\pi_{nc1} = 1/4$, $\pi_{nc2} = (4 + \sigma_{23})/12$, and $\pi_{nc3} = (5 - \sigma_{23})/12$, with $\sigma_{23} \in [0, 1]$. The chair's agenda strategy is given by: $\mathcal{T}_c = (4, 2, 3)$ if $\sigma_{23} > 1/2$, $\mathcal{T}_c = (4, 3, 2)$ if $\sigma_{23} < 1/2$, and indifference between either strategy if $\sigma_{23} = 1/2$. Given these strategies by the other voters, it is not difficult to verify that a non-chair member is indeed better off casting his bonus vote on P_1 if $v_{nc1} = 4$. Thus, these are indeed equilibrium strategies, and by the arguments above, the only possible *FI* equilibrium strategies with $\pi_{c1} = 1$. Consider now a candidate equilibrium with $\pi_{c1} = 0 = \pi_{c2}$, $\pi_{c3} = 1$. Following exactly the same logic, if there is an equilibrium, it must be such that $\pi_{nct} \geq \pi_{nc3} > 0$ for $t = 1, 2$. The only non-chair's strategy that satisfies such constraints is: cast the bonus vote on P_1 if either $v_{nc1} = 4$ or $v_{nc1} = 3$; on P_2 if either $v_{nc2} = 4$ or $v_{nc2} = 3$ and $v_{nc1} \in \{1, 2\}$; and on P_3 otherwise. Again, calculating expected utilities, it can be verified that no deviation is profitable, and these are indeed equilibrium strategies. Finally, consider a candidate equilibrium with $\pi_{c1} = 0$, $\pi_{c2} = 1$, $\pi_{c3} = 0$, which implies $\pi_{nct} \geq \pi_{nc2} > 0$ for $t = 1, 3$. If the equilibrium exists, the non-chair's strategy must be: cast the bonus vote on P_1 if either $v_{nc1} = 4$ or $v_{nc1} = 3$; on P_2 if $v_{nc2} = 4$ and $v_{nc1} \in \{1, 2\}$; and on P_3 otherwise. The calculation of expected utilities shows that deviation is not profitable and the strategies are equilibrium strategies. Equilibrium strategies and welfare properties of the fully informative equilibria are summarized in Table T4.2a below, where, for ease of reading, the values reported correspond to $\sigma_{23} = 1$.[1]

1. Recall that non-chair equilibrium strategies in $E1$ are $\pi_{nc1} = 1/4$, $\pi_{nc2} = (4 + \sigma_{23})/12$, and $\pi_{nc3} = (5 - \sigma_{23})/12$, with $\sigma_{23} \in [0, 1]$. The chair's agenda strategy is $\mathcal{T}_c = (4, 2, 3)$ if $\sigma_{23} \geq 1/2$, and $\mathcal{T}_c = (4, 3, 2)$ if $\sigma_{23} \leq 1/2$. The effect of different σ_{23} values on expected welfare is so small as to be barely detectable.

Table T4.2a Storable votes: Equilibrium strategies and expected utilities with $\sigma_{23} = 1$. $n = 3$; $\mathcal{V} = \{1, 2, 3, 4\}$.

Equilibrium	$\pi_{c1}, \pi_{c2}, \pi_{c3}$	$\pi_{nc1}, \pi_{nc2}, \pi_{nc3}$	T_c	EV_{0c}	EV_{0nc}	EV_0
E1	1, 0, 0	1/4, 5/12, 1/3	4, 2, 3	5.98	4.92	5.28
E2	0, 1, 0	1/2, 1/6, 1/3	2, 4, 3	6.07	4.86	5.267
E3	0, 0, 1	1/2, 1/3, 1/6	2, 3, 4	6.07	4.87	5.273

Partially informative equilibria – such that there exists a t for which $\pi_{ct} \in (1/3, 1)$ – exist, too. One such example is an equilibrium in which the chair orders $P_c^* = P_2$ with some probability $r \in [1/2, 9/11]$, and $P_c^* = P_3$ with probability $1 - r$, and always spends his bonus vote on P_c^*; non-chair voters cast their bonus vote on on P_1 if either $v_{nc1} = 4$ or $v_{nc1} = 3$, on P_2 if either $v_{nc2} = 4$ and $v_{nc1} \in \{1, 2\}$, or if $v_{nc2} = 3$ and $v_{nc1} = 2$, and on P_3 otherwise. Its welfare properties are analogous to fully informative equilibria (for example, with $r = 1/2$, $EV_0 = 5.29$), and the comparison to majority voting is unaffected.

If the agenda is sequential but exogenous and random, there is no distinction between chair and non-chair voters. In a symmetric equilibrium, the impact of the bonus vote on the probability of winning is given by: $(p_{Bt} - p_{1t}) = (1/6)[1 - (\pi_t)^2]$. From the arguments in (i) above, $\pi_t = \pi$ for all t cannot be an equilibrium, because in this case only the comparison of expected intensities would matter, supporting strategies that contradict $\pi_t = \pi$ for all t. A similar logic rules out candidate equilibria with $\pi_1 \geq \pi_2 \geq \pi_3$, and slightly less obvious arguments, not reproduced here, rule out $\pi_1 \leq \pi_2 < \pi_3$. The following strategies, however, are an equilibrium: every voter casts the bonus vote on P_1 if $v_1 = 4$, or with probability $q_1 = 0.14$ if $v_1 = 3$; on P_2 if either $v_2 = 4$ and the bonus vote is available, or $v_2 = 3$ and $v_1 = 2$, or, finally, with probability $q_2 = 0.43$ if $v_2 = 3$ and $v_1 = 1$; and on P_3 otherwise. The strategies correspond to $\pi_1 = 0.285$, $\pi_2 = \pi_3 = 0.357$, and they yield the expected utility reported in Table T4.2b below. I conjecture, but have not shown, that the equilibrium is unique. Majority voting calculations, with and without a chair, are trivial, taking into account that unanimity is ruled out, and thus the probability of being in the majority when everyone casts a single vote equals 2/3. When the chair controls the

Table T4.2b Majority voting with chair; Exogenous agenda with storable votes or majority voting. $n = 3$; $\mathcal{V} = \{1, 2, 3, 4\}$.

EW_{0c}	EW_{0nc}	EW_0	EU_0^X	EU_0^{XM}
6.00	5.00	5.33	4.97	5.00

agenda, he benefits from being able to choose proposals with intensities {4, 3, 2}. The order of the proposals is irrelevant.

3. Suppose now $n = 4$. In this case, $(p_{ncBt} - p_{nc1t}) = (1/14)[2 + (\pi_{nct})^2 + (1 - 2\pi_{nct})(1 - \pi_{ct})]$, and $(p_{cBt} - p_{c1t}) = (3/14)[1 - \pi_{nct} + (\pi_{nct})^2]$. The calculations are straightforward. Equilibrium strategies and welfare properties of the three informative equilibria are reported in Table T4.3a, where the notation $\mathcal{T}_c = (4, \{2, 3\})$ indicates that the chair is indifferent between $\mathcal{T}_c = (4, 2, 3)$ and $\mathcal{T}_c = (4, 3, 2)$. The equilibrium probabilities $(\pi_{nc1}, \pi_{nc2}, \pi_{nc3})$ correspond to the following strategies: E1: cast the bonus vote on P_1 if $v_{nc1} = 4$; on P_2 if $v_{nc2} = 4$, or if $v_{nc2} = 3$ and $v_{nc1} = 2$, or, with probability 1/2 if $v_{nc2} = 3$ and $v_{nc1} = 1$; on P_3 otherwise. E2: cast the bonus vote on P_1 if $v_{nc1} \in \{3, 4\}$; on P_2 if $v_{nc2} = 4$ and $v_{nc1} \in \{1, 2\}$; on P_3 otherwise. E3: cast the bonus vote on P_1 if either $v_{nc1} = 4$, or, with probability 0.727, if $v_{nc1} = 3$; on P_2 if $v_{nc2} \in \{3, 4\}$ and the bonus vote has not been cast on P_1; on P_3 otherwise.

Table T4.3a Storable votes: Equilibrium strategies and expected utilities. $n = 4$; $\mathcal{V} = \{1, 2, 3, 4\}$.

Equilibrium	$\pi_{c1}, \pi_{c2}, \pi_{c3}$	$\pi_{nc1}, \pi_{nc2}, \pi_{nc3}$	T_c	EV_{0c}	EV_{0nc}	EV_0
E1	1, 0, 0	1/4, 3/8, 3/8	4, 2, 3	6.00	4.98	5.238
E2	0, 1, 0	1/2, 1/6, 1/3	2, 4, 3	6.07	4.96	5.238
E3	0, 0, 1	0.43, 0.36, 0.21	2, 3, 4	6.03	4.98	5.242

With a sequential but exogenous and random agenda, $(p_{Bt} - p_{1t}) = (3/14)[1 - \pi_t + (\pi_t)^2]$, and the following strategies are an equilibrium: every voter casts the bonus vote on P_1 if $v_1 = 4$, or with probability $q_1 = 0.028$ if $v_1 = 3$; on P_2 if either $v_2 = 4$ and the bonus vote is available, or $v_2 = 3$ and $v_1 = 2$, or finally with probability $q_2 = 0.49$ if $v_2 = 3$ and $v_1 = 1$; and on P_3 otherwise. The strategies correspond to $\pi_1 = 0.257$; $\pi_2 = \pi_3 = 0.3715$, and yield the expected utility reported

Table T4.3b Majority voting with chair, and exogenous agenda with storable votes or majority voting. $n = 4$; $\mathcal{V} = \{1, 2, 3, 4\}$.

EW_{0c}	EW_{0nc}	EW_0	EU_0^X	EU_0^{XM}
5.79	4.82	5.06	5.00	4.82

in Table T4.3b above. With simple majority, a voter's probability of winning, either because he is in the majority or because the two sides are equally split and the tie break favors his side, is 9/14.

This concludes the analysis for $n \in \{2, 3, 4\}$, and $\mathcal{V} = \{1, 2, 3, 4\}$. All statements in Result 4.1 follow. ■

4.9 Proof of Result 4.2

(i) Suppose that a non-informative equilibrium exists: $\pi_{ct} = 1/3$ for $t = 1, 2, 3$. If $\pi_{nct} = 1/3$ for $t = 1, 2, 3$, then a voter who is not chair decides on which proposal to cast the bonus vote on the basis of intensities only. With $\mathcal{V} = \{1, 2, 3, 6\}$, this implies casting the bonus vote on P_1 if $v_{nc1} = 6$; on P_2 if $v_{nc2} = 6$; and on P_3 otherwise.

But then $\pi_{nc1} = 1/4$, $\pi_{nc2} = 1/4$, and $\pi_{nc3} = 1/2$, contradicting $\pi_{nct} = 1/3$ for $t = 1, 2, 3$. Thus, if a non-informative equilibrium exists, it cannot be with $\pi_{nc1} = \pi_{nc2} = \pi_{nc3}$. There must exist at least one t and one $t' \in \{1, 2, 3\}$ such that $\pi_{nct} < \pi_{nct'}$. The rest of the proof continues identically to the proof of point (i) for Result 4.1.

(ii)-(iv) Given the expressions for $(p_{nctB} - p_{nc1t})$ and $(p_{ctB} - p_{c1t})$ reported in the proof of Result 4.1, and following the same logic described there, it is not difficult to verify that for all $n \in \{2, 3, 4\}$, the unique equilibrium strategy for voters who are not chair is to cast their bonus vote on P_1 if $v_{nc1} = 6$; on P_2 if $v_{nc2} = 6$ and on P_3 otherwise, yielding $\pi_{nc1} = 1/4$, $\pi_{nc2} = 1/4$, and $\pi_{nc3} = 1/2$. The chair is thus indifferent between $\mathcal{T}_c = (6, 3, 2)$ and $\mathcal{T}_c = (3, 6, 2)$, both of which are best response strategies. Thus, there are two fully informative equilibria, with identical strategies for voters who are not chair, and identical expected utilities for all. Their welfare properties are summarized in Table T4.4.

All statements in Result 4.2 follow. ■

Table T4.4 Welfare comparisons. $n \in \{2, 3, 4\}$; $\mathcal{V} = \{1, 2, 3, 6\}$.

n	EV_{0c}	EV_{0nc}	EV_0	EW_{0c}	EW_{0nc}	EW_0	EU_0^X	EU_0^{XM}
2	6.87	5.50	6.19	5.50	4.50	5.00	5.50	4.50
3	7.54	6.02	6.53	7.33	6.00	6.44	6.09	6.00
4	7.56	6.11	6.47	7.07	5.79	6.11	6.13	5.79

4.10 Derivation of Table 4.5

In Table 4.5, the available surplus is calculated using as floor expected earnings with random decision-making and random agenda (ER_0). For example, with $n = 2$, $\mathcal{V} = \{1, 2, 3, 4\}$, and random agenda, $ER_0 = (1/2)(3/4)(1 + 2 + 3 + 4) = 3.75$ (relative to $EW_0 = 4.125$, with simple majority, and $EV_0 \in [4.67, 4.68]$ with storable votes). Calculating expected earnings corresponding to the first best outcome (EV_0^*) is slightly more involved. For each possible profile of preferences, each proposal is resolved in favor of the side with higher total intensities, and the three proposals yielding highest total earnings are selected. Maximal expected aggregate earnings are the sum of the earnings so obtained, weighted by the probability of the corresponding preferences profile. For example, with $n = 2$ and opposite preferences, there are (4!)(4!) preference profiles. With $n = 2$ and $\mathcal{V} = \{1, 2, 3, 4\}$, highest expected earnings in per capita terms are 5.292. In this case, the expected surplus share appropriated with storable votes (and $\sigma_{23} = 1/2$) is then: $(4.67 - 3.75)/(5.292 - 3.75) = 59.7$. Table T4.5 reports expected maximal earnings per capita, and expected earnings with random decision-making and random agenda for the parameters used in the experiment. For convenience, the table includes EV_0 and EW_0.

Table T4.5 Constructing the bounds of the surplus measure.

	$\mathcal{V} = \{1, 2, 3, 4\}$					$\mathcal{V} = \{1, 2, 3, 6\}$			
n	ER_0	EV_0^*	EV_0	EW_0	n	ER_0	EV_0^*	EV_0	EW_0
2	3.75	5.29	4.67[a]	4.125	2	4.5	7.04	16.19	15.00
3	3.75	5.64	5.27[a]	5.33	3	4.5	7.21	16.53	16.44
4	3.75	5.6	5.24	5.06	4	4.5	7.09	16.47	16.11

[a]For ease of reading, the table reports only one value, here the lowest bound in the range of equilibrium values.

5

Storable Votes in Large Elections

5.1 The Formal Model—Version 5

A large number n of voters are asked to vote, contemporaneously, on a set of $K > 1$ unrelated referendums. Each voter is asked to cast one vote in each referendum, but in addition is given one extra bonus vote that can be cast freely. The bonus vote is worth $B > 0$ regular votes, where B is either an integer or the inverse of an integer and is small relative to $\sqrt{n}$, but otherwise arbitrary. Each referendum is decided in the direction that receives more votes; in case of an exact tie, either side prevails with probability 1/2. Voter i attaches valuation v_{ik} to referendum k. If $\mathrm{v}_{ik} < 0$, i is against the referendum, if $\mathrm{v}_{ik} > 0$, i is in favor of the referendum. For each referendum k, voter i receives utility $u_{ik} = |\mathrm{v}_{ik}| \equiv v_{ik}$ if the decision goes in his preferred direction, and 0 otherwise, where the absolute valuation v_{ik} is called the intensity of voter i's preferences over referendum k. Voter i's utility from the full set of referendums, U_i, equals $\sum_{k=1}^{K} u_{ik}$.

Individual valuations are drawn, independently across individuals and across referendums, from probability distributions $\mathbf{G} \equiv \{G_k(\mathrm{v}), k = 1, .., K\}$, each with full support normalized to $[-1, 1]$. The distributions $\mathbf{G}$ can vary across referendums but are common knowledge. Individual i knows v_{ik}, for all $k = 1, .., K$, but only the probability distributions of the others' valuations and their statistical independence across individuals and referendums. There is no cost of voting.

The analysis focuses on symmetric Bayesian equilibria in undominated strategies where, conditional on their set of valuations, all voters select the same optimal strategy. Since there can be no gain from voting against one's preferences, in these equilibria voters vote sincerely. The only decision is the referendum on which to cast the bonus vote.

With an electorate of size n, denote by EV_{0n} expected utility with the bonus vote ex ante, before the realization of preferences; by EW_{0n} expected ex ante utility with a series of simple majority referendums, and by ER_0 expected ex ante utility with random decision-making (when each proposal is resolved in either direction with probability 1/2). Define $\omega_n \equiv (EV_{0n} - ER_0)/(EW_{0n} - ER_0)$ as the measure of welfare improvement from the bonus vote, relative to majority voting. Storable votes are said to improve efficiency if there exists an electorate size above which $\omega_n \longrightarrow \omega > 1$.

The core question is how robust is the expected welfare impact of the bonus vote mechanism to different properties of the distributions of valuations. Call *symmetry* of a distribution the lack of systematic differences between supporters and opponents of a referendum: a distribution of valuations is *symmetric* when the corresponding distributions of intensities, for supporters and opponents, are identical. Call *homogeneity* of the distributions the lack of systematic differences across referendums: distributions are *homogeneous* when $G_k(\mathrm{v}) = G(\mathrm{v})$ for all k. Then:

Proposition 5.1 Symmetric homogenous distributions. Suppose $G_k(\mathrm{v}) = G(\mathrm{v})$ for all k. Then, for any distribution $G(\mathrm{v})$ symmetric around 0 and any number of referendums $K > 1$, there exist $B'(G, K) > 0$ and some n' finite such that for all $n > n'$ and $B < B'$, $\omega_n \rightarrow \omega > 1$.

Proposition 5.2 Symmetric heterogeneous distributions. Suppose $G_{k'}(\mathrm{v}) \neq G_k(\mathrm{v})$ for some or all $k' \neq k$. Then, for any set of distributions $\mathbf{G}$ all symmetric around 0 and any number of referendums $K > 1$, there exist $B''(G, K) > 0$ and some n'' finite such that for all $n > n''$ and $B < B''$, $\omega_n \rightarrow \omega > 1$.

Although storable votes deliver positive percentage gains in expected welfare relative to simple majority voting, when the distributions of valuations are symmetric and the electorate is very large, the absolute magnitude of the gains must be vanishingly small. With independent preference draws, the sum of the intensity draws must approach the theoretical mean, and the assumption of symmetry imposes equal mean intensity for opponents and supporters of each proposal. Hence, in each referendum the two alternatives are asymptotically welfare equivalent. By implication, asymptotically *any* decision rule is interchangeable. Storable votes can only reward occasional empirical asymmetries, sample deviations from the theoretical distribution whose quantitative importance must disappear as the population becomes large.

The assumption that the distributions **G** are symmetric around 0 has a second strong implication. It states that each voter supports each proposal with known probability equal to 1/2, or equivalently that a large electorate will be equally split with probability very close to 1. Suppose instead that in each referendum the probability of approval is not known ex ante. Before preferences are realized, each voter has probability ψ_k of being in favor of referendum k, and $1 - \psi_k$ of being against, where ψ_k is stochastic and distributed according to some distribution H_ψ defined over the support [0, 1] and symmetric around 1/2. Each realized ψ_k is an independent draw from H_ψ. For both supporters and opponents of each referendum k, intensities are drawn independently across voters and referendums from distributions $\mathbf{F} \equiv \{F_k(v),\ k = 1, .., K\}$, each with full support [0,1]. The model is symmetric and homogeneous ex ante, but *not* ex post, since in general the realized ψ_k will differ from 1/2 and differ across referendums. Then:

Proposition 5.3 Symmetric homogeneous distributions with stochastic median. Suppose $prob(\mathrm{v}_{ik} > 0) \equiv \psi_k \sim H_\psi$, and $v_{ik} \sim F_k(v) = F(v)$ for all k. Then, for all distributions H_ψ symmetric around 1/2 and all F, and for any number of referendums $K > 1$, there exist some n' finite such that for all $n > n'$, $\omega_n \rightarrow \omega > 1$ for all $B > 0$.

Alternatively, we can maintain the assumption that ψ_k is known and equal to 1/2, but introduce systematic differences in intensities between supporters and opponents of each referendum. Call $\mathbf{F_P} \equiv \{F_{Pk}(v),\ k = 1, .., K\}$, with full support [0, 1], the distributions of intensities of voters in favor of a referendum, and $\mathbf{F_C} \equiv \{F_{Ck}(v),\ k = 1, .., K\}$, with full support [0, 1], the distributions of intensities of voters against a referendum. Suppose $F_{P_k}(v) = F_P(v)$ and $F_{C_k}(v) = F_C(v)$ for all k, and call ϕ_P the ex ante probability of casting the bonus vote in favor of a referendum, and ϕ_C the ex ante probability of casting it against. In equilibrium:

$$\phi_P = \left(\frac{1}{2}\right)^{K-1}\left[\sum_{k=0}^{K-1}\binom{K-1}{k}\int_0^1 F_C(v)^{K-1-k}F_P(v)^k dF_P(v)\right]$$

$$\phi_C = \left(\frac{1}{2}\right)^{K-1}\left[\sum_{k=0}^{K-1}\binom{K-1}{k}\int_0^1 F_C(v)^{K-1-k}F_P(v)^k dF_C(v)\right].$$

Call $E_P(v)$ the expected intensity of a supporter of referendum k, and $E_C(v)$ the expected intensity of an opponent of referendum k. Then:

Proposition 5.4 Asymmetric homogeneous distributions with 0 median. Suppose that for all k, $prob(\mathrm{v}_{ik} > 0) = 1/2$, $v_{ik} \sim F_P(v)$ if $\mathrm{v}_{ik} > 0$, and $v_{ik} \sim F_C(v)$ if $\mathrm{v}_{ik} < 0$, with $E_P(v) > E_C(v)$. For any $B > 0$ and $K > 1$, if $\phi_P > \phi_C$ then there exist some n' finite such that for all $n > n'$, $EV_{0n}/EW_{0n} \rightarrow 1 + [E_P(v) - E_C(v)]/[E_P(v) + E_C(v)] > 1$, and $\omega_n \rightarrow \infty$.

The important assumption is that the two distributions of intensities have different means. Assigning higher mean to the "pro" side comes with no loss of generality: which side has higher mean is irrelevant, and the model can be generalized trivially to allow the side with higher mean to change across proposals. The condition $\phi_P > \phi_C$ is not very transparent. A more intuitive but stronger sufficient condition is first-order stochastic dominance: if $F_P(v)$ first-order stochastically dominates $F_C(v)$, $\phi_P > \phi_C$ and Proposition 5.4 applies.

5.2 Three Preliminary Results

Three preliminary results must be established before proving the propositions. Define votes in favor as positive votes and votes against as negative votes, and the votes differential, the sum of all votes cast in referendum k, as V_k.

Lemma 5.1. Consider the voting problem in the absence of bonus votes when everybody votes sincerely. Call p_k a voter's probability of obtaining the desired outcome in referendum k. Then, if $G_k(v)$ is symmetric around 0, as $n \to \infty$, $V_k/\sqrt{n} \to N(0,1)$ and $p_k = 1/2 + 1/\sqrt{2\pi(n-1)} + o\left(n^{-1/2}\right)$.

Proof of Lemma 5.1. The derivation of the asymptotic distribution of the votes differential is standard (see for example Feller (1968), pp. 179 – 182). The distribution is normal with mean given by the sample mean $(1/2(-1) + 1/2(1) = 0)$ and variance given by the sum of the variances of the summands: $n[(1/2)(-1)^2 + (1/2)(1)^2] = n$. Because the distribution does not depend on $G_k(v)$, we can ignore the subscript k. Taking into account possible ties, voter i's probability of obtaining his desired outcome is as follows:

$$p = (1/2)(1 + prob(V^i = 0)) + (1/2)prob(V^i = 1),$$

where V^i is the votes differential excluding voter i. Given the discreteness of the votes, we can use Gnedenko's local theorem (Gnedenko and Kolmogorov (1968), ch. 9):

$$prob(V^i = x) = \frac{1}{\sqrt{2\pi(n-1)}} \exp\left[-\frac{x^2}{2(n-1)}\right] + o\left(\frac{1}{\sqrt{n}}\right),$$

where $o\left(\frac{1}{\sqrt{n}}\right)$ indicates a term that converges to zero faster than $1/\sqrt{n}$, i.e. such that $\sqrt{n} \cdot o\left(\frac{1}{\sqrt{n}}\right)$ converges to 0 as $n \to \infty$.

$$\begin{aligned}
p &= \frac{1}{2}\left(1 + \frac{1}{\sqrt{2\pi(n-1)}} + o\left(\frac{1}{\sqrt{n}}\right)\right) \\
&\quad + \frac{1}{2}\left(\frac{1}{\sqrt{2\pi(n-1)}} \exp\left[-\frac{1}{2(n-1)}\right] + o\left(\frac{1}{\sqrt{n}}\right)\right) \\
&= \frac{1}{2} + \frac{1}{2\sqrt{2\pi(n-1)}} + o\left(\frac{1}{\sqrt{n}}\right) \\
&\quad + \frac{1}{2\sqrt{2\pi(n-1)}}\left(1 - \frac{1}{2(n-1)} + o\left(\frac{1}{n}\right)\right) + o\left(\frac{1}{\sqrt{n}}\right) \qquad (5.1) \\
&= \frac{1}{2} + \frac{1}{\sqrt{2\pi(n-1)}} + o\left(\frac{1}{\sqrt{n}}\right).
\end{aligned}$$

■

Now introduce the bonus vote: a vote can assume a value in the set $\{-1-B, -1, 1, 1+B\}$. Call ϕ_k a voter's ex ante probability of casting the bonus vote in referendum k (before observing his valuations), where $\sum_{k=1}^{K} \phi_k = 1$. When the distributions **G** are symmetric, from the point of view of voter i, the value of the vote cast by every other voter in referendum k is an independent random variable with mean $\mu_k = 0$ and variance given by:

$$\sigma_k^2 = \begin{cases} 1 + \phi_k(2B + B^2) & \text{if } B \geq 1 \\ B^{-2}[1 + \phi_k(2B + B^2)] & \text{if } B < 1. \end{cases} \tag{5.2}$$

The difference arises because when $B < 1$ it is preferable to normalize the value of the bonus vote to 1 and the value of the regular vote to $1/B > 1$ and integer (see the discussion in Casella and Gelman, 2008). Using this normalization if necessary, and again making use of Gnedenko local theorem, from the point of view of voter i, in any referendum k the probability that the votes differential V^i assumes value $r \in \mathbb{N}$ is such that:

$$\sigma_k \sqrt{n-1} prob\{V^i = r\} = \frac{1}{\sqrt{2\pi}} Exp\left[\frac{-r^2}{2\sigma_k^2(n-1)}\right] + o_{n\to\infty}(1), \tag{5.3}$$

where $o_{n\to\infty}(1)$ is a residual that converges to 0 as $n \to \infty$. It is then possible to show:

Lemma 5.2. Call p_{1k} the probability that voter i obtains the desired outcome in referendum k when casting a regular vote only, and p_{Bk} the corresponding probability when adding the bonus vote. If the distributions **G** are symmetric around 0, then:

$$\begin{aligned} p_{1k} &= \frac{1}{2} + \frac{1}{\sqrt{2\pi(n-1)\left[1 + \phi_k(B^2 + 2B)\right]}} + o\left(\frac{1}{\sqrt{n}}\right) \\ p_{Bk} &= \frac{1}{2} + \frac{1 + B}{\sqrt{2\pi(n-1)\left[1 + \phi_k(B^2 + 2B)\right]}} + o\left(\frac{1}{\sqrt{n}}\right). \end{aligned} \tag{5.4}$$

Asymptotically, voter i's optimal strategy is to cast a bonus vote in referendum k if and only if:

$$\frac{v_{ik}}{v_{ik'}} > \sqrt{\frac{1+\phi_k(B^2+2B)}{1+\phi_{k'}(B^2+2B)}} \qquad \forall k' \neq k. \tag{5.5}$$

Proof of Lemma 5.2. The first part of the lemma follows immediately from (5.3). If $B \geq 1$, $p_{1k} = (1/2)[1 + prob(V_k^i = 0)] + (1/2)prob(V_k^i = 1)$, and $p_{Bk} = (1/2)[1 + prob(V_k^i = 0)] + \sum_{m=1}^{B} prob(V_k^i = m) + (1/2)prob(V_k^i = 1 + B)$, or:

$$\begin{aligned}
p_{1k} &= \frac{1}{2} + \frac{1}{2}\frac{1}{\sigma_k\sqrt{2\pi(n-1)}} + o\left(\frac{1}{\sqrt{n}}\right) \\
&\quad + \frac{1}{2}\left(\frac{1}{\sigma_k\sqrt{2\pi(n-1)}} Exp\left[\frac{-1}{2(n-1)\sigma_k^2}\right] + o\left(\frac{1}{\sqrt{n}}\right)\right) \\
&= \frac{1}{2} + \frac{1}{2}\frac{1}{\sigma_k\sqrt{2\pi(n-1)}} + o\left(\frac{1}{\sqrt{n}}\right) \\
&\quad + \frac{1}{2}\left(\frac{1}{\sigma_k\sqrt{2\pi(n-1)}}\left[1 - \frac{1}{2(n-1)\sigma_k^2}\right] + o\left(\frac{1}{\sqrt{n}}\right)\right).
\end{aligned}$$

Substituting σ_k from (5.2):

$$p_{1k} = \frac{1}{2} + \frac{1}{\sqrt{2\pi(n-1)[1+\phi_k(B^2+2B)]}} + o\left(\frac{1}{\sqrt{n}}\right).$$

Similarly,

$$\begin{aligned}
p_{Bk} &= \frac{1}{2} + \frac{1}{2}\frac{1}{\sigma_k\sqrt{2\pi(n-1)}} + o\left(\frac{1}{\sqrt{n}}\right) \\
&\quad + \sum_{m=1}^{B}\left(\frac{1}{\sigma_k\sqrt{2\pi(n-1)}} Exp\left[\frac{-m^2}{2(n-1)\sigma_k^2}\right] + o\left(\frac{1}{\sqrt{n}}\right)\right) \\
&\quad + \frac{1}{2}\left(\frac{1}{\sigma_k\sqrt{2\pi(n-1)}} Exp[\frac{-(1+B)^2}{2(n-1)\sigma_k^2}] + o\left(\frac{1}{\sqrt{n}}\right)\right) \\
&= \frac{1}{2} + \frac{1}{2}\frac{1}{\sigma_k\sqrt{2\pi(n-1)}} + \sum_{m=1}^{B}\left(\frac{1}{\sigma_k\sqrt{2\pi(n-1)}}\right)
\end{aligned}$$

$$
\begin{aligned}
&+\frac{1}{2}\frac{1}{\sigma_k\sqrt{2\pi(n-1)}}+o\left(\frac{1}{\sqrt{n}}\right)\\
&=\frac{1}{2}+\frac{1+B}{\sqrt{2\pi(n-1)[1+\phi_k(B^2+2B)]}}+o\left(\frac{1}{\sqrt{n}}\right).
\end{aligned}
$$

If instead $B < 1$, then $p_{1k} = prob(V_k^i \leq 0) + \sum_{m=1}^{1/B-1} prob(V_k^i = m) + (1/2)prob(V_k^i = 1/B)$, and $p_{Bk} = prob(V_k^i \leq 0) + \sum_{m=1}^{1/B} prob(V_k^i = m) + (1/2)prob(V_k^i = 1 + 1/B)$, or:

$$
\begin{aligned}
p_{1k} &= \frac{1}{2}+\frac{1}{2}\frac{1}{\sigma_k\sqrt{2\pi(n-1)}}+o\left(\frac{1}{\sqrt{n}}\right)\\
&+\sum_{m=1}^{1/B-1}\frac{1}{2}\left(\frac{1}{\sigma_k\sqrt{2\pi(n-1)}}Exp\left[\frac{-m^2}{2(n-1)\sigma_k^2}\right]+o\left(\frac{1}{\sqrt{n}}\right)\right)\\
&+\frac{1}{2}\left(\frac{1}{\sigma_k\sqrt{2\pi(n-1)}}Exp\left[\frac{-(1/B)^2}{2(n-1)\sigma_k^2}\right]+o\left(\frac{1}{\sqrt{n}}\right)\right)\\
&=\frac{1}{2}+\frac{1}{B}\frac{B}{\sqrt{2\pi(n-1)[1+\phi_k(B^2+2B)]}}+o\left(\frac{1}{\sqrt{n}}\right)\\
&=\frac{1}{2}+\frac{1}{\sqrt{2\pi(n-1)[1+\phi_k(B^2+2B)]}}+o\left(\frac{1}{\sqrt{n}}\right)\\
p_{Br} &= \frac{1}{2}+\frac{1}{2}\frac{1}{\sigma_k\sqrt{2\pi(n-1)}}+o\left(\frac{1}{\sqrt{n}}\right)\\
&+\sum_{m=1}^{1/B}\frac{1}{2}\left(\frac{1}{\sigma_k\sqrt{2\pi(n-1)}}Exp\left[\frac{-m^2}{2(n-1)\sigma_k^2}\right]+o\left(\frac{1}{\sqrt{n}}\right)\right)\\
&+\frac{1}{2}\left(\frac{1}{\sigma_k\sqrt{2\pi(n-1)}}Exp\left[\frac{-(1+1/B)^2}{2(n-1)\sigma_k^2}\right]+o\left(\frac{1}{\sqrt{n}}\right)\right)\\
&=\frac{1}{2}+\left(\frac{1}{B}+1\right)\frac{B}{\sqrt{2\pi(n-1)[1+\phi_k(B^2+2B)]}}+o\left(\frac{1}{\sqrt{n}}\right)\\
&=\frac{1}{2}+\frac{1+B}{\sqrt{2\pi(n-1)[1+\phi_k(B^2+2B)]}}+o\left(\frac{1}{\sqrt{n}}\right).
\end{aligned}
$$

This establishes the first part of the lemma.

Voter i will choose to cast the bonus vote in referendum k over referendums k' if and only if $v_{ik}p_{Bk} + v_{ik'}p_{1k'} > v_{ik'}p_{Bk'} + v_{ik}p_{1k}$. Substituting (5.4), we obtain (5.5). If (5.5) holds for all k''s different from k, then the voter will cast the extra vote in referendum k. ■

Lemma 5.3. Suppose $G_k(\mathrm{v}) = G(\mathrm{v})$ for all k, and $G(\mathrm{v})$ symmetric around 0. Then: (i) there exists a unique equilibrium; (ii) in equilibrium, each voter casts the bonus vote in referendum s if and only if $v_{is} \geq v_{ir}\ \forall r$.

Proof of Lemma 5.3. Given Lemma 5.2, the proof of Lemma 5.3 is straightforward. Start with point (ii). To see that the candidate strategy is indeed an equilibrium strategy, suppose that all voters but i cast their bonus vote in the referendum with the highest intensity. Since all valuations are drawn from the same probability distribution, with K independent draws each has probability $1/K$ of being the highest, implying $\phi_k = \phi_{k'} = 1/K\ \ \forall k, k'$. Thus, the square root in (5.5) equals 1, and voter i's best response is to follow the same strategy, establishing that it is indeed an equilibrium. (i) To see that the equilibrium is unique, suppose, to the contrary, that there is an equilibrium such that not all ϕ_k's are equal, and call s the referendum such that $\phi_s = \max\{\phi_k\}$. Then $\sqrt{[1 + \phi_s(B^2 + 2B)]/[1 + \phi_k(B^2 + 2B)]} \equiv \alpha(s, k) \geq 1\ \forall k \neq s$, with at least one strict inequality. Call r one of the referendums for which the strict inequality holds (at least one r must exist). Then, by (5.5), in the bilateral comparison between s and r the expected share of voters casting their bonus vote on s is lower than on r. We can have $\phi_s = \max\{\phi_k\}$ only if there exists at least one r' such that $\alpha(s, r') < \alpha(r, r')$. But this requires $\phi_r > \phi_s$, contradicting $\phi_s = \max\{\phi_k\}$. ■

We can now prove Proposition 5.1.

5.3 Proof of Proposition 5.1

Call $F(v)$, defined over $[0, 1]$, the distribution from which each voter's intensity is drawn independently, and denote by Ev its mean and by $Ev_{(j)}$

the expected jth order statistics among the K independent draws (where therefore $Ev_{(K)}$ is the expected value of each voter's highest intensity). From Lemma 5.3, $\phi_k = 1/K\ \forall k$ and thus $p_{1k} = p_1, p_{Bk} = p_B\ \forall k$. Because voters cast their bonus vote in the referendum associated with the highest intensity, expected ex ante utility with an electorate of size n, EV_{0n}, is given by:

$$EV_{0n} = Ev_{(K)}p_B + \sum_{j=1}^{K-1} Ev_{(j)}p_1 = K(Ev)p + Ev_{(K)}(p_B - p_1).$$

Substituting (5.4) and $\phi_r = 1/K\ \forall r$:

$$EV_{0n} = Ev\left(\frac{K}{2} + \frac{K\sqrt{K}}{\sqrt{2\pi(n-1)(K+B^2+2B)}}\right) + Ev_{(K)}\left(\frac{B\sqrt{K}}{\sqrt{2\pi(n-1)(K+B^2+2B)}}\right) + o\left(\frac{1}{\sqrt{n}}\right).$$

Given Lemma 5.1, EW_{0n}, expected ex ante utility with a series of simple majority referendums, is given by:

$$EW_{0n} = Ev\left(\frac{K}{2} + \frac{K}{\sqrt{2\pi(n-1)}}\right) + o\left(\frac{1}{\sqrt{n}}\right).$$

Call ER_0 expected ex ante utility when each referendum is decided by a coin toss (i.e. with random decision-making). Since $ER_0 = KEv(1/2)$, we immediately derive:

$$\omega_n = \left(\frac{EV_{0n} - ER_0}{EW_{0n} - ER_0}\right) = \frac{(KEv + BEv_{(K)})\left(\frac{\sqrt{K}}{\sqrt{2\pi(n-1)(K+B^2+2B)}}\right) + o\left(\frac{1}{\sqrt{n}}\right)}{Ev\left(\frac{K}{\sqrt{2\pi(n-1)}}\right) + o\left(\frac{1}{\sqrt{n}}\right)}.$$

Or:

$$\omega_n \longrightarrow \frac{\sqrt{K}\left(KEv + BEv_{(K)}\right)}{Ev\sqrt{K + B^2 + 2B)}} = \omega.$$

Therefore:

$$\omega > 1 \quad \begin{cases} \forall B > 0 & \text{if } (Ev_{(K)})^2 \geq K(Ev)^2 \\ \forall B < \frac{2KEv(Ev_{(K)}-Ev)}{K(Ev)^2-(Ev_{(K)})^2} & \text{if } (Ev_{(K)})^2 < K(Ev)^2, \end{cases} \tag{5.6}$$

proving the proposition. ■

Given ω, we can derive the optimal B, the value of the bonus vote that maximizes the asymptotic efficiency gains, which we denote by B^*:[1]

$$B^* = \frac{K(Ev_{(K)} - Ev)}{KEv - Ev_{(K)}}.$$

The results can then be applied directly to specific distributions F. Figure 5.1 illustrates the following example:

Example 5.1. Suppose that $F(v)$ can be parameterized as a power distribution: $F(v) = v^b$, $b > 0$. Then, ignoring integer constraints: (i) For all K, $\omega > 1$ if $B < 2/b$. (ii) For all K, $B^* = 1/b$. (iii) If $B = B^*$, the optimal number of referendums K^* equals $2 + 1/b$.

5.4 Proof of Proposition 5.2

The first step is the characterization of the equilibrium.

Lemma 5.4. Call $F_k(v)$, defined over [0, 1], the distribution of intensities in referendum k, where now we allow $F_k(v) \neq F_{k'}(v)$ for $k' \neq k$. Voter i's optimal strategy is to cast a bonus vote in referendum k if and only if:

$$\frac{v_{ik}}{v_{ik'}} > \sqrt{\frac{1 + \phi_k(B^2 + 2B)}{1 + \phi_{k'}(B^2 + 2B)}} \equiv \alpha(k, k') \quad \forall k' \neq k, \tag{5.7}$$

1. For arbitrary $F(v)$,

$$Ev_{(K)} = K \int_0^1 v[F(v)]^{K-1} dF(v),$$

ensuring that B^* is always well-defined.

where:

$$\phi_{k'} = \int_0^1 \prod_{k \neq k'} F_k(\min(\alpha(k, k')v, 1)) f_k(v) dv. \tag{5.8}$$

Lemma 5.4 follows immediately from Lemma 5.2. ■

Lemma 5.5. The equilibrium is unique.

Proof of Lemma 5.5. Consider an equilibrium $\{\phi_k'\}$. Posit a second equilibrium $\{\phi_k''\}$ such that without loss of generality there exists some referendum r such that $\phi_r'' > \phi_r'$. Call z the referendum for which ϕ_z''/ϕ_z' is maximal. Call $\alpha'(z, r)$ the ratio defined in (5.7) in the original equilibrium $\{\phi_k'\}$, and $\alpha''(z, r)$ the equivalent ratio in the second candidate equilibrium $\{\phi_k''\}$. By (5.7), if z is the referendum for which ϕ_z''/ϕ_z' is maximal, $\alpha''(z, r) < \alpha'(z, r)\ \forall r \neq z$. But if $\alpha''(z, r) < \alpha'(z, r)$ $\forall r \neq z$, by Lemma 5.4 $\phi_z'' < \phi_z'$ establishing a contradiction. ■

To understand the equilibrium strategy intuitively, consider the following example. Suppose $B = 1$, $K = 2$ and $F_k(v) = v^{b_k}$, with $b_1 = 1$ and $b_2 = 2$. Then $\alpha(1, 2) = 0.89$ – a voter casts the bonus vote on issue 1 as long as $v_1 \geq 0.89\ v_2$ – and the expected shares of bonus votes cast in the two referendums are $\phi_1 = 0.41$ and $\phi_2 = 0.59$. If $b_2 = 4$, the numbers become $\alpha(1, 2) = 0.82$, $\phi_1 = 0.34$ and $\phi_2 = 0.66$.

Proposition 5.2 can now be proved.

Proof of Proposition 5.2. Recall the definition of ω_n:

$$\omega_n = \left(\frac{EV_{0n} - ER_0}{EW_{0n} - ER_0} \right)$$

Denote by $E_k(v)$ the mean of distribution $F_k(v)$. With heterogeneous distributions:

$$EV_{0n} = \sum_k E_k(v) p_{1k} + \sum_{k=1}^{K} \left[\left(\int_0^1 \prod_{s \neq k} F_s(\min(\alpha_{sk} v, 1)) v f_k(v) dv \right) (p_{Bk} - p_{1k}) \right]$$

$$EW_{0n} = \sum_k E_k(v)p_k$$

$$ER_0 = \sum_k E_k(v)(1/2).$$

Keeping in mind the definition of ϕ_k in (5.8), call:

$$\beta_k(B) \equiv \frac{1}{\sqrt{1 + \phi_k(B)(B^2 + 2B)}}.$$

We can write:

$$\omega_n \longrightarrow \frac{\sum_{k=1}^{K} E_k(v)\beta_k(B) + \sum_{k=1}^{K}\left[B\beta_k(B)\left(\int_0^1 \prod_{s\neq k} F_s(\min(\alpha_{sk}v, 1))vf_k(v)dv\right)\right]}{\sum_k E_k(v)} = \omega, \tag{5.9}$$

and $\omega > 1$ if and only if:

$$\sum_{k=1}^{K} E_k(v)\beta_k(B) + \sum_{k=1}^{K}\left[B\beta_k(B)\left(\int_0^1 \prod_{s\neq k} F_s(\min(\alpha_{sk}v, 1))vf_k(v)dv\right)\right]$$
$$> \sum_{k=1}^{K} E_k(v). \tag{5.10}$$

At $B = 0$, $\omega = 1$ – as must be the case by the definition of ω_n and as can be verified by setting $B = 0$ in (5.9). Proposition 5.2 must hold if ω is increasing in B at $B = 0$: although B must be a rational number larger than $1/\sqrt{n}$, there is always a value of n such that B can take values arbitrarily close to 0. Because in addition ω is continuous in B in the neighborhood of $B = 0$, in this neighborhood we can treat B as a continuous variable. Showing $d\omega/dB > 0$ at $B = 0$ amounts to differentiating the left hand side of (5.10), taking into account (5.7) and (5.8). The derivative is greatly simplified by being evaluated at $B = 0$. It is not difficult to show that it reduces to:

$$\left.\frac{d\omega}{dB}\right|_{B=0} > 0 \Longleftrightarrow \sum_{k=1}^{K}\left[\left(\int_0^1 \prod_{s\neq k} F_s(v)vf_k(v)dv\right)\right] - \sum_{k=1}^{K} E_k(v)\, \phi_k|_{B=0} > 0. \tag{5.11}$$

Integrating by part the first summation:

$$\sum_{k=1}^{K}\left[\left(\int_0^1 \prod_{s\neq k} F_s(v)vf_k(v)dv\right)\right] = \int_0^1\left(1-\prod_{k=1}^{K} F_k(v)\right)dv = Ev_{(K)}.$$

Thus, (5.11) can be rewritten more simply as:

$$\left.\frac{d\omega}{dB}\right|_{B=0} > 0 \Longleftrightarrow Ev_{(K)} > \sum_{k=1}^{K} E_k(v)\ \phi_k|_{B=0}\,.$$

Since $\sum_{r=1}^{k} \phi_k|_{B=0} = 1$, the expression must be strictly positive, and the proposition is established. ■

In addition, call $\omega^R \equiv \omega(\alpha_{sr} = 1\ \forall s, r)$. Note that, evaluated at $B = 0$, $d\omega/dB = d\omega^R/dB$. Thus, the argument is unchanged, and the result must remain true if voters do not maximize fully but set $\alpha_{sr} = 1\ \forall s, r$. The following corollary is established:

Corollary to Proposition 5.2. Suppose voters set $\alpha_{sr} = 1\ \forall s, r$. Proposition 5.2 continues to hold.

5.5 Proof of Proposition 5.3

Call p^s_{1k} the probability of obtaining one's desired outcome in referendum k when the probability of approval ψ_k is stochastic (hence the s superscript) and the voter does not cast the bonus vote, and p^s_{Bk} the corresponding probability when the voter casts the bonus vote. The notation will be simplified by writing $\psi_k \equiv 1/2 + \delta_k$, where δ_k is distributed according to $H_\delta(\delta)$ defined over the support $[-1/2, 1/2]$ and symmetric around 0, and each realized δ_k is an independent draw from H_δ. Given H_δ symmetric around 0, and $F_k(v) = F(v)$ for all k, if each voter casts his bonus vote on his highest-intensity referendum, it must follow that $p^s_{1k} = p^s_1$ and $p^s_{Bk} = p^s_B$ for all k. Thus the strategies are an equilibrium.

For given δ_k, call $V(\delta_k)$ the votes differential in referendum k. $V(\delta_k)$ converges asymptotically to a normal distribution whose mean is the limit of the sample mean and whose variance is the limit of the sample variance. Given the equilibrium strategy, $E(V(\delta_k)) = n[\psi_k(1/K)(1+B) + \psi_k(1-1/K)(1) + (1-\psi_k)/K(-1-B) + (1-\psi_k)(1-1/K)(-1)] = n[(2\psi_k - 1)(1+B/K)]$, where $\psi_k = prob(v_{ik} > 0)$ for all i, k and $1/K = prob(v_{ik} = \max\{v_i\})$ over all k, and thus $1/K$ is the probability that voter i casts the bonus vote in referendum k. Using $\psi_k = 1/2 + \delta_k$, we can write $EV(\delta_k) = 2n\delta_k(1+B/K)$. Similarly, the sample variance of the votes differential is given by $n[(\psi_k + 1 - \psi_k)(1/K)(1+B)^2 + (\psi_k + 1 - \psi_k)(1-1/K)(1) + O(\delta_k^2)] = n[(B^2 + 2B + K)/K + O(\delta_k^2)]$. Taking into account the discreteness of the distribution and ignoring terms of order δ_k^2 and higher, p_1^s and p_B^s can be approximated as:

$$p_1^s(\delta) \simeq \widetilde{\Phi}(0) + \frac{\sqrt{K}}{\sqrt{2\pi n(K+B^2+2B)}} \exp\left[-\frac{4n\delta^2 K(1+B/K)^2}{2(K+B^2+2B)}\right]$$

$$p_B^s(\delta) \simeq \widetilde{\Phi}(0) + \frac{(1+B)\sqrt{K}}{\sqrt{2\pi n(K+B^2+2B)}} \exp\left[-\frac{4n\delta^2 K(1+B/K)^2}{2(K+B^2+2B)}\right],$$

where $\widetilde{\Phi}(0)$ is the cumulative function at 0 of a normal distribution with mean $2\delta n(1+B/K)$ and variance $n(K+B^2+2B)/K$. (The probabilities simplify to the values in (5.4) above for $\delta = 0$).

Because the expected intensity in each referendum is independent of the direction of the preferences, ex ante expected utility with stochastic approval, EV_{0n}^s, is as follows:

$$EV_{0n}^s = \int_{-1/2}^{1/2} [K(Ev)p_1^s(\delta) + Ev_{(K)}(p_B^s(\delta) - p_1^s(\delta))]dH_\delta(\delta).$$

With H_ψ symmetric around 1/2, $\int_{-1/2}^{1/2} \widetilde{\Phi}(0)dH_\delta(\delta) = 1/2$.

Thus,

$$EV_{0n}^s - ER_0 = [K(Ev) + BEv_{(K)}] \int_{-1/2}^{1/2} \frac{\sqrt{K}}{\sqrt{2\pi n(K+B^2+2B)}} \times \exp\left[-\frac{n4\delta^2 K(1+B/K)^2}{2(K+B^2+2B)}\right] dH_\delta(\delta).$$

At large n, only realizations of δ close to 0 yield positive probabilities. Thus at large n we can write:[2]

$$\int_{-1/2}^{1/2} \frac{\sqrt{K}}{\sqrt{2\pi n(K+B^2+2B)}} \exp\left[-\frac{n4\delta^2 K(1+B/K)^2}{2(K+B^2+2B)}\right] dH_\delta(\delta)$$
$$= \frac{\sqrt{K}}{\sqrt{2\pi n(K+B^2+2B)}} \sqrt{2\pi} \frac{\sqrt{(K+B^2+2B)}}{\sqrt{Kn}2(1+B/K)} h_\delta(0)$$
$$= \frac{1}{2(1+B/K)} \frac{1}{n} h_\delta(0).$$

Therefore,

$$EV_{0n}^s - ER_0 = [K(Ev) + BEv_{(K)}]\left[\frac{1}{2(1+B/K)} \frac{1}{n} h_\delta(0)\right]. \qquad (5.12)$$

At $B = 0$, equation (5.12) reduces to the expected improvement over randomness with simple majority, or:

$$EW_{0n}^s - ER_0 = K(Ev)\left[\frac{1}{2}\frac{1}{n} h_\delta(0)\right].$$

We obtain:

$$\omega_n^s \longrightarrow \omega^s = \frac{K(Ev) + BEv_{(K)}}{(Ev)(K+B)}.$$

It is then immediate that $\omega^s > 1 \iff Ev_{(K)} > Ev$, a condition that is always satisfied. ■

2. Exploiting the Gaussian integral:

$$\int_{-\infty}^{\infty} e^{-ax^2} dx = \sqrt{\pi/a},$$

with large n:

$$\int_{-c}^{c} g(x) e^{-\frac{nx^2}{2q}} dx = g(0)\sqrt{2q\pi/n}.$$

5.6 Proof of Proposition 5.4

If $\phi_P > \phi_C$, in each referendum the sample mean of the votes differential is $EV = (n/2)B(\phi_P - \phi_C) > 0$, and the sample variance $\sigma_V^2 = (n/2)[(\phi_P + \phi_C)(2B + B^2) - B^2/2(\phi_P - \phi_C)^2 + 2]$. The probability that the referendum passes equals:

$$prob(V > 0) = prob\left[\left(\frac{V - EV}{\sigma_V}\right) > -\frac{EV}{\sigma_V}\right].$$

For large n, the term $\left(\frac{V-EV}{\sigma_V}\right)$ converges in distribution to a standard normal, with 0 mean and unitary variance, while $-EV/\sigma_V \to -\infty$. Hence $prob(V > 0) \to 1$.

If all proposals pass with probability approaching 1, we can write ex ante utility as:

$$EV_{0n} \to \frac{K}{2} E_P(v),$$

where 1/2 is the ex ante probability of being in favor of any proposal.

With simple majority voting, on the other hand:

$$EW_{0n} \to K\left(\frac{1}{2} + \frac{1}{\sqrt{2\pi n}}\right)\left(\frac{E_P(v) + E_C(v)}{2}\right).$$

Because $E_P(v) > E_C(v)$, we can conclude that there always exists a large but finite n' such that for all $n > n'$, $EV_{0n} > EW_{0n}$. The result holds for any positive B, independently of its precise value. In addition, if we consider a sequence of referendums with increasing n, as $n \to \infty$, $EW_{0n} \to ER_0 = K/2\left(\frac{E_P(v)+E_C(v)}{2}\right)$, while $EV_{0n} \to \frac{K}{2}E_P(v) > ER_0$. ■

Note that since both $F_P(v)$ and $F_C(v)$ are strictly increasing in v, if $F_P(v)$ first-order stochastically dominates $F_C(v)$, each term summed in ϕ_P is larger than its corresponding term in ϕ_C, and thus $\phi_P > \phi_C$. The condition $\phi_P > \phi_C$ in Proposition 5.4 can be substituted by the stronger condition that $F_P(v)$ first-order stochastically dominates $F_C(v)$.

Figure 5.4 illustrates the following example:

Example 5.2. Suppose that both $F_P(v)$ and $F_C(v)$ are power distributions with parameters b_p and b_c, where $b_p > b_c$. Then, for any $B > 0$ and $K > 1$, as $n \to \infty$, $EV_{0n}/EW_{0n} \to 1 + (b_p - b_c)/(b_p + b_c + 2b_p b_c) > 1$ and $\omega_n \to \infty$.

6

A Field Test of Storable Votes in Large Elections: Student Elections on the Columbia Campus

6.1 Testing the Representativeness of the Samples

Table T6.1 reports the statistical evidence suggesting the imperfect representativeness of the data samples, relative to the full populations of voters in the two schools.

Table T6.1 Comparison of abstention rates and margins of victory in and outside the samples

Table T6.1a: GS

	Abstentions			Share of votes for the winner		
	Nonsample	Sample	Diff.	Nonsample	Sample	Diff.
President	0.21	0.02	0.19*	0.63	0.53	0.10*
Alumni Affairs	0.54	0.26	0.28*	0.59	0.48	0.11
Int'l Repr.	0.46	0.23	0.24*	0.63	0.65	−0.02

Table T6.1b: CC

	Abstentions			Share of votes for the winner		
	Nonsample	Sample	Diff.	Nonsample	Sample	Diff.
Exec Board	0.08	0.02	0.06*	0.57	0.60	−0.03
Senate-1	0.15	0.12	0.03	0.69	0.73	−0.04
Senate-2	0.13	0.08	0.05*	0.56	0.55	0.01
AcademicAffrs.	0.18	0.15	0.03	0.65	0.54	0.11*

The star indicates that the hypothesis that both the rest of the electorate and the samples of respondents are random draws from a common population is rejected at the 5 percent confidence level. Both in the electorate as a whole and in the samples: (i) abstention rates are calculated for each election for students who voted at least once, and thus do not reflect the fraction of students who did not take part in voting at all; and (ii) the share of votes for the winner is calculated among voters in each election, and thus ignores abstentions.

6.2 Measures of Inequality

Table T6.2 reports different synthetic measures of inequality in bootstrap samples in which the minority wins at least one election.

Table T6.2 Measures of inequality when outcomes differ

Table T6.2a: GS

Gini Coefficient

	Maj	A	B	C	D
Mean	0.347	0.353	0.353	0.353	0.354
95% CI	(0.20, 0.40)	(0.21, 0.40)	(0.21, 0.40)	(0.22, 0.40)	(0.22, 0.39)
Prob bv lower (%)		47.9	52.8	58.2	58

Ratio of average utility of bottom 20 percent to sample average

	Maj	A	B	C	D
Mean (%)	9.08	7.89	7.44	7.14	6.78
95% CI	(0, 47.1)	(0, 45.0)	(0, 44.9)	(0, 43.7)	(0, 43.1)
Prob bv higher(%)		52.5	51.2	53.5	49.4

Table T6.2b: CC

Gini Coefficient

	Maj	A	B	C	D
Mean	0.280	0.246	0.243	0.243	0.243
95% CI	(0.24, 0.30)	(0.22, 0.29)	(0.22, 0.28)	(0.22, 0.27)	(0.22, 0.27)
Prob bv lower (%)		90.5	95.3	97.1	97.7

Ratio of average utility of bottom 20 percent to sample average

	Maj	A	B	C	D
Mean (%)	27.27	33.88	34.42	34.42	34.38
95% CI	(22.5, 37.7)	(24.9, 41.8)	(25.9, 41.5)	(27.2, 41.0)	(27.4, 41.2)
Prob bv higher (%)		88.6	94.0	96.6	97.0

Because the focus here is on bootstrap samples in which majority voting and the bonus vote lead to different outcomes, to each bonus vote rule corresponds a slightly different data set. The values reported in the table for majority rule correspond to bootstrap samples in which majority and Rule A lead to different outcomes (the values in the other cases are almost identical).

Appendix: Experimental Instructions

The Appendix is a collection of sample instructions for all experiments discussed in the book. While the experimenter read the instructions aloud, relevant screen shots were typically shown to the subjects. Here they are reproduced only for the experiment on Chapter 1; all others are similar.

A.1 Experiment in Chapter 1

SAMPLE INSTRUCTIONS: four-person, three-proposal treatment

INTRODUCTORY REMARKS

Thank you for agreeing to participate in this decision-making experiment. During the experiment, we require your complete, undistracted attention, and ask that you follow instructions carefully. You may not open other applications on your computer, chat with other students, or engage in other distracting activities, such as using your phone, reading books, etc. Please turn off your cell phone.

Before we begin, please read and sign the consent form, which is located at your terminal.

[Collect consent forms]

You will be paid for your participation in cash at the end of the experiment. Different participants may earn different amounts. What you earn depends partly on your decisions, partly on the decisions of others, and partly on chance.

The entire experiment will take place through computer terminals, and all interaction between you will take place through the computers. It is important that you not talk or in any way try to communicate with other participants during the experiments.

We will start with a brief instruction period. During the instruction period, you will be given a complete description of the experiment and will be shown how to use the computers. If you have any questions during the instruction period, raise your hand and your question will be answered out loud so everyone can hear. If you have any questions after the experiment has begun, raise your hand, and an experimenter will come and assist you.

DESCRIPTION

The experiment you are participating in is a committee voting experiment. You will participate in 12 voting sessions. Before each voting session you will be randomly matched with three other people to form a committee of four. Each group follows exactly the same rules and what happens in one group has no effect on the other groups.

In each session you and the other members of your group will be asked to vote over three successive proposals. The proposals are called the Green Proposal, Blue Proposal, and Red Proposal. As a result of voting, each of the three proposals can either pass or fail. Each member of a group has one regular vote to be cast on each proposal. In addition, each member will be given a single extra bonus vote. You will choose in which of the three proposals you want to cast the bonus vote in addition to your regular vote.

At the beginning of a voting session you will be randomly assigned a personal Green Proposal Value, Red Proposal Value, and Blue Proposal Value. In this experiment, values are denominated in francs, and each of the three proposals' values is equally likely to be any integer amount between −100 and 100 francs, but not 0. The values are assigned randomly and thus will generally be different. The other members of your group are also randomly assigned their own Green, Red, and Blue Proposal Values, each of which is equally likely to be any integer amount between −100 and 100 francs, but not 0. Because the values are random, each person is likely to have different values for the three proposals, and the values of each proposal (for example, the Green Proposal Values) are also likely to be different for different persons. You are not told what the values of the other members of your group are.

If your value is positive, you are in favor of the proposal, and earn your value if and only if the proposal passes. If your value is negative, you are against the proposal and earn the absolute value of your value if and only if the proposal does not pass. Otherwise you earn 0 francs. For example, if your Green Proposal Value is −55, then you earn 55 francs if Green does not pass, and 0 francs if Green passes (and similarly for Blue or Red). Because the values are randomly assigned, being in favor of one proposal has no implication for how you feel about the other.

Your screen will look like this: (The values in the screen shots are for illustration only).

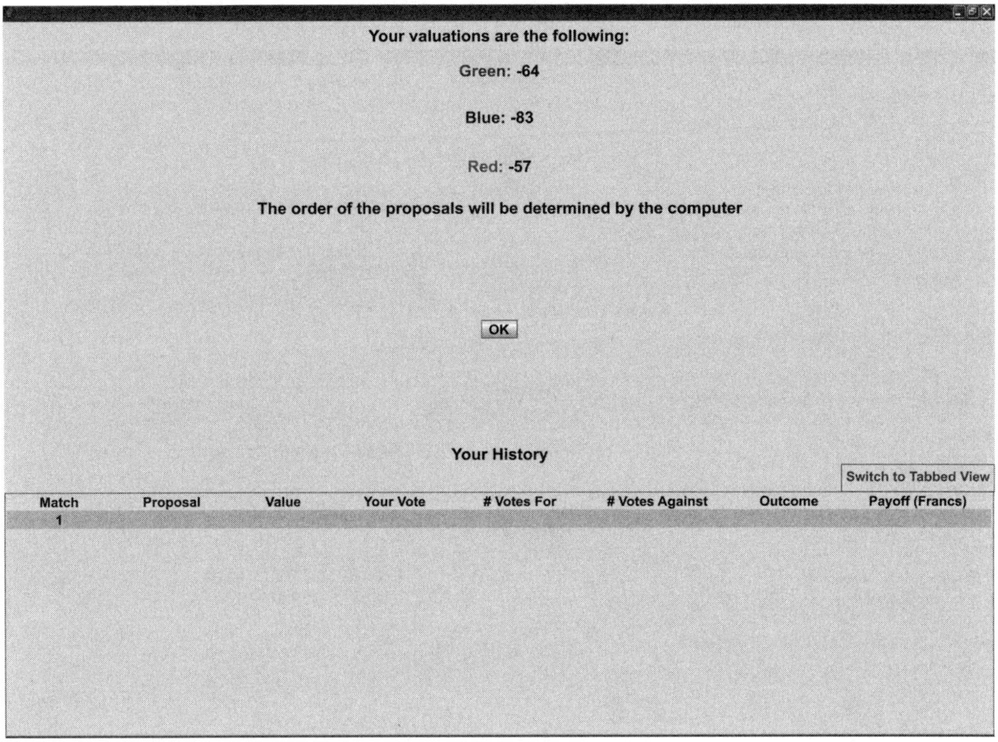

After all personal values have been assigned, the computer randomly chooses the order in which the three proposals will be voted on. You will be informed about the order chosen by the computer.

The three elections are held sequentially. As mentioned earlier, each member of the group will cast one regular vote on each proposal. In addition, each member will be given one extra bonus vote and will choose on which of the three proposals s/he wants to cast the bonus vote in addition to the regular vote. Suppose for example that the first election is on the Green proposal. Then you will decide whether to cast one or two votes in the Green election: your regular Green vote only, or your regular Green vote and the bonus vote. The other members of your group may also cast up to two votes in the Green election. If you are in favor of the Green proposal (that is, your Green Proposal Value is positive), any votes you cast will automatically be counted as yes votes. If you are against Green (that is, your Green Proposal Value is negative), any votes you cast will be automatically counted as no votes.

Your screen will look like this:

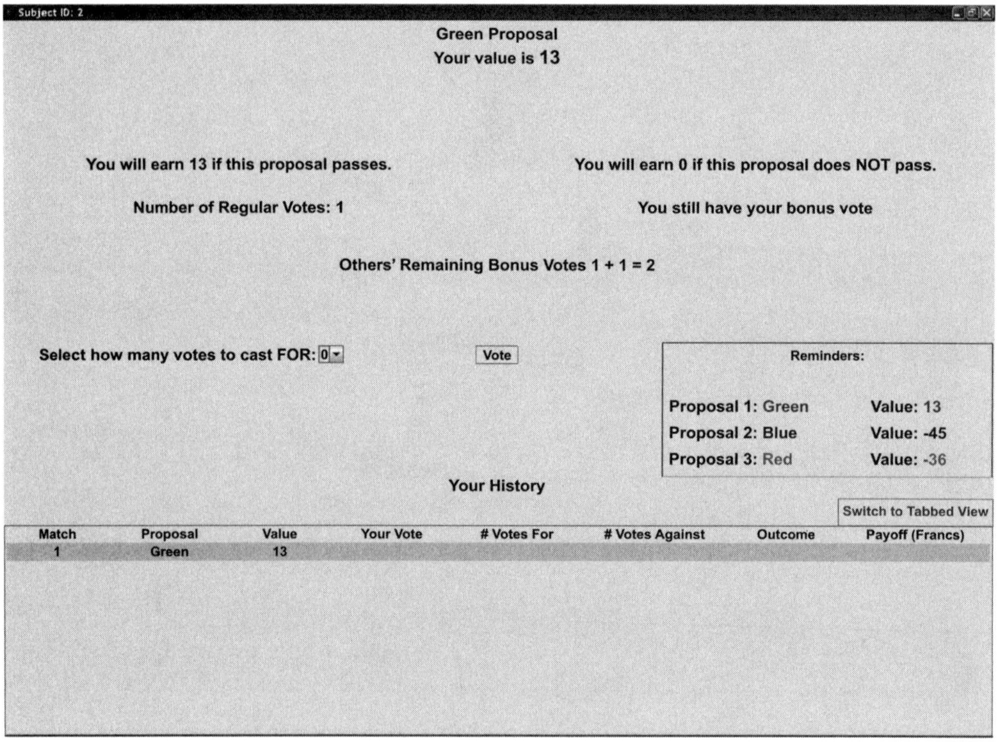

Notice that the screen displays how many bonus votes you and the members of your group have left.

The Green proposal passes in your group if there are more yes votes than no votes cast by members of your group, and fails if there are more no votes than yes votes. Ties are broken randomly by the computer. After you and the other members of your group have made voting decisions for the first proposal, the computer will tell you the number of votes cast for and against the proposal, and the outcome of the vote for your group.

Your screen will look like this:

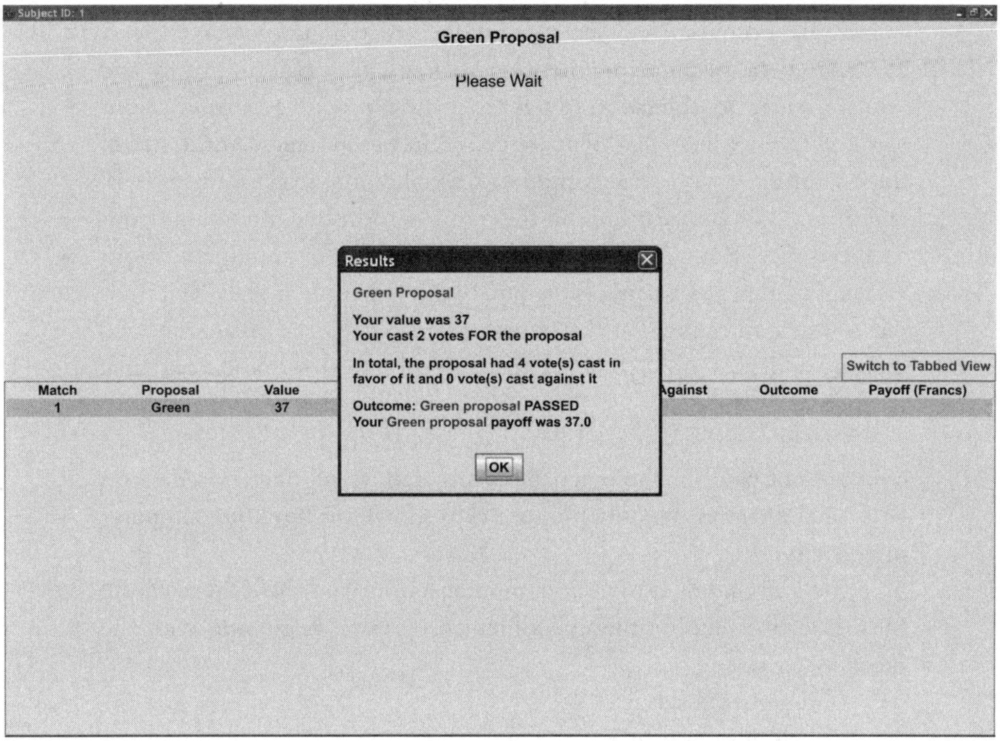

You will then proceed to the next proposal. Continuing with the example above, suppose that the second election is the Blue election. In the Blue election each member of your group (including you) is left with his or her regular Blue vote, plus the bonus vote, if the bonus vote has not been cast earlier in the Green election. If you have cast two votes in the Green election, you will have only your regular vote in the Blue election. But if you cast one vote in the Green election, then you still have your bonus vote, and will be able to cast up to two votes in the Blue election.

In the third and final election, the Red one in this example, you will cast all your remaining votes by clicking the "Vote" button. You do not have any choice about how many votes to cast in this third election.

When everyone has finished, we will go to the next voting session. The groups will be rematched randomly by the computer, and the procedure described above will be repeated. Each voting session has three successive elections over the three proposals. The proposals values are reassigned anew for every session, and in every session you will have one regular vote for each election and one single bonus vote.

At the end of the experiment, everyone will be paid in private and you are under no obligation to tell others how much you earned. Your earnings during the experiment are denominated in francs. At the end of the 12 voting sessions, the computer will randomly select four sessions, and the sum of your earnings in these four sessions will determine your total earnings. Your dollar earnings are determined by multiplying your earnings in francs by a conversion rate. In this experiment, the conversion rate is 0.025, meaning that 100 francs equal 2.5 dollars. This amount will then be added to the $10.00 participation fee to determine your final payment.

Are there any questions before we proceed to the practice session? You are not paid for the practice session, and it will have no effect on your final earnings. Its only purpose is to show you how the computer interface works.

You will find next to your computer terminal a record sheet. Please fill the record sheet as the experiment progresses, beginning with the practice session.

[Start game on server]

We will now proceed to the practice session. Please complete it on your own. Feel free to raise your hand if you have any questions.

[Practice session]

[Wait for subjects to complete the practice session]

The practice session is now over. Any questions?

If you have any questions from now on, raise your hand, and an experimenter will come and assist you. We will now begin the 12 paid sessions. Please remember to fill the record sheet.

[Play 12 real matches]

END OF EXPERIMENTAL PROTOCOL

This is the end of the experiment. Please record your total earnings at the bottom of the record sheet. Add the $10.00 show-up fee enter the sum as the total.

We will pay each of you in private in the next room in the order of your Subject ID numbers. Remember you are under no obligation to reveal your earnings to the other players.

Please put the mouse behind the computer screen and do not use either the mouse or the keyboard at all. Please be patient and remain seated until we call you to be paid. Do not converse with the other participants or use your cell phone. Thank you for your cooperation.

Could the person with lab number ... please go to the next room to be paid? Please bring all your belongings with you, including your payment receipt sheet.

A.2 Experiment in Chapter 2

SAMPLE INSTRUCTIONS: two-person, two-proposal treatment

INTRODUCTORY REMARKS

DESCRIPTION

The experiment you are participating in is a voting experiment, where you will be asked to allocate a budget of several votes over two successive elections. We will have a practice session before we proceed to the paid session. The paid session will consist of 30 rounds. Each round will have two elections, and you will receive a new budget of votes at the beginning of each round.

At the end of the paid session, you will be paid the sum of what you have earned in each of the 30 rounds, plus a show-up fee of $5.00. Everyone will be paid in private and you are under no obligation to tell others how much you earned. Your earnings during the experiment are denominated in francs. Your dollar earnings are determined by multiplying your earnings in francs by a conversion rate. In this experiment, the conversion rate is 0.007, meaning that 100 francs is worth $0.70.

At the beginning of the first match, you will be randomly divided into six groups with two persons in each group. Each group follows exactly the same rules, but what happens in your group has no effect on the members of the other groups, and vice versa. You and the other member of your group will vote on two different proposals, in sequence. You will cast one regular vote in each election. In addition, you will be given two bonus votes that you will be able to add to your regular votes in any way you wish.

The first proposal your group votes on is called Proposal A. You may cast up to three votes in the A election, your regular A vote plus either 0, one, or two of your bonus votes. Before making a decision of how many votes to cast, you will be assigned your personal Proposal A Value, which is equally likely to be any integer amount between −100 and 100 francs, but not 0. The other member of your group is also randomly assigned his or her own Proposal A value, which is equally likely to be any integer amount between −100 and 100 francs, but not 0. Because the values are random, you and the other member of your group will usually have different values. You are not told what his or her value is. The other member of your group may also cast up to three votes in the A election. This is indicated on your screen where it says, "Other's available votes for current proposal."

If your value is positive, you are in favor of Proposal A and earn your value if and only if A passes. If your A value is negative, you are against proposal A and earn the absolute value of your value if and only if A does not pass. Otherwise you earn 0 francs. For example, if your proposal A value is –55, then you earn 55 francs if A does not pass, and 0 francs if A passes. Proposal A passes in your group if there are more yes votes than no votes cast by members of your group. Proposal A fails in your group if there are more no votes than yes votes cast by members of your group. Ties are broken randomly by the computer.

After being told your proposal A value, you must decide whether to cast one vote, two votes, or three votes in the proposal A election. If you are in favor of A (that is, your proposal A value is positive), any votes you cast will be automatically counted as yes votes for A. If you are against A (that is, your proposal A value is negative), any votes you cast will be automatically counted as no votes. Whatever bonus votes you do not use in the A election, will be saved for you to use in the B election. For example, if you cast one vote in the A election, both your bonus votes will be saved. If you cast two votes in the A election, only one of your bonus votes will be saved. If you cast three votes in the A election, none of your bonus votes will be saved. You will be told how the other member of your group voted in the proposal A election after you have made your voting decision.

After you and the other member of your group have made voting decisions, you are both told the outcome of your group's proposal A election. You then proceed to the proposal B election. You are grouped with the same member in the proposal B election as you were grouped with for the proposal A election.

When you and the other member of your group are ready to proceed, each of you will be randomly assigned proposal B values in the same manner that your proposal A values were assigned. Again, because the values are random, they will typically be different from each other and different from your proposal A values. You are not told what the proposal B value of the other member of your group is. Your screen will display how many votes the other member of your group has left over from the A election. This is indicated on your screen where it says "Other's available votes for current proposal."

You will then cast your regular B vote, plus all of your remaining bonus votes by clicking on the "Vote" button. These votes will automatically be cast as yes votes for proposal B if your B value is greater than 0 and as no votes if your B value is less than 0. Your group's outcome of the B election is then reported to you. You do not have any choice about how many votes to cast in the B election. The number of votes you cast in the B election is equal to one plus the number of bonus votes you saved from the A election.

When everyone has finished we will go to the next match. In the next match, you will be reassigned into new groups of two persons each, and will repeat the procedure described above. This will continue for 30 matches.

[Practice session]

We will now give you a chance to get used to the computers with a short practice session. Do you have any questions before we begin the practice session?

[Answer questions]

You will not be paid for this session; it is just to allow you to get familiar with the experiment and your computers. During the practice session, do not press any keys or click with your mouse, unless instructed to. When we instruct you, please do exactly as we ask. Go ahead and double click on the icon that says "MULTISTAGE CLIENT."

FIRST SCREEN [Display screen-shot of their current screen on the video projector.]

Please enter your subject ID number, click OK/SUBMIT, and wait for further instructions.

SECOND SCREEN [Display screen-shot of their current screen on the video projector.]

This is the decision screen. The match number, the current proposal, the number of voters in your group (which is always two in this experiment), and your ID# are listed at the top of the screen. At the bottom of this screen is a table that will contain the history of all elections that you participate in. Since there have been no elections yet, it is blank. [Experimenter points to the appropriate areas of the screen on the projected image in the front of the room.]

Go ahead and open your envelope. You should have two record sheets.

Please record your ID number at the top of your record sheets. Please record your proposal A value on your record sheet in the row labeled "Practice 1 A." Then choose how many votes you want to cast in the A election, by clicking on the up or down arrows next to the number of votes. You may cast either one, two, or three votes in this election. Any unused votes in this election will be saved for you to use in the B election of this match.

If your proposal A value is positive, then all votes you cast will count as yes votes for A, and if your proposal A value is negative, then all votes you cast will count as no votes. When you have selected the number of votes you wish to cast in this election, please click on the "Vote" button. Please record the number of votes you cast on your record sheet. Then wait for all other participants in the room to finish casting their Proposal A votes.

THIRD SCREEN [Display screen-shot of their current screen on the video projector.]

Once everyone has made their vote decision for the A election, the votes are tallied and the results for your group are displayed on your screen. The screen displays the number of yes votes and the number of no votes cast by each member of your group. Please record these numbers on your record sheet. The proposal passes if there are more yes votes than no votes. Tie votes are broken randomly by the computer. The outcome for your group is displayed on your screen. Please record the outcome on your record sheet.

The screen also displays your earnings from the A election. Please record this number on your record sheet. This screen also displays your cumulative earnings so far in the experiment, which you do not need to record. Please press OK when you are ready to proceed to the proposal B election.

FOURTH SCREEN [Display screen-shot of their current screen on the video projector.]

We are now in the B election. You will not make any choices in the B election. Your voting decision is completely determined by how many votes you cast in the A election. But you will need to read the information on the screen and record it. Please record your proposal B value on your record sheet in the row labeled "Practice 1 B." This screen reminds you how many votes you have remaining. Please record this number on your record sheet in the column labeled "your vote." This number equals the number of bonus votes you did not use for proposal A, plus one additional vote. When you have recorded all the information, click on the "Vote" button. All these votes are now automatically cast by the computer. They are recorded as yes votes for proposal B if your B value is positive, and as no votes if your B value is negative.

FIFTH SCREEN [Display screen-shot of their current screen on the video projector.]

Once everyone has voted in the B election, the votes are tallied and the results for your group are displayed on your screen. The screen displays the number of yes votes and the number of no votes cast by each voter in your group. Please record these numbers. Proposal B passes in your group if there are more yes votes than no votes cast by voters in your group. Tie votes are broken randomly by the computer. The outcome for your group is displayed on your screen. Please record the outcome on your record sheet.

The screen displays your earnings from the B election. Please record this number on your record sheet. This screen also displays your cumulative earnings so far in the experiment, which you do not need to record.

We have now completed the first practice match. We will now proceed to the second practice match. Remember that you will be regrouped with a new participant in this match. This regrouping is done between every match in the experiment, and is determined randomly by the computer. Please complete the second practice match by following the same directions as in the first practice match. Don't forget to record the information as it appears on the screen. Remember, you are not paid for these practice matches. Feel free to raise your hand if you have any questions.

When everyone has made their vote decisions for proposal A and proposal B in this practice match, the practice session will be over.

Your total earnings for the practice session are displayed on this screen in francs and dollars. Since it is a practice match, the dollar amount equals 0. You do not need to record this because it is a practice match. But at the end of the experiment, it is essential that you record both of these numbers on your record sheet. Please click on the done button and wait for the experiment to begin

Any questions? [Answer questions]

Please pull out your dividers so we can begin the paid session of the experiment

[Proceed through paid matches 1–30]

END OF EXPERIMENTAL PROTOCOL

This completes the experiment. Please make sure to record your total payoffs on your record sheet, including your show-up fee of $5.00. Please remain in your seat. Do not talk with the other participants or play with the computers. We will come by to check your total. We will pay each of you in private in the next room in the order of your ID numbers. Please take all belongings with you when you leave to receive payment. You are under no obligation to reveal your earnings to the other players. Thank you for your participation.

A.3 Experiment in Chapter 3

SAMPLE INSTRUCTIONS: CChat treatment.

INTRODUCTORY REMARKS

DESCRIPTION

The experiment you are participating in is a voting experiment, where you will be asked to allocate a budget of several votes over two different proposals. We will begin with a practice session. The practice session will be followed by the paid session, which will consist of

20 matches. Each match will have elections for two different proposals, and you will receive a new budget of votes at the beginning of each match.

At the end of the paid session, you will be paid the sum of what you have earned, plus a show-up fee of $10.00. Everyone will be paid in private and you are under no obligation to tell others how much you earned. Your earnings during the experiment are denominated in francs. Your dollar earnings are determined by multiplying your earnings in francs by a conversion rate. For this experiment the conversion rate is 0.01, meaning that 100 francs equal 1 dollar.

At the beginning of the first match, you will be randomly assigned with four other persons in the room to form a five-voter committee, which votes over two different proposals, in sequence. Of the five voters of this committee, two voters belong to the *for* group; the remaining three voters belong to the *against* group. Whether you belong to the *for* or to the *against* group is decided randomly by the computer and will be displayed on your computer monitor.

The groups not only differ in size, but also differ in their preference over proposals. Specifically, all voters in the *for* group are always in favor of all proposals; all voters in the *against* group are always against all proposals.

Each voter is given one regular vote to cast in each of the two proposal elections. You must always use this vote in each proposal election. In addition, each voter is given a total of two bonus votes at the beginning of each match that you will use in addition to the regular votes.

The first proposal your committee votes on is called Proposal A. You may cast up to three votes in the A election (your regular A vote plus either 0, one, or two of your bonus votes.) Before proceeding to the vote, you are assigned your personal Proposal A value. If your value is positive, you are in favor of Proposal A; if your value is negative, you are against Proposal A. Each voter of the *for* group is in favor of Proposal A and has a positive value for Proposal A which is equally likely to be any amount between 1 and 100 francs. Every member of the *for* group is assigned the same Proposal A value by the computer. Each voter of the *against* group is against Proposal A and has a negative value for Proposal A which is equally likely to be any amount between −1 and −100 francs.

Every member of the *against* group is assigned the same Proposal A value by the computer.

If you are in the *for* group, you earn your value if A passes. If you are in the *against* group, you earn the absolute value of your value if A does not pass. For example, if your are in the *against* group and your proposal A value is −55, then you earn 55 francs if A does not pass, and 0 francs if A passes. A passes if there are more yes votes than no votes in the A election. A does not pass if there are more no votes than yes votes. Ties are broken randomly. In this example, you also know that the other two members of the *against* group also have Proposal A values of −55.

After being told your proposal A value, you will be allowed two minutes to exchange messages with the other members of your group. The messages you send and receive are not seen by members of the other group. They are private messages within your group. The messages must conform to the following rules. 1. Your messages must be relevant to the experiment. Do not engage in social chat. 2. You are not permitted to send messages that are intended to reveal your identity or participant ID number. 3. The use of threatening or offensive language, including profanity, is not permitted.

At any time during this two-minute period, you can make your individual voting decision. You must decide whether to cast one vote, two votes, or three votes in the proposal A election. If you are in the *for* group, any votes you cast will be automatically counted as yes votes for A. If you are in the *against* group, any votes you cast will be automatically counted as no votes.

The experimenter will announce when the two-minute period is finished. If you haven't yet voted, please vote when the announcement is made, so we can all proceed to the next proposal. You are not told how the other people have voted until after you cast your vote, although you are free to say whatever you wish about your voting decision to the other members of your group during the two minute message stage.

Whatever bonus votes you do not use in the A election, will be saved for you to use in the proposal B election. For example, if you cast one vote in the A election, all your bonus votes will be saved for the B election. If you cast two votes in the A election, only one of your bonus votes will be saved, and if you cast three votes in the A election, none of your bonus votes are saved.

After you and the other voters in your committee have made voting decisions, you are told the outcome of the proposal A election, and the total number of votes for and against. You then proceed to the proposal B election. You are in the same committee for the proposal B election as you were for the proposal A election. In addition, if you were in the *for* group in the A election, you remain in the *for* group in the B election (and if you were in the *against* group, you remain in the *against* group).

There is no message stage for Proposal B. When you and the voters in your committee are ready to proceed, you will each be assigned proposal B values in the same manner that your proposal A values were assigned. Each voter's assigned value for proposal B will typically be different than their proposal A values. All voters in the *for* group still receive positive values, and these values are the same for all members of the *for* group. All voters in the *against* group receive negative values, and these values are the same for all members of the *against* group. All your remaining votes will automatically be cast as yes votes for proposal B if you are a *for* voter, and as no votes if you are an *against* voter. The outcome of the B election is then reported to you.

When everyone has finished, this completes the first match, and we will then go to the next match. You will be rematched with four other people to form a new five-person committee, and repeat the procedure described above. The voters in your new committee will be selected randomly by the computer, but if you were a *for* voter in the first committee, you will still be a *for* voter for the rest of the experiment. And if you were an *against* voter in the first match, you will still be in the *against* group for the rest of the experiment. As in the first match, your new committee has two *for* voters and three *against* voters.

After your new committee has finished voting on both proposals in the second match, you will again be rematched into a new committee in a similar way, and this will continue for 30 matches. Remember that each match consists of 2 proposals, every committee has two *for* voters and three *against* voters. Also remember, if you are a *for* voter, you will always be a *for* voter, and if you are an *against* voter, you will always be an *against* voter.

[Practice session]

We will now give you a chance to get used to the computers with a brief practice session. Are there any questions before we begin the practice match?

[Answer questions]

You will not be paid for this practice session; it is just to allow you to get familiar with the experiment and your computers. During the practice session, do not press any keys or click with your mouse, unless instructed to. When we instruct you, please do exactly as we ask. We will now hand out record sheets for you to record important information during the experiment. Please raise your hand if you need a pen or pencil.

[Hand out record sheets and pens]

Please pull out your dividers so we can begin the practice session.

[Start game on server]

FIRST SLIDE

This is the decision screen for Proposal A in match 1. Your ID# is printed at the very top left of your screen. Please record this on your record sheet.

The screen tells you your proposal A value, whether you are in the *for* group or in the *against* group, and the number of people in each group (always two for the *for* group and three for the *against* group in this experiment). Then the screen tells you the number of votes you have available. The bottom window of your screen is the history table, which is blank now because nothing has happened yet.

Please record your proposal A value on your record sheet in the row labeled "Practice 1 A". Remember that everyone in your group has the same value as you do. That is, everyone in the *for* group of your committee has the same positive proposal A value in this round, and everyone in the *against* group of your committee has the same negative proposal A value this round. For example, if you are in the *for* group and your proposal A value is 41, then this tells you that both of the other members of your committee's *for* group also have a proposal A value equal to 41. The *against* group members of your committee also share a proposal A value, but all you would know is that it is some negative number between −1 and −100.

It is important that you understand how these values are assigned. Are there any questions before we proceed with the practice round?

After recording this information, we begin the two-minute message stage. Messages are entered by typing on the line at the very bottom of the screen and then clicking the send button. Everyone please practice this once by sending the message "Hello" now. Notice that this is echoed in the message display box, and your message is also displayed on your screen. Also notice that each of your has been assigned a temporary number that identifies you anonymously to the other members of your group. For example, the two members in a *for* group are assigned temporary id numbers 1 and 2. The three members in the *against* group are assigned temporary id numbers 1, 2, and 3.

At any time during the two-minute message stage, you may choose how many votes to cast in the A election, by clicking on the arrow key. You may cast either one, two, or three votes in this election. Any unused votes in this election will be saved for you to use in the B election of this match.

If your proposal A value is positive, then all votes you cast will count as yes votes for A, and if your proposal A value is negative, then all votes you cast will count as no votes. When you have selected the number of votes you wish to cast in this election, please click on the "Vote" button. Please record the number of votes you cast on your record sheet. Then wait for all other voters in the room to finish casting their Proposal A votes. The proposal passes if there are more yes votes than no votes. Tie votes are broken randomly by the computer.

SECOND SLIDE

The experimenter will announce when the two-minute message stage is over. Please make your voting decision at this time, if you have not done so already. Once everyone has made their vote decision for the A election, the votes are tallied and the results for your match are displayed in the results window. The window displays your Proposal A value, the number of votes you cast, the total number of yes votes cast in the election, the total number of no votes, the outcome, and your payoff from the A election. Please record all of this information on your record sheet.

Then click OK when you are ready to proceed to the proposal B election.

THIRD SLIDE

We are now in the B election. Notice that the history screen has been updated and includes a summary of the previous proposal A election. There is no message stage for Proposal B, and your voting decision is determined completely by how many votes you cast in the A election. But you will need to read the information on the screen and record it. Please record your proposal B value on your record sheet in the row labeled "Practice 1 B". This screen reminds you how many votes you have remaining. This number equals the number of bonus votes you did not use for proposal A plus your regular proposal B vote. Please record this number on your record sheet in the column labeled "your vote". Then click on the "Vote" button. All these votes are now automatically cast by the computer. They are recorded as yes votes for proposal B if you are in the *for* group, and as no votes if you are in the *against* group.

FOURTH SLIDE

Once everyone has made their vote decision for the B election, the votes are tallied and the results for the people in your committee are displayed in the results window. The screen displays the number of yes votes and the number of no votes, the outcome, and your payoff in francs. Please record this information on your record sheet.

Please press OK when you are ready to proceed.

FIFTH SLIDE

Once everybody has pressed OK, a new window appears and displays what your dollar payoff would have been if this were a paid match instead of a practice match. It also displays your total dollar payoff from all previous matches, which so far is 0. You do not need to record your cumulative payoff after each match. But you will need to record it at the very end of the experiment. Please press OK when you are ready to proceed.

We have now completed the first practice match. We will now proceed to the second practice match. Remember that you are assigned to a new committee in this match, although you will continue to be a *for* voter if you were a *for* voter in the first committee; you will continue to be an *against* voter if you were an *against* voter in the first committee. Everyone is randomly assigned to a new committee after every match in the experiment. Notice that the full-view history contains the information about what you did in the first match. Please raise your hand if your history screen does not show this information.

Please complete the second practice match on your own, by following the same directions as in the first practice match. Don't forget to record the information as it appears on your screen. Remember, you are not paid for these practice matches. Feel free to raise your hand if you have any questions.

When everyone has made their vote decisions for proposal A and proposal B in this practice match, and the screen with the proposal B results has appeared at the end of the match, please wait for further instructions. Do NOT click OK on that screen.

[Wait for subjects to complete practice match 2]

Practice match 2 is now over. Please press OK to go to the final screen of the practice session, displaying your payoff from the current match, and your total payoff in the experiment so far. Do not press OK yet. You do not need to record your total payoff because this was a practice session. You will have to record it at the end of the paid session. Any questions?

Please press OK when you are ready to proceed.

If you have any questions from now on, raise your hand, and an experimenter will come and assist you.

Please pull out the dividers to ensure your privacy and the privacy of others.

Please click OK and begin the first paid match.

[Play matches 1 – 20]

END OF EXPERIMENTAL PROTOCOL

This completes the experiment. Please make sure to record your total payoffs on your record sheet, including your $10 show-up fee. Please remain in your seat and we will come by to check your total. Do not use the computers or talk with each other. We will pay each of you in private in the next room in the order of your seat numbers. Please sign and turn in your record sheet when you receive payment. You are under no obligation to reveal your earnings to the other participants. Thank you for your participation.

A.4 Experiment 4.1 in Chapter 4

SAMPLE INSTRUCTIONS: Three-person, three-proposal treatment

INTRODUCTORY REMARKS

DESCRIPTION

The experiment you are participating in is a committee voting experiment. You will participate in 18 voting sessions. At the beginning of the experiment you will be randomly matched with two other people to form a committee of three. You will remain in the same group for the duration of the experiment. Each group follows exactly the same rules and what happens in one group has no effect on the other groups.

In each session you and the other members of your group will be asked to vote over three successive proposals. The proposals are called the Green Proposal, Blue Proposal, and Red Proposal. As a result of voting, each of the three proposals can either pass or fail. Each member of a group has one regular vote which is to be cast for each proposal. In addition each member will be given a single extra bonus vote. You will choose in which of the three proposals you want to cast the bonus vote in addition to your regular vote.

At the beginning of a voting session you will be randomly assigned a personal Green Proposal Value, Red Proposal Value, and Blue Proposal Value. In this experiment, values are denominated in francs, and each of the three proposals' values is equally likely to be any integer amount between −100 and 100 francs, but not 0. The other members of your group are also randomly assigned their own Green, Red, and Blue Proposal Values, each of which is equally likely to be any integer amount between −100 and 100 francs, but not 0. Because the values are random, each person is likely to have different values for the three proposals, and the values of each proposal (for example the Green Proposal Values) are also likely to be different for different persons. You are not told what the values of the other members of your group are.

If your value is positive, you are in favor of the proposal, and earn your value if and only if the proposal passes. If your value is negative, you are against the proposal and earn the absolute value of your value if and only if the proposal does not pass. Otherwise you earn 0 francs. For example, if your Green Proposal Value is -55, then you earn 55 francs if Green does not pass, and 0 francs if Green passes (and similarly for Blue or Red). Because the values are randomly assigned, being in favor of one proposal has no implication for how you feel about the other.

After all personal values have been assigned, the computer selects a member of the group to be the Chair. Each member of the group will be Chair for six consecutive voting sessions. The Chair decides the order in which the three elections are held. Thus, for example, the Chair decides whether to vote first for the Blue proposal and then for the Green followed by the Red, or first for the Green and then for the Red followed by the Blue (or any other combination). You will see on your computer monitor whether you have been chosen to be the Chair. If so, you will be asked to make the ordering choice.

Your screen will look like this: [SCREEN SHOT: PROPOSER]

If you are not the Chair, your screen will also tell you:

[SCREEN SHOT: NOT_PROPOSER]

The computer will let you know the order of elections chosen by the Chair. The three elections are held sequentially. Each member of the group will cast one regular vote on each proposal. In addition, each member will be given one extra bonus vote and will choose on which of the three proposals s/he wants to cast the bonus vote in addition to the regular vote. Suppose for example that the first election is on the Green proposal. Then you will decide whether to cast one or two votes in the Green election: your regular Green vote only, or your regular Green vote and the bonus vote. The other members of your group may also cast up to two votes in the Green election. If you are in favor of the Green proposal (that is, your Green Proposal Value is positive), any votes you cast will automatically be counted as yes votes. If you are against Green (that is, your Green Proposal Value is negative), any votes you cast will be automatically counted as no votes.

Your screen will look like this: [SCREEN SHOT: MAIN]

Notice that the screen displays how many bonus votes you and the members of your group have left.

The Green proposal passes in your group if there are more yes votes than no votes cast by members of your group, and fails if there are more no votes than yes votes. Ties are broken randomly by the computer. After you and the other members of your group have made voting decisions for the first proposal, the computer will tell you the number of votes cast for and against the proposal, and the outcome of the vote for your group.

Your screen will look like this: [SCREEN SHOT: RESULTS]

You will then proceed to the next proposal. Continuing with the example above, suppose that the second election is the Blue election. In the Blue election each member of your group (including you) is left with his or her regular Blue vote, plus the bonus vote, if the bonus vote has not been cast earlier in the Green election. If you have cast two votes in the Green election, you will have only your regular vote in the Blue election. But if you cast one vote in the Green election, then you still have your bonus vote, and will be able to cast up to two votes in the Blue election.

In the third and final election, the Red one in this example, you will cast all your remaining votes by clicking the "Vote" button. You do not have any choice about how many votes to cast in this third election.

When everyone has finished, we will go to the next voting session and will repeat the procedure described above. Each voting session has three successive elections over the three proposals, in the order chosen by the committee Chair. The proposals values are reassigned anew for every session, and in every session you will have one regular vote for each election and one single bonus vote.

At the end of the experiment, everyone will be paid in private and you are under no obligation to tell others how much you earned. Your earnings during the experiment are denominated in francs. At the end of the 18 voting sessions, the computer will randomly select five sessions, and the sum of your earnings in these five sessions will determine your total earnings. Your dollar earnings are determined by multiplying your earnings in francs by a conversion rate. In this experiment, the conversion rate is 0.04, meaning that 100 francs equal 4 dollars. This amount will be added to your participation fee to determine your final payment.

Are there any questions before we proceed to the practice session? You are not paid for the practice session, and it will have no effect on your final earnings. Its only purpose is to show you how the computer interface works.

You will find next to your computer terminal a record sheet. Please fill the record sheet as the experiment progresses, beginning with the practice session.

[Start game on server]

We will now proceed to the practice session. Please complete it on your own. Feel free to raise your hand if you have any questions.

[Practice session]

[Wait for subjects to complete practice session]

The practice session is now over. Any questions?

If you have any questions from now on, raise your hand, and an experimenter will come and assist you. We will now begin the 18 paid sessions. Please remember to fill the record sheet.

[Play 18 real matches]

END OF EXPERIMENTAL PROTOCOL

This is the end of the experiment. Please record your total earnings at the bottom of the record sheet. Add the $10.00 show-up fee and enter the sum as the total.

We will pay each of you in private in the next room in the order of your Subject ID numbers. Remember that you are under no obligation to reveal your earnings to the other players.

Please put the mouse behind the computer screen and do not use either the mouse or the keyboard at all. Please be patient and remain seated until we call you to be paid. Do not converse with the other participants or use your cell phone. Thank you for your cooperation.

Could the person with lab number . . . please go to the next room to be paid. Please bring all your belongings with you, including your payment receipt sheet.

A.5 Experiment 4.2 in Chapter 4

SAMPLE INSTRUCTIONS: Three-person, three-proposal,
$V = \{100, 200, 300, 400\}$.

INTRODUCTORY REMARKS

DESCRIPTION

The experiment you are participating in is a committee voting experiment. You will participate in 16 voting sessions. At the beginning of the experiment you will be randomly matched with two other individuals to form a committee of three. You will be matched randomly with different committee members at the start of each voting session. Each committee follows exactly the same rules and what happens in one committee has no effect on the other groups.

In each voting session, your committee will face four different proposals, called the Green, Blue, Orange, and Red proposals. However, only three of these proposals will be voted upon. Which of the proposals are brought to a vote is determined by one of the three members of each committee, himself or herself randomly chosen by the computer to act as committee chair. The proposals are presented for a vote sequentially. After the third proposal has been voted upon, the voting session ends.

Each of the proposals that are brought to a vote can either pass or fail. Each committee member has one regular vote to cast on each proposal and, in addition, a single extra bonus vote. You will choose on which proposal you want to cast the bonus vote in addition to your regular vote.

At the beginning of a voting session you will be assigned the value you attach to the Green proposal, the Blue proposal, the Orange proposal, and the Red proposal. If the value you attach to a proposal is positive, you are in favor of that proposal, and earn your value if and only if the proposal passes. If your value is negative, you are against that proposal and earn the absolute value of your value if and only if the proposal does not pass. Otherwise you earn a value of 0. Values are denominated in francs, and the possible values are plus or minus 100, plus or minus 200, plus or minus 300, and plus or minus 400. For example, if your Green Proposal Value is −200, then you earn 200 francs if Green does not pass, and 0 francs if Green passes.

If you are in favor of a proposal, then at least one of the other members of your committee will be against that proposal: there is always a committee member with preferences opposite to the other two members'.

How many francs each proposal is worth is determined randomly in each voting session for each committee member, and thus in general will differ between the three members. For example, if your Green proposal value is −200, then the other members' values can be +/−100, +/−200, +/−300 or +/−400 with equal probability, but with at least one member's value being positive. In the first eight voting sessions, you will know your own values for each proposal, but you will not be able to see the values of the other members of your committee, and they will not be able to see your values. In the second eight voting sessions, each committee member's values will be revealed to the entire committee (so you will see both your own values and the values of your other committee members, and they will see yours).

In each voting session, as all values are assigned, the computer will also choose randomly which member of the committee will act as Chair. The role of the Chair is to choose, one after the other, which three of the four proposals should be brought to a vote. A new Chair is chosen randomly in each voting session (i.e., for each new sequence of three votes) and you will see on your computer monitor whether you have been chosen to be the Chair. If so, your screen will look like this: [SCREEN SHOT: CHAIR INCOMPLETE INFORMATION] (the values in the screen shots are for illustration purposes only). If you are not the Chair, your screen will also tell you. The screen will look like this: [SCREEN SHOT: NON-CHAIR INCOMPLETE INFORMATION] In this example you are player 1.

The Chair will begin each session by choosing the first proposal to be voted upon. The Chair and the other committee members then cast their regular vote on the chosen proposal. In addition, each of them must decide whether to cast their extra bonus vote, or to save it for a future proposal. Remember: each voter, including the Chair, has one, single bonus vote.

Suppose, for example, that the Chair in your committee begins by calling a vote on the Green proposal. Each member of the committee, the Chair and the other members, then decide, independently, whether to cast one or two votes in the Green election: the regular Green vote only, or the regular Green vote and the bonus vote (you must always cast at least your one regular vote). If you are in favor of the Green proposal (that is, your Green Proposal Value is positive), any votes you cast will automatically be counted as yes votes. If you are against Green (that is, your Green Proposal Value is negative), any votes you cast will be automatically counted as no votes. The monitor will look like this: [SCREEN SHOT: VOTE INCOMPLETE INFORMATION]. In this example, you are the Chair. [Show why] Notice that the screen displays whether the members of your committee have any bonus vote left and also reminds you of your values.

The Green proposal passes in your committee if there are more yes votes than no votes, and fails if there are more no votes than yes votes. Ties are broken randomly by the computer. The computer will tell you the number of votes cast for and against the proposal, and the outcome of the vote for your group. Your screen will look like this: [SCREEN SHOT: RESULTS]

After voting on the first proposal is completed, the Chair will choose the second proposal to be brought to a vote, and each committee member will again cast their regular votes on the chosen proposal. If you did not cast your bonus vote on the first proposal, you may decide to cast it now. Alternatively, you may choose to wait further. All votes you cast will be automatically be counted in favor of your preferred direction.

After voting on the second proposal is completed, the Chair will choose the third and final proposal to be brought to a vote. If you have not cast your bonus vote on either of the first two proposals, it will be cast automatically on the third and last proposal. You do not have any choice about how many votes to cast in this third election: you will cast all your remaining votes by clicking the "Vote" button. Remember: only three of the four proposals will be brought up for a vote.

This concludes the first voting session. Individuals are them randomly re-matched into committees of three voters; committee members are endowed again with three regular votes (one for each proposal to be voted upon) and the single bonus vote; proposal values are reassigned; and the experiment proceeds to the second voting session. Remember; in each session, if your bonus vote is not spent on the first proposal, it can be spent on the second, or again saved, in which case it will be cast automatically on the third and final proposal voted upon. Also, in the first eight sessions, you will only know your own values (you will not be able to see the values of the other committee members, and they will not see yours). In the second set of eight sessions, all committee members will be able to see their own and each other's values. The chair and the other committee members' screens for this second set of sessions will therefore look like this: [SCREEN SHOTS: CHAIR; NON-CHAIR WITH INFORMATION]. Correspondingly, in the voting screen, you will be reminded of both your own and the other committee members' values [SCREEN SHOT: VOTE WITH INFORMATION].

At the end of the experiment, everyone will be paid in private and you are under no obligation to tell others how much you earned. The computer will select randomly four of the 16 voting sessions and you will be paid your cumulative earnings for these four sessions. Your dollar earnings are determined by multiplying your earnings in francs by a conversion rate. In this experiment, the conversion rate is 1/100, meaning that 100 francs equal 1 dollars. This amount will then be added to the $10.00 participation fee to determine your final payment.

Are there any questions before we proceed to the practice session? You are not paid for the practice session, and it will have no effect on your final earnings. Its only purpose is to show you how the computer interface works. In this practice session, you will only know your own proposals values. When you reach the end of the practice session, please wait. Do not ask the computer to advance to the next match.

You will find next to your computer terminal a record sheet. Please fill the record sheet as the experiment progresses, beginning with the practice session. It is important that you do so. Please write your value in the appropriate column including the sign. In the column marked "Order" please write 1 next to the proposal voted upon first, 2 next to the one voted upon second, and 3 for the one voted third.

[Start game on server]

Please write your subject ID number at the top of the record sheet. We will now proceed to the practice session. Please complete it on your own. Feel free to raise your hand if you have any questions.

[Practice session]

[Wait for subjects to complete practice session]

The practice session is now over. Any questions?

If you have any questions from now on, raise your hand, and an experimenter will come and assist you. We will now begin the 16 paid sessions. In the first eight sessions you will only know your own proposal values; in the following eight sessions all proposal values in a committee will be know by all committee members. Please remember to fill the record sheet.

[Play 16 real matches]

END OF EXPERIMENTAL PROTOCOL

This is the end of the experiment. Please record your total earnings at the bottom of the record sheet. Add the $10.00 show-up fee and enter the sum as the total.

We will pay each of you in private in the next room in the order of your Subject ID numbers. Remember you are under no obligation to reveal your earnings to the other players.

Please do not use either the mouse or the keyboard at all. Please be patient and remain seated until we call you to be paid. Do not converse with the other participants or use your cell phone. Thank you for your cooperation.

Could the person with lab number .. please go to the next room to be paid. Please bring all your belongings with you, including your payment receipt sheet.

A.6 Experiment in Chapter 6

[What follows is the form received by CC students who participated in the survey]

Columbia University Economics Department

Voting Experiment

Thank you for choosing to participate in this experiment. By entering your number below and attaching your post-it to the questionnaire, you acknowledge that you have read and understand the consent form (attached to the ballot box). Please enter your number here: ____________

A lottery will be conducted among all participants who have followed the instructions of the experiment and written the number above legibly. The winner will receive an iPod.

This experiment asks you how much you care about the outcome of some of the elections.

Each election can be scored on a scale of 1–10, with 10 meaning "care very much" and 1 meaning "care not at all." In order to indicate a box, please cross out the relevant number with an X like this: [X]

E-Board	1	2	3	4	5	6	7	8	9	10
Senate (1 year)	1	2	3	4	5	6	7	8	9	10
Senate (2 year)	1	2	3	4	5	6	7	8	9	10
Academic Affairs	1	2	3	4	5	6	7	8	9	10

Suppose now that, in addition to the regular votes you cast earlier, you had 1 additional vote to cast in favor of your candidate in one of the elections. You can choose any of these four elections as you see fit. Which one would you choose? (NOTE: This is for experimental purposes only. Your answer will not change the outcome of the actual elections in any way).

Please check the box under the election you choose. Please check **only one** box.[1]

E-Board	**Senate (1 year)**	**Senate (2 year)**	**Academic Affairs**
Evolution	David	Tiffany	Ehizoje
Open Columbia	Yihe (Eric)	Gerry	Alidad
☐	☐	☐	☐

Thank you for participating. And good luck with the lottery!

1. The original instructions included the last names of the candidates, omitted here.

Bibliography

Austen-Smith, David, 1990, "Information Transmission in Debate," *American Journal of Political Science*, 34:124–152.

Battaglini, Marco, 2002, "Multiple Referrals and Multidimensional Cheap Talk," *Econometrica*, 70:1379–1401.

Binder, Sarah and Steven Smith, 1997, *Politics or Principle? Filibustering in the United States Senate*, Washington, D.C.: Brookings Institution Press.

Blume, Andreas, Douglas DeJong, Yong-Gwan Kim, and Geoffrey Sprinkle, 2001, "Evolution of Communication with Partial Common Interest," *Games and Economic Behavior*, 37:79–120.

Bowler, Shaun, Todd Donovan, and David Brockington, 2003, *Electoral Reform and Minority Representation: Local Experiments with Alternative Elections*. Columbus: Ohio State University Press.

Brams, Steven, 2005, "Fair Division," in Weingast, Barry R. and Donald Wittman, *Oxford Handbook of Political Economy*, Oxford and New York: Oxford University Press.

Brams, Steven and William H. Riker, 1973, "The Paradox of Vote Trading," *American Political Science Review*, 67:1235–1247.

Brams, Steven and Alan D. Taylor, 1996, *Fair Division: From Cake Cutting to Dispute Resolution*, Cambridge and New York: Cambridge University Press.

Brams, Steve, Kilgour D. Marc, and William S. Zwicker, 1998, "The Paradox of Multiple Elections," *Social Choice and Welfare*, 15:211–236.

Briffault, Richard, 2004, "Voting Systems for the Election of Representatives to a State Constitutional Convention, New Jersey Constitutional Reform," Background Paper #6, Center for State Constitutional Studies, Rutgers University.

Broder, David S., 2000, *Democracy Derailed: Initiatives Campaigns and the Power of Money*, New York, NY: Harcourt.

Buchanan, James M. and Gordon Tullock, 1962, *The Calculus of Consent*, Ann Arbor: University of Michigan Press.

Campbell, Colin M., 1999, "Large Electorates and Decisive Majorities," *Journal of Political Economy*, 107:1199–1217.

Casella, Alessandra, 2005, "Storable Votes," *Games and Economic Behavior*, 51:391–419.

Casella, Alessandra, 2008, "Storable Votes and Agenda Control. Theory and Experiments," NBER W.P. No 14487, November.

Casella, Alessandra, 2011, "Agenda Control as a Cheap Talk Game. Theory and Experiments with Storable Votes," *Games and Economic Behavior*, 72:46–76.

Casella, Alessandra and Andrew Gelman, 2008, "A Simple Scheme to Improve the Efficiency of Referenda," *Journal of Public Economics*, 92: 2240–2261.

Casella, Alessandra, Andrew Gelman, and Thomas R. Palfrey, 2006, "An Experimental Study of Storable Votes," *Games and Economic Behavior*, 57:123–154.

Casella, Alessandra, Thomas R. Palfrey, and Raymond Riezman, 2008, "Minorities and Storable Votes," *Quarterly Journal of Political Science*, 3:165–200.

Casella, Alessandra, Shuky Ehrenberg, Andrew Gelman, and Jie Shen, 2010, "Protecting Minorities in Large Binary Elections: A Test of Storable Votes Using Field Data," *The B.E. Journal of Economic Analysis & Policy*: Vol. 10: Iss. 1 (Advances), Article 98.

Casella, Alessandra, Aniol Llorente-Saguer, and Thomas R. Palfrey, 2010, "Competitive Equilibrium in Markets for Votes," NBER W.P. No 16315, August.

Chakraborty, Archishman and Rick Harbaugh, 2007, "Comparative Cheap Talk," *Journal of Economic Theory*, 132:70–94.

Chamberlain, Gary and Michael Rothschild, 1981, "A Note on the Probability of Casting a Decisive Vote," *Journal of Economic Theory*, 25:152–162.

Chwe, Michael, 1999, "Minority Voting Rights Can Maximize Majority Welfare," *American Political Science Review*, 93:85–97.

Clarke, Edward H., 1971, "Multipart Pricing of Public Goods," *Public Choice*, 11:17–33.

Coleman, James S., 1966, "The Possibility of a Social Welfare Function," *American Economic Review*, 56:1105–1122.

Cooter, Robert, 2002, "Constitutional Consequentialism: Bargain Democracy versus Median Democracy," *Theoretical Inquiries in Law*, 3:1–20.

Cox, Adam B., 2007, "The Temporal Dimension of Voting Rights," *Virginia Law Review*, 93:361–413.

Cox, Gary, 1990, "Centripetal and Centrifugal Incentives in Electoral Systems," *American Journal of Political Science*. 34:903–935.

Crawford, Vincent and Joel Sobel, 1982, "Strategic Information Transmission," *Econometrica*, 50:1431–1452.

Crawford, Vincent, 1998, "A Survey of Experiments on Communication via Cheap Talk," *Journal of Economic Theory*, 78:286–298.

Crémer, Jacques, Claude d'Aspremont, and Louis-André Gérard-Varet, 1990, "Incentives and the Existence of Pareto-Optimal Revelation Mechanisms," *Journal of Economic Theory*, 51:233–254.

d'Aspremont, Claude and Louis-André Gérard-Varet, 1979, "Incentives and Incomplete Information," *Journal of Public Economics*, 11:25–45.

Dahl, Robert, 1956, *A Preface to Democratic Theory*, Chicago: University of Chicago Press (third edition: 2006).

Dahl, Robert, 1989, *Democracy and Its Critics*, New Haven: Yale University Press.

Davidson, Russell and James G. MacKinnon, 2006, "Bootstrap Methods in Econometrics," in Kerry Patterson and Terence C. Mills (eds.), *Palgrave Handbook of Econometrics: Vol. 1 Econometric Theory*, Palgrave Macmillan Ltd, Houndmills, Basingstoke, Hampshire RG61 6XS, UK.

Dodgson, Charles, 1884, *The Principles of Parliamentary Representation*, London: Harrison and Sons (Supplement, 1885).

Efron, Bradley, 1979, "Bootstrap Methods: Another Look at the Jackknife," *Annals of Statistics*, 7:1–26.

Efron Bradley and Robert J. Tibshirani, 1993, *An Introduction to the Bootstrap*, Chapman and Hall: New York.

Feller, William, 1968, *An Introduction to Probability Theory and Its Applications*, Vol. 1, New York: John Wiley & Sons.

Ferejohn, John, 1974, "Sour Notes on the Theory of Vote Trading," Social Science W.P. No. 41, Caltech.

Gelman, Andrew, Jonathan N. Katz, and Francis Tuerlinckx, 2002, "The Mathematics and Statistics of Voting Power," *Statistical Science*, 17: 420–435.

Gelman, Andrew, John B. Carlin, Hal S. Stern, and Donald B. Rubin, 2004, *Bayesian Data Analysis*, London: CRC Press.

Gerber, Elisabeth R., 1999, *The Populist Paradox: Interest Group Influence and the Promise of Direct Legislation*, Princeton, N.J.: Princeton University Press.

Gerber, Elisabeth R., Rebecca B. Morton, and Thomas A. Rietz, 1998, "Minority Representation in Multimember Districts," *American Political Science Review* 92:127–144.

Gerken, Heather K., 2005, "Second-Order Diversity," *Harvard Law Review*, 118:1099–1195.

Gnedenko, Boris V. and Andrey N. Kolmogorov, 1968, *Limit Distributions for Sums of Independent Random Variables*, Reading, Ma: Addison-Wesley.

Good, I.J. and Lawrence S. Mayer, 1975, "Estimating the Efficacy of a Vote," *Behavioral Science*, 20:25–33.

Goeree, Jacob and Jens Großer, 2007, "Welfare Reducing Polls," *Economic Theory*, 31:51–68.

Green, Jerry R. and Jean-Jacques Laffont, 1979, *Incentives in Public Decision Making*, Amsterdam: North-Holland.

Grofman, Bernard and Chandler Davidson, eds., 1992, *Controversies in Minority Voting*, Washington, D.C.: The Brookings Institution.

Groves, Theodore, 1973, "Incentives in Teams," *Econometrica*, 41:617–631.

Guinier, Lani, 1994. *The Tyranny of the Majority*. New York: Free Press.

Haefele, Edwin, 1971, "A Utility Theory of Representative Government," *American Economic Review*, 61:350–365.

Harsanyi, John, 1953, "Cardinal Utility in Welfare Economics and in the Theory of Risk-Taking," *Journal of Political Economy*, 61:434–435.

Harsanyi, John, 1955, "Cardinal Welfare, Individualistic Ethics and Interpersonal Comparisons of Utility," *Journal of Political Economy*, 63:309–321.

Hortala-Vallve, Rafael, 2010, "Qualitative Voting," *Cuadernos de Economia*, 33:5–44.

Hortale-Vallve, Rafael, and Aniol Llorente-Saguer, 2010, "Qualitative Voting in Conflict Resolution Situations," *Games and Economic Behavior*, 70:375–391.

Illinois Assembly on Political Representation and Alternative Electoral Systems, 2001, *Final Report and Background Papers*, IGPA, University of Illinois.

Issacharoff, Samuel, 1995, "Supreme Court Destabilization of Single Member Districts," *The University of Chicago Legal Forum*, 205–240.

Issacharoff, Samuel, Pamela Karlan, and Richard Pildes, 2002, *The Law of Democracy: Legal Structure and the Political Process*, second edition, Westbury, N.Y.: Foundation Press.

Jackson, Matthew and Hugo Sonnenschein, 2007, "Overcoming Incentive Constraints by Linking Decisions," *Econometrica* 75:241–257.

Karlan, Pamela, 1995, "Our Separatism? Voting Rights as an American Nationalities Policy," *The University of Chicago Legal Forum*, 83–110.

Kirman, Alan and Mika Widgrén, 1995, "European Economic Decision-making Policy: Progress or Paralysis?," *Economic Policy*, 21:421–460.

Koger, Gregory, 2010, *Filibustering: A Political History of Obstruction in the House and the Senate*, Chicago: University of Chicago Press.

Krasa, Stefan and Mattias Polborn, 2009, "Is Mandatory Voting Better than Voluntary Voting?," *Games and Economic Behavior*, 66:275–291.

Laffont, Jean Jacques and Eric Maskin, 1983, "The Theory of Incentives: An Overview," in Werner Hildenbrand (ed.), *Advances in Economic Theory*, Cambridge: Cambridge University Press.

Laslier, Jean-Francois and Karine Straeten, 2008, "A Live Experiment on Approval Voting," *Experimental Economics*. 11:97–105.

Ledyard, John O., 1984, "The Pure Theory of Large Two-Candidate Elections," *Public Choice*, 44:7–41.

Ledyard, John O. and Thomas R. Palfrey, 2002, "The Approximation of Efficient Public Good Mechanisms by Simple Voting Schemes," *Journal of Public Economics*, 83:153–171.

Mailath, George J. and Andrew Postlewaite, 1990, "Asymmetric Information Bargaining Problems with Many Agents," *Review of Economic Studies*, 57:351–67.

Margolis, Howard, 1977, "Probability of a Tie Election," *Public Choice*, 31:135–138.

Matsusaka, John G., 1992, "Economics of Direct Legislation," *Quarterly Journal of Economics*, 107:541–571.

Matsusaka, John G., 2004, *For The Many or The Few. The Initiative Process, Public Policy, and American Democracy*, Chicago: University of Chicago Press.

McLennan, Andrew, 1998, "Consequences of the Condorcet Jury Theorem for Beneficial Information Aggregation by Rational Agents," *American Political Science Review* 92:413–418.

Milgrom, Paul R. and Robert J. Weber, 1985, "Distributional Strategies for Games with Incomplete Information," *Mathematics of Operations Research*, 10:619–632.

Mueller, Dennis C., 1973, "Constitutional Democracy and Social Welfare," *Quarterly Journal of Economics*, 87:61–79.

Ordeshook, Peter C. and Thomas R. Palfrey, 1988, "Agendas, Strategic Voting, and Signaling with Incomplete Information," *American Journal of Political Science*, 32:441–466.

Palfrey, Thomas R. and Howard Rosenthal, 1991, "Testing for Effects of Cheap Talk in a Public Goods Game with Private Information," *Games and Economic Behavior*, 3:183–220.

Philipson, Tomas and James Snyder, 1996, "Equilibrium and Efficiency in an Organized Vote Market," *Public Choice*, 89:245–265.

Piketty, Thomas, 1994, "Information Aggregation through Voting and Vote-Trading," unpublished, MIT (available at: http://www.jourdan.ens.fr/piketty/fichiers/public/Piketty1994c.pdf.).

Pildes, Richard H., 2007, "What Kind of Right is the Right to Vote?," *Virginia Law Review* In Brief, 93:45–52

Pildes, Richard H. and Kristen A. Donoghue, 1995, "Cumulative Voting in the United States," *The University of Chicago Legal Forum*, 241–313.

Rawls, John, 1971, *A Theory of Justice*, Cambridge, Mass: Harvard University Press (revised edition, 1999).

Sawyer, Jack and Duncan MacRae, 1962, "Game Theory and Cumulative Voting in Illinois: 1902–1954," *American Political Science Review*, 56: 936–946.

Spence, Michael, 1973, "Job Market Signalling," *Quarterly Journal of Economics*, 87:355–374.

Spiegelhalter, David, Andrew Thomas, Nicky Best, Walter Gilks, and David Lunn, 1994 and 2002, *BUGS: Bayesian Inference Using Gibbs Sampling*, Cambridge, England: MRC Biostatistics Unit, www.mrc-bsu.cam.ac.uk/bugs.

Taylor, Curtis R. and Huseyin Yildirim, 2010, "Public Information and Electoral Bias," *Games and Economic Behavior*, 68:353–75.

Vickrey, William, 1961, "Counterspeculation, Auctions, and Competitive Sealed Tenders," *Journal of Finance*, 16:8–37.

Index

Boxes indicated by letter *b*, figures by *f*, tables by *t*.